SPIRIT
—IN THE—
ROCK

SPIRIT
—IN THE—
ROCK

—THE—
FIERCE BATTLE FOR
MODOC HOMELANDS

JIM COMPTON

WSU
PRESS

Washington State University Press
Pullman, Washington

Washington State University Press
PO Box 645910
Pullman, Washington 99164-5910
Phone: 800-354-7360
Fax: 509-335-8568
Email: wsupress@wsu.edu
Website: wsupress.wsu.edu

First printing 2017
Third printing 2023

Library of Congress Cataloging-in-Publication Data

Names: Compton, Jim, 1941-2014.
Title: Spirit in the rock : the fierce battle for Modoc homelands / Jim
    Compton.
Description: Pullman, Wash. : Washington State University Press, 2017. |
    Includes bibliographical references and index.
Identifiers: LCCN 2017022062 | ISBN 9780874223507 (alk. paper)
Subjects: LCSH: Modoc Indians--Wars, 1873. | Indians of North
    America--California--Wars. | Indians of North America--Oregon--Wars.
Classification: LCC E83.87 .C66 2017 | DDC 979.4004/974122--dc23
LC record available at https://lccn.loc.gov/2017022062

On the cover: design by Scott Swanger
    based on the photography of Bill Stafford.

UPI photo/Carlos Gutierrez

Spirit in the Rock

A Modoc grandmother gave the boy a spear and said: "Go to the rock out there and try this spear. Stand on the right side of the rock and strike it five times." He struck four times, and each time great pieces of rock fell. The fifth time the rock split in the center. Every time it struck, the spear looked like a flash of lightening.

—Modoc Legend
From Curtin, *Myths of the Modocs*

Contents

Illustrations

Maps

Editor's Note

Jim Compton, my husband, was a television news reporter. More than anything, he loved to chase a story, track down the facts, interview the players. For much of his life he told anyone who would listen the "great yarn" about the Modoc War and the Modoc Nation's struggle for a homeland on Lost River near the Oregon-California border.

Carol Arnold and Jim Compton.
Photo by Bill Stafford.

Growing up in Klamath Falls, Oregon, Jim and his family visited the Lava Beds along the California border. There he saw the stronghold where a century before Captain Jack and his band of Modoc warriors humiliated the U.S. Army. He learned about the capture and execution of Captain Jack and the theft of his Lost River homeland. Jim grew up in the 1950s, a time when vicious stereotypes about Native people were unquestioned. He often recalled how his father, an orthopedic surgeon, lost his temper one day at a Native patient and vowed never again to treat another "Indian."

Maybe it was this gross injustice that turned Jim into a champion of the Modocs. Maybe it was the heroism of Captain Jack's improbable victory over the army that hooked him on the Modoc War. Maybe it was Jim's never-ending curiosity. What hidden schemes and plots lurked behind the tragedy in the Lava Beds?

For whatever reason, Jim nurtured a decades-long passion to tell the Modoc story. In 1979 a feature by Lee Juillerat in the Klamath Falls *Herald and News* got him started. Jim was intrigued by Juillerat's reporting on the skulls of Captain Jack and the others who were hanged in October 1873. The skulls had been missing for nearly a century, and Jim wanted to solve the mystery.

Finally, in 2006 when retired from television news and the Seattle City Council, Jim had the time to turn his considerable journalistic talents into writing this book. A few years earlier, Jim received a lucky gift of materials from Francis "Van" Landrum, a Klamath Falls historian who had worked for decades on the Modoc War. Van kept detailed records of the battles and prepared meticulous maps and surveys.

Travelling to museums and libraries, Jim added a mountain of materials to Van's collection. He filled his Seattle office with newspapers, maps, antique photographs, and historic books—all about the Modocs and the Modoc War. He visited Modocs in Oklahoma. He made friends with Klamath Falls historians like Todd Kepple, Ryan Bartholomew, and Steve Kandra. A warm friendship grew between Jim and Debra Riddle, whose amazing knowledge of Modoc history and genealogy he respected and admired.

Jim wrote the Modoc story like the journalist he was, pursuing leads and checking facts. In January 2014 Jim finished the manuscript, originally titled *Kill The Chief.* Unfortunately, he died suddenly only a few months later. At that point, the task fell upon the rest of us to see the Modoc story published.

After Jim's death, Bill Stafford—Jim's long-time friend and a noted Seattle photographer—offered to create a photographic record of Modoc country to help illustrate the book. Bill traveled to southern Oregon and shot the gorgeous landscapes of Lost River and the Modoc homeland. Stephanie Stafford joined in the photo shoot, and she became my good friend and helpmate. Allison Kerr rebuilt and corrected the maps the University of Washington Department of Geography had prepared for Jim. Richard Gates prepared the historic photographs for publication.

Vivian Arviso—a classmate of Bill's from Colorado College—graciously agreed to write the preface. A former Miss Navajo and Miss Indian World, Vivian is a noted educator and author. Vivian's deep understanding of Native American culture and spiritual life—especially her expertise on traditional healers—contributed enormously to this book. Working with Vivian has been a journey of discovery for me personally, and I am grateful for her sensitivity and generosity.

Many reviewers read and commented on the manuscript. As a result, Jim's book has been substantially edited. At the suggestion of several reviewers, we renamed it. The new title— *Spirit in the Rock: The Fierce Battle for Modoc Homelands*—is a tribute to the Modocs' rich oral heritage and a reminder of their heroic struggle in the Lava Beds.

Ryan Bartholomew reviewed and corrected the manuscript based on his encyclopedic knowledge of the Modoc War. He and Steve Kandra spent a day driving us around in Ryan's truck to see Modoc Country and photograph the important sites around the Lost River. Todd Kepple contributed his expertise on Klamath basin history. Lee Juillerat reviewed the manuscript, and his recent *Lava Beds National Monument (Images of America)* informed the historical photographs.

David Brewster, Steve Dunphy, and Max Power of Seattle all generously gave of their time and their professional skills to review and critique the manuscript. John C. Gardner, chief executive officer of the WSU Foundation, introduced us to WSU Press. Eric Eberhard, the Distinguished Indian Law Practioner in Residence at the Seattle University School of Law, critiqued the book in detail and shared his expertise in Indian law. Eric's wisdom and sensitivity enormously enhanced the narrative.

Jim loved the Lava Beds and he loved Modoc country. *A Spirit in the Rock* is Jim's work. But it has fallen upon all of us to fulfill his life-long dream of telling the world about the Modoc War. Rest in peace, Jim, for here is your story.

Carol Arnold
Seattle, Washington

Author's Preface: The Modoc Story

We live on haunted ground, on land that is layers deep in human
passion and memory.
— Patricia Nelson Limerick, *Something in the Soil*

The Modoc War of 1872-73 was fought by a handful of Modocs
along the California-Oregon border. But for me, the battles echo
through the arid landscapes of my childhood—the stark plateau and
the Lava Beds, rough land crisscrossed by black rocky flows, bounded
by mountains and dark pine forests.

Growing up in Klamath Falls, we saw the Indians—Modocs and
Klamaths—as a shadowy presence. They came to town from time to
time to collect their share of tribal timber sales, often thousands of
dollars. Vicious stereotypes were unquestioned. My father, an orthopedic surgeon, treated their wounds and fixed their broken limbs. But
one night Dad announced at dinner, "I'll never treat another Indian."

Our family made summer treks to the vast Lava Beds where the
Modoc War was fought. It was a long, hot drive down a dusty county
road passing through miles of potato and alfalfa fields. The destination
was Captain Jack's Stronghold, the stone redoubt where the Modoc
chief and his fifty-three warriors barricaded themselves.

Later on, I learned that chief Keintpoos—known to whites as Captain Jack—had humiliated the U.S. Army, fighting with his band of warriors from the impregnable lava wilderness. The Modoc War ended only
when four of Captain Jack's people betrayed him to the army. An army
commission tried him as a war criminal, and hanged him. His corpse
was cut down from the gibbet and taken to an improvised mortuary,
where an army doctor scalped and decapitated him. Captain Jack's skull,
with three others, was sent to an army museum in Washington, D.C., an
atrocity his Modoc descendants did not discover for nearly a century.

But what was the Modoc War about? Why was it so important to
move Captain Jack's tiny band of Modocs from their homeland? Why

couldn't the Modocs keep the postage stamp of land around Captain Jack's village on Lost River? Why were they forced to live on a distant reservation with the rival Klamath tribe?

The answer, of course, was land and water. Captain Jack never knew his Lost River village stood in the path of a railroad, or that his riverside home was a barrier to a massive irrigation scheme. If the campaign to remove him seemed wildly disproportionate to the stakes, it is now evident why the white men had to drive Captain Jack from his homeland.

Historian Patricia Limerick wrote: "All the cultural understanding and tolerance in the world would not have changed the crucial fact that Indians possessed the land and the Euro-Americans wanted it."[1] Economic forces underlying the Modoc war were well disguised—hidden in incorporation documents I found in a dusty courthouse annex. We now know that among the first white arrivals to the Modoc homeland were keen-eyed entrepreneurs who saw more than farmland. They recognized immense resources of water for irrigation, and they knew only railroads were lacking for the region to flourish. They sought to control those resources by treaty or the appropriation of land.

Standard accounts of the war, largely shaped by the prominent pioneer Applegate family, diverted attention from the powerful economic forces at play. Their narrative of the Modoc war attributes the conflict to the collision between yeoman farmers and rebellious natives, typifying what one historian calls "selective rhetorical gestures" told by a literate elite.[2] Their plans to "replumb" the area's lakes and rivers and put a railroad through a Modoc village have escaped notice.

I have sought to bring the techniques learned in thirty years of professional journalism to these pages. If the historian's role is to sift details for themes, the journalist's job is to "parachute in," find a story line in the tangled facts, and enliven the narrative with the memorable personalities. Patricia Limerick observed, "Journalists and historians often labor in separate spheres, unaware of the themes that unite their work."[3] It is my hope this study—written from a journalist's point of view—will promote our understanding of the Modoc War and the "haunted ground" upon which it was fought.

The Modoc War has never achieved the iconic status of Custer's final battle or the assassination of Crazy Horse. But I still find richer soil alongside Lost River and in the Lava Beds of northern California than I could ever find at Little Big Horn. The loss of Modoc lands and culture, Captain Jack's trip to the gallows, and the mutilation of his remains are disturbing tales of white greed and depravity that still haunt the blackened ground.

On a windy October afternoon a few years ago while visiting the Modoc fortifications, I was startled by the noisy flapping of wings. It was a great horned owl, descending from its lair in a lava cliff stained white with droppings. The bird was equally surprised to see me, and we shared a moment of nervous eye contact. It labored to fly past me and disappeared into a ridge of sagebrush. For me, the dark rocks of Captain Jack's Stronghold are alive with such spirits.

Jim Compton
Seattle, Washington
January 2014

Foreword
by Vivian Arviso

Spirit in the Rock: The Fierce Battle for Modoc Homelands is the product of decades of work by a nationally known journalist, Jim Compton. It offers historians and Native American scholars and students a thoroughly researched book on the factors contributing to the Modoc War. The aftermath of this war led to the classification of Modoc men, women, and children as enemy combatants. This case study describes the incredible struggle for control by military and  civil administrations as part of western expansion into Oregon Territory, a struggle which nearly erased the Modoc as a people. Compton illuminates, through new sources, the circumstances in which Captain Jack assumed a leadership role for two Modoc bands. Captain Jack and his tiny band of warriors prevailed in three of the four military engagements against federal troops. The Modoc reality became the standard treatment for Native American tribes whose homelands faded away as a result of the disregard for Indian rights and perceived cultural inferiority.

Compton describes the mind-set of American emigrants who, upon encountering the Modoc people, saw them as metaphorical "rocks in the road" in their quest for land. His descriptions of Tule Lake and the lush Lake Country where Modoc lodges flourished for eons brings us into the center of their universe and gives us a glimpse into their spiritual and emotional connection with the homeland that ordered their lives. How they come to be declared as "belligerents of a foreign power" and forcibly removed from their universe is the compelling narrative delivered by Compton.

Educators will find in-depth depictions of the circumstances that dictate Native American reliance on cultural knowledge to safeguard their very existence and their homelands. Native American students who are versed in their own tribal history will gain knowledge of the internal decision making of a tribal leader during a war period. Compton's book encapsulates the multiple forces that pressure the Modoc tribe whose homelands lay in the path of settlers. It is a timeless case study whose lessons mirror what other tribes endured under the weight of federal policies.

After the Oregon Trail opened in 1843, the country changed rapidly as white settlements sprang up west of the Mississippi. White settlers lacked an understanding of the amount of land area needed to sustain a tribal hunting-and-gathering livelihood, as opposed to sedentary, individual family farming, and erroneously concluded that a small number of Indians coveted large expanses of "unused" land. White settlers, as well as federal, state, and local governments, used this misguided narrative to justify land seizure without regard for Indian ownership. Their enforcement tools were federal troops, local militias, and legislative action. As a result, many tribes, starting in 1830 and continuing throughout the next six decades, were displaced from their lands.

The Modoc developed varying adaptations to white settlers. They participated in the economic life of the settlers, whom they called Bostons, providing needed labor for nearby farmers and townspeople. They wore Boston clothing and carried "talking papers" as resumes for prospective employers. It was not unusual to have intermarriages between Modoc women with white men who lived in towns. Yet, despite this apparent melding of cultures, townspeople instigated continuing violent acts in order to displace and remove the Modoc people. Some saw extermination as the solution.

Compton demonstrates how tribal lands were actually taken in the saga of the Applegate family. Among the early Oregon pioneers arriving in 1843, the Applegates helped open the Applegate or Southern Trail to Oregon, providing a route for immigration and for settlers taking advantage of the Oregon Donation Act of 1850 to access rich lands in Lake Country. The trail passed directly through the villages of the Modoc people, creating conflict and dislocation. When the Klamath reservation was created, Applegates assumed positions of authority and established a monopoly on contracting rations for the tribe, offer-ing goods and services of poor quality at the highest prices. Applegates also played a key role in the Modoc War. Relentless, they consolidated Modoc lands into family ownership at every opportunity and pushed to spread their influence in Congress and the White House, seeking finan-cial gain from railroad development and the control of water rights.

The state and federal office holders faced a political dilemma in dealing with the Modoc and other tribes when California became the 31st state in 1850, and Oregon the 33rd in 1859. For the Modoc, whose Lake Country lands were situated on the disputed border between Cal-ifornia and Oregon (ironically a state conflict unresolved until 1896), treaty-making by competing political entities to accomplish land acqui-sition in exchange for rations of food and clothing became an unwieldy solution when the Modoc leadership signed conflicting treaties in 1864 with both states. The California treaty permitted them to remain in their village, while the Oregon treaty removed them to the Klamath res-ervation alongside their historical rivals. Unfortunately for the Modoc, who preferred the California treaty, Congress in 1869 ratified the Ore-gon Treaty, thereby severing the Modoc from their homelands.

In this early period, Indian tribes had been under U.S. military and civilian supervision. However, in 1869 administration of the reserva-tions was placed under religious denominations as part of a "Peace Policy," framed by President Ulysses Grant as the "Christianization and Civilization" policy that would change the livelihood and culture of Indian people to more closely resemble white cultural norms. This policy divided seventy existing Indian reservations among thirteen Christian denominations, positioning church leadership to choose each Indian Agent who in turn became the sole authority and administrator for a reservation.

In the Northwest Methodist and Catholic denominations admin-istered the reservations. The effect of the Peace Policy was that tra-ditional tribal communities, whose internal values and social practices had sustained them for generations, found their lifestyles subject to the judgment and control of a reservation Indian Agent. Indians were pres-sured and coerced to abandon cherished tribal customs and exchange their lifestyle practices for those of the Euro-American. When Indians resisted, their lifeline of rations was withheld until they complied. The degree to which many Indians were Christianized is evidenced during the Modoc War by Warm Springs scouts who held a Christian prayer service before leaving to hunt down the Modoc warriors.

Compton unravels many elusive facts through Modoc and other voices preserved over time. He raises the question of who really caused the Modoc War. The conduct of the war, when set against notions of military order and common sense, is challenged by his examination of the motives and actions of the religious, military, and civilian individuals representing different states and the federal government. He reveals the vacillation of government actors over leaving the Modoc in their homeland, removing them to Indian Territory, or exterminating them. Into this deep chasm of conflicted policymaking must also be added the eventual breakdown in chains of command, blundering administrative skills, and cultural misunderstandings framed by the quest for economic enrichment and political ends.

This narrative foretells the destiny of the Modoc whose dire circumstances were predictable in 1864 when they are lured by promises to live alongside their enemy on the Klamath reservation while awaiting treaty ratification. Years passed during which sparse rations and clothing either dwindled or ceased altogether. Attempts by Modoc men to support their families by felling trees and cutting rails were thwarted when their historic enemy boldly stole and sold their rails. After long waits, the few arriving rations were unfit for human consumption. The Modoc clearly acted to avoid starvation by resuming their hunting and gathering livelihood outside the Klamath reservation, only to find their homelands now under survey by the Applegates for a railroad line.

Leaving the Klamath reservation in 1869, Captain Jack, considered the war leader, defied federal authorities and led the return of the Lost River band of some forty or so Modocs back to Lost River. Further complications arose when Captain Jack killed a Klamath healer in accordance with Modoc cultural mores, whereby a healer could be killed for failure to cure the patient. At that time, federal policy saw tribes as nations and left such matters to be resolved internally in accordance with tribal custom. The state of Oregon, however, saw this as murder and secured a grand jury indictment and order for Captain Jack's arrest as a lawless renegade.

Compton describes the subsequent military attack on Captain Jack's village, which in turn instigated a chain of events in which his Lost

River band and the nearby Hot Creek band converged in the Lava Bed Stronghold against one thousand federal soldiers and volunteer militia from both California and Oregon. Certainly, the Modoc were well aware of military conflicts elsewhere which ended in massacres. It is here that Modoc cultural beliefs and faith in the powers of their native healer bear a large influence on their war strategies and leadership decisions. The Lava Beds became their only hope for survival against overwhelming military odds.

Throughout this book, Captain Jack's decision-making is apparent against the obstacles. He sees laws applied to him do not apply to Bostons accused of wrongdoing. He accepts he will die if he surrenders, and he will die if he fights. Illiterate, Captain Jack is uninformed as to the written manual governing laws of war used by the army which will later convict him. What persists is the strength of Modoc cultural ways that influence their war strategies. This is reflected in the internal leadership struggles when Captain Jack is taunted by placement of a woman's shawl on his shoulders. It is also seen in the Modoc war strategy that killing the chief of the opposing war party results in war abandonment. All of this converges with the killing of General Edward Canby and a minister in their roles as Peace Commissioners under a white flag.

Compton's research reveals the bitter defeat of Captain Jack at the hands of the same Hot Creek warriors who fought alongside him in the Lava Beds. Hired scouts for the army, they are given the label of Bloodhounds. Sadly, there is no traditional cremation for Captain Jack and the Modoc warriors deemed guilty of war crimes by the military court and executed. The 153 remaining men, women, and children are imprisoned as enemy combatants and escorted to Indian Territory where their numbers dwindle due to new diseases and inhospitable lands. Inauspiciously, they are subject to years of corruption at the hands of an Indian Agent chosen by Quakers, who hired eleven members of his family for reservation jobs and conspired with them to divert federal dollars intended for the Modoc. By 1904, the Modoc Tribe of Oklahoma was reduced to 54 individuals.

The work of Jim Compton is an extensive depiction of an Indian leader's attempts to make decisions that protect the homeland of his people against decisions by state, federal, and religious authorities. Compton demonstrates that the Modoc presented a far greater presence and persistence than "rocks in the road" to American domination. The

Modoc story, in its portrayal of resistance to external threats to their homeland, livelihood, and universe, casts light on the flaws in American federal and state policies, including conflicts between states, the colonizing efforts of the federal government, Euro-American beliefs about race, culture, and inequality, and the peculiar ways in which federal policy was consolidated in the hands of ambitious families in collaboration with missionaries and politicians. In fighting the Modoc War, the Modoc people accurately mapped the growth and development of the American nation-state.

Spirit in the Rock reveals the responsibility of a leader in placing concern for the welfare of his band above all else, and struggling to avoid failure in all external dealings. The fact the Modoc people exist today is a tribute to this leadership, the participation of women and children in defending Modoc land and livelihood, and the Modoc cultural spirit.

Prologue: The Hanging

I am a Modoc. I am not afraid to die.

—Captain Jack
Riddle, *Indian History*

They delayed the hanging of the four Modocs. Colonel George Hoge, the officer in charge, had to call a brief halt while he cut Captain Jack's dense black hair so the noose would fit around his neck. At the foot of the towering gallows stood seven Union officers in dress blue tunics, brass buttons gleaming, the cavalrymen wearing their swords. A celebrated Civil War officer was in command. A corporal, a private, and a colonel stood on the tall gallows with the Indians. A blacksmith had removed Captain Jack's iron shackles. His arms and legs were pinioned "with savage jerks," and a used haversack was placed over his head in lieu of a hood.[1] The Modoc chief was visibly weak. Cutting his hair severed Captain Jack's final link with his past and readied him for the white man's justice. It was October 3, 1873.

Witnesses said Captain Jack stood proudly to the end and died quickly. Some of the others died hard. "The bodies swung round and round," wrote one reporter. "As the drop fell with a terrible deadly thud, four poor, wretched human beings fell into eternity, and a half smothered cry of horror went up from the crowd of over 500 Klamath Indians, who witnessed the awful spectacle." Wails of deep and bitter anguish went up from the stockade, where wives and children were blocked from full view of the shocking scene.[2]

It was a textbook hanging. Regulations called for Manila rope, boiled so it would not stretch. The traditional knot was employed, lubricated with soap to slide freely, and placed behind the prisoner's left ear. Not until 1913 did the army require the condemned be weighed to calculate the required length of the fall. If the rope is too long, there is danger of decapitation; if too short, death occurs by strangulation. The Modocs fell about six feet—probably about right, by modern standards.

A few curious souvenirs of the execution survive. Colonel Hoge collected a lock of Captain Jack's hair, affixed it to a letter with a red ribbon, and mailed it to his brother in upstate New York.[3] The Post Commander, Lieutenant George Kingsbury, sent a lock of Captain Jack's hair to his hometown paper in Vermont, where it was available for viewing at the office of the *Bellows Falls Times*.[4]

The evening before Captain Jack's execution, he put his "X" on little squares of paper inscribed, "True signature of the Modoc Chief Captain Jack, the night before his hanging, October 3, 1873." A Doctor F. J. Hearn of Yreka claimed in 1874 that he owned the hangman's knots from the ropes.[5] Leonard Case, a sightseer from Ohio who witnessed the hanging, said he had collected both hair and "halter" (noose) souvenirs.[6]

Today the site of the hanging at Fort Klamath is a place of grassy meadows, rimmed with pine forests. Cattle graze in the nearby pastures east of Crater Lake. Only the guardhouse where the condemned men were held can still be seen, a duplicate built after a 2001 fire destroyed the original building and its modest trove of artifacts. Gone is the little wooden chair where Captain Jack silently held his five-year-old daughter, Rosie, the night before he was hanged. Gone is the set of manacles that held one of the prisoners. Gone for more than a century are the whitewashed barracks and stables, the officers' quarters, and the gallows.

Fort Klamath was an isolated frontier backwater in 1873. The fort had a 125-foot flagpole, flying the thirty-seven star flag. Officers were housed in six duplex buildings of sawn boards, whitewashed, with generous porches. Several officers, including the post commander, had installed their wives in the new quarters. "Here one finds," reported the *San Francisco Bulletin*, "even in the bachelor homes, the refinements of civilization, articles of *virtu* [antiques] and objects d'art."[7] Infantry and cavalry noted their barracks were adequate, although less comfortable than the stables. Lieutenant Frazier Boutelle, who had led New York Volunteers during the Civil War, found the post chaotic; "all is a hubbub," he wrote, and he complained he could not find a place to sit quietly for a few minutes and write to his fiancé, Dolly.[8]

On that October 1873 morning, Fort Klamath was crowded with tents and wagons, and campgrounds for spectators had sprung up. The army post, on its great meadow of native grass, had turned into an expanse of mud. Food vendors set up tents, and cook fires filled the air with smoke. Throngs of Indians, most from the neighboring (and rival) Klamath tribe, grew daily as the execution of the condemned men neared. Oregon's Indians had adopted the dress of the settlers—the men wore woolen trousers (often from army uniforms), flannel shirts, and slouch hats. The Indian women acquired a taste for ankle-length calico skirts, and wore traditional basket hats that looked like inverted bowls. Some of them made and sold souvenir moccasins.

The cool fall weather was perfect for those travelling to the hanging. Mountain roads in Oregon from Jacksonville and Ashland, seventy miles west, were clotted with wagons and carriages crossing the Cascade Range. A school in Ashland gave students the week off, "to enable the preceptor [teacher] and pupils to come here and gloat over the ghastly scene," wrote one reporter.[9] The road into Fort Klamath was notoriously bad; wagons and buckboards creaked and rattled for two days crossing the Cascades before emerging from the woods at Fort Klamath. An Oregon farmer who thought there would be a charge to attend the hanging brought a barrel of cider; he was surprised to learn that admission was free.[10] A trio of businessmen left Cleveland two months earlier to cross the country and witness the hanging. Three others came from Pittsburgh for the spectacle of military justice.

In the days leading up to the executions, the town of Linkville, thirty-five miles south, was a bedlam of "horse races and soldiers drinking." Travelers played dice and billiards "until the lamp blew up." One spectator from Ohio bound for the hangings won fifty dollars in a poker game but awoke to find thirty of his winnings had been stolen. Leonard Case and his two companions from Cleveland reveled in the excitement when they finally reached Fort Klamath. Quartered in the post hospital, the post surgeon took the trio to see the condemned men. Case saw Captain Jack's "old wife Mary" (actually his sister) while she was visiting the chief, and she in turn wanted to see Case's gold teeth.[11]

As the execution day approached, the army admitted a parade of journalists and tourists. Upon request, the jailers would open the cell doors for the curious newsmen to look at the prisoners. Being first to report the hangings was the great prize, and reporters from six major newspapers in New York and California awaited the execution. The army provided a table for the press just at the left foot of the gallows. The journalists had ponies and riders waiting to ride relays with their dispatches seventy miles to the telegraph in Jacksonville. They reckoned it would take nine horses and seven hours to make the mad trip over the Cascades.

The prisoners awaiting execution had been confined in an over-hot guardhouse throughout the long summer of 1873. Initially, six men had been condemned to death: Captain Jack; his three lieutenants, Schonchin John, Black Jim, and Boston Charley; and two confused Indian youths, Barncho and Slolux, whose pardon by President Grant was announced on execution day.

Captain Jack, whose Modoc name was Keintpoos ("Sour Stomach"), was a trim man of about thirty-five, five feet eight inches tall. His striking appearance—stony and stoical, dressed in the collarless striped flannel shirt he wore to the gallows—is evident in the photographs taken immediately after his capture. Muscular and compact, his body made lean by months of near-starvation, Captain Jack stares placidly at the lens. His ear-length hair, parted at midline, is glossy and dark.

Captain Jack shared his gloomy cell with his subchief, Schonchin John, a grizzled man of about fifty whose name meant "square jaw." The cell was dark, unlit except for an air vent at the top of the nine-foot walls. Captain Jack was initially shackled at the ankle with Schonchin John, but they were now separate, each keeping his anklet of iron. One photo exists of them standing barefoot together, wearing short-billed caps and grubby blue jeans rolled up six inches at the ankle. Schonchin John looks elderly and broken.

Nearly 153 Modocs were imprisoned in a stockade—a pen, really, about 100 x 150 feet wide, near the guardhouse where Captain Jack was held. The army erected the large enclosure for the prisoners, mostly women and children, with walls of twenty-five-foot pine logs standing on end, driven several feet into the ground. There were internal log barricades partitioning the stockade, to keep feuding bands and families from fighting. The logs had been sharpened to a point at the top. Twenty-four soldiers stood shifts as sentries.

The Modoc families pitched tents in the stockade, and the women cooked the rations given them over campfires. Over the summer, the families and relatives of the condemned were sometimes allowed out of the stockade to visit the men in the guardhouse. "They chafe under restraint, and those who can speak a little English inquire anxiously when they will be given their liberty."[12] On the day of the execution, the Modoc families watched the crowd through cracks between the logs of the stockade, but they were not allowed to see the men die. From their enclosure, they could only glimpse the top of the gallows and the six nooses.

Among the Indian spectators awaiting the hanging was Scarface Charley, once Captain Jack's principal strategist and translator. Just twenty-two, he had fought by Captain Jack's side through most of the war. His name originated from a striking scar running from his right temple and down across the cheekbone, clearly seen in photographs. In the end, he avoided punishment by giving himself up to the army. Four Modoc turncoats, known as the Bloodhounds, were also given freedom of the post. The day before the hangings, the Bloodhounds sat in their tent outside the stockade walls playing cards.

The free Modocs were now celebrities of a sort, mingling with the sightseers who thronged Fort Klamath. As the execution neared, Scarface Charley walked around the fort, selling souvenirs to tourists. He bartered his beaded moccasins to the businessman from Cleveland for two dollars. Bogus Charley and Shacknasty Jim, two of the Bloodhounds, sold rings for one dollar.[13]

On execution day, Colonel Hoge and his soldiers experimented with sandbags to test the trap doors and the strength of the rope. The

"He bore himself with dignity, and sat there like a Roman hereo." Souvenir card of Captain Jack. *Courtesy author's collection.*

gallows was huge for the era, erected from Ponderosa pine logs. With six trap doors, it was three feet wide and thirty feet long. The traps were designed to fall simultaneously when the rope securing them was cut with an ax. Six graves had been dug outside the guardhouse.

By the day of the execution, October 3, army, spectators, and Indians numbered more than two thousand. On a perfect fall morning the hangings at Fort Klamath took place with precision and ceremony. "Birds are singing, and nothing in nature indicates that it is Hangman's day," wrote one newspaperman. Morning routines were followed, although horses were saddled a half hour early. At 9:00 A.M. all troops were assembled in a column and readied to march the four hundred yards from the parade ground to the execution site in the great meadow south of the fort. Promptly at 9:15 the seven companies of infantry and artillerymen, marching at quickstep and preceded by a company of mounted cavalry, arrived at the guardhouse to escort the convicted men to the rope. There were about 250 soldiers in all. A wagon with a four-horse team carrying coffins was brought for the prisoners. The officer of the day unlocked their cells, and a blacksmith chiseled off their shackles. The men were directed to mount the wagon and sit on the coffins.

With muffled drums, the column raised "a great cloud of dust" as the soldiers slowly escorted the prisoners the short distance to the scaffold. The column divided and formed squares on three sides of the gallows. Three senior officers stood in front. Three post surgeons, a translator, and several other officers and privileged civilian spectators, including Case and the Cleveland party, were grouped behind them. Six reporters sat at their table at the corner of the gallows. Cavalrymen on horseback held back the crowds milling behind the military formations. The designated hangmen, two enlisted men, and Colonel Hoge waited on the scaffold in preparation for the execution. "Four or five dogs belonging to the garrison basked in the shadow of the gallows, which was thrown forward, the bright sun being behind the condemned," wrote one reporter. A "gentle breeze" swept across the field. One paper reported: "Visitors were gathered in large numbers—ranchmen from the adjacent valleys; merchants, lawyers and people of leisure from across the mountains, half-breeds, Snakes, Klamaths and Modocs from the reservation, making a motley and picturesque crowd."[14]

General Wheaton ordered the prisoners to mount the scaffold. The post commander, Lieutenant Kingsbury, read lengthy orders and declarations from President Grant and his secretary of war. A translator explained the sentences to the condemned, which had to be translated first into the Chinook trade jargon, and then from Chinook into Modoc. Boston Charley chewed a plug of tobacco and spat. Chaplain Huquemborg read the Episcopal service for the condemned and wept when finished. The prisoners' arms were roughly trussed behind their backs, black hoods made from haversacks placed over their heads.[15]

Captain Jack was very weak by this time. He wore a collarless striped cotton shirt open at the breast, revealing a red flannel shirt beneath. The other men wore some items of army clothing. Black Jim wore a full-dress officer's coat, probably stripped from General Canby's corpse. Schonchin John wore an army blouse and trousers. Boston Charley defiantly wore the uniform cap of Lieutenant Arthur Cranston, who had died in a gruesome Modoc ambush.

At 10:15, in a hushed silence, Colonel Hoge took out a handkerchief and dropped it as a signal. Then "Corporal Ross raised his hatchet, and with a flourish, it severed the rope, and the drop fell with a report as though one plank had fallen on another. The four bodies swung round several times." The cry "Parade Rest!" broke the stillness.[16]

Captain Jack and Black Jim died instantly. Schonchin John and Boston Charley struggled, their legs convulsing up and down, strangling. Their bodies remained hanging for thirty minutes before they were cut down and put in simple coffins of rough pine boards.[17]

A half hour after the execution, the coffins were taken to a surgeon's tent just behind the guardhouse where assistant surgeon Dr. Henry McElderry had improvised a mortuary. It stood a few dozen yards from the stockade, where the families of the dead Indians were still confined. McElderry ordered the bodies taken from their pine coffins and placed on an India-rubber sheet like those used in dissecting rooms. Colonel H.S. Shaw, city editor of the *San Francisco Chronicle,* saw a macabre scene that night in McElderry's tent. A Modoc cadaver stretched out on the black waterproof sheet, the body evidently the subject of embalming or dissection.[18] Later there were rumors the body of Captain Jack had been stolen, preserved, and shown to the public "at ten cents a sight."[19] In fact, the corpses were decapitated, and only the torsos were buried.

McElderry had removed the heads, scalped them, soaked them in a lime solution to part the flesh from the bone, packed the skulls in a barrel, and shipped them to a colleague in Washington, D.C.

More than a century passed before the Modocs learned the fate of Captain Jack's skull. An old catalog of specimens in the army medical collection of 1909 recorded seven Modoc skulls, four of which were received from McElderry. In the mid-1980s, Debra Riddle, a forceful and striking Modoc woman with waist-length auburn hair and an extraordinary resemblance to her famous Modoc ancestor, set out to recover the remains of Captain Jack and the other Modoc warriors. Highly knowledgeable in Modoc history and genealogy, Riddle was determined to bring the skulls home. She launched an odyssey through tribal, state, and federal bureaucracies that finally took her to the Smithsonian headquarters in Washington, D.C. In 1984 Riddle succeeded in her quest. The skulls were delivered to her, and she brought them home to Oregon. But to this day no one—except Riddle herself—knows where the skulls rest.

Photo by Carol Arnold.

Part One
The Screeching of the Owl

Nî'shta hä'ma mû'kash txû'txuk: "máklaks k'läk!
Nä'nu wíka-shítko múkash hä'ma.

All night long the big owl screeches, presaging "People Die!
I hear the owl's cry and very near it seems to be.

—From Modoc Song for Funeral of Warriors
Gatschet, *The Klamath Indians*

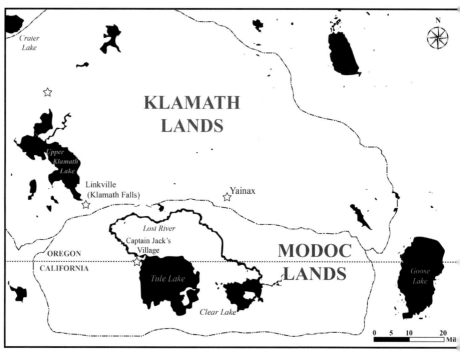

Modoc and Klamath Lands, Pre-1864.

1

A Harmonious World

My people, we were born in this country; this is our land. God put our fathers and mothers here. We have lived here in peace.

—Captain Jack's Father
Riddle, *Indian History*

The Modocs traditionally cremated their fallen warriors. According to custom, the dead and their possessions were solemnly cremated on a funeral pyre, their horses sometimes killed and cremated along with them, head to the west, within five days. "The weeping of the chief mourners was audible over the crackling of the flames, but friends attempted to soothe them and urged them not to exhaust their strength by mourning." The faces of mourners were blackened with soot; and widows and children of the deceased cut their hair and smeared their bodies with pine pitch.[1] Houses of the dead were burned immediately to remove any reminder of the dead person.

But Keintpoos' few belongings had been seized as souvenirs on the day of his capture, and the army had taken his horses. His death by hanging was considered shameful to the Modocs as well as to Keintpoos himself: "I am ashamed to die the way I am to die," he said.[2]

Modoc culture, one of many different Native cultures in the Pacific Northwest, was ancient. Archeologists have evidence of Modoc ancestors living in Lake Country as early as 5,500 BCE.[3]

The homeland of the Modoc and neighboring Klamaths consisted of a five-hundred-square-mile basin straddling what is now the modern Oregon–California state line. The name "Modoc" comes from the Modoc word "Móatokini," which means "Southerners." The Klamaths lived around Upper Klamath Lake in the north, while the Modocs lived in the southern villages around the Sprague River, Lower Klamath Lake,

Hot Creek, northwest of Tule Lake, and along the Lost River. Early writers tended incorrectly to refer to all the Indians in the Lake Country as "Klamaths." But according to Modoc oral history, the Modocs had seceded from the Klamath tribe, "seven times ten years ago." The two groups had a separate culture, but "a relationship of cool friendship."[4] Linguistically, the Klamath language was the root for the Modoc tongue, and the Modocs and the Klamath could converse.[5]

"The Modoc homeland was the center of their universe and the hub of their spiritual world." Marshland around Tule Lake. *Photo by Bill Stafford.*

For centuries the Modocs lived in extraordinary isolation. Cheewa James, Modoc historian, observed, "Above all, the Modocs loved their land. It was, in every sense, their world. They understood the land. The environment sometimes could be adversarial, but Modocs knew ways to cope. It was that knowledge that made them powerful in combat."[6] In 1780, there were only four to eight hundred Modocs. Along with the Klamaths, the total population in the Lake Country was about 2,000 Indians.[7] Individual Modoc bands rarely numbered more than forty. The Modocs were so few and so isolated in their Lake Country, no one knew much about them, and no one really cared. Keintpoos most likely did not see a white person for the first decade of his life.

The Modocs shared their land with legions of spirits who inhabited every rock and stream. One anthropologist described it this way: "Virtually every unique rock feature, mountain, cave, body of water . . . had a spirit and everything with a spirit had power."[8] Chief among the spirits was the creator named Kumash, the Old Man of the Ancients, who was always dwelling among them. He resembled mortals in every strength and frailty; like the Modoc people, he loved to gamble and play tricks.[9] Dreams offered spiritual guidance, but some—like a dream of a recently deceased person—could be dangerous.[10]

A young Modoc man was expected to go alone into the mountains on a "crisis quest" to gather spiritual powers for success in hunting and other life activities. The crisis quest demanded several days of fasting, strenuous physical activity, and isolation—all in rough country.[11] Among other tasks, a young man was required to pay respect to stones and to the mountains.

Adult Modocs also embarked on crisis quests during difficult times such as the death of a child, illness, death of a spouse, or gambling losses. Such a crisis signaled the need to renew a person's spiritual powers. Someone on such a quest would build a rock cairn and a prayer seat to focus his spirit and as an offering to the spirit powers. No one other than the creator should touch these sacred places. Today, the sacred rock piles are still there: one anthropologist recently found rock cairns on "virtually every high peak or ridge" in Modoc and Klamath territory.[12]

The Modocs created pictographs on the rocks in and around the Lava Beds, some of which date back 4,500 years. The Modoc rock art embodied spiritual matters like the medicine doctor's quest, the curative powers of rocks, and the spiritual force of the landscape. Shamans created rock art as part of their healing powers "in order to store their medicine spirits for anticipated use."[13]

Powerful spirits inhabited the rocks. Rock spirits were alive. They could talk, flirt with pretty young girls, and magically transform into fish. Men sometimes turned to stone, but their spirits lived on in the rocks and their bodies could return later as men.[14] Gatschet collected songs or incantations for every kind of rock—"mountain, rock-cliff, rocks spotted, upright rocks, upright rocks small, rocks in river."[15] Even today, nearby tribes prohibit touching or photographing sacred rock art.[16]

"The Modoc rock art embodied spiritual matters like the medicine doctor's quest, the curative powers of rocks, and the spiritual force of the landscape." *Photo by Jim Compton.*

The Modocs of Keintpoos' band wintered beside Lost River in semi-subterranean lodges sometimes called wickiups. These were oval-shaped dwellings dug in the earth, spanned by a wooden framework, crisscrossed with mats woven from tules, and covered with dirt. Depending on size, these lodges usually housed from one to three families. The residents entered from above by a ladder through a single hole that also let smoke escape. Their summer homes were more temporary structures made of mats and bent willow poles. They always approached the house from the east, as the land of the dead lay to the west ("fearful influences emanated from that direction"). Those who slept at the west end of the house turned their feet to the wall, "otherwise they would suffer frightening dreams in which the dead would appear; they would be impelled to eat snakes and walk into fires."[17]

The land gave generously but not extravagantly. As snows melted, Modoc families moved from their permanent warm winter camps.

They caught and dried the spring suckerfish on wooden racks. Women dug and dried wild parsley and camas (the bulb of a wild hyacinth). A second run of suckerfish arrived in the fall, and women dried berries for winter. They fished from canoes crafted from tree trunks hollowed with burning coals and scraped with stone tools.[18] The Modoc caught several species of fish, including trout, salmon, and suckerfish. The lakes were bountiful: Indian Agent Alfred Meacham fishing in Klamath Lake reported catching twenty-four trout in an hour, weighing together 104 pounds.[19]

In late spring the Modocs moved their camps to lakes in the high meadows, where they could harvest ipos, the bulb of a small wild lily they ate fresh, or dried and stored. In the late summer the women used canoes to harvest wocus, the seedpods of a pretty yellow pond lily that grows in profusion in the lakes. Families hid caches of wocus and other food to prepare for the long winter, and they guarded these locations carefully.

The Modocs used tule and bulrush from Tule Lake to make everything from mats to clothing, leggings, shoes, and baskets, a distinguishing characteristic of their culture. Modoc baskets were set apart from those of other tribes by the use of tule material and plain twining. [20]

Gaming played an important part of Modoc life. Both men and women played elaborate games of betting and skill involving sticks, dice, and kick balls.[21] Later misunderstood by pious Indian Agents and preachers, gambling and gaming were deeply rooted in Modoc culture and were considered a test of skill, not vice.

The Modocs were organized not as a tribe, but in small bands, their leaders chosen through consensus. The leader's job was to keep peace in the community, mediate disagreements, and make decisions such as when to change fishing camps or dig roots. Wealth and fighting ability figured large in choosing leaders, but skill at oratory trumped other qualities as a qualification for leader. Modoc leaders with authority over more than one band appeared only when whites demanded an Indian "chief" to speak for all. The band chose a war leader only when the Modocs went slaving or fought neighboring Indians.[22]

Known as doctors or healers, shamans were the most potent figures in Modoc culture and served for life. The shaman lived in the largest house in the village.[23] To become a shaman, a man (or occasionally a woman) would first receive a spiritual calling in a dream. Following a quest to contact the spirits, an elaborate initiation ceremony was held with lavish gifts of food. The initiation of the Modocs' famous Doctor George attracted two hundred people, and he sang fifty songs.[24]

A shaman might construct a ceremonial pole to be displayed at his house. The pole, about nine feet high with the limbs and bark removed, was painted red. Tail feathers of a hawk were fastened to the top along with streamers or pendants, three or four feet long, made of twisted grass and tied with bright symbolic feathers, such as the red plumage of the woodpecker, to display the spirits of the shaman.[25]

When a Modoc fell ill, the family called in a doctor or healer. Sickness was thought to be caused by the intrusion of a morbid growth or foreign object in the body—sometimes a grapelike growth in the chest.[26] The doctor's medicine was strong if he had many spirits, and the success of diagnosis and cure depended on how many spirits he could command.

The family of the patient was allowed to kill a shaman or healer if the sick person died, particularly if the patient was a child. A healer who failed to cure "was thought to be giving prima facie evidence of evil intent," wrote anthropologist A.L. Kroeber. "Earnest attempts to kill him almost invariably followed."[27]

Prayers were an important part of Modoc spiritual life. There were prayers to the sun, moon, stars, and earth as well as mountains and bodies of water.[28] Nineteenth-century ethnographer Stephen Powers described how the Modocs "intoned an orison" (chanted a prayer) before leaving their homes at first light. A soldier, quoted by Powers, reported "a thrill of strange and superstitious awe" when he heard the Modoc singing.[29]

Modoc culture had a comforting rhythm that embraced life and death, spirits and passages. Lizzie Schonchin, whose husband Peter remembered the Modoc War as a child of ten, said, "Water evaporates, trees die. I used to think it was too bad to get old and die; but I see everything grow up and then die. So now, I think it is all right. Trees mature, and they fall, and new trees spring up."[30]

Keintpoos was born into this harmonious world about 1835, around the time when horses first arrived in Lake Country.[31] His village on the Lost River near Tule Lake was most likely the one called "Wachamshwash."[32]

Keintpoos probably married for the first time in his teens. Keint-poos' family included his first wife Spe-ach-es (later called Rebecca) and his young wife Whe-cha (later called Lizzie).[33] It was unusual for a Modoc man to have two wives; there is no record of any of the other warriors who fought with him having more than one spouse.

Keintpoos had one living child, his daughter Rosie Jack. Another child may have died in infancy. Rosie was born in the late 1860s, when Keintpoos was in his mid-thirties. Modoc parents loved their children. Small children were carried during the day, and at night they slept with the mother. Children were allowed to run free and play.[34]

Keintpoos clearly loved little Rosie. He was deeply moved and could not speak when she visited him in the guardhouse at Fort Klamath the night before he was hanged. After his execution, Rosie, who had spent the bitter winter of 1872–73 barricaded with her father inside the Lava Beds, was sent to exile in Oklahoma. She died in April 1874, just six months after the hanging. She was not quite five years old.

There is one photograph from the period in which Keintpoos' young wife Lizzie, his half-sister who was called "Queen" Mary, his old wife Rebecca, and little Rosie all pose moodily for the camera. Lizzie looks particularly resentful and probably posed unwillingly. Rosie looks quizzical but bored, ready for her nap.

CAPTAIN JACK'S FAMILY
"Keintpoos' young wife Lizzie, his half-sister who was called Queen Mary, his old wife Rebecca, and little Rosie all pose moodily for the camera."
Courtesy author's collection.

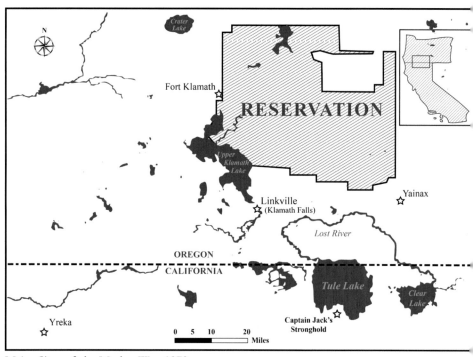

Major Sites of the Modoc War, 1873

2

The White World Arrives

On the Fourth of July 1846, an exploring party that included brothers from a prominent Oregon pioneer family appeared in Modoc country. Emerging from the Cascade Mountains, they trudged to the top of a ridge and beheld a dazzling sight—a high basin sparkling with lakes and rivers, stretching eastward "as far as the eye could see." It was an exciting moment. After days traversing the dark forests of the Cascades, their party broke forth in cheer after cheer. The sight stunned Jesse and Lindsay Applegate. There were "columns of smoke in every direction," marking the villages of scattered Modoc bands. Lindsay wrote in his diary, "We were entering a country where the natives had seen but few white people." He found the area "of peculiar interest, [which] only intensified our desire to see more of this then wild land."[1] The Applegates in fact were gazing at the Lake Country and Lost River where Modoc people had been living for millennia.

The homeland of the Modoc and neighboring Klamaths was called Lake Country by early white explorers. It was a place of "extravagant geographic diversity," a high plateau dotted with sparkling lakes and rivers, blessed with fish and game and nourishing plants. Their territory extended fifty miles north and east, bisected by a long informal boundary—the Klamaths to the north, the Modocs to the south.

During the first three decades of the nineteenth century, white visitors to Modoc country found little to interest them. Both Canadian and American trappers and traders probed into southern Oregon in the 1820s and '30s, only to find the trapping mediocre and the travel difficult. A great bear of a man named Finan McDonald pushed his way south to try trapping in Lake Country in 1825. But he found no bounty of beavers or otters, and he went home.[2]

In 1826 the Canadian trapper and explorer Peter Skene Ogden arrived in a blizzard. His party had fought their way through dense snow, their provisions exhausted, and they had just killed a horse to eat.

"Modoc country was blessed with fish and game and nourishing plants." Tule Lake. *Photo by Bill Stafford.*

Ogden had come to the riverside settlement of "Clamittes" in bitter November weather. He described "fine men, wretchedly clad." He saw only poverty, writing: "In the winter they live on roots. In summer on Antelope and fish." Ogden reported they had no guns and only one horse, but they were "well supplied with bows and arrows."[3]

Explorer-politician John Fremont marched through Modoc-Klamath country twice. On his second trip in 1846, he failed to post sentries when he camped, and he awoke to the sound of an ax being driven into the head of his lieutenant, Basil LaJeunnesse. The Klamath attackers also killed Fremont's favorite Delaware Indian guide. He was enraged at the Indian attack, and retaliated by firing artillery into their village and burning their dwellings to the ground, killing fifteen Indians, including women and children.

Even the early settlers arriving in Oregon did not impact the Modocs because the vast majority settled west of the Cascade Range, not in the Lake Country of southeastern Oregon. The mountain-ringed basin of lakes where the Modocs lived held little interest for the westering tide of white settlers. Visiting their remote domain required travel through three hundred miles of unmapped forest from the north, or a trek across 150 miles of desert from the east. For these immigrants, rich farmland was easily accessible in the Willamette Valley in north-central Oregon. Until those lands filled up, there was no need to cross the Cascade Range.

The Modocs might have come to the attention of western settlers a decade earlier had they not been bypassed by the many western gold rushes, a major factor in many of the Indian wars between 1844 and 1877. As the miners rushed into parts of California and Idaho, the Modocs were left in relative isolation. The only influence of this precious metal on Modocs' lives was the explosion of population in the small northern California town of Yreka, eighty miles to the west, where the Modocs began to visit for work and trade.

By the late 1840s new routes opened to Lake Country, and white settlers began pouring into Modoc lands. Instead of heading west across the Snake River Plain, a new road known as the Southern Route (later called the Applegate Trail) followed the California Trail down the Humboldt River, leaving it above the Humboldt Sink and bearing northwest into Modoc country.[4] Oregon's territorial government wanted treaties signed quickly to extinguish tribal titles and clear the way for homesteaders.[5] The Oregon Donation Land Act of 1850 made land available to settlers in Oregon territory, but—perversely—some grants were given on lands that still belonged to the tribes.[6] Tribal lands on the Sprague River were surveyed and opened for sale, and Congress made land grants to railroads and others before the tribes had ceded the territory by treaty.[7] Immigrants moved into the Lake Country area by the thousands, oblivious to evidence of Modoc homes and hunting grounds. The tribes meant nothing more to them than features of the landscape, rocks in the road on the way to settlement.

Between 1840 and 1860, tens of thousands of people immigrated to Oregon. Historian Jeff LaLande wrote: "A stranger arriving in southern Oregon during the 1850s would have encountered an agricultural and mining frontier region with a population of about 10,000."[8] Of the region, John H. Reed wrote in 1859: "[It] is rapidly filling up with people; all of the available land in it is claimed and improved. The settlers are already beginning to feel that restlessness, and sense of suffocation which so peculiarly belongs to a pioneer population."[9]

In the beginning, the Modocs—like many tribes along the immigrant route—were friendly and even welcoming to newcomers. In 1860, Lieutenant Piper, a soldier stationed on the frontier, reported the Modocs did not object to settlers stopping and cutting grass on their lands nor did they have "the least idea of molesting settlers" to the west of Lake Country.[10] Captain Jack said, "I always told white men when they came to my country, that if they wanted a home to have there they could have it, and I never asked for any pay for living there as my people lived. I liked to have them come there and live."[11]

But the crescendo of wagons rumbling through Modoc territory soon provoked the Modocs. Too often, the white newcomers treated the Modocs with gross disrespect and cruelty. One boy, traveling with one of the first groups on the Applegate Trail, told how he and his brother sneaked up on an Indian man fishing in Tule Lake and killed him, just for sport.[12] Another brutal incident was reported by Winema—the Modoc woman who served as translator and messenger during the Modoc war—who said blood was spilled when whites captured an "old Modoc woman," slashed her feet, cut a rope through both heels, dragged her behind a horse, and killed her.[13]

Late in the 1840s, Modocs began to retaliate, staging regular attacks on wagon trains on the Applegate Trail. They ambushed slow-moving wagons at a point on the trail where rocks forced settlers to travel a narrow passage along Tule Lake. In a September 1852 raid on an emigrant train, Modocs reportedly killed 65 men, women, and children. The site became known as Bloody Point.[14]

In 1852 a notorious act of white vengeance altered Modoc-white relations forever.[15] It all began when a group of Modocs ambushed a small party of eight or nine California-bound gold hunters at Bloody Point. The Indians killed all but one, a man named Coffin, who cut the packs off his horse, charged through the Indians, and escaped to Yreka, California. Coffin reported the massacre to a horrified public. The people of Yreka drafted Ben Wright, a professional Indian fighter—some would say killer—to lead the counterattack against the Modocs. Wright organized a volunteer company of twenty-seven men, and townspeople supplied Wright's men with arms, horses, and provisions.

Wright wore a buckskin suit, and his "glossy black hair, falling in waving tresses on his shoulders . . . made his resemblance to an Indian very striking when his back was turned." He took pride in scalping the fallen and committing other barbarities, such as "cutting off the ears, noses, and finger joints of the wounded, before the breath of life had taken their bodies." On this occasion, Wright equipped himself with a vial of strychnine and rode across the mountains from Yreka to Modoc country. There he invited the Indians to dine with him. Wright "roasted a beeve," which he laced with the poison, and then urged them to come to a feast. But a Warm Springs Indian traveling with Wright warned the Modocs not to eat the meat.

Having failed to poison, Wright invited the Modocs to a peace parlay at a spot on the bank of the Lost River a few hundred yards from the Natural Bridge. An account recorded in the Klamath language quoted Wright as saying: "Meet in council I desire God's white flag raising [*sic*]."[16] The trusting Indians came to the meeting, sat with the white men, and unstrung their bows as a sign of peace. At a signal (Wright lowered his pipe), his men attacked the unarmed Modocs. Many—including women and children—drowned trying to escape by leaping into the river. Wright's men killed as many as 64 Modoc men, women, and children.[17] In Modoc history, there were two (and perhaps five) survivors of the Ben Wright Massacre, possibly Schonchin John and the shaman Curley-Headed Doctor, both of whom would play central roles in the Modoc War twenty years later. Captain Jack's father was one of the Modocs killed.

When Wright's murderous gang returned to Yreka, there was a grand triumphal march. "Indian scalps dangling on the barrels of guns, their caps, and horses. Cheers and shouts rent the air . . . The enthusiastic crowd lifted them from their horses and bore them . . . to the saloons. Whiskey was free, and a big dinner was given them."[18] Judge Elijah Steele prophetically warned Wright that "the [massacre] would sometime react fearfully upon some innocent ones of our people."[19] Wright's dark reputation caught up with him. In 1856, a scant three years later, Indians on the Oregon coast killed Wright.[20]

The Ben Wright Massacre, committed under a white flag, embittered the Modocs for decades, and the betrayal would be resurrected during the catastrophic peace conference during the Modoc War.[21]

Relations between the whites and the Modocs continued to be ugly throughout the 1860s. Visitors to Modoc and Klamath Country brought back frightening stories. The British naturalist John Keast

Lord visited the Modocs in 1860. Terrified, he called them "ugly, half-naked demons, who are evidently doubtful whether to be friend or foe." Lord thought the Indians were trying to intimidate him with a wild horseback show: "A strange sight it is to see a dozen of these demons nearly naked, painted from their heads to their waists, in all colors and patterns, skying and whirling around on their half-tamed beasts, yelling and shouting, with no apparent object that I could discover but that of exhibiting themselves and trying to frighten me."[22]

Another visitor, Sergeant John Feilner of the First Dragoons stationed near Yreka, had a shocking experience when he took a furlough from the army to lead an ornithological expedition into Lake Country in May 1860. His party of four, including one Indian, met "hostiles"—undoubtedly Modoc—near Lower Klamath Lake. He reported that a man he called "head of the hostiles" named "Ike" (possibly the Modoc warrior later imprisoned with Captain Jack) said he had "killed both men and cattle, and it was his intention to do it again; that whites had no business here, and that he would drive them off."[23] Feilner canceled the bird-watching trip and went home.

But most of the time, the standard complaint by the white settlers against the Modocs was simply "impudence." In 1862 Indians demanded one hundred dollars from one Joseph H. Chaffee to establish a ferry across the river at the white hamlet of Linkville. Indians were said to be charging immigrants a dollar a night for grass. Chaffee said: "[They] are well armed, having in most instances 2 revolvers apiece, plenty of rifles and a good supply of ammunition. The Indians engaged in this work are Modocs, Paiutes, and Klamaths."[24]

Lieutenant Piper warned that people from west of the Cascade Mountains wanted to claim lands in Lake Country, but without proper arrangements with the Indians, "troubles will occur." Settlement of the area "would be very imprudent if not hazardous." Piper correctly predicted that an army presence in Modoc-Klamath country would open the floodgates for settlers: "The very first movement that is made by troops in direction of the Lakes will be the signal for these people to rush out and dispossess the Indians of their lands."[25]

Settlers in southern Oregon called upon the federal government for protection, demanding an army base and an Indian Agency, and the Applegate family lobbied for a fort in central Oregon to protect travelers on the Applegate Trail. With the Civil War raging, however, it was hopeless to ask for soldiers. Most available troops—including volunteers from Oregon—had gone east to fight on the Union side in the Civil War, and the federal government initially turned down the request for protection.

A military base was finally authorized in 1863 at Fort Klamath, an outpost just north of Linkville (present-day Klamath Falls) to oversee the Modocs, Klamaths, and Yahooskins (a band of Snakes). As expected, settlers began to rush over the mountains into Modoc territory. Historian Van Landrum wrote: "We can feel the pressure for extermination building against the red man." He explained: "All those lands [sought by settlers] were Modoc homelands—homelands for which the Indian tribe had not been paid, and most importantly, had not agreed to abandon. A treaty . . . was becoming necessary."[26]

3

The Applegate Factor

Captain Jack's story is entwined from the beginning with the fortunes of the Applegates, a famous Oregon pioneer family. The Modoc War cannot be understood without examining the Applegates' influence in shaping their version of the story. Two family members—Jesse Applegate and his nephew Oliver—had close association with historian Frances Fuller Victor, who penned Bancroft's two-volume *History of Oregon*.[1] These volumes are sharply critical of many figures in the Modoc War, often scathing in criticism of the Indians, and unfailingly flattering to the Applegates.

The Applegate brothers were descended from New Englanders. The family had drifted west to Missouri, where the brothers joined the first large migration to Oregon in 1843. The brothers' westward trip on the Oregon Trail was five months of hunger, thirst, and punishing travel.[2] Their arrival in Oregon began with tragedy, as two of the Applegate brothers watched their young sons drown in the treacherous rapids of the Columbia River. The brothers, like many other emigrants, had unwisely tried to pass through the rapids by manning their own boats rather than portage around the dangerous water. Their overconfidence and lack of skill were catastrophic: "[Their boat] was caught by one of those currents which, forming an open funnel shaped vacuum in the water to the bottom of the river, called a whirlpool . . . The boat was swallowed up in the roaring vortex."[3]

The death of their sons, and other emigrants, helped galvanize the settlers' determination to find a safer route to Oregon. In July 1846 an exploring party, including Jesse and Lindsay Applegate, set out to chart a new route for immigrants coming to Oregon. They rode south, then east, from their homes in central Oregon toward Fort Hall on the Snake River in today's Idaho. Crossing the Cascade Range east into Modoc territory, they at first did not see any Indians, but noticed moccasin tracks and picked up "broken and shattered arrows." Lindsay later wrote: "We were but a handful of men surrounded by hundreds of Indians with their poisoned arrows, but by dint of great care and vigilance we were able to pass through their country safely."[4]

Nine days into the terra incognita, they stepped out on the bluff overlooking the misty landscape of lakes and meadows of the Modoc plateau. The beauty of the land stunned the Applegates. They stood on a promontory near Buck Mountain, thirty-five miles southwest of modern-day Klamath Falls. Lindsay's diary recorded the dazzling sight of the Modoc country extending eastward, as far as the eye could see.[5] From their high perch, they had an uninterrupted view of the Modocs' traditional territory, the hills and mountain, the arc of land sweeping fifty miles to the southeast, lakes sparkling in the foreground.

"The Applegates trudged to the top of a ridge and beheld a dazzling sight—a high basin sparkling with lakes and rivers, stretching eastward as far as the eye could see." *Photo by Bill Stafford.*

When the party reached Lost River, it seemed to present an impassable obstacle. But a Modoc man showed the Applegate party the unique natural bridge across Lost River, a quarter mile from Captain Jack's village. The party thanked the Modoc "by gestures" and crossed the "smooth flat roadway across the river, over which the water rippled, swift and clear, about six inches deep."[6] Later known as the "stone bridge," the geological formation became a key landmark for west-bound travelers on the Applegate Trail.

Natural Bridge Across the Lost River (1936). *Courtesy author's collection.*

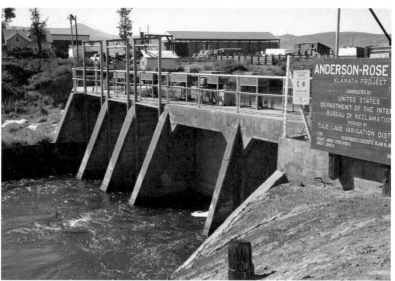

Site of the Natural Bridge (2015). *Photo by Bill Stafford.*

The Applegates' interest in Modoc lands continued for a half century. In 1846 Jesse brought a bill to the Territorial Legislature (of which he was a founding member) to charter a "Klamet [*sic*] Company," which would have given the right "to treat with the Indians, and purchase lands from them." The legislature refused "to grant a charter to any individual [to write] treaties with the Indian tribes to purchase their lands."[7]

The Applegates won a victory the following year when the Territorial Legislature declared the Applegate Trail "a safe and easy road for immigrants in this country."[8] But the new alternate route turned out to be longer than the original Oregon Trail—700 miles and three weeks longer—and it was dangerous. In 1847 several emigrant groups, relying on Jesse Applegate's description of the new route, ran out of food, were forced to abandon their animals and wagons, and were saved only by a seven-week rescue mission. Territorial Governor George Abernethy issued a warning to emigrants with families and wagons to avoid the Applegate Trail and "keep the old road."[9] Newspaper reports of the disaster triggered a war of words in the newspapers that eventually led to dueling pistols. Opponents charged Jesse Applegate with underestimating the distance of the trail (which he did) and overestimating the condition of the roads. Jesse Applegate, under the pseudonym "Z," fought back in letters insisting the new southern route was much superior and hinting that "diligent" emigrants would not have the problems experienced by the "slothful and indolent."[10]

The Applegates were ever enterprising, and the family thrived for decades on Modoc lands and Indian affairs. In 1863 the Applegates built a ranch on Clear Lake in Modoc country where they raised sheep and eventually had over a thousand head of cattle.[11] In 1865 J.W.P. Huntington, superintendent of Indian affairs for California and married to Jesse Applegate's niece, appointed fifty-seven-year-old Lindsay Applegate to run the Klamath reservation, at an annual salary of $1,000.[12] Lindsay then put two of his sons on his payroll: Ivan Decatur Applegate was hired as commissary at a salary in 1872 of almost $2,000; and Oliver Cromwell Applegate (often known as O. C.) served in dual jobs as a "commissary" at $983 per year and "teacher" at $1,700 per year.[13] Later several of the Applegate children purchased tracts of land near Jesse Applegate's ranch at Clear Lake. When a change in federal policy threatened Lindsay Applegate's job as Indian Agent, Oliver wrote to his brother Lucien saying, "I have done all possible towards having Papa sustained." As to the new arrangements, Oliver assured Lucien: "I think *we* can make as much out of the Indian Service as ever—perhaps more."[14]

But by the late 1860s, good fortune had eluded Jesse Applegate. He experienced financial reverses and suffered from depression (which eventually sent him to a mental institution). His cattle herds had been twice decimated by cold weather and his first plan for a railroad through southern Oregon had failed. In 1871 Jesse settled on land near Clear Lake country—supposedly swamp land—that was owned by California cattle baron Jesse Carr.[15] The Applegate ranch was in Modoc country, and in an attempt to revive his fortunes, Jesse embarked on business schemes that would destroy Captain Jack's village, forever sever the Lost River Modocs from their homeland, and bring on the Modoc War.

In standard histories the Applegate family is synonymous with the pioneer settlement and growth of early Oregon—their name given to a mountain, town, and river—but their central role in the Modoc War has been hidden by their own manipulation of history. The flattering treatment of the family in the landmark *History of Oregon* can better be understood when examining their letters, particularly those between Oliver Applegate and author Frances Fuller Victor.

The letters detail Victor's surprisingly close ties to the family. She first visited Jesse Applegate at his home in fall 1865, staying for an extended period and gathering history on the early days. "Mrs. Victor pumped me so dry of historical matter that the stores of both memory and imagination were utterly exhausted," wrote Jesse. "There was nothing I could conceal or withhold from the keen scrutiny of this lady."[16]

In 1873 Oliver and Jesse invited Victor to visit the Applegates in Klamath County and write a history of the Modoc War. They camped outdoors, roasting fish and venison on sticks over a log fire. Victor spent much of her six-week visit at the Indian Agency with Oliver, learning about the war and the life and customs of the Modocs.[17] Victor later candidly admitted she depended heavily on Oliver's written account of the Modoc War. "This is a full and competent account of Modoc affairs from 1864 to 1873," she wrote. "No one has a more thorough and intelligent knowledge of the customs, manners, and history of this tribe than Mr. Applegate."[18]

Following her visit to Modoc country, Victor continued to correspond with Oliver, whom she addressed as "Bliwas" or "Eagle." She often gushed with sentimentality and almost romantic affection: "I take great pleasure in liking you and esteeming you . . . It is a privilege to cherish and enjoy the sentiment. In the language of a true poet, 'God sends us love, Something to love he lends us. When love is grown to ripeness, love is left alone.'"[19]

In the 1880s Victor again visited Jesse Applegate at his home, and described him as she stepped from the stage at his gate: "His philosophical head, close shaven, with its large ears standing almost at right angles to his face, his large mouth stretched wide in a cordial yet half-quizzical smile, together with his gaunt figure and farmer's garb, made altogether a most unexpected picture." The historian spent ten days with Jesse, "the evenings of which were devoted to historical reminiscences."[20]

The Victor/Bancroft version of the events surrounding the Modoc War is rich in detail and bespeaks Victor's enormous research and knowledge of early Oregon. But its portrayal of the story is hardly impartial. The murderous Ben Wright was "a genial gentleman, honest, frank, brave."[21] Indian Agent Alfred Meacham is described as a hack, and Captain Jack as an incessant libertine who couldn't stay away from Yreka. As a result, Victor's flattering portrait of the Applegates and her bias toward the settlers have clouded our understanding of this complex episode in western history.

4

Dueling Treaties

In 1864 Judge Elijah Steele arrived at his home to find several hundred Indians—many of them Modocs—camped in the yard of his colonnaded Victorian mansion on Third Street in Yreka, California. His wife, Elizabeth, had been lecturing the assembly for three days on how to live like white folks. Steele, the Indian Agent for Northern California, regarded as one of Yreka's "leading citizens,"[1] was one to whom the Modocs often turned for help. This time they came to him to settle the fighting among several tribes, including Klamaths, Shastas, and Modocs, as well as to help the Indians make peace with white settlers.[2]

Steele was a friend to the Modocs from the start. He sometimes wrote letters for Indians to carry as a sort of pass they could present to whites, allowing them to travel freely.[3] Once, when a white prankster had installed a padlock in an Indian's perforated nose (which he said the Indian considered a "fine present"), the Indian complained to Judge Steele. Steele intervened and made the perpetrator remove the padlock. On another occasion, the judge successfully mollified a Rogue River Indian named Old Chief Joe, who threatened harm if he did not get "a white girl for a squaw for his son."[4]

Many of the judge's early dealings had been with a Modoc leader known as Old Schonchin, the older brother of Schonchin John who fought in the Modoc War and was executed along with Captain Jack. Old Schonchin had abandoned his pledge to kill settlers and now he wanted peace. "I threw down my gun," he said. "I will not fight again."[5] When the quarrelling groups of Indians came to Judge Steele's home to settle matters in 1864, Captain Jack emerged as leader of the Modocs. Old Schonchin remained as the figurehead of the "cooperative" Modocs who later willingly stayed on the Klamath reservation and did not fight in the Modoc War.[6]

On February 14, 1864—two days after the Indians' visit to his home—Steele made a treaty in which the Modocs were guaranteed a home in their own country. In return, the Modocs would allow "free and uninterrupted passage by whites through their country." A. M. Roseborough, a California judge, endorsed and approved the principles of Steele's treaty.[7] Steele submitted this California treaty to the Commissioner of Indian Affairs in March 1864, noting his pact with the Oregon tribes was "somewhat irregular," but necessary to avoid war. He reported the Indians intended to fully comply with the treaty and warned that trying to remove the tribes from their lands by force would be a costly and prolonged effort. "Their country is but little needed by our citizens," he added, "and much of the difficulty arises from evil-disposed white men who reside among the Indians."[8]

Unfortunately, Congress never even considered Steele's treaty.[9] Steele made the agreement in good faith, believing he had responsibility for tribes on both sides of the California-Oregon state line. But the Oregonians relentlessly condemned Steele's treaty for years, and within a few months Congress charged the Oregonians with negotiating a new one.

The new treaty was signed in October 1864 at beautiful Council Grove, Oregon, in Klamath territory following an intense week of pipe smoking, oratory, and bargaining. Lindsay Applegate, the acting Oregon Indian Agent, is said to have served as a counselor and translator to the Indians.[10] Superintendent J.W.P. Huntington, related by marriage to Jesse Applegate, represented the white settlers at the treaty negotiations. Huntington had visited the Klamaths several weeks earlier and jawboned them about the benefits of a treaty, hoping to get as many Klamaths as possible to attend and sign. No one spoke about the California treaty signed by both Klamaths and Modocs, or worried about the overlapping signatures on the two treaties.

A Klamath from Sprague River country named Monchnkasgit later described the Oregon summit: "Huntington met [us] there with the man who wrote for him, and another white man. We were there about a week and talked three days about the treaty. We built our first fire under the big pine tree which I think is still there. Huntington made a speech and said, 'I have come from Washington from the Great Father, to see about buying your land and have brought the things to pay for it.' He then showed us fishhooks, beads, buttons, coarse blankets, and red paint."[11] The chiefs at first asked for a large reservation that would include the original lands of both tribes. But Huntington told them: "That's too much land for you to take care of and hold." So the Indians caucused for several more hours and came back with a proposal for a much smaller reservation, with no Modoc land, which Huntington accepted, leaving the Modocs with none of their traditional territory.

Fewer than two dozen Indians representing bands from three tribes signed the 1864 Oregon treaty.[12] Each Indian signatory put his "X" next to his name. Although some Indians later acquired Anglicized names like Allen David, they are identified in the treaty only by the phonetic renditions of their Native names. Captain Jack signed the Oregon treaty with his Modoc name Keintpoos.[13] His "X" appears on the lengthy parchment document, with its red ribbon and wax seals, that now rests in the National Archives.

To celebrate the signing of the Oregon treaty, Lindsay Applegate gave presents to the Indians. He preserved an inventory of the gifts: Old Schonchin signed with his "X" for goods received by the assembled Modocs: 6 axes, 350 pounds of flour, 1½ pounds of gunpowder, 6 pounds lead, 1,050 fish hooks, 107 blankets, 3 cotton handkerchiefs, 1 box of matches, bolts of calico, and woolen pants. On the following day, Old Schonchin accepted an additional 755 pounds of beef and 1,700 pounds of flour.[14]

In the Oregon treaty, the tribes gave up their claim to twenty-three million acres—almost thirty-six thousand square miles of land. That staggering cession of territory—one of the largest ever agreed to by any tribe—was made in return for a guarantee of peace, a reservation where the tribes agreed to live together, and the promise of goods and money. The tribes thus surrendered title to the vast basin of timber, lakes, and high plateau where they had lived for millennia. The reservation they received in return was about one-twentieth the area of the lands they gave up, even though immense—800,000 acres or 12,500 square miles, larger than the state of Rhode Island.[15] But the Klamath reservation excluded the Modoc's Lost River homeland. It included only territory traditionally occupied by the Klamath tribe. Historian Keith Murray wrote, "No Modoc was allowed one acre of his traditional hunting grounds."[16]

The disputes over the reservation borders were not finally settled for decades, but the Applegate family worked hard to make sure the boundary lines favored their holdings. Ivan Applegate made his way to Washington and emerged as part of the commission that eventually approved a southern border that excluded the extensive Applegate holdings at Swan Lake.[17] As historian Theodore Stern noted, "Inevitably [the Applegates'] property interests and their wide and intimate relationships with the white community eventually confronted them with a grave conflict of interest."[18]

The October 1864 Oregon treaty became the official one, supplanting the unratified California treaty. But because of the distraction of the Civil War and its aftermath, five years passed before the U.S. Senate ratified it. President Grant did not sign it until 1870.[19] The conflicting documents—one signed in California and the other in Oregon—confused and bedeviled government relations with the Indians for nearly two decades. Had the government approved and honored the California treaty, it might have prevented the Modoc War. But for the Modocs, the Oregon treaty of 1864 was destined not to work.

For Captain Jack and his band, the conflicting treaties made no sense. Elijah Steele reported: "The [Modocs] asked me why the [California] treaty was not lived up to. They said they would give up their lands [outside the Lost River village]; would take care of themselves, as fish and fowl were abundant there; and that white men's cattle might graze there and they would not disturb them; and when people came there to cross the river they would assist them. I told them they made a new treaty with the Oregon agency and that done away with this one."[20]

The Modocs were forced to agree to move to a reservation on Klamath land called the "Klamath" reservation, a name that ignored the existence of the Modocs and Yahooskins who were also parties to the Oregon treaty. And it soon became clear the Modocs had signed away what the white men considered the best agricultural land in the area. When settlers poured in through the decades afterwards, the newcomers headed for the rich farmland around Tule Lake and Lost River, the heart of the Modocs' historical domains.

The signing of the Oregon treaty also had the unintended effect of creating "chiefs" among a people previously organized in bands, and this soon created factions among the Modocs. Captain Jack's Lost River band, along with the two other groups of Modocs, could never be satisfied with relocation to the Klamath reservation. The compliant

Modoc band led by Old Schonchin moved without resistance to the new Klamath reservation, thirty-five miles north of their traditional homes. The tiny Yahooskin band, linguistically and culturally different from the Klamaths and Modocs, settled in the eastern part of the reservation and played no part in the Modoc War.

The Oregon treaty led to deep mistrust among the tribes of the government and its promises. In authorizing the 1864 Oregon treaty, Congress had appropriated twenty thousand dollars to buy gifts for the tribes. But when the Oregon treaty was finally approved, few of the blankets and none of the eight-thousand-dollar per year subsidies promised to the tribes had been paid. All the Indians had to show for the Oregon treaty were some cattle brought to them by Huntington, and the fishhooks and beads given them the day they had signed the treaty almost five years earlier.

Despite an inauspicious beginning for Captain Jack, he and his band of Modocs left their Lost River homeland and moved to Yainax, a village created for the Modocs, on the Klamath reservation.

5

Captain Jack Flees

Captain Jack soon recognized that he had made a bad deal. The Modocs and the Klamaths clashed on the newly created reservation. The government solution was to keep them apart by creating a "subagency," a kind of reservation-within-a-reservation with a subagent for the Modocs. The subagency was headquartered at Yainax, a settlement of three hundred or so Modocs along the Sprague River, thirty miles from the main concentration of the Klamath tribe and about forty-five miles northeast of Linkville, today's Klammath Falls. The village expanded quickly as most of the "compliant" Modocs, led by Old Schonchin, gathered there and waited for the federal bounty.

Captain Jack and his band reluctantly made their way north from Lost River to Yainax in the depth of winter 1864. The journey took two days for the dozens of families. Food shortages were inevitable. The Modocs brought slender provisions gathered the previous spring and summer, and Yainax had no lake where the Modocs could fish and hunt waterfowl. It was at least thirty-five miles from the closest place to gather wocus. Captain Jack's band was now penned in among a people whom they did not like and who did not like them.

Modoc prestige and freedom were greatly diminished. Lindsay Applegate, Indian Agent for the Klamath reservation, got a Klamath named Allen David elected "chief" of the Klamaths.[1] Captain Jack had always bristled at any suggestion that white soldiers could rule his people, but now Indian Agents, Klamaths, and the army all oversaw the Modocs on the Klamath reservation. The Modocs were expected to comply immediately with the Oregon treaty; Captain Jack was told the agreement he had negotiated with the California Indian Agent, Judge Elijah Steele, was null. He complained to John Fairchild, a settler with whom the Modocs had good relations, that he had not sold his country. "The treaty was a lie," he told Fairchild.[2]

By spring 1865 Captain Jack had had enough. Caged, powerless, and separated from traditional sources of food, he bolted from the reservation and took his band back home to Lost River.

After Jack and his band left the Klamath reservation, some of the promised treaty goods arrived at Yainax—three years late. But the treaty payment would only benefit the Klamath tribe. Captain Jack's band of Modocs could share in the goods only if they returned to the Klamath reservation. Superintendent Huntington went to Lost River to deliver some annuity goods to entice Captain Jack back. He refused to accept them, angrily took his band across the river, and warned Huntington not to cross to the other side or he would shoot. Huntington asked the army at Fort Klamath to use troops to arrest Captain Jack, but the commanding officer said his forces were inadequate and refused. This was the first of several attempts made from 1865 to 1868 by the military and civilian Indian Agents to persuade Captain Jack to return to the Klamath reservation—to no avail.

Captain Jack left Lost River periodically to visit his friend Judge Steele in Yreka. Captain Jack protested the loss of his land and demanded that the February 1864 California treaty be recognized. Steele, sympathetic to the Modoc cause, wrote letters on Captain Jack's behalf, arguing the Modocs should be allowed to live along Lost River. Steele vouched for the Modocs' good faith, and their pledge not to harass settlers. He advised "that they not be molested, [so that] an unpleasant complication will be avoided."[3]

Captain Jack's rebelliousness began a full-blown contest for Modoc leadership. Old Schonchin kept the more compliant Modocs at Yainax. The army and the settlers accepted him as the legitimate head chief of the Modocs. The Modocs who left the Klamath reservation were divided among Captain Jack's band at Lost River, and another group led by Schonchin John, who settled across the Lost River from Captain Jack's village. Still another band—the Gombuntwas or "Hot Creeks"— settled twelve miles west of Tule Lake, just over the California line near the farm of John Fairchild. By 1869 half of the Modoc people were in revolt against the government, living away from the Klamath reservation.

At Lost River, Captain Jack's followers had periodic squabbles with their white neighbors. Jeff Riddle, writing in 1914, related how a farmer named Abe Ball befriended a Modoc named Skukum Horse. One evening Skukum dropped in to see Ball, who turned unfriendly. They had words, and Ball drove Skukum away "at a trot, at the end of a gun." Ball later tried to explain to Skukum that he had a guest—an Indian woman. Skukum was outraged. "They became hated enemies as the time rolled by," Riddle wrote, and "never showed friendship towards one another again."[4]

The best land for homesteading in Lake Country was on traditional Modoc territory around the Lost River, and the edge of Tule Lake. An 1859 letter described the region: "The grass it affords so luxuriantly, if nothing else, would make it a tempting place to the owners of our immense bands of cattle, particularly as the latter have consumed all the wild grass on [the other] side of the Cascade range of mountains."[5] But as the Modoc woman Artinie explained to a reporter, the settlers and ranchers were destroying the Modocs' food sources: "[The settlers] steal [Captain Jack's] land where he hunts and try to push him off his fishing-place on Lost River. By-and-by the buckaroos come and bring heap of cattle and drive off the games, and build houses on Capt. Jack's land. He got mad."[6]

As the tempo of white settlement increased, the little town of Linkville boomed. A prosperous ferry was established across the Klamath River, and lots were offered for sale beside the river. Pioneer Bob Whittle and his Modoc wife Matilda (both of whom would later play major roles in the Modoc War) built a barge that carried supplies up the lake for the military.[7]

By 1866 the Applegate family was running the Klamath reservation. Lindsay Applegate, Indian Agent, employed two of his sons: Ivan Applegate as subagent at Yainax, and Oliver Applegate as commissary in charge of ordering and providing supplies for the reservation Indians. In January 1865 Lindsay wrote to his nephew-by-marriage, Oregon Superintendent of Indian Affairs Huntington, that some Modocs "regretted their move [off the reservation], and want to talk. I am satisfied that in the event of the ratification of the treaty of October 15th 1864 they would willingly come to the reservation and acknowledge the authority of their Old Chief Schonchin."[8] In another letter dated the same day, Lindsay urged treaty ratification: "Klamaths and Modocs are growing mistrustful, and prompt action on the part of the Government is necessary to inspire them with proper confidence in it."[9]

Five summers and five winters passed as Captain Jack—who could not understand why one treaty was more binding than another—stayed at Lost River. There he could roam across two hundred square miles of familiar land, hunt and fish, and visit mining towns. Warnings from military and civilian officials to return to the Klamath reservation proved empty, and efforts to force Captain Jack to live among the Klamaths were futile. A dangerous impasse was emerging.

6

Jesse Applegate Meets Captain Jack

On a late summer day in 1869, Jesse Applegate had an unexpected and harrowing face-to-face encounter with Captain Jack. The Modoc chief, considered by the white community to be a lawless renegade after fleeing the reservation, was spending the summer beside Lost River. When Applegate and a team of surveyors blundered into his village, Captain Jack appeared, "suddenly and unexpectedly," demanding to know what they were doing. Jesse's worried group were not sure they would escape with their hides. They had been surveying to lay out a railroad route through Modoc country. One of the surveying party later said: "His highness, Captain Jack" confronted them, thinking they came to build farms. Captain Jack told them: "[he] did not want his dominions surveyed," and he had "no intention of joining the 'Bostons' [whites] in agricultural pursuits."[1]

When Applegate explained a rail line was planned, Captain Jack grew more obstinate: "[Jack] said that he did not want a railroad, his ponies being good enough for him and his people." After a talk that lasted through the night, costing the group "all the tobacco it possessed and nearly everything eatable," Jack gave permission to proceed. But Captain Jack warned the Modocs were "hiyu sullix copa Boston" ["angry at the whites"], saying that he would not be responsible for their lives or property if Applegate and his party continued. No one seems to have doubted Captain Jack, and at dawn the surveyors fled to Linkville, "with feelings of considerable relief that [they] were well out of a bad scrape."[2]

Jesse had been promoting rail development for several years. There were federal subsidies to be won, and he was an early investor in a proposed railroad route from Portland to California along the Willamette. He had invested in another unsuccessful venture to bring the rails to his home in Yoncalla, and now hoped other efforts would succeed.

When a high-rolling Californian, colorful stagecoach baron Ben Holladay, arrived on the scene, Jesse's plans—and Oregon's railway future—were altered forever.[3] Holladay lavished legendary amounts of bribes on the Oregon legislature and swiped the prized contract to build the railroad south from Portland. Holladay snookered everyone, and within five years he controlled most of Oregon's railroads. "He was a very big fish, for such a small pond as Oregon," wrote rail historian Larry Mullaly.[4]

Holladay was pursuing an immense economic reward. In 1865 Congress enacted a massive subsidy to build a north-south railroad in Oregon. For every mile of track completed, the builders would be granted twenty miles of land alongside the route, containing timber worth one hundred million dollars.[5]

It was clear to Jesse Applegate—sensing a rich opportunity—that it was in his best interests to join Holladay. The rails were finally reaching southern Oregon, and Jesse's hopes were aligned with the rail baron's plans. Holladay hired Applegate as a surveyor at two hundred dollars a month, and he laid out the route south toward the California border.[6] Holladay planned to start by building the railroad 197 miles south through Roseburg, near the center of the state. The planned line then took a swing to the east, bypassing the major towns of southern Oregon—Jacksonville and Ashland—and headed over the Cascade Range toward Modoc country. A rail line going to the east would be a godsend to Jesse, and he mounted his horse to survey Holladay's new proposed route.

Holladay was determined to cross the richly wooded Cascades in order to win the huge grants of public land and timber. Applegate likewise wanted to direct the line toward his business ventures in Modoc country and get in on some of the action if Holladay succeeded with his grand plan. The railroad would follow the Applegate Trail and pass just north of Tule Lake, crossing the natural stone bridge across Lost River.[7] Applegate and Holladay planned the route to pass almost directly through Captain Jack's village along the bank of the Lost River. For Holladay and Applegate, the village of Captain Jack's Modoc people was nothing but an obstacle.

When Applegate arrived home from his surveying trip in Captain Jack's homeland, he was energized. He now could promote his scheme to send a railroad east along the Applegate Trail. He entertained the vice president of the United States, Schuyler Colfax, for dinner at his stately white two-story house in Yoncalla, to talk railroads. His hospitality was well known.[8] Colfax was traveling with the influential publishers of the *Chicago Tribune* and the *Springfield* [Massachusetts] *Republican.* Jesse wrote to the riverboat magnate J.C. Ainsworth in Portland: "These three men, who exercise as great a control over public opinion, and wield as large an influence in the Govt. as any three men in it, thought of the Rail Road itself, and the proper means to secure its speedy construction."[9] In the end, Jesse secured a promise from Colfax to support rail development in Oregon.

Meanwhile Holladay was on the move, seeking money from German investors, marketing bonds in Frankfurt, Stuttgart, and Heidelberg. His securities were sold at attractive prices—it was believed in Europe that America was a foolproof place to invest. But Jesse's alliance with Holladay faced one final test: there was a powerful challenge to Holladay's plan. In 1870 the Central Pacific set out to build a line north through Oregon, with federal subsidy, that would cross the Cascade Mountains farther north and terminate at Eugene, Oregon, one hundred and forty miles north of Jesse's home. If built, the line would have rendered Holladay's Oregon Central line obsolete. The Central Pacific rail tycoon C. P. Huntington was ready to bankroll the competing route. It would probably bankrupt Holladay.

No stranger to brass knuckle politics, Holladay went to Washington. He lobbied Oregon's Senator George Williams to declare Holladay's route from Portland through Modoc country and south the main rail line through Oregon. At Holladay's urging Williams proceeded "in Holladay's interests."[10] From all appearances, Jesse cashed in some political chits, too.[11] Senator Williams broke ranks with other Oregon legislators, and Congress declared that a railroad by the name of Oregon Branch Pacific would take the route through southern Oregon along the Applegate Trail. In a single action, Congress blocked the plans of Central Pacific, and threw the windfall toward Holladay and Applegate.[12]

Jesse was prepared for Congress to take action. He had begun to raise money in Jacksonville, rounding up thirty-two well-heeled burghers and friends from southern Oregon and bringing them to the Jackson County Courthouse to incorporate a railroad. The investors were a virtual who's who of the successful farmers and businessmen around Ashland and Jacksonville.[13] Applegate incorporated his railroad in August 1870, just before Congress decided in December it would favor Applegate's route. He had named his railroad the Oregon Branch Pacific, the name prescribed by Congress. This suggests extraordinary prescience—or that Jesse Applegate had inside information about what would transpire in Congress.[14]

Old Jackson County Courthouse. *Photo by Bill Stafford.*

Holladay, now controlling all routes in and out of the state, was aggressively marketing Oregon land. In March 1872, on the eve of the Modoc War, he circulated a map showing the Applegate Trail as the chosen route to the east. Holladay announced with great fanfare the creation of the European and Oregon Land Company, and he opened offices in San Francisco and New York. Its prospectus trumpeted "RAILROAD LANDS IN WESTERN ORE- GON. EXTRAORDINARY INDUCEMENTS TO EMIGRANTS." The route passed through the Rogue River valley, then east to "the great basin of the Klamath Lakes." The "South-East Division" crossed part of Tule Lake and the Lost River. The company sold land in Oregon at bargain prices on credit, requiring only 20 percent in cash, the balance due over the next five years.[15]

The Applegates promoted the rail route relentlessly. A glowing endorsement of "South East Oregon and Railroads" in a handwritten unsigned manuscript in Lindsay Applegate's papers appears to be in Jesse Applegate's hand. Perhaps drafted as a letter to the editor, it extols "beautifully timbered hills [and] golden trout in pellucid waters . . . a moderately good image of paradise." The letter promises an easy route by rail all the way to the Humboldt River in Nevada.[16]

There is a most interesting map of Applegate's proposed rail line that survives in military records. Supposedly, if there were a war, a railroad could supply troops in Modoc country. The map, with a slender black line of ink, indicated the route of Jesse's proposed railway, which would go east across the mountains from central Oregon to Modoc lands and continue to Idaho and Nevada. The ink line is crosshatched to signify a railroad and bears the inscription "C and ORR railroad as now surveyed."[17]

But Applegate's scheme for railroad lines along the Applegate Trail never got the lavish federal subsidies he and Holladay had hoped for. Oregon's Republican politicians offered another resolution to fund the Holladay/Applegate route, but the 1871 Congress failed to approve the appropriation. The Democrats, who wanted no financial favors given to their political enemies, sabotaged the resolution, and Oregon's Republican senators Henry Corbett and George Williams could not produce another miracle. An *Oregonian* "letter from Washington" said, "It is too late to save the bill from oblivion. It sleeps the last sleep, and 'Gabriel's trumpet' can't wake it to life again."[18]

There was another final blow to Jesse's hopes. Holladay, on whom all of Jesse's plans had depended, was running a Ponzi scheme. The money he was raising in Germany was used to pay dividends to stock-holders of his other enterprises. Holladay's line down the center of the state stalled. As a financial panic swept the country in 1873 he ran out of money. The route favored by Jesse—veering east toward Modoc country—was never built.

Jesse, undaunted, held out hope for a federal subsidy. Proposals for rail subsidies often perished in the labyrinth of congressional com-mittees—where scores of appeals were considered—and support was granted to few. Committees were so rife with bribery and corruption that they became effective "choke points" through which few schemes would pass.[19] But no rail proposal was ever dead; Congress could reverse itself on rail subsidies, and the Applegate route could have been resurrected by a simple resolution in the next session. The continuing possibility of a rail line along the Applegate Trail played significantly into Jesse's other massive farming and irrigation plans for Modoc coun-try. Convenient rail transportation was vital, and Jesse was slow to give up his dream that the railroad would follow his namesake trail.

7

Alfred Meacham

"Of all the figures in the story of the Modoc War, Meacham probably deserves the most credit for trying to preserve the peace."
Courtesy author's collection.

Minutes before midnight on New Year's Eve 1869, a tall bearded white man named Alfred Meacham held aloft his pocket watch and told six hundred assembled Klamath and Modocs that they were on a momentous cusp when the past would die and the future commence. Newly appointed as United States Superintendent for Indian Affairs for Oregon, Meacham had come to southern Oregon a few months earlier to deal with the nettlesome Modoc problem.

The Indians awaited the magic moment. It was a moonlit night, with the wind howling off Upper Klamath Lake. The night was bitterly cold, wrote reporter Samuel A. Clarke, and "the crash of cracking and breaking ice came from the lake side with fearful significance."[1] Meacham told the Indians that when the little sticks of his watch were in a row together, the old year would die in the West and another would be born in East. The Indians crowded around to see the hands of his watch move toward the New Year. "They waited in deathlike stillness," wrote Clarke, "as if they expected to see some vision of the Apocalypse burst forth on the frozen air."[2]

Klamath chief Allen David said not all could see the watch, and asked that a pistol be fired at the moment of midnight. Meacham described the scene: "A blaze of light flash[ing] over the dusky faces . . . a report reverberating up the rocky canyons, and before it died away, six hundred voices joined in an almost unearthly farewell to 1869." As the New Year 1870 began, Meacham sat after midnight with three chiefs by the great bonfire. He remembered it as an ominous event. "I was surrounded then with elements of power for mischief that were only waiting . . . to open a chapter with a finger dipped in . . . blood."[3]

A day earlier, Meacham had accomplished the seemingly impossible: he had persuaded Captain Jack to return again to the Klamath reservation. The chiefs—Captain Jack and the Klamath chief Allen David—had buried a hatchet in the frozen ground, symbolically reconciling the Klamaths and Modocs. The tribes agreed to live together in peace on the reservation located entirely on Klamath territory. "We are enemies no longer," said Captain Jack to the Klamath leader. "We have buried all the bad blood."[4]

Of all the figures in the story of the Modoc War, Meacham probably deserves the most credit for trying to preserve the peace. Despite his irritating grandiosity (he sometimes referred to himself in the third person as "our keen-sighted, grey-eyed man"), he was genuinely devoted to Indian welfare and nearly prevented the war. Ironically, he would later be forced from office at the moment when he was the only person to bring forth a viable solution to the Modoc conundrum.

Meacham was endlessly energetic and always talking. The Indian Agent T. W. Davenport, who probably wanted Meacham's job, wrote caustically in 1907: "He [Meacham] was given to egotistical display and florid if not fanciful speech, [and] in works he was not ahead of others who made no pretensions to excellence in ideas or practice."[5] Bancroft's *History of Oregon* was scathing: "Meacham was a man with a hobby. He believed he knew all about the savage race, and how to control it. He was flattered by the distinction of being the friend of those wild people, and his theory was that he could govern them through his hold on their esteem."[6]

Meacham had moved to Oregon in 1863, where he bought a toll road and operated a stagecoach station and roadhouse with his brother. He boasted his wife Orpha's cooking at the hotel was the best in Oregon.[7] Meacham dabbled in Oregon politics and became a prominent Republican, his rise in the party "meteoric."[8] He campaigned energetically for Ulysses S. Grant in the 1868 presidental race. Even though Grant did not win Oregon that year, Meacham was rewarded for his efforts. The new president appointed Meacham Oregon Indian Super-intendent at an annual salary of twenty-five hundred dollars.

Meacham energetically took office on May 1, 1869. He made a quick tour of the Indian agencies under his control and discovered affairs in Oregon were a quagmire of land confiscations, broken treaties, need-less wars, and hangings. The reservation system was a shambles: many Indians were simply absent from their assigned reservations as whites lured them into towns to work. Meacham met his first Klamaths in the far eastern part of Oregon, wandering at least a hundred miles from the Klamath reservation.

The Oregon Indian service was broken. Employees were getting no wages, and contracts for goods were unpaid. Agents were hostile to the tribes supposedly under their care. One Indian agent gave Mea-cham a disdainful description of the Native people: "A more degraded set of beings I am sure did not exist on the earth."[9] Another agent thought "the best way to civilize the Indians was to *wash out* the color." Meacham's own attitude toward the tribes was humane, but paternalis-tic. He later wrote, "I had never stood, until now, before a people just emerging from the chrysalis of savage life."[10]

Meacham found simmering resentment among the tribes. The Ore-gon treaty had still not been ratified, and the Indians had received little of the food and trade goods promised. The tribes also knew wagon roads were planned to pass through their lands and road-builders had been awarded sections of reservation land along the route.[11] Meacham warned Washington that pushing the road-building issue could bring war: "[The government should] make compensation to the Indians equivalent to the sacrifices they may make; otherwise more blood will be shed. Let [Indian title] be recognized still; treat them with justice, and war and its bloody attendants will be averted."[12]

The Modocs posed Meacham's biggest challenge. Captain Jack and his band were still living in their homes along the Lost River, away from the Klamath Reservation. Ivan Applegate complained the Modocs were "now roving" over lands the tribe purportedly ceded by the Ore-gon treaty.[13] To address the issue, Meacham boldly announced he would personally talk with Captain Jack. As Christmas approached in 1869, Meacham set out to meet Captain Jack at his village by the Lost River, fifty-five miles south. The army provided Meacham a squad of twelve soldiers, and he also took Ivan Applegate, Indian Agent Knapp and his assistant W. C. McKay, Modoc chief Old Schonchin, Frank Riddle, and Winema. The party rode south, followed by a wagon of supplies, on December 22, 1869. Meacham ordered the soldiers to wait in the little town of Linkville, and the party headed south across the sagebrush plain to Lost River. Meacham's group was confronted a few miles from Captain Jack's camp by four Modocs in war paint, each armed with a pistol and rifle, demanding to know his business. They warned them to turn back, but Meacham rode past them and toward Captain Jack's camp.

Meacham's account of his visit in *Wigwam and Warpath* is overwrought, but makes for lively reading. When he rode into the camp, the December weather was execrable, the snow two feet deep. Meacham asked to meet Captain Jack, and a sentry hollered, "One man come. No more!" Meacham knew it was necessary to go through with the meeting to avoid loss of face, so he went alone to Captain Jack's house and looked down the hole into the earthen home. Fifty armed warriors were looking up at him.[14]

The earthen home had to be entered through an opening that acted both as entrance and chimney, down a rawhide ladder through the smoke into a dark chamber below. When Meacham reached the bottom, Captain Jack refused to shake hands, would not speak, and treated him as an intruder. Meacham feared for his life but stayed calm: "Coolly lighting my pipe, and trying to make the best of a bad job; meanwhile enduring the stare from all eyes—an expression cold and scornful, but burning with hatred, was on every countenance." Meacham reckoned the trick was to outwait the Modocs, so he sat and smoked. Captain Jack's principal lieutenant, Scarface Charley, supposedly asked Meacham, "What for you come? Jack he not send for you!" Meacham told them he was a chief sent by the Big Chief in Washington. Captain Jack finally spoke, calling all white people liars and swindlers. "I do not believe half that is told me," he said. But Captain Jack finally agreed to meet the others in Meacham's entourage. The tone changed, the ice was broken, and Captain Jack offered to let them stay overnight. He had tents of reed matting erected for his white visitors, and they were each given a fish.

The next day negotiations began. Captain Jack pulled out his packet of talking papers—testimonials to his character from various whites—and everyone duly acknowledged their importance. Captain Jack then denied he had ever signed the Oregon treaty, but Meacham had brought along a copy and showed Captain Jack where he had put his "X." The rival Modoc chief Old Schonchin vouched Captain Jack had signed. After a time, Captain Jack began to ask questions about where he would live if he went back to the Klamath reservation. He was curious whether he would get the promised blankets and other gifts.

Curley-Headed Doctor was present, and he suddenly disrupted the meeting by jumping up and shouting at the Modocs not to cooperate. Everyone drew guns and, according to Meacham, there were tense minutes when the whites feared they would be killed. Captain Jack stood to leave the meeting, but Meacham claims he coaxed him back. He warned Captain Jack the army would come after him if he did not cooperate.

Fearing for their lives, Meacham sent a courier to summon the troops waiting in Linkville. By the time reinforcements arrived several hours later, Curley-Headed Doctor was conducting a noisy dance and making war incantations. Most of the soldiers arrived drunk and rowdy ("They had secured the company of a bottle"). But their arrival was enough to scare Captain Jack, who fled with all his warriors, riding around Tule Lake to the Lava Beds, leaving women and children behind. To everyone's surprise, a day later Captain Jack sent word he would agree to go on the Klamath reservation, effectively surrendering.

The Modoc band arrived at the Klamath reservation just before New Year's Eve, ending five years of resistance. "Most of the tribe surrendered gracefully," wrote Ivan Applegate, who met them midway with blankets.[15] As his band traveled north, Captain Jack asked Meacham to send the cavalry ahead so the Klamaths would not ridicule him for surrendering to the army. Captain Jack brought forty-three people with him—about ten men and the remainder women and children. Upon his arrival at the Klamath reservation, more Modocs gravitated to his camp, and 371 Modocs—perhaps two thirds of the tribe—arrived and were waiting for the long-promised rewards for signing the Oregon treaty.[16]

Captain Jack and his people moved to a chaotic environment on the northern shore of Upper Klamath Lake. A new small pox epidemic was ravaging the Klamath population. Lindsay Applegate was instructed to "collect the Squaws, vaccinate them, provide quarters and subsistence."[17] Young Klamaths arrived and crowded the camp, "to negotiate for new wives."[18] Gambling was rampant among the Klamaths, to the chagrin of the righteous Meacham, who issued an order prohibiting the Klamaths from gambling.[19]

Control of the Klamath reservation slipped from the Applegate family's hands when Congress decided to put Indian reservations under military, not civilian, command. In October 1872 Army Captain O.C. Knapp was appointed Indian Agent to take the place of Lindsay Applegate. The Applegates girded for political war against Knapp, and the new agent was no match for the Applegates. Damaging allegations of drunkenness, "cohabiting with squaws," and other improprieties were made against him by people in Jacksonville—charges perhaps planted by the Applegates. Ivan Applegate wrote his brother Oliver, complaining Knapp "was on a drunk." Oliver wrote to a friend in Salem about Knapp's "immoral and licentious course," hiring people "entirely wanting in honesty."[20] When Knapp found out, he fired Oliver as subagent for the Modocs.

To make matters worse, Knapp favored the Klamaths and mistreated the Modocs. The Modocs were not allowed to leave the reservation to gather food, and often did not have enough to eat.[21] Food supplies were running low and were completely exhausted within a few months.[22] "To die, shot with a bullet, don't hurt much," said Captain Jack. "To go on a Reservation and die of starvation, hurts great deal."[23] Some Klamaths made sure to be around when the cattle were slaughtered, and they grabbed the "head and pluck"—the prized delicacies from the offal. Captain Jack claimed he had been given nothing to eat but some "sour wheat" and he had to slaughter seventeen of his horses to feed the women.[24]

Knapp put the Modoc men to work cutting down pines, making rails, and hewing logs to build houses. They cut and stacked thousands of fence rails, a valuable commodity on the frontier. Gangs of young Klamaths promptly brought their wagons to the site, however, and hauled away loads of the fence rails—by one account, more than nine hundred. When Captain Jack confronted the Klamaths, one old man retorted, "I am a Klamath Indian. This is my land. You have got no business to cut my trees down. This is not your country or land."[25] One contemporary observer remembered: "[The Klamaths] did everything that savages are so ingenious in doing to make another tribe miserable.

Only the presence of troops prevented bloody outbreaks from occurring constantly."[26]

Captain Jack now appealed to Knapp to intervene, but Knapp refused to control the thieving Klamaths. When Captain Jack visited the agent's office, Knapp would not let him enter and made him stand on the porch. He ordered Jack to move his whining Modocs somewhere else and get back to work.[27]

Within three months after the Modocs' arrival at the Klamath reservation, Captain Jack was fed up. He called together the various Modoc bands and proposed they leave the reservation again and return to their homelands. A stormy all-night quarrel took place on April 25, 1870. Some of the Modocs insisted on staying; others advocated war. Curley-Headed Doctor wanted to fight.

Captain Jack prevailed, convincing several hundred Modocs to leave peacefully. Captain Jack's band of seventy-five Modocs returned to their old village on Lost River; about sixty Modocs led by Schonchin John (the brother of Old Schonchin) settled directly across the river from Captain Jack's village; and another group, fewer than fifty, made their homes near Hot Creek, sixteen miles to the southeast. For the next two and a half years, the Modocs (now called "renegades" by some whites) lived away from the Klamath reservation, roaming their traditional lands, over two hundred square miles stretching from Goose Lake on the east to the Siskiyou Mountains and the Cascade Range on the west.

8

General E.R.S. Canby

In August 1870 President Ulysses S. Grant sent a trusted general to deal with the Indians in the Pacific Northwest. He chose an officer known as solid and reliable, a soldier more plodding than dashing. General Edward Richard Sprigg Canby was a fifty-five-year-old veteran with decades of experience in Indian wars, the Civil War, and Reconstruction in the South. He was a tall and rather handsome man in his official Signal Corps portrait. Thirty-four years after he left West Point, his dark hair was flecked with white. Canby won praise for leadership in the Civil War but was known less for brilliant soldiering than his organizational skills. "His great ambition was the proper performance of his duties."[1]

Nevertheless, his decades of experience in all types of combat more than qualified him to command the army in the Pacific Northwest and, if it became necessary, to deal with the Modoc renegades. Against the Navajos in 1860 Canby had learned the futility of chasing fast-moving Indians across lands they knew intimately, so he simply drove the Navajos deep into the mountains and scattered their sheep. He became convinced that Indians could not be pacified if they were denied their own land, and concluded that the only solution to the Navajo uprising was to give them a reservation.[2]

Despite Canby's wide experience, in 1872 there was no army doctrine or strategy available that fit the Modoc situation. Canby was cautious—his biographer called him a "prudent soldier"—and he knew the cost of using excessive force against the Indians. Colonel George Custer's slaughter of a camp full of women and children at the Battle of Washita in 1868 had triggered an angry backlash of public opinion. To some the massacre became a symbol of white barbarity against the Indians.[3]

Canby assumed his duties in 1870 at Fort Vancouver, Washington, across the Columbia River from Portland. He and his wife, Louisa,

General E.R.S. Canby. "Canby
was truly a prudent soldier."
Courtesy author's collection.

settled into the colonnaded three-story quarters of the commanding
officer that dominated Officers' Row. They found some quiet at his
new post in the "settled damp," as he called it, commanding 1,225 officers and men scattered thinly across nine posts in the sprawling military
district that spanned the entire Northwest. Canby's stately new quarters
belied the woeful state of the army's forces in the Northwest in 1871.
Most regular troops were fighting Indian wars in the southwest, and
there were only 72 men at Fort Klamath. Of 71 Springfield breech
loading rifled muskets, only 64 were "serviceable."[4] Undermanned and
under armed, Canby warned officials in Washington that he could not
deal with a serious emergency with such scant resources. His immediate
challenge was to stem the high rate of desertion, as troops skipped out
for the gold mines of Idaho. No fewer than 268 soldiers—20 percent
of his force—deserted in 1871. Another 239 were absent without leave
in 1872.[5]

Too many treaties strained army resources. Most worrisome was
"the hostile disposition" of the Modocs in southern Oregon. Captain
Jack and his people were living once again on Lost River, and settlers
were pressuring the army to arrest him and return him to the Klamath reservation. Canby worried that anxious settlers might create "a

collision" with the Modocs. Canby was also concerned (correctly, it turned out) that planned "draining operations" would impair vital Indian water resources like Lost River.[6]

Some settlers believed the situation was already beyond the tipping point, and they demanded immediate military intervention to control the Modocs. But Canby, like Meacham, feared that action against the Modocs would provoke a conflagration. In spite of good intentions, Canby's peace strategy was doomed from the start.

9

Storm Clouds for Captain Jack

In 1870 when Captain Jack's band of Modocs returned to their village beside Lost River for the second time, it was spring and the land was bountiful. The river swarmed with suckerfish and trout, so abundant it was said you could walk across the river on their backs. There is a point on Lost River, at the town of Olene, where Indians are known to have caught fifty tons of suckerfish in 1900.[1] Men fished and women worked to split and dry the catch. The abundant fish and water plants supported huge populations of migratory waterfowl. A wildlife expert who visited in 1904 found a colony of nine thousand white pelicans and "the most extensive breeding ground in the West for all kinds of inland water birds."[2] As summer went on, the Modocs hunted deer, which were herded into traps and killed with clubs. They ranged the adjacent hills, where women harvested roots.

The Modocs also resumed visits to Yreka for work and trade. From the 1850s on there had been an uninterrupted presence of the Modocs in Yreka, where they often occupied a rural encampment or "rancheria" on the outskirts of town. In 1864 the *Yreka Union* reported a large band of Modocs had come in from the lakes and camped near the town. "They are very much dissatisfied with the arrangements made by the Indian Agent at the Lakes," the article stated, "and express a desire to leave their old hunting grounds and to relocate near Yreka."[3]

Captain Jack and his band periodically visited Yreka, but always returned to their traditional villages by Lost River. In the warmer weather of late spring the Modocs most likely moved around, using temporary shelters made of woven reed mats. They followed the food—fishing the rivers, hunting waterfowl and finding duck eggs at Tule Lake, and gathering roots and berries in the foothills.

The arriving white settlers saw the Modocs as a nuisance. There were persistent charges of theft and petty thuggery, and the Modocs' relations with settlers soured in 1870 and 1871. One settler complained the Modocs had taken down his fence and their horses ate his hay.[4] Others complained the Modocs were killing their cattle. A settler named C. (probably Charley) Blair wrote to Indian Agent Knapp on April 26, 1870, the day Captain Jack arrived home on Lost River, claiming the Modocs were menacing him. The Indians have been "very sulky" and were "making some threats of killing white men." One day they scattered their fish over the ground, raised a "war whoop," and left for Lost River. "They intend to fight. There is no doubt of it," he asserted.[5]

Another settler, Mr. Pos, dictated a statement swearing the Modocs tried to steal flour from his wife, and Mr. Davis complained the Modocs were "saucy and impudent." Joseph Seeds objected because one of Captain Jack's men demanded pay for hay: "Said the Indians must be paid for it as it was out on their land." Other settlers complained the Indians showed up at their farms when men were absent, lounged on the beds, and demanded the women cook them meals.[6]

But the Modocs were not hurting anyone. Harry Wells wrote that Captain Jack and his band "lived quietly at their camp on Lost River and though harmless were no doubt unpleasant neighbors."[7] Neither the Army nor Indian Agents saw an immediate threat of violence. Captain James Jackson wrote that there was no imminent danger from the Modocs: "I have no doubt they are insolent beggars, but so far as I can ascertain no one has been hurt, robbed or seriously threatened." The Indian Agency commissary similarly assured the Superintendent of Indians Affairs "there is no danger at present of any serious trouble between the Modoc Indians and the settlers of Lost River."[8]

Captain Jack offered peaceful assurance: "We are good people and we will not kill or frighten anybody. We are willing to have whites live in our country but do not want them to locate on the west side and near the mouth of Lost River where we have our winter camps. The settlers are continually lying about my people and trying to make trouble."[9] But in spring 1871 Captain Jack triggered a wave of white anger when he killed a Klamath medicine man. The murder, incomprehensible to white authorities and settlers, was perfectly consistent with Modoc law. If a healer who had been paid in advance for his services failed to deliver a cure, he could be killed. Captain Jack's niece, a daughter of his widowed sister, had become ill, and Captain Jack had sought the services of a Klamath healer, Com-Po-Twas. It is unclear why the Modoc healer, Curley-Headed Doctor, did not treat the girl. But the Klamath doctor promised he could do the cure, and when the patient died, Captain Jack exercised his right to kill him.

It was just the ammunition Captain Jack's critics needed, and they went after him. The murder was depicted in lurid detail in an unsigned letter from Fort Klamath: "[The shaman was] shot and instantly killed by an Indian named 'Captain Jack.' The murder was committed in cold blood, the murdered man being shot while asleep. The insolence of this man and his followers has seriously alarmed citizens through out Lost River."[10] Ivan Applegate demanded Captain Jack be arrested for murder.[11] Applegate guessed Captain Jack would take refuge in Yreka, and as expected, he showed up there on June 28 at Judge Elijah Steele's door. Obviously worried, Captain Jack wanted to know how the whites intended to deal with the death of the healer. The ever-tolerant Judge Steele warned the Oregon authorities that involvement in internal tribal affairs was hazardous. He wrote a letter admonishing them not to meddle with the Modoc and their laws, "further than to try to persuade them out of their foolish notions."[12]

Captain Jack, who put great store in his "talking papers"—testimonials and permissions from white authorities—persuaded Yreka judges Elisha Steele and A. M. Roseborough to write a new document for him, a copy of which survives. The judge worded his endorsement noncommittally: "Captain Jack of the Modoc Tribe wishes me to write this paper to tell white people who are not acquainted with him that he is friendly with all the whites."[13]

Captain Jack also got a testimonial from prominent Oregonians when the Modocs were in Yreka on July 4, 1871. A fire had broken out during the Independence Day festivities, and some Modocs had helped the volunteer firefighters. Although most of the town burned to the ground, the grateful townspeople thanked Captain Jack and signed a proclamation: "We the undersigned have had an interview with the Modoc chief know [*sic*] as Captain Jack. He wishes us to make know [*sic*] to whom it may concern that he will not resist the soldiers, nor in any way disturb the settlers in the Modoc country." Jesse Applegate, Henry F. Miller, John F. Miller, and Judge A. M. Roseborough signed the proclamation.[14]

There is an intriguing, if unexplained, scrap of notepaper in Oliver Applegate's papers at the University of Oregon. It is headed "Blairs, Nov. 29th, 1870" and seems to record a meeting between Oliver, Captain Jack, and Charley Blair, the quarrelsome white farmer who had tangled with Captain Jack before. The record suggests an unfriendly encounter. Oliver, with his long beard, was most likely clad in his customary fringed buckskin jacket and stovepipe hat. Captain Jack, who favored browbeating people from horseback, probably didn't dismount. Captain Jack liked being recorded on a talking paper, and Oliver may have scribbled the note, which says, "I want my Country + East Side Lost River California. White people know my Country + and all Yreka people all know. 'One talk' I talk big chief Washington."[15]

Oliver's note of this conversation is consistent with other reports: Captain Jack just wanted his land, and he thought everyone supported him in this, particularly the Californians. He believed the "big chief" in Washington—President Grant—would understand about the Modoc homeland if he had a chance to talk with him. Captain Jack couldn't understand why "everyone was mad" at him and he continued to demand to see the "big chief" until the day he was hanged.

10

A Lost River Reservation

Even as the controversy about Captain Jack's killing of the healer continued, Indian Superintendent Meacham and prominent players began promoting a separate reservation for the Modocs near their home by Lost River. Jesse Applegate was out surveying near Clear Lake in July 1871 when he and a companion met up with a band of Modocs. Things did not begin well, according to Applegate. "Some 10 or 15 Indians all fully armed, mistaking us for immigrants, came charging into our camp evidently aiming to intimidate us into compliance with their demands for food, ammunition, &c. This band was headed by [Black] Jim, a very saucy impudent fellow but possessing good sense; when he found out who we were he seemed very anxious to discuss the situation & seemed to suffer to an equal degree the anxiety and fear manifested by the settlers." As they talked, the usually cranky Applegate warmed to Black Jim, and he later wrote a long description of their frank discussion. Black Jim demanded to know why the Modocs were not allowed to live in peace on their homelands and why the soldiers were pursuing the Modocs into the mountains where there were no roots or fish for them to eat. "Life has no pleasure for us and <u>we are ready to die</u>," he said. But when Applegate mentioned giving the Modocs a small reservation on the lake, "it seemed to fill him with joy—he said it was all they asked for—a place at the mouth of Lost River for a home."[1]

That same day Jesse wrote to Meacham, saying Jim's speech made a "good deal of good sense."[2] Meacham promptly replied, "I will make the effort to secure a home for [the Modocs] in Lost River."[3] Jesse paid a visit to Meacham, and they discussed the merits of a Lost River reservation.[4] Meacham later reported that Jesse Applegate believed "the only sure way for permanent peace was to give [the Modocs] a small Reservation at the mouth of the Lost River—the old home of Captain Jack." He said Applegate even drew up a map showing a proposed reservation on Lost River, which he sent to Meacham's office.[5] A few months later,

Applegate confirmed to Meacham: "I fully approved of your purpose last summer to place these Indians on a reservation to themselves."[6]

Judge Elijah Steele, who had negotiated the California treaty of February 1864, also thought the Modocs were entitled to their land, pointing out that he had promised the Modocs a home on their customary territory.[7] Steele requested a description of the land Captain Jack wanted so he could draw up papers to be filed with the land commissioner.[8]

Meacham fully supported a Lost River reservation for the

"Life has no pleasure for us and we are ready to die." Souvenir card of Black Jim. *Courtesy author's collection.*

Modocs. He forwarded Jesse Applegate's letter to General Canby requesting that military action be delayed. Then he dispatched his brother John Meacham and Ivan Applegate to meet with Captain Jack to negotiate peace. He requested Jesse Applegate go with them. The negotiators were authorized to tell the Modocs that Meacham "will try to get a small reserve for them in their country."[9]

In October 1871 Meacham made good on his promise and submitted a request for a Modoc reservation to the Commissioner of Indian Affairs in Washington, D.C. He recommended creation of "a small reservation of six miles square, lying on both sides of the Oregon and California, near the head of the Tule Lake."[10] A month later, Meacham wrote to Ivan Applegate: "I have recommended to the dept. to allow them a home at or near the mouth of Lost River with the understanding that they would consent to locate [there] permanently and become like other Reservation Indians."[11]

The governor of California also urged the government to reverse the order sending the Modocs to the Klamath reservation and give them 3,000 acres on their ancestral ground by the Lost River. The California press agreed. Give the Modocs the land, argued one writer, "which from time to time immemorial they have regarded as their own."[12] Set aside the order removing the Modocs back to "inhospitable country," urged the *Sacramento Union*. "Give them instead 3,000 acres of land on Lost River. If 3,000 acres will save many lives, we say let there be peace on such cheap terms."[13]

General Canby endorsed a separate reservation for the Modocs, possibly on the Lost River. "I am not surprised at the unwillingness of the Modocs to return to . . . the reservation where they would be exposed to the hostilities and annoyances they have heretofore experience from the Klamaths" he wrote, "but they have expressed a desire to be established upon Lost River, where they would be free from this trouble."[14] He later added, "[A reservation] would not only give greater security against Indian troubles, but will materially diminish the expense of the military establishment in that part of the country."[15]

At the same time Canby prepared for the worst, positioning troops to quell trouble if it began, and reminding his officers to avoid tangling with the Modocs until the reservation issue was decided, "unless the hostile attitude of the Indians should leave you no alternative."[16]

In his October 1871 report recommending a Lost River reservation for the Modocs, Meacham had warned that "land hungry persons would oppose the demand." Meacham's warning was prophetic. By early 1872 the conflict between the white settlers and the Modocs was growing even more heated. Some of army officers began to warn of war. The much-respected cavalryman Captain R. F. Bernard, writing after the first great battle of the war from "Camp Applegate," sympathized with the Modoc cause: "The only thing they claim or ask is a home at the mouth of Lost River, where they were born and raised."[17]

But Washington ignored the urgent request for a Lost River reservation, and soon the Modocs grew frustrated and belligerent. In April 1872 Canby sent Colonel Elmer Otis to investigate and, if possible, get the situation under control. Otis, a battle-seasoned forty-one-year-old cavalry officer, decided to make a show of force to get the Modocs' attention. Accompanied by Ivan Applegate, Indian Agent Leroy Dyar, and Oliver Applegate, Otis took two troops of cavalry and a dozen mules laden with supplies and set up a camp in the heart of Modoc country, about ten miles from Captain Jack's camp on Lost River.

After much haggling, Captain Jack agreed to meet Otis at Lost River Gap, a dramatic site where Lost River flowed through a deep notch in Stukel Mountain, ending its long meander and becoming a swift-running river. It was a favorite place of the Modocs because of the large fishery there. It was also on their favored route into the mountains to harvest camas roots. Lost River has high banks at the Gap that drop sharply toward the river. Otis and his cavalry took up a position on the north bank. The Modoc chief arrived on the opposite bank with "thirty to thirty-five braves, heavily armed." Both sides laid their weapons on the ground, and Captain Jack and Otis crowded into a small cabin. Seven local settlers jammed in to listen. Captain Jack had invited several people to testify that the Modocs were not troublesome, but other settlers complained about the Modocs' bad behavior, stealing horses and annoying homesteaders.[18]

Someone, probably Ivan Applegate, made a transcript of their meeting. Otis talked tough with the Modocs: "Colonel Otis [To Captain Jack]: I was sent into this country to see what was the matter between you and the whites here, and ask you if you have got anything to say to me. I have got fifty (50) soldiers over there. I have got plenty more soldiers behind if I want them." Otis told Captain Jack he had reports his men were going into houses in groups of fifteen or twenty, where no one was home but women. "I want to know what you have to say about it," he demanded. He asked about reports that Captain Jack's men had torn down fences and stolen hay.

Captain Jack asked who had made the charges, and insisted he have a chance to confront his accusers. Otis fired back. "Can you control your men? Can you make them do as you want them to?" he said. It was a skillful gibe. Otis said that if Captain Jack was a chief, he should know where his Indians were and what they did. Captain Jack tried to put blame on other bands: "It ain't only my people that travel up and down this river. There are some Indians not mine who travel that way too."

Captain Jack's manner veered from defensive and whining to cocky and defiant. He was not impressed with Otis's threats: "You are not the first white man I ever saw," Captain Jack said. "I have seen lots of white men before." Otis acknowledged the bitter relations between Modocs and whites. "I know that you fought them a long time; now you are at peace." Captain Jack responded that his warriors were blameless, and he now had nothing but good feelings toward whites. Captain Jack brought out his "talking papers," including the testimonial

Lost River Gap, where the river flows through a deep notch in Stukel Mountain. *Photo by Bill Stafford.*

signed by Jesse Applegate. Ivan Applegate's transcript recorded Captain Jack's remark: "You see my book [placing a pocket-book on the floor], I watch my Indians, same as I watch the book. Good many white men tell stories; my Indians all right . . . My book says that my men never meddle with their cattle."

Captain Jack made a vigorous but debatable defense on the charge of killing cattle. He pointed out there was a poisonous wild parsnip that killed cattle. He said Modoc women sometimes butchered and cooked cattle that died from eating poisonous parsnips, but he would not eat the meat. Otis found the replies evasive, and threatened harsh action if there was further trouble. But he held out the ultimate carrot for the Modoc chief—the prospect of getting his land back as a permanent reservation. "When Mr. Meacham talked to you last summer," Otis told Captain Jack, "he said you could stay here, and he would write to the Big Father at Washington to give you a piece of land here. I don't know whether he will or not. You must wait and see what the Big Father says."

But the Modocs' hope that the "Big Father" would set aside a res-ervation on their Lost River homeland was darkening. Land in western Oregon was becoming scarce, and immigrants were still spilling over the mountains. Ivan Applegate acknowledged that the arrival of settlers was creating a tinderbox: "Every acre [of the country] fit for use is now claimed by Citizens. Thousand of cattle, sheep, and horses are ranging over it." He warned that locating the Modocs in the Lost River area would be "regarded with hostility and opposition will be sufficient to keep up an endless Conflict."[19]

To prevent a "collision' between the Modocs and the settlers, Canby recommended the Modocs be kept "under quiet supervision" by maintaining a detachment of cavalry nearby. "The temper of both parties is such that a very slight cause may give rise to serious consequences," he warned. And a Lost River reservation, which would meet with serious opposition from the settlers, was probably "not advisable."[20] Meacham continued to hold out for a separate reservation for the Modocs as the best hope of avoiding an Indian war. But Meacham would soon be gone, Jesse Applegate would reverse his support for a Modoc reservation, and Canby would be ordered to arrest Captain Jack and return the Modocs to the Klamath reservation. The scale was tilting sharply against the Modocs.

11

Captain Jack Must Go

A Modoc reservation on Lost River had been a long shot from the start. Settlers were rushing in, and the government was delaying a decision. But the fatal blow to the Modocs' hopes for a riverside home was struck when Jesse Applegate abruptly turned against the plan.

In February 1872 Applegate wrote to Meacham, reversing his support. The "arrogance" and "impudence" of the Modocs, he argued, discouraged new settlers. Indians, he said, couldn't be trusted to behave on their own reservation: "The 'untutored savage' is also a 'wild man' and like other wild animals they chafe and fret under any kind of restraint." A separate reservation would put the Modocs out of the reach of authorities: "It will scarcely be possible to introduce or enforce discipline. They had better be removed out of harm's way and the city of refuge on Modoc Lake be broken up."[1]

Applegate's extraordinary reversal came—not coincidentally—a few months after he partnered up with the California land baron Jesse Carr. The two eventually became known as "The Two Jesses." By mid-1871 Jesse Applegate had suffered a series of financial reverses, including the collapse of his plans for a railroad through Lake Country. Applegate was a skilled surveyor, with experience at laying out the maps and grids that are the basis for acquiring land. Jesse Carr retained Applegate's services as a surveyor in the fall of 1871—just months before Applegate changed course on his support for a Modoc reservation.[2]

The Two Jesses were an odd match: Applegate, straight-laced Puritan pioneer, and Jesse Carr, pugnacious California land speculator who liked cigars, racehorses, and land grabs. Carr had used brass-knuckle tactics to create an immense "rancho" near Salinas, California, one of the largest stock operations in the United States. By 1871 Carr set out to build a huge cattle ranch in the traditional Modoc territories, straddling the Oregon-California state line. "A Modoc Ranch," as he called it, would be "the crowning achievement" of his long career in land acquisition. Only two things were missing—irrigation and transportation.[3]

The Two Jesses had a plan to answer both those needs. Jesse Applegate brought to the partnership his long-planned project to build an east-west railway line to move goods to market along the Applegate Trail. But the success of the venture hinged on the ability to control the water of the Modoc basin. To seize the water, Applegate and Carr planned to do nothing less than replumb the region's entire water system, damming rivers and draining lakes in the heart of the Modocs' traditional territory.[4] Diverting the Lost River would water some of their properties, and they would sell water to adjacent farms. They also planned to drain Tule Lake, creating thousands of acres of new farmland. Historian Robert Johnston wrote: "It was a magnificent concept . . . It encompassed a large portion of the land and virtually *all* the water resources of a significant portion of the 'Modoc Lava Plateau.'"[5]

Captain Jack and his village on Lost River were squarely in the way of the Two Jesses' grand design. Diverting Lost River would cut off the water supply to the village. Draining Tule Lake would destroy one of the Modocs' chief sources of fish and birds. The Two Jesses did not care if their scheme cut out the heart of the Modocs' traditional territories and destroyed the center of their spiritual universe.

Applegate and Carr began to acquire land. Applegate's shrewd skill as a surveyor was the key. Later Carr praised Applegate's skills: "He was a very educated man on land matters." Applegate agreed to survey three townships—108 square miles. He was to be paid by Carr an amount "not to exceed $2,500 to $3,000" to map out a plan for the huge cattle ranch Carr envisioned around Clear Lake and on the eastern shore of Tule Lake.[6]

In 1903 Carr explained his water strategy in Modoc country: "It didn't take me long to see that water rights are more valuable than the broad acres themselves. So I picked my land accordingly . . . [I acquired] about eight or ten miles of frontage on Tule Lake and over twenty-two miles of border around—completely around—Clear Lake. My land lies in long strips between the water and the other fellows' land. If they wanted to raise cattle, they had to have water and they couldn't get it without driving their cattle over my property."[7]

Carr also bought land designated as "swamp or overflowed" for one dollar an acre with an initial payment of twenty cents, the remaining eighty cents due if the buyer could harvest three crops of hay in ten years. The law, intended by the federal government to raise money for schools, was widely abused.[8] The trick, of course, was to stake out the good land and buy it at the swampland price. One cattleman got land from the government by loading a rowboat onto a wagon, driving the wagon around, and swearing he had covered the territory in a boat.[9]

The dubious methods of land acquisition used by the Two Jesses successfully avoided scrutiny from state or federal officials until decades later. Applegate settled several members of his large family on Clear Lake at a site later known as "Fiddler's Green." Carr also used Applegate family members to acquire land for him, probably illegally. Sallie Applegate, Jesse's twenty-two-year-old daughter, quitclaimed 160 acres of land just a mile north of the Modoc village to Carr on February 27, 1872. Daniel Webster Applegate, her twenty-seven-year-old brother, quitclaimed 160 acres to Carr on the same date. But the State of Oregon did not convey the land to either until a week later on March 4.[10] The Applegate children probably got a commission for a transaction no more arduous than going to the courthouse and signing papers.

Three of Jesse's children (Sallie, Daniel Webster, and twenty-one-year-old Peter Skene Ogden Applegate) made other land purchases for Jesse Carr. Ten such transactions occurred between November 1871 and February 1872.[11] Jesse Carr himself applied for the purchase of over thirteen thousand acres of swampland (including seven thousand acres around Clear Lake) on June 24, 1873, just as the Modoc War ended.[12]

Eventually Carr controlled almost twenty miles of waterfront on the east shore of Tule Lake. Carr also acquired two additional sections—two square miles—northwest of the lake, which he planned to irrigate with water diverted from Lost River.[13] Captain Jack's village at the heart of the Modoc homeland was being encircled by the Carr/Applegate enterprises.[14]

In October 1871 the Two Jesses traveled over the Cascades to Jacksonville, Oregon, then the Jackson County seat to incorporate the "Link and Lost River Irrigating, Manufacturing, and Navigation Company." The company planned to dam Lost River and convey the head waters "along the foothills for irrigating and manufacturing purposes."

The incorporators were Jesse Carr, Jesse Applegate, and a third partner, Benjamin Berry. Four witnesses, including Applegate's son, Peter O. Applegate, signed the three-page handwritten document, and filed with county clerk Silas J. Day.[15]

Carr and Applegate's scheme got immense play in the *New Northwest*, a Portland newspaper. In September 1872 Jesse Applegate paid a call on the staff, and a few weeks later the newspaper ran a glowing report of their grand project:

GREAT ENTERPRISE IN SOUTHERN OREGON

[The] advantages of irrigation will shortly be tried on a grand scale in the Klamath country. Jesse D. Carr has made a contract with Jesse Applegate to cut a ditch or canal from Lost River into Klamath River, a distance of ten miles as a cost of $50,000. This ditch will tap Lost River . . . and drain Tule Lake . . . and thereby drain at least 350,000 acres of what is now known as swampland . . . and convert the whole valley into wheat fields. Mr. Carr has the capital and Mr. Applegate has the brains to accomplish the work.[16]

Applegate and Carr were on the march. A board of directors was formed, officers chosen, and a first meeting held. Jesse Applegate was elected president, bylaws were passed, and plans were laid for commencement of the work in the spring.[17]

During the Modoc War, *San Francisco Chronicle* correspondent Robert Bogart (not always a pillar of accuracy, but probably correct this time) charged several times that a land grab caused the Modoc War. Bogart asserted that the Two Jesses were using the time-honored method of having others buy land as their surrogates, then buying it back. Bogart wrote: "In fact, if the truth were known, every rood [sic] of ground in that section in Lost River is being held by the settlers for the two Jesses—Carr and Applegate."[18]

The methods being used by Carr and Applegate to assemble land may have been illegal. The practices were widely used to fraudulently gain ownership of timber, oil-producing land, and mineral resources all across the United States. But the scale and ruthlessness of Carr's tactics to assemble his huge Modoc Rancho were breathtaking. He eventually acquired huge tracts of the traditional lands that the Modoc tribe had supposedly relinquished by the Oregon treaty in 1864.[19] Carr's ranch would virtually cover all the original territory of the Modoc tribe, even including the rocky and desolate Lava Beds where the Modocs would make their last stand.[20]

Carr's most arrogant exploit was his famous "Chinese Wall," a rock wall at Clear Lake which illegally enclosed over eighty-four thousand acres along the Oregon/California boundary. The *Kansas City Gazette*, after interviewing Carr in 1901, called him "the King of Squatters." "There are squatters and squatters," the *Gazette* opined, "Beside [Carr] the others fade into insignificance."[21]

Historical maps of the area in the possession of Steve Kandra, a farmer whose family homesteaded nearby in 1911, show how important and shrewd was the Two Jesses' irrigation scheme. Spreading antique maps on his dining room table, Kandra, a wiry, sunburned man who has worked a half century on the family farms, explains that the hydrology—the movement of water—was the key to capturing the wealth of the basin of lakes and rivers. [22] Unfortunately for Captain Jack, the Modoc village beside the meandering Lost River was at the nexus of the Two Jesses' emerging enterprises. Their plans would have been disastrous for the Modocs. Kandra said, "For the Modocs, Lost River was their artery of life."[23]

The proposed Modoc reservation on Lost River, which would have included both Captain Jack's village and Schonchin John's village across the river, would have been just a postage stamp of land, six by six miles (a township), less than five percent of the desirable land along Lost River. But—as Kandra pointed out—the proposed Modoc reservation would have been at the heart the region's principle transportation and agriculture hub (through the modern town of Merrill) and encompassed several miles of the legendary Applegate Trail, the main route for wagons entering Oregon from the southeast.[24]

General Canby, at his headquarters three hundred miles north, understood the particular danger that the irrigation schemes posed for the Modocs. He wrote insightfully on February 7, 1872: "It is understood that drainage operations are in contemplation, which, although they are to be carried on outside its limits, will have the effect of destroying the value of large portions of the reservation, for the purpose to which it was reserved."[25] Cheewa James quotes a letter written by Lieutenant Harry DeWitt Moore, who fought in the Lava Beds, that neatly summed up the situation: "Too much Applegate, too much steal."[26]

The Lava Beds. *Photo by Bill Stafford.*

Part Two
A Spirit in the Rock

The Lava Beds are a black ocean tumbled into a thousand fantastic shapes, a wild chaos of ruin, desolation, barrenness—a wilderness of billowy upheavals, of furious whirlpools, of miniature mountains rent asunder, of gnarled and knotted, wrinkled and twisted masses of blackness, and all these weird shapes, all this turbulent panorama, all this far-stretching waste of blackness, with its thrilling suggestiveness of life, of action, of boiling, surging, furious motion was petrified.

— Colonel William Thompson, *Reminiscences*

12

Meacham Is Fired

In late 1871 Oregon Indian Superintendent Alfred Meacham, champion of a Lost River reservation for the Modocs, was abruptly fired. A letter to the state's largest paper, the Portland *Oregonian*, credited Senator Henry Corbett with getting Meacham, who opposed his reelection, fired from his job for political reasons.[1]

Meacham didn't learn the news of his dismissal for almost a month, and he was furious with Corbett for not telling him. "King Corbett says he knew it Nov. 25th [1871] but did not write to me about it until Dec. 26th," Meacham wrote to a friend, "and then does not tell me what the reasons are."[2] The news of Meacham's ouster did not reach Oregon until January 3, 1872, when it was reported in the Salem *Statesman*. Some Oregon newspapers expressed surprise and regret.

Meacham wrote to Ivan Applegate: "I have made up my mind to fight to the end."[3] He battled to keep his job for the next four months, penning a blizzard of letters, some barely legible in his hurried script. Meacham seemed genuinely grief stricken that he was losing his chance to help the Indians. "To be decapitated without any reasonable cause does hurt me and it ever will when I think of any of these people who have given me their hearts."[4]

Meacham entertained several explanations for his firing. He finally concluded that politicians had sabotaged him. In an avalanche of letters he pointed repeatedly to a mysterious political cabal he called "The Brigade," "The Ring," "The Political Brigade," or "the Unscrupulous Ringmasters."[5]

The reasons for Meacham's dismissal have been debated for a century. One historian thought it was for incompetence.[6] But, if anything, Meacham did his duties too well. He was a vigorous proponent of President Grant's poorly articulated and woefully administered "Peace Policy," which sought to deal with the Indians through compassion.

Meacham's suspicions may have been right. The correspondent for the *New York Herald,* Edward Fox, wrote that Meacham's zeal for Indian welfare and his support of the Modocs, in particular, had cost him his job. "In consequence of the lively interest Mr. Meacham assumed in behalf of these Indians," Fox wrote, "interest was brought to bear in Washington which caused his removal."[7]

Unfortunately for Meacham, the Republicans were organizing the 1872 reelection campaign at the same time Meacham was lobbying for a Modoc reservation, and the politicians knew Oregonians were in no mood to accommodate the Modocs. The Oregon Republican leadership wasted no time getting Meacham's replacement appointed. His successor was Thomas Benton Odeneal, chairman of the State Republican Central Committee. Odeneal was a newspaper editor and lawyer from Corvallis, in Benton County, who had moved to Portland to become editor of the pro-Republican *Portland Gazette.*[8] He had been identified with secessionists but "converted to President Lincoln." More importantly, he brought valuable political influence from his home in Benton County to assure reelection for the Republican candidate. Meacham knew Odeneal's appointment would "secure three senatorial votes for the Republican party."[9]

In the midst of this political firestorm, on February 1, 1872, Jesse Applegate withdrew his endorsement of a Modoc reservation on Lost River.[10] A week later, Meacham—perhaps realizing he had made a political mistake—reversed himself as well. On February 8 Meacham forwarded a copy of Applegate's letter to General Canby. Meacham now asked for Canby "to arrest [Captain Jack] and five or six of the headmen, and hold them in confinement."[11]

The Modocs, wintering quietly in their warm lodges beside Lost River, most likely had no idea these political maneuvers were going on. But Meacham's reversal of support for a reservation, followed immediately by his dismissal, sealed their fate.

Meacham's replacement, Thomas Odeneal, brought no experience to the job, and lacked Meacham's vision and compassion in dealing with the Modocs. In early summer 1872, Odeneal sent a copy of Jesse Applegate's February 1 letter to the Superintendent of Indian Affairs and recommended, "The Klamath reservation is the best place in that whole country for the Modoc Indians."[12]

On July 6, 1872, the Commissioner of Indian Affairs ordered Odeneal to remove the Modocs from their homes and place them on the Klamath reservation, arresting their leaders if necessary. The Modocs were to be removed "peaceably if you possibly can, forcibly if you must."[13]

13

A Grave Mistake

S now blanketed southern Oregon in winter 1871-72. When an occasional warm spell melted the snow, roads turned to mud, and it was difficult to visit a farm even a mile away. Travel to Linkville (with the only saloons) from Fort Klamath required a twenty-five-mile ride south on the wretched road around Klamath Lake. The Cascade Mountain passes were completely blocked for months.

Captain Jack had been away from the Klamath reservation for nearly two years. In winter, the Modocs didn't do battle or move about. Mid-winter was a spiritual season for the Modocs when the spirits communicated directly with the shamans. The Modocs clustered in their villages, catching suckerfish and trout, living on provisions stored the previous summer and fall, and hunting on the immense migrations of waterfowl at Tule Lake. They did not steal hay or pester settlers, who were miles away through the snow. Some of the soldiers posted at Fort Klamath favored striking Captain Jack and his people while winter held when the Modocs could not scatter in the mountains nor hide their tracks in the snow. But there was no rush; the Modocs were snowbound on Lost River.

The commanding officer at Fort Klamath, cavalry officer Major G. G. Hunt, wrote to Canby on February 18, 1872: "At present these [Modoc] Indians are not disturbing the settlers, or giving any trouble."[1] Canby instructed Odeneal that until the reservation question was resolved, "force will not be used by the military to compel the return of the Modocs to the [Klamath] reservation." He should not, Canby continued, assume reports from settlers about robberies and other disturbances showed a "hostile attitude" on the part of the Modocs, although the individual offenders could be arrested and punished.[2]

But in early February 1872, Jesse Applegate started campaigning for the immediate arrest of Captain Jack and his men. "If this not done before spring opens, it cannot be done this year," he wrote. "As well expect to collect the coyotes out of that region of rock, mountain, and morass, as the Indians in the summer season."[3] Perhaps not coincidentally, in early February a group of "citizens" from the Tule Lake area submitted a petition to Canby and Meacham demanding removal of Captain Jack and his "20 desperados and a squalid band of these hundred miserable savages." They complained of "years of annoyance from the presence of the Modoc Indians," and suggested Ivan Applegate would be the "suitable man to take charge of any forces or expedition looking to their removal."[4]

A few weeks later, Major Otis reported that the white settlers in the neighborhood of the Modocs "appear to be considerably alarmed, and consider that both their lives and property are in danger."[5] Ivan Applegate wrote Odeneal that the white settlers were very much opposed to setting aside a reservation for the Modocs and added that in winter the Modocs could be moved quite easily by the troops stationed at Fort Klamath. The arrest of Captain Jack and his leaders would "settle all the trouble."[6]

Odeneal—who was not even in Lake Country, but was residing miles away in Salem, Oregon—then began lobbying Washington to move against the Modocs. Captain Jack's people, he wrote, were "desperadoes, brave, daring and reckless" and they "imagine they are too powerful to be controlled by the Government." The Modoc leaders, he urged, should be arrested and held at some remote place, and the Modocs forced back to the Klamath reservation as soon as practicable.[7] The Modoc problem, in Odeneal's view, was caused by corrupt Californians, including Steele, who were profiting from "illicit traffic" with the Indians.[8]

The July 1872 order by the Commissioner of Indian Affairs to remove the Modocs killed any hope for a Modoc reservation at Lost River. Military preparations were begun to force the Modocs back to the Klamath reservation. In October Canby instructed General Frank Wheaton, commander of the Lakes District stationed in eastern Oregon, to bring the cavalry over the mountains to Fort Klamath, a force "so large as to secure the result at once and beyond peradventure."[9] Still, it was generally agreed careless action by the army would provoke the Modocs to violence and removal should be conducted as peacefully as possible.

The Modoc War began with a fateful decision made by Indian Superintendent Odeneal. In late November 1872, Odeneal departed from his warm office in Salem, Oregon, and made the winter trip to Modoc country, three hundred miles south. The weather was horrendous—deep snow in the mountains and freezing rain at his destination. Odeneal rode sixty-nine miles by rail to Eugene City, where he boarded a stagecoach that took him another 170 miles south to the Rogue River Valley. From there it was 105 miles on horseback over a Cascade Mountain pass. It took Odeneal three days to reach Linkville, just north of the California line, the only town near the Modocs.

Linkville had saloons, a hotel, a land office, and a livery stable. The town was best known as a watering hole for card players and carousing soldiers. An Irish immigrant described it as a meager place, "mostly buckaroos."[10] Its citizens were given to vigilante justice toward Native peoples, and the Modocs generally gave the town a wide berth. Captain Jack's Modoc village was still another twenty miles south, so Odeneal checked into Linkville's lone hotel. Whether from fear or prudence, he chose not to go and talk directly with Captain Jack as his predecessor, Alfred Meacham, had done.

On November 25, 1872, Odeneal told General Wheaton he was in the area to remove the Modocs to Yainax and the Modoc "headmen" were to meet him at Linkville and be persuaded to return to the Klamath reservation.[11] Two days later, at Odeneal's instructions, Ivan Applegate and a small party of whites rode south to invite Captain Jack and the Modocs to come to Linkville and talk. When Odeneal's emissaries reached him, Captain Jack declined to talk, saying he had no intention of meeting with Odeneal at Linkville or of moving to the Klamath reservation. Ivan hurried back to Linkville to give the bad news to Odeneal, who reported to Major John Green, the commanding officer at Fort Klamath, that the Modocs "defiantly decline to meet me."[12]

Modoc bargaining was desultory, as was customary, testing white resolve. The Modocs assumed talks would continue and there would be additional meetings. Both Captain Jack and Schonchin John later insisted that Ivan had promised to return the next day with two or three men to continue talks. Instead, Ivan returned with a squadron of cavalry. Schonchin John raged to the *New York Herald* correspondent Edward Fox: "Applegate's son [Ivan] tell me lie! Applegate's son tell me he [come] back tomorrow; he tell me lie, me feel bad . . . he bad man."[13] Bogus Charley said much the same: "Ivan come down two days before, say he come back, two men, have big talk, *hi hi* ['amused laughter']." Instead, Ivan brought soldiers. "Major Jackson no talk," Bogus said.[14] Captain Jack further explained this misunderstanding at his trial: "Ivan Applegate was to come and have a talk with me, and not to bring soldiers, but to come alone."[15]

On the evening of November 28 Odeneal received Ivan Applegate's report of Modoc defiance, and he made the fateful decision to instruct the army at Fort Klamath to immediately arrest Captain Jack and his subchiefs. Odeneal ordered Ivan to race north to Fort Klamath with a message to Green asking for immediate military action "sufficient to compel said Indians to go to Camp Yainax, on said reservation." Perhaps concerned that he, as a civilian, lacked authority to give orders to the army commander, Odeneal assured Green the army would be carrying out instructions from the Commissioner of Indian Affairs.[16] Elijah Steele later said, "I believe that if Superintendent Odeneal had gone down there [to talk to Jack] instead of sending the soldiers to surprise them in the night, all could have been quietly settled."[17]

Odeneal had promised he would inform Canby and Wheaton if he ordered action, but he made no effort to do so. Odeneal tragically disregarded the danger to nearby settlers, later claiming he had not known there were homesteads near the Modocs. He tried to shift the blame to Green, saying he had transferred the whole matter to the army, "without assuming to dictate the course."[18] When Odeneal's instructions led to major trouble and loss of life, he quickly left Linkville and returned to Salem.

Ivan Applegate rode all night to deliver Odeneal's message to Green, making the thirty-mile trip from Linkville and arriving before dawn on a bitterly cold winter morning. The overnight fires had burned down to coals in the barracks, and soldiers had not yet risen for breakfast when Applegate arrived, his horse in a lather. Sentries took him to the young Lieutenant Frazier Boutelle, the officer on duty.

Boutelle, reading the message at 5 A.M., was surprised. He thought it unlikely any request for troops would be honored. "I told [Ivan Applegate] to make himself comfortable until later as I knew [Major] Green would not send troops," Boutelle explained. "About eight o'clock, I was amazed at receiving orders to make ready for a trip to Lost River; that we were ordered to move the Modocs." Boutelle worried the command being sent was "altogether inadequate—just enough to provoke a fight."[19]

Green, pressed by Applegate, decided to ignore Canby's directions and go after the Modocs immediately without waiting for reinforcements or trying to talk further with Captain Jack. He replied to Odeneal, advising he was sending troops who would hopefully be at Captain Jack's camp by morning.[20] Captain James Jackson, one of his cavalry officers, rode out at 11 A.M. for Lost River to arrest Captain Jack, Black Jim, and Scarface Charley. Jackson's hastily assembled force was composed of thirty-six mounted troops from Troop B, First Cavalry, with Lieutenant Boutelle second in command. The post surgeon, Dr. Henry McElderry, volunteered to accompany them, and a few mule-skinners followed with rations.

Ivan Applegate guided the cavalry as it made its way from Fort Klamath through Linkville and on to the villages on Lost River in punishing weather. The troops didn't make it to Linkville until after sunset where they stopped for dinner, and then continued their trip in the dark. The exhausted cavalrymen traveled fifty miles in freezing rain and darkness, in their saddles for more than eighteen hours before they reached the Modoc camp.

Green defended his decision to ignore Canby's instructions. "If I didn't send the troops," he said, "they (the citizens of Klamath Basin) will think we are all afraid."[21] He thus ignored standing orders from his commanding officer to postpone action, granted a request made by an inexperienced civilian, and did not wait for additional troops to arrive. Ironically, just six weeks later, Green won the Medal of Honor in the first fight at the Stronghold in the Lava Beds for "most distinct gallantry in action."

General Wheaton, Green's immediate superior, did not receive word of the action until several days after the order had been given. Confined to his bed with "quinsy" (tonsillitis) at distant Camp Warner, Wheaton was furious upon learning the army had yielded to the civilian Odeneal's request for an immediate attack. He wrote to Canby: "In my opinion, if Indian Superintendent Odeneal had exercised a little more judgment and discretion in selecting his agents to deal with the

Modocs, . . . instead of urging and insisting on Green's attacking them *at once* . . . all of the horrid massacres would have been prevented, and great expense avoided." Wheaton was angry that Ivan Applegate had pressured the army. "Mr. Ivan Applegate was sent by Odeneal to *insist* upon an *immediate* movement of Jackson's troop on the Modocs," he complained.[22]

Canby later reported "a grave mistake" had been made.[23] And Canby, who had repeatedly ordered extreme caution, would later pay the ultimate price for Ivan Applegate's haste and Odeneal's grave misjudgment.

14

Attack On Lost River Village

On the night of November 28, 1872, the Modocs slumbered in their warm winter lodges on Lost River where it empties into Tule Lake. The two villages, straddling Lost River near its mouth, were just a mile north of the modern California state line. It was a bitterly cold and starless night. The dogs barked all night and the old women didn't sleep well, but Captain Jack had posted no sentries. He was expecting another visit from Ivan Applegate and the negotiators in the morning.

Along with Captain Jack in the large permanent village on the west side of the river were fourteen men and their families.[1] The group included Black Jim, a powerful warrior who had repeatedly demanded that the whites leave, and Schonchin John, the fiercely militant leader. Other men in Captain Jack's camp, identified by the names given them by whites, included One-Eyed Mose, Watchman, Humpy Joe, Big Ike, Old Tails, Old Tail's Boy, Old Longface, and four unnamed

Lost River Near the Modoc Village. *Photo by Bill Stafford.*

others. Captain Jack's lieutenant, Scarface Charley, joined Captain Jack after shooting started. In the camp on the east bank of the Lost River were Modocs from the Hot Creek band, including Hooker Jim and Curley-Headed Doctor. The Modocs in the camps on both sides of the river were armed with outdated muzzle-loading muskets, or bows and arrows.[2]

Meanwhile, Oliver Applegate spent the night of November 28 in Linkville. Hearing that his brother was leading the cavalry to Captain Jack's village, Oliver assembled a group of civilian volunteers to march south to the Lost River. Oliver—subagent on the Klamath reservation—had come to Linkville to arrest two Indians who had left the reservation to gamble, and he was worried these two might warn Captain Jack's village that the cavalry was coming.[3] In the dark of night Ivan Applegate led the soldiers toward Captain Jack's village. Ivan reported they left the road and traveled through heavy sagebrush "to avoid being discovered by the wily Indians."[4] Oliver and his volunteers detoured through the sagebrush and were lost.

When the cavalry reached Lost River, the men dismounted and waited in the darkness a mile from Captain Jack's village. Lieutenant Frazier Boutelle took off his woolen greatcoat and tied it across his saddle, saying to Captain Jackson: "If I was going into a fight I wanted my deck clear for action."[5] The cavalrymen did the same. The temperature had fallen, their wet coats were partly frozen, and rain collecting on their blue woolen blouses began to freeze. As dawn approached, Jackson ordered the troops to remount and ride forward at a rapid rate. When they reached a small rise overlooking Captain Jack's camp, they again dismounted. They formed a line and readied their weapons.

Accounts differ about what happened next. Meacham (who was not there) wrote three years later that there was a half hour of negotiation in which Captain Jack seemed ready to surrender. Meacham said Captain Jack's people laid down their weapons.[6] But Ivan Applegate (who was there) says he was sent into the camp by Captain Jackson to find Captain Jack but never located him.[7] Testifying at his trial months later, Captain Jack said he expected Ivan to return alone for further talks and was therefore shocked to find the army at his door:

> It scared me when Major Jackson came. When Major Jackson and his men came to my camp, they surrounded it, and I hollered for them not to

shoot, that I would talk. I told Bogus Charley to go and talk, until I could get my clothes on. They all got down off their horses, and I thought we were going to have a talk. I thought then, why are they mad at me?[8]

Ivan Applegate's account described mounting disorder as the startled Modocs emerged from their lodges. There is agreement that Scarface Charley crossed the river to Captain Jack's camp on the west side when the army arrived and that he fired his rifle to alert Captain Jack's people about the ambush. Ivan said Scarface Charley began "haranguing his people and demanding that they fight to the death; telling them that if they be quick enough, they could kill every soldier without loss of a man."[9]

There may have been words between the soldiers and some of the Modocs. As far as can be confirmed, however, the army never saw Captain Jack. His band grew agitated, and Scarface Charley waved his rifle. Boutelle believed a fight was imminent: "Captain Jackson finally rode over to me and said, 'Mr. Boutelle, what do you think of the situation?' I replied, 'There is going to be a fight, and the sooner you open it the better, before there are any more complete preparations [by the Modocs].'"[10] Jackson ordered Boutelle to advance with four soldiers toward Scarface Charley and arrest him. Modoc author Jeff Riddle wrote forty years later that Boutelle hurled a storm of profane language at Scarface.[11] The line of dismounted cavalry waited to see if Scarface Charley would surrender. Things were at a flash point.

The first shots of the Modoc War were fired just before dawn on November 29, 1872. Boutelle and Scarface Charley shot at each other simultaneously, beginning what was later known as the Battle of Lost River. As Boutelle (who shot his pistol left-handed) raised his arm, Charley's rifle bullet cut through his sleeve, slicing his tunic and the sweater he wore underneath, and exited without drawing blood. Boutelle shot a hole in the scarf tied around Scarface's head, not even leaving a scratch. As Boutelle and Scarface Charley exchanged gunfire, the soldiers sent a fusillade at the Modocs. Ivan Applegate later described the chaotic battle that ensued:

> Then all was din and commotion; men were falling in the line, the riderless horses were dashing here and there and kicking among us, but instantly came the brave Major, 'Fire'! The attack was so sudden and desperate, the Modocs rushing on us with demon-like yells, that the men were forced

back a step or two, and it seemed for a moment the thinned line would yield and break. But immediately came the order 'Forward!' and it was like an inspiration. The men sprang forward, under the brave Boutelle, delivering a deadly fire, and the Indians were forced back.[12]

At the village on the east side of Lost River the civilian volunteers led by Oliver Applegate had arrived before dawn, after riding in freezing rain all night. Some of the volunteers wanted to protect the settlers living in the area; others just hoped to see a good fight. The volunteer group had grown to twelve men as they rode south. They hid in a gulch and watched the village from the sagebrush as a few Modocs moved about lighting their morning fires.

Oliver and his volunteers wanted to see what was happening on the west bank across Lost River, and a settler named O. A. (One-Armed) Brown galloped up to take a look. He returned to say all was well, so the volunteers decided to ride into the village and arrest the Modocs. Oliver, who was liked by the Modocs, rode calmly to the village center and told them that the long squabble was over; they should surrender their weapons and come with him to the Klamath reservation. But he recalled that only a few sullen warriors were talking with him.

When the Modocs on the east bank of the river heard the first shots fired across the river, however, their warriors attacked Oliver and his volunteers with heavy gunfire. A settler named Thurber was killed in the first volley, and shortly thereafter Wendolin Nus was mortally wounded. The volunteers moved back in disarray. Oliver fled on horseback. The Modocs charged, he wrote, "sounding the war cry, shooting with both guns and arrows at the retreating men." Many of the panicked volunteers ran on foot toward their horses. Writing three decades later, Oliver claimed he ordered a daring countercharge, firing his revolver "with great effect" and yelling, "You scoundrels, go back to your camp!" He said the Indians abandoned their attack and retreated to shoot from a distance, still riding back and forth on their horses, "shouting the war whoops." Women and children fled.[13]

Jackson filed a report (later corrected) boasting that he "poured in volley after volley among their worst men, killing most of them, capturing the camp, and driving the Indians to the refuge of the brush and hills."[14] In fact, only a single Modoc warrior was killed in the fight.

No-Sing-Ko-Pos (Watchman), a relative of Captain Jack and "one of the most prominent Indians," according to Oliver Applegate's later account, was killed.[15] In addition, Black Jim, a major lieutenant of Captain Jack's, was wounded in both arms.

The attack on the east-side village soon broke off, and Oliver galloped north to report the Modocs were at war. The other white fighters

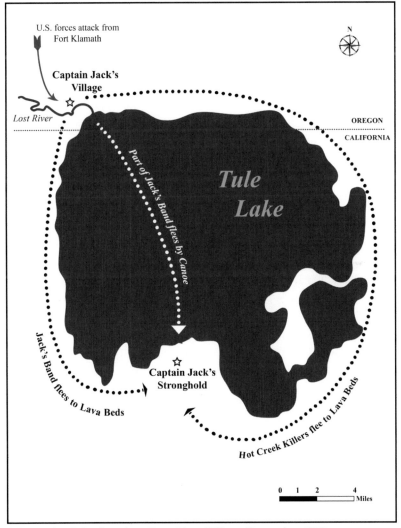

Aftermath of the Attack on Lost River Village, November 1872.

on the east bank quickly withdrew to a nearby settler's cabin. The civilian volunteers retreated to Linkville. The fighting on the west side of the river at Captain Jack's camp also ended within minutes. The initial gunshots had stampeded the army's horses, and the cavalrymen struggled frantically to recover them. Boutelle led a brief counterattack, but the cavalry quickly retired.[16] It was first reported that ten army soldiers had died, but the army actually lost only one, a Private Harris, and suffered seven additional casualties.

Following the battle, Captain Jack's fighting men retreated around the west side of Tule Lake, riding seventeen miles to sanctuary in the volcanic formations of the Lava Beds. The Modoc women and children and the few wounded were loaded into shovel-nosed dugout canoes and paddled down Lost River to Tule Lake. Crossing twelve miles of open water across Tule Lake was a harrowing trip for the Modocs, through the night and into the next day. The wind and rain threatened several times to swamp them, but the band arrived at the south end of the lake late the next morning. They arrived on the south shore, soaked and exhausted, almost twenty-four hours after the warriors on horseback.[17]

As the sun came up after the fight, the army soldiers occupied the Modoc villages and told a few old men and women who had stayed behind to leave so they could burn the lodges. According to one account the soldiers piled tule mats on an old blind Modoc woman—"like a load of straw"—and burned her alive.[18] The volunteers on the east side of the river murdered a Modoc woman and two small children.[19]

As Oliver and the volunteers abandoned the fight, Hooker Jim's warriors stayed on the east side of the river and laid harassing fire on the retreating men. When the shooting ended, a small group of Modoc warriors left on horseback and rode around the east side of Tule Lake, looking for whites to kill to revenge the unprovoked attack on the villages and the killing of the women and children. Captain Jack's band, escaping from the army across Lost River, was not involved in the killings. The killers of the settlers eventually went free, but Captain Jack and three of his lieutenants were not so fortunate.

15

Revenge: Fourteen Settlers Murdered!

On the cold dawn of November 29, 1872, settlers near Tule Lake remained unaware of the skirmish on Lost River and the threat of attacks in reprisal. The alarm was to have been carried to homesteads along the east shore of Tule Lake by One-Armed Brown and Dennis Crawley, who had ridden south with Oliver Applegate. Inexplicably, they stopped at Crawley's cabin on Lost River and did not continue on to alert the farmers. In the end, fourteen settlers were killed.[1]

Hooker Jim, a Hot Creek warrior, led the retaliatory attack.[2] There is one surviving picture of Hooker Jim, wearing a wrinkled shirt and a kind of beaded choker or necklace, looking sullen. His chief lieutenant (or co-commander) was Curley-Headed Doctor, the Modoc medicine man. Other Hot Creeks on the rampage were Scarface Charley, Long Jim, One-Eyed Mose, Old Doctor Humphrey, Little Jim, Boston Charley, and Dave.

The sky spit snow as the angry Hot Creeks began their ride around Tule Lake, looking for revenge. Their two-day rampage began at Charlie Monroe's farm where they burnt haystacks. Three miles to the east, they came upon four recent immigrants from Australia cutting wood— William Boddy, his son-in-law Nicholas Schira, and Boddy's two stepsons. The men were about a mile and a half from the Boddy cabin on Tule Lake.

The Boddy women first realized there was trouble when they spotted a horse dragging an empty wagon back to the Boddy homestead, covered with blood. The terrified Louisa Boddy and her daughter-in-law, Mrs. Schira, rushed into the woods where they met the party of Modocs leaving the scene of the massacre. Hooker Jim's men assured the women there was no problem, but inquired ominously if there were more men at the house. The women soon came upon the four men, their bodies lifeless in the bloodstained snow. William Boddy, who apparently tried to defend himself with an axe, was shot four times. All were stripped of clothing. "One [boy] was found a few rods from his work," a later account said, "his bowels beside him, his heart taken from his body, and hacked to pieces. This was the work of Hooker Jim."[3] The women fled, hiking all night in the snow twelve miles over towering Stukel Mountain to reach safety at the Galbraith homestead.

Hooker Jim's group overnighted in the woods, watching for pursuers. On the morning of November 30, 1872, they resumed their deadly work, continuing eight miles east to the Brotherton farm. Meeting the Brothertons along the way, they killed all three men. A German named Nicholas Shearer, tending sheep with young Joseph Brotherton, saw the Modocs approaching and tried to flee, but was gunned down. As the Modoc men stopped to strip the clothes from Nicholas' body, Joseph ran toward the family cabin. His mother saw Joseph approaching with the Modocs in pursuit, and she ran out and confronted them with a rifle. She retreated into the cabin with her son, and fortified it by stacking twenty bags of flour against the walls. Mrs. Brotherton supposedly used an augur to bore holes in the wall through which they fired at the Modocs. The Modocs finally left, but the Brothertons did not dare step outside until a rescue party arrived a day and a half later.

Hooker Jim's band continued down the east side of Tule Lake in pursuit of Henry Miller, an advocate and friend to the Modocs. He had employed them as ranch hands and vouched for them when the army had visited. Miller had an understanding with the tribe: he gave them provisions and ammunition, and they left him alone. Once he provided a "talking paper," saying the Modocs were peaceful. Just the day before, Miller—who could not have known about army movements—assured the same Modocs there was no plan to attack them, and promised to warn them if there were. Hooker Jim now saw Miller's assurances as treachery. Wanting revenge, he shot Miller dead standing next to his pump, alongside a hayfield.

Ivan Applegate knew Jesse Applegate was at Fiddler's Green, his home on Clear Lake, and several other Applegate kin lived nearby. To warn his family and the other settlers who were in harm's way, Ivan sent Arthur Langell to make sure they were safe. The next morning Langell and his party headed back to Tule Lake, where they discovered Mrs. Brotherton and her children alone and seven men dead within a mile and a half of her home.[4]

By evening of the second day, fourteen settlers were dead. The Modocs boasted they only killed men, and indeed they had spared

women and children.[5] But only one of the dead had escaped mutilation—the cowboy Adam Shillingbow. Shot with an arrow in the chest,
Shillingbow had ridden eight miles before falling from his horse and
dying at Bloody Point, escaping the Modocs' knives. The Modocs later
wore the clothes stripped from their victims' bodies, and the survivors
could sometimes identify the clothing. The full extent of the carnage
was not discovered for three days, when Captain Jackson sent a cavalry squad to pursue the fugitives, led by the indefatigable Lieutenant
Boutelle. The squad found the mutilated bodies of the Boddy men and
reported to Jackson the bloody aftermath of the army's attack on the
Modocs at Lost River.

In an ironic twist, land baron Jesse Carr's pursuit of land along
Tule Lake's eastern shore benefited from the slaughter. Carr bought the
Brotherton property from the surviving widow shortly after the war,
and later purchased the Henry Miller ranch from Miller's heirs. Jesse
Applegate's son and daughter later purchased land belonging to other
victims just to the north and turned it over to Carr.[6]

Rumors and misinformation about the murder of the settlers
swirled up and down the coast as newspapers published the first stories. A "reign of terror existed all through the Lake country," wrote
one paper. The San Francisco *Evening Bulletin* reported that "all the
male settlers on Tule Lake have been killed." Another paper announced
that "all the settlers on Link River have been massacred." The Modocs
"opened war upon the settlers," wrote another, and two companies of
militia were raised in Yreka "on a few hours' notice."[7] Meacham later
described the frenzy: "People were aroused to madness at the sight of
the mangled bodies of the soldiers and citizens . . . Who shall ever find
words to describe the horror of the night following this treacherous
butchery?"[8]

Hooker Jim's Hot Creek band, with "plunder and horses," rode
south to find sanctuary in the Lava Beds, where Captain Jack's people
were already hiding. Fresh from murdering and pillaging, the Hot Creek
men announced to Captain Jack they were joining him in his rocky
sanctuary. When he heard what they had done, Captain Jack tried to
turn Hooker Jim's band away, but they refused to leave. Captain Jack's
people—innocent of the killings—would soon suffer white wrath for
the massacre of these settlers.

16

Captain Jack's Stronghold

Captain Jack's people—fleeing the army—sheltered in the Lava Beds, an astonishing twenty-five-square-mile moonscape of rocks and chasms. The Lava Beds in northern California would provide the Modocs an unparalleled natural fortification. On the south shore of Tule Lake, the Lava Beds were uncharted land, considered so rough and remote white men didn't think it even worth exploring. But the Modocs knew these lands, and they followed sketchy trails deep into the jumble of lava rocks and camped in caves and under ledges. The Modocs had abandoned their lodges in such haste they left behind their winter caches of dried fish and roots. Hunger soon set in.

The Lava Beds—site of Captain Jack's Stronghold—present a landscape of forbidding beauty: a stark volcanic plateau, flooded millennia earlier with molten rock that cooled into a sea of jumbled and jagged basaltic lava, capturing in stone the violence of its creation. Fumaroles—chimneys that release underground gas from deep volcanic formations—belched their foul breath at sites just nine miles from Captain Jack's Lost River home. The black scoria (a kind of foamy lava turned to stone) radiates menace mixed with beauty. The harsh land was a potent setting for war.

The Lava Beds are virtually uninhabitable. They bake under an implacable sun for half the year. The summer sun flattens the land, erasing shadows and inflicting brutal heat; the horizon seems to recede, the land becomes a hot disc, and the Lava Beds a shimmering Golgotha. A scant overlay of soil supports some bunch grass, fragrant sage, and a few twisted juniper trees. In winter, low overcast skies, uncomfortably bright, merge with the horizon, and the flat light seems to sharpen the ragged rocks. Winter temperatures sometimes stay below zero for days, and snow softens the sharp contours of the jagged rocks.

The extraordinary geology of the Lava Beds—geologic turmoil and rocks that still seem alive—would play a critical role in the Modoc War.

The Lava Beds are crisscrossed with a geologic form called "schollen-domes." In prehistoric times the advancing lava froze into stone on its surface, but its hot core continued to flow, and sometimes expand, leaving behind tunnels, voids, and domes beneath a hardened crust. Many of the spaces later collapsed to form ravines, cluttered trenches, and sinkholes. Captain Jack and his family sheltered in a cave that was a partial schollendome, a concavity open on one side to the weather, with little protection against snow and rain. Schollendomes created the ramparts for Modoc defensive positions.

"Captain Jack lived under a ledge in a cave with his two wives, Rebecca and Lizzie, and three-year-old Rosie, through the winter months of 1872–73." *Photo by Bill Stafford.*

At the southern end of the Lava Beds there are dozens of caves and tunnels. Inside the tunnels the rippling surfaces make the tubes seem like wandering intestines and the unlit caves like gloomy sub-terranean rooms. Some caves had floors of ice, later mined for water when the army denied the Modocs access to the lake. One shallow cave has a collapsed roof, open to filtered half-light that nourishes a surreal underground field of lime green ferns. Inside the Stronghold itself, the dark rocks are splashed with brilliant lichens, in yellow, orange, and incandescent green. In their oral history, Modocs described seeing peri-odic volcanic eruptions of nearby Mount Lassen, when the lava poured across the land. Although they lived near the Lava Beds for millennia, they had no reason to enter the sea of twisted stone except to escape danger. It is not a congenial place.

Captain Jack's Stronghold hides within the Lava Beds. Today, entering from a parking area, the visitor can walk up a trail toward what appears to be a small hill in a rolling landscape. There is a jumbled crown of blackish stone, and low rocky ridges appear on either side. The rolling land hides the complex of natural stone fortifications as secure as a medieval keep. The depth of the Stronghold complex becomes clear when viewed from the inside. The rock fortification rises just enough above its surroundings to give an unobstructed view for several miles in each direction to the steep bluffs on the west, the lake to the north, the broken prairie and lava rock on the east, and a massive lava field and group of sandy buttes to the south.

From this redoubt Modoc snipers fired from hidden walkways, caves, and convenient apertures. There was no way for an enemy to approach the Stronghold unseen. Every opening had a wide field of

"Inside the Stronghold, the Modoc families experienced five months of immense hardship, ensconced in a rock pile with only caves for shelter, dwindling food, and little water." *Photo by Bill Stafford.*

fire, and each marksman could protect his neighbor. When combat began, the Modoc warriors moved from one position to another; the army saw "puffs of smoke" but rarely a warrior, which caused the military to greatly overestimate the Modoc numbers.

Keith Murray, park ranger at Lava Beds National Monument, correctly described the chasms and fissures of the Lava Beds as "a series of roughly parallel gullies a quarter of a mile long, possibly a hundred feet wide, and averaging perhaps twenty feet deep."[1] To infantryman, approaching the rock-strewn gullies with Modoc snipers firing down on them, the chasms were a deadly moat. The landscape is littered with sharp rocks, "varying in size from a match-box to a church," wrote General Wheaton.[2] Walking was slow and difficult. Soldiers complained the lava shredded their boots.

The terrain allowed the Modocs to overcome their disadvantages in numbers, firearms, and ammunition. They were fighting from a stone fortress, shooting from a dozen places at once. Jesse Applegate wrote to a Portland newspaper, "From the top of these stone pyramids, an Indian can shoot a man without even exposing a square inch of himself. He can, with due haste, load and shoot a common muzzle-loading rifle ten times before a man can scramble over the rocks and chasms between the slain and the slayer."[3]

General Wheaton, who commanded the first, disastrous assault on the Stronghold, later said it would take a thousand men to dislodge the Modocs from their "almost impregnable position."[4] Cavalry were useless; horses could hardly cross the stony landscape without stumbling and breaking their legs. The army brought "mountain howitzers" of Civil War vintage, notoriously heavy and cumbersome to move. The guns fired at such a shallow trajectory their projectiles crashed harmlessly off the rocks. Only a mortar could loft shells (mortar bombs) inside the natural fortifications, and the army didn't employ them for another four months.

When the fighting began, the Modocs had only obsolete weapons, muzzleloaders purchased at frontier trading posts, discarded, or sold by the military. But these weapons were more than a match when fired from rocky fortifications. After each fight, Modoc women would comb the battlefield to collect the weapons of fallen soldiers and strip them of uniforms and ammunition. The Modocs also stole army provisions and were able to smuggle some food from the south. Captain Jack once offered a piece of dried beef to a visiting reporter, perhaps to show him the fighters in the Stronghold had adequate food. The Modocs had an emaciated herd of cattle—some claim there were a hundred—which grazed on the sparse grass around the rocky fortress. But by the end of the siege, the Modocs were eating their horses.

Inside the Stronghold, the Modoc families experienced immense hardship, ensconced in a rock pile with only caves for shelter, dwindling food, and little water. Through months of snowstorms and freezing weather, they endured with only small sagebrush fires. Captain Jack lived under a ledge in a cave with his two wives, Rebecca and Lizzie, and three-year-old Rosie, through the remaining winter months of 1872–73. Children born in the Stronghold lived their first months in these caves. Cheewa James, whose grandfather—the son of Shacknasty Jim—was born in the Stronghold, wrote that the infant "struggled to survive that snowy, bloody winter of the war [but] that delicate thread of life dug in and held on."[5]

The first person to visit Captain Jack's cave after U.S. Army troops recaptured the Lava Beds was the English artist and writer William Simpson, touring the world for the *Illustrated London News*. He saw "bones, some of them picked; others with the pickings still left; horns of cattle; hoofs; skins, with the hair on; hides and pieces of deer skin . . . Fish in a putrid state, and fish bones, were in shelves of the rock; pieces of fat, and dark questionable-looking lumps lay about which were said to be meat."[6] The cave where Captain Jack and his family lived through the war offered little protection. Snow blew into the shelter, and the darkness beneath the black scoria ledge was oppressive.

On New Years Eve of 1992, with permission from officials of the Lava Beds National Monument, this author slept in Captain Jack's cave. It was bitterly cold, with a light snow falling and a sharp wind from the north. The cave is at the bottom of a deep bowl of jumbled boulders, and the irregular ceiling requires that a person crouch to enter. It is really nothing more than a craggy ledge affording a few feet of shelter under the rock. Patches of sandy pumice form small areas of floor barely large enough to unroll a sleeping bag. This dwelling was (and still is) a testimony to the bravery and endurance of the Modocs who survived there those long winter months.

17

Ready for War

The bloody rampage of Hooker Jim and the other Hot Creeks terrified the settler community. With rumors swirling of Indian war, they fortified their cabins and sent women and children over the mountains for safety. After the assault on the Modoc village at Lost River and the revenge murders of the settlers, A. J. Burnett and Oliver Applegate raced to Jacksonville to telegraph the terrible news to Oregon governor L. F. Grover in Salem. They reported the military had sent an inadequate force, enraged the Modocs, and caused the slaughter of civilians. The governor demanded details from General Canby, who was angry at the suggestion the military was to blame. The governor announced he was approving a request from "more than a hundred respectable citizens in Ashland" to recruit a volunteer militia "sufficient to quell disturbances and to protect the settlements."[1] No doubt irritated by the suggestion the army needed the help of civilian volunteers, Canby replied: "If not already in Modoc country, sufficient force to suppress [the Modocs] and give protection [is] close at hand."[2]

On December 26 a noisy meeting in the engine house of Yreka Fire Company Number One organized an appeal to the California state government "for the suppression of Indian hostilities." Settler Presley Dorris, who lived twenty miles west of the Lava Beds, was deputized to go immediately to Sacramento and put the matter before California Governor Newton Booth.[3] There is no record of the details of their meeting, but Booth responded that Indian control was a federal matter and declined to call up the California Volunteers. He did agree to send arms and ammunition to Yreka for self-defense, but the rifles were old and the ammunition too large.[4]

For Canby, after months of caution, the outbreak of war with the Modocs was the worst possible outcome. Not only were Captain Jack and his Modocs now fugitives, but fourteen white settlers had been killed. With one soldier dead and seven wounded, some grievously, the Modocs were now barricaded in the near-impregnable Stronghold. Canby was furious his careful planning and orders for patience had been ignored. He grumbled to headquarters, "The original arrangement should have been carried out."[5]

Canby issued a flurry of orders dispatching troops toward Modoc country from all directions. This time he would make sure an overpowering force was assembled before any more attempts were made to arrest the Modocs. Major Green, who had disobeyed Canby's orders not to disturb the Modocs, scrambled to regain the initiative. He sent an infantry company to reinforce Captain Jackson, still camped near the site of the ambush on Captain Jack's village, but they arrived three days after the initial fight. Green, a portly man with a generous beard, wrote sarcastically to Canby that Indian superintendent Thomas Odeneal, who had requested the military attack, had left Linkville in a hurry when the fighting began. Green issued twenty muskets and carbines to Linkville citizens, and sent ten more carbines to the Indian Agent at Yainax. He gave away most of his ammunition, emptied his barracks, and personally marched south to Crawley's cabin on Lost River to take command of the troops still in the field.

Canby put Wheaton in command of the troops preparing to fight the Modocs. Wheaton, who had been bedridden during the ambush at Lost River, crossed the mountains from Fort Warner, a hundred miles to the east, and took over from the discredited Green. Like most of Canby's officers, Wheaton had a distinguished Civil War record, cited five times for "gallant and meritorious service." But the botched attack on Captain Jack's village happened on his watch, and although it was not his decision, he was blamed for the disastrous aftermath. His reputation took a serious blow.

Wheaton arrived at Crawley's "miserable cabin" on Lost River just before Christmas 1872 where he began planning an assault on the Lava Beds. The first challenge was to assemble sufficient arms and men. Materiel—guns, ammunition, and food—had to be shipped to Fort Klamath from the San Francisco Bay area three hundred miles south, or from the army garrison at Vancouver, Washington, three hundred miles north. From either direction there was a railroad part way, but infantry soldiers had to slog the last hundred miles or so to Fort Klamath on foot. The closest town was Yreka, eighty-one miles over the mountains to the west, at least a two-day trip in mud and snow during winter.

Wheaton decided to wait for arms and men from distant garrisons in Oregon and California. He telegraphed Fort Vancouver to provide two howitzers "to demoralize the Indians."[6] He waited weeks for their delivery, and when they finally arrived without ammunition, he had to send back for powder and shells. Unfortunately for Wheaton, Green had already issued most of the small arms ammunition to frightened civilians in Linkville. "Some of the troops today have but 5 or 10 rounds each," Wheaton noted.[7] He sent for more.

Canby asked about supplies on hand and was told a few shabby uniforms were available, including "38 Greatcoats, 13 damaged, 249 prs Stockings, Trousers, thirty (30) damaged."[8]

Canby scrambled to assemble a fighting force. He pillaged the small forts strung from northern California through eastern Oregon for any available troops to send to Wheaton, but the pickings were slim. The posts at Fort Bidwell and Camp Warner had been depleted of manpower during the Civil War and never reinforced.

Most of the officers he ordered to southern Oregon were Civil War veterans, and several had decorations for "gallantry and valor." Most served with Grant's huge northern armies in set piece battles where columns of thousands marched, wheeled, and attacked massed Confederates, resulting in terrible carnage. These officers could not imagine how a few dozen poorly armed Modocs could repel a mass attack. Within weeks, the army assembled more than 350 troops, and eventually a thousand arrived. Removing a band of renegade Modocs from a pile of rocks seemed no more than a training exercise for these hard-boiled veterans. "We will be prepared to make short work of this impudent and enterprising savage," Wheaton boasted. "I feel confident the guns [artillery] will astonish and terrify them, and perhaps save much close skirmishing and loss of life."[9]

Oregon governor LaFayette Grover, true to his word, ordered two companies of Oregon Volunteers into the field—one militia from Jacksonville and one from Fort Klamath. Soon the ubiquitous Oliver Applegate was commissioned as "Captain" Applegate (a title he used for the rest of his life), and he showed up at Crawley's cabin on Lost River with seventy Oregon Volunteers. Half of his volunteers were

Klamath, Modoc, Shoshone, and Pit River Indians recruited from around Yainax. Applegate's Indians were deployed as "scouts" charged with intercepting any emissaries Captain Jack might send to recruit additional Modocs from the Klamath reservation.

Wheaton wasn't impressed with the volunteers. He told Canby: "The entire force has been constantly drilled, and practiced at targets, and they needed it."[10] Oliver Applegate's mismatched band of farmers and drifters, with three dozen Indian scouts, were easily the most inexperienced and disorganized of the troops in the force. Applegate drilled his homespun recruits, marching them up and down a muddy field, some off step, mismatched rifles askew, many hatless, all in clothing that would fill a rag museum. Applegate himself was quite tall, towering over both the Indians and whites in photographs, wearing a stovepipe hat, which he later changed for a coonskin.

The Oregon Volunteers had signed up for a month and made up roughly a third of the 350-man total. They received as much as three dollars a day, plus a dollar a day to feed their horses. Their pay scale must have been a source of resentment to army regulars—privates got thirteen dollars a month and a sergeant thirty-four dollars.[11] The volunteers hoped their thirty-day enlistments would expire so they could return home, and if possible, avoid fighting. They knew they would not be allowed to leave once hostilities began, and Wheaton hoped he could get his forces assembled in time to make them stay. Modoc warriors held the civilian volunteers in contempt, believing they were cowards. Modoc author Jeff Riddle, writing in 1914, created a dialogue of a fearful volunteer recruit: "Bill, these reds [Indians] will be hell, gol darn it. I wish I had stayed at home."[12] In fact, when combat began, the militiamen fought poorly, and in the end were more trouble to Wheaton than they were worth.

Meanwhile army regulars continued to arrive from across the region. From Fort Vancouver, Washington, across the Columbia River from Portland, came Major E. C. Mason and a battalion of sixty-four infantrymen. Mason was a decorated veteran of the Civil War battles of Fredericksburg, the Wilderness, and Spotsylvania. His troops were "enchanted by [Mason's] interesting and conspicuous behavior, mounted upon a snow-white war steed and wearing a fur cap."[13]

Mason and his infantrymen had a horrendous trip to the front. After crossing the Columbia River, they boarded a train to Roseburg. They arrived in a driving rain, commandeered wagons, and struggled in mud and rain for seven more days to haul their supplies south to Jacksonville. When they finally struck east over the mountains to Modoc country, they had to camp in the snow. One officer collapsed from exhaustion and had to return to Portland. As the snow turned to rain, they marched in mud. Some soldiers deserted.

By this time, several outstanding officers had joined Wheaton's command. Captain David Perry, later a Brigadier General, had Indian fighting experience in Idaho and eastern Oregon. He was ordered west to Fort Klamath from Goose Lake by forced march, and his troops were fired upon twice as they traveled. Captain J. G. Trimble, stationed at Camp Harney three hundred miles away to the north, was ordered to rush his infantry companies to the front. He groused bitterly about the order for "light marching order . . . [with no wagons], without tents and our numberless blankets." Supplies were loaded on "unfortunate mules." Trimble later described a harrowing trip through the frozen plain, dragging the horses, sometimes in armpit deep snow.[14]

Captain Reuben Frank Bernard, a hardboiled Tennessee cavalryman known to his troops as "Old Itchy Whiskers," was a beloved and sometimes controversial figure in the Indian Wars, known for freely expressing his doubts and disagreements to his superiors.[15] Bernard rushed his Twenty-Fourth First Cavalry troops north from Fort Bidwell, California. Traveling as lightly as possible, Bernard's troops made the 96-mile trip to Fort Klamath in two days. General Wheaton at first thought Bernard would be used to "give a sense of confidence to the settlers" and probably not enter combat, but that idea quickly changed. Bernard was soon directed to request supplies and prepare to be in the field for an extended time.[16]

Inside the growing army camp at Fort Klamath soldiers began grumbling over the cold and the food. Meals in the mess hall were frozen by the time they were served. A sergeant based at Fort Klamath in 1865 said the most odious victual was a Civil War invention called "desiccated vegetables," a kind of tablet that could be cooked into a soup or stew.[17] To the sergeant, they were "a compound that could be smelled for one hundred yards away, and contained every form and flavor of vegetable known to the temperate zone. There were cabbage leaves, pumpkin leaves, and vines, tomatoes, turnips, carrots and numerous other ingredients which when cooked up with the proverbial government sowbelly, would cause angels to weep or fiends to laugh in ghoulish glee."[18]

At the camp at Lost River, the soldiers had neither mess hall nor barracks, camped fifty miles from their base in the cold snow beside a muddy river. Army food in the field was seldom plentiful and often inedible, and there are endless accounts from the Indian wars of maggoty beef and weevil-ridden hardtack. Later, troops in the field were able to supplement their army rations with more edible food by buying it at exorbitant prices from "sutlers," traders who followed the army. But the sutlers did not join the Modoc campaign for two more months.

Two weeks after he arrived, Wheaton began to move cavalry, infantry, and artillerymen into position. He ordered Captain David Perry to take his cavalry to the tiny farmhouse at Dan Van Brimmer's ranch on the high bluff twelve miles west of the Lava Beds. Van Brimmer's soon became a principal army base for the operations that followed. Hundreds of troops, camp followers, civilian muleskinners, and sutlers eventually camped on the fields around the Van Brimmer ranch. On New Year's Day of 1873, Wheaton moved his staff headquarters there. He had hoped to attack by December 27, but he still had weeks to wait for his howitzers and small arms ammunition to arrive.

In early January 1873 the Oregon Volunteers also moved to Van Brimmer's, one company from Jacksonville and Oliver Applegate's militia from the Klamath reservation area. The citizen soldiers from Jacksonville were quickly chastened when they had their first encounter with the Modocs. Captain Kelley, a dozen Oregon Volunteers from Company A, and six Indian scouts were riding toward the bluff above the Lava Beds when they saw a party of Modocs. Lieutenant J.W. Berry of Company A wrote a breathless letter to his friend Lieutenant E.R. Reames on January 6, reporting that his patrol caught sight of some Modocs. "[We] started in pursuit of the red devils, and came up on them in the neighborhood of the juniper grove." There was an exchange of gunfire, but the skirmish between the amateur soldiers and the Modocs ended quickly. More warriors appeared, and "our boys thought it best to make the retreat to camp." No one was hurt, but Berry said, "I thought of meeting my saviour [*sic*]."[19]

The army viewed with suspicion the thirty Indian mercenaries recruited by Oliver Applegate, as the officers feared they would side with the Modocs. Whenever they were near enough, the Modocs would call out to the Klamaths and other Indians, encouraging them to defect to their side. "It was certainly unsafe allowing the Indian allies to converse with the Modocs, who appealed to them so strongly for help. The regular officers afterward entertained the belief that the Klamaths were deceitfully promising to help Captain Jack's warriors in the Modoc/Klamath tongue."[20]

Oliver Applegate believed the Klamaths trustworthy, but the skeptics were probably right. Captain Jack testified at his military trial the Klamaths had indeed provided his warriors with guns and ammunition, and fired their guns in the air rather than at the Modocs. One Klamath who was most helpful to the Modocs, Captain Jack said, was Link River Jack, who crept into the Modoc camp to warn them when the soldiers were coming. Even though he was one of Captain Jack's tormentors on the reservation, "taunting them with their poverty and cowardice," Link River Jack later became a Modoc friend and—to the army—"a natural traitor."[21]

Eventually a small militia of California volunteers arrived to help with the fighting, but with no official blessing. California governor Newton Booth declared it was the business of the U.S. Army to deal with the Modocs, and he seemed to side with those who wanted lenience for the tribe. He had recommended three thousand acres be set aside for the Modocs as a reservation. The total California contribution to the growing fighting force was twenty-four men recruited locally by rancher John Fairchild, considered by the Modocs to be a friend. Most of the California volunteers were farmhands who worked nearby for Fairchild and Presley Dorris.

Wheaton's first task was positioning the troops for an attack. From their base at Van Brimmer's, soldiers had to cross a series of parallel ridges before reaching the eight-hundred-foot bluffs above the shore of Tule Lake and the Lava Beds. Modoc sentries hid in the rock ridges watching for an attack, and Modoc snipers skillfully disrupted Wheaton's patrols. Nevertheless, Wheaton's sunny optimism continued: "We hope to make very quick work of them very soon after our ammunition comes up."[22]

As the weather worsened, hostilities began to intensify. Major Reuben Bernard, now readying for a long assignment, had been ordered to deliver supplies to the army camp at Jesse Applegate's ranch. While waiting for stores and supplies from Fort Bidwell, over one hundred miles away, he camped at the farm of Louis Land just east of the Lava Beds. The Modocs were also short on supplies, and when Captain Jack's scouts spotted a wagon loaded with ammunition just two miles from their destination at Jesse Applegate's ranch, they decided the soldiers would be easy prey for an ambush. A surprise Modoc volley on December 21 killed one soldier, mortally wounded a second, and killed six horses.[23] Captain Bernard, two miles away, could hear the gunfire and quickly sent a rescue party. Led by Second Lieutenant John Kyle, ten cavalry troops drove off the Modocs and saved the supplies. The night after the raid the Modocs built a large fire in the Lava Beds and danced to celebrate the victory within sight of the soldiers.[24] The boldness of the foray unnerved the army as Bernard reported about sixty-five Indians had attacked him, a gross exaggeration.[25] Bernard requested reinforcements, and efforts were redoubled to keep the Modocs from leaving the Lava Beds.

"Schonchin John was a fiercely militant warrior." Souvenir card. *Courtesy author's collection.*

The Modoc force inside the Stronghold had grown to about four dozen warriors, living with their families in caves and under ledges in the lava wilderness. Hot Creek warriors escaping vigilantes had joined Captain Jack's original group, but it was an unhappy coalition. Two factions were emerging within the Stronghold: one supporting Captain Jack, the other more militant and warlike. Captain Jack's band—which had fled from the army and killed no settlers—was now trapped in the rocks with the violent Hooker Jim and his Hot Creek group, who had slain and mutilated fourteen men. The divided Modocs began to argue about whether to sue for peace or stand and fight. Captain Jack favored settlement. But Hooker Jim and the Hot Creeks resisted because they would have to surrender to authorities if there were any peace agreement. The balance of power within the Modoc factions began to shift toward the militants, who now included Schonchin John, Curley-Headed Doctor, Bogus Charley, Hooker Jim, Shacknasty Jim, Steamboat Frank, Rock Dave, Big Joe, Curley Haired Jack, and others.[26]

The army often sighted the Modocs moving on horseback around the perimeter of their fortified camp, sometimes attempting to draw the army into ambushes. Somehow the Modocs were able to venture out for miles and mount bold harassing attacks—one on troops at Lost River, and another on soldiers camped on the ridge above the Lava Beds. Scouts and other Indians warned General Wheaton the Modocs would fight desperately, but he remained chirpy with optimism. "I don't understand how [the Indians] can think of attempting any serious resistance. If the Modocs will only try to make good their boast to whip 1,000 soldiers, all will be satisfied."[27]

Surprisingly, the Modocs often frequented the army camps and mingled with the same soldiers they were fighting on the battlefield. A good number of Modocs emerged from the Stronghold, dropped in to chat, negotiate, and barter with the troops (and of course, to spy). As the conflict wore on, Modoc women brought bags of duck feathers to sell to soldiers for beds, and Modoc men and women carried messages and negotiation offers back and forth to the army. Captain Jack's half-sister, Queen Mary—a "regal looking" young woman with "considerable influence with her tribe and good natural sense and brain power"—frequently moved between the Modocs and the military camps, becoming a principal intermediary.[28]

It took General Wheaton six weeks—a month longer than expected—to assemble 350 men in arms. By mid-January his grand plan was coming together, and he began to position forces to attack the Modocs from east and west. He set Friday January 17, 1873, for the attack. "I am happy to announce that after all our annoying delays . . . we leave for Captain Jack's Gibraltar tomorrow morning." He added optimistically, "A more enthusiastic, jolly set of regulars and volunteers I never had the pleasure to command."[29]

18

Modoc Victory at the Stronghold

The arriving troops poised near the Lava Beds craved action, and a sergeant promised they would soon be eating "Modoc steak for breakfast."[1] It was mid-January of 1873, and the soldiers were happy to escape boring garrison duty at other posts. They expected an easy victory. Sergeant Maurice Fitzgerald, Troop K, First Cavalry, had been hoping for a chance to fight. He and his fellow recruits "longed for adventure and excitement and fervently wished that some *casus belli* might speedily arise to give them an opportunity to show of what kind of stuff they were made."[2] "[When] Major Green goes after those Indians," Lieutenant William Boyle wrote, "he will clean them out sooner than a man can say 'Jack Robinson.' Didn't he when he went after the Apaches?"[3]

Within the Stronghold, the Modocs laid plans to defend themselves. Mid-winter was the season when the spirits spoke directly to Modoc medicine men. Curley-Headed Doctor prayed and made a long rope of tule reeds, which he painted red and stretched around the Modoc positions to deflect bullets and make the Stronghold invulnerable. He called it "the line of death" and warned the Modocs that they themselves should not step across it.[4] The people believed him, and danced with him all night, "singing all the while."[5]

The Modocs also posted "medicine flags" at three high points on the Stronghold. One flag, later captured by the army, hung on a four-foot pole, standing upright, with a mink skin, some feathers, and a single medicine bead.[6] The soldiers who captured the pole did not know the meaning of the powerful ceremonial staff. A Modoc spiritual leader—probably Curley-Headed Doctor—made the staff of feathers and other objects that symbolized his spirits. The ceremonial pole typically was stationed outside a shaman's house, and the one at the Stronghold most likely stood near Curley-Headed Doctor's dwelling as a symbol of spiritual power.[7]

But Captain Jack was deeply worried. To keep peace, he contacted several trusted settlers and met with John Fairchild, Press Dorris, farmer Nate Berwick, and a man named Ball on a juniper ridge north of the Lava Beds. Captain Jack was tense and apprehensive. He told them his band of Modocs were not involved in the killings of the fourteen settlers, but that Long Jim, Curley-Headed Doctor, and Hooker Jim were the murderers. He said they could safely use the Tickner Road around the north end of Tule Lake, but warned that anyone traveling the South Immigrant Road—the Applegate Trail—was in danger of being shot. Ominously, a few days later, settlers George Fiocke and Charles Monroe ran into an unidentified group of Modoc scouts and "barely escaped with their lives."[8]

Several members of the Hot Creek band, led by their eighty-year-old chief Old Sheepy, who had not been involved in killing the settlers, were living near Fairchild's ranch twenty miles west of the Lava Beds. Fairchild had an informal arrangement with the Hot Creeks to whom he paid a small "rent" to leave him in peace. He was sympathetic to their desire to keep their land. These Hot Creeks wanted to avoid trouble, so Fairchild offered to take the fourteen men and thirty or so women and children north to safety in Fort Klamath. When the army agreed, he readied them for the trip. Fairchild and his neighbor Presley "Press" Dorris would provide an escort. Unfortunately, their trek north took them past the unfriendly town of Linkville.

War fever was high in Linkville. In December, a lynch party had been formed, and a drunken German settler named "Fritz" had rounded up eight friends to intercept the Fairchild convoy of Modocs as they headed north. Some said Fritz was driven to a frenzy by the death of his friend Wendolin Nus at Lost River.[9] Fortunately, Fairchild and his charges were warned in time, and he kept the Modocs from crossing the Klamath River to Linkville. Indian Agent Leroy Dyar proposed to sneak the Modocs across the river at dawn. But Shacknasty Jim believed they would certainly be killed, so the Hot Creeks rounded up all the horses they could find (including Fairchild's) and fled south to the safety of the Lava Beds, now casting their lot with Captain Jack.[10]

General Canby, three hundred miles north in Portland, understood the danger of backlash from the army's blunder at Lost River. The Modocs' Lava Bed fortifications were now secure as a citadel, and

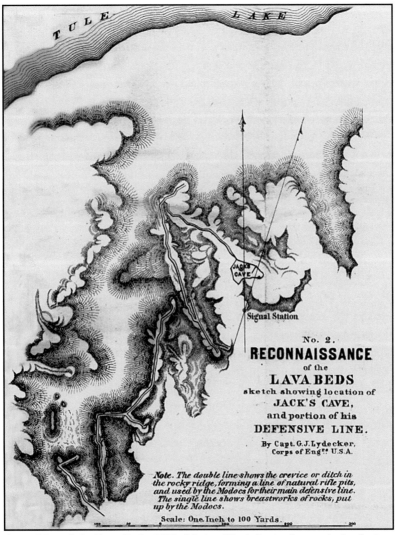

Army Map of the Lava Beds, 1873. *National Park Service, from author's collection.*

despite the presence of a growing army, the Modocs moved about freely, making regular sorties into the surrounding sagebrush plain to steal cattle, get water from Tule Lake, and harass the army's scouts.

General Wheaton knew there was no precedent for the challenge he now faced—war in the roadless, isolated wilderness where the Modocs were barricaded. The area was so sparsely settled that the only shelter the army could requisition were a few log cabins with dirt floors. Maps were sketchy and without detail. Whites viewed the Lava Beds as a trackless badland. Lieutenant Boutelle later mused: "There was no officer experienced in such work; he did not live."[11]

When the army looked down on the Lava Beds from the high bluffs to the west, the area looked deceptively flat, like a plain with scattered gullies and piles of rock—not a stone "Gibraltar," as Wheaton called it—incapable of withstanding a concerted siege. There was little visible forage for the Modocs' animals, and the Stronghold was three hundred yards from the shore of Tule Lake. Wheaton believed that once surrounded, the Modocs could not be resupplied. But encircling the volcanic badlands would not be that easy.

Wheaton was a veteran of siege warfare. He had fought under General Grant at Petersburg, where the Union Army surrounded and compressed the Confederate forces using thirty miles of trenches. Nine months later, General Lee finally yielded to overwhelming pressure when his supply lines were cut. Grant's patient—if costly—siege of Petersburg seemed a good model for a campaign of encirclement and gradual compression against the trapped Modocs, but Wheaton failed to apply the lessons learned at Petersburg to the Lava Beds. Rather than blockade the Modocs and wait them out, he decided to hurl concentrated forces at them from two directions and drive them from their refuge. Tule Lake would serve as a barrier to keep the Modocs from escaping north. All forces—infantry, artillery, and cavalry—would advance on foot with the cavalrymen's horses left behind. Wheaton had planned his attack in December 1872, and it was largely unchanged when he laid out his final order of battle.

The attack would come on January 17, 1873. The majority of Wheaton's forces, now camped at Van Brimmer's ranch, were to strike the main blow from the west, with Major John Green, First Cavalry, in command. Green had three infantry companies, two companies of

Oregon Volunteers, one of California Volunteers, one cavalry troop, and an artillery company with mountain howitzers—about two hundred fighting men altogether. On the far side of the Lava Beds, crusty Captain Bernard commanded a smaller force that would attack from the east. He would have two infantry companies and a group of twenty Klamath Indian scouts under Dave Hill, the Klamath chief, making about 150 troops total. The two forces advancing on the Modoc positions were to "wheel" or rotate inward as they marched and, in theory, converge south of the Stronghold. Troops carried three days' rations, full canteens, two blankets, and one hundred rounds of ammunition. The long-awaited howitzers, which finally arrived, were to signal the attack. The Modocs were to be offered ten minutes to surrender before the assault would begin.

Unexpectedly, the weather presented Wheaton with a devastating problem. As troops began to move into position on January 16, a heavy fog descended over the Lava Beds, "so dense that objects a few yards distant could hardly be distinguished."[12] Undaunted, Wheaton did not postpone the attack. Green marched part of his command, including the two mountain howitzers, on a long roundabout route to avoid detection by Indian sentries. Marching in dense fog, the advance took all day. Their long trek placed them two miles west of the Stronghold on Tule Lake, where they overnighted and waited for the remainder of the force.

At dawn on January 17, the fog still lay heavily over the Lava Beds. Some thought it was even thicker than the day before. Cavalry and infantry units based at Van Brimmer's, twelve miles west, rose at 4 a.m. and marched to the ridge overlooking the Lava Beds. "As the troops looked down from the high bluff upon the lava beds, the fog which overhung it resembled a quiet sea, and the troops [had] to plunge down into this," wrote one historian.[13] They descended eight hundred feet down a steep mule trail into a sea of mist. Lieutenant Boyle recognized that the weather would be a mixed blessing: "The morning of the 16th dawned smoky and foggy, so much so that it was almost impossible to discern an object ten paces from you. The officers were pleased, as they were of the opinion that they could the more easily come upon the enemy without their seeing them. But what seemed a godsend for our troops was also to the advantage of the enemy."[14]

When Lieutenant David Perry saw the fog, he quoted Dante: "All hope abandon, ye who enter here."[15] The blinding fog deprived the army of a key advantage: "semaphores" (flagmen) could not send wig-wag orders and information between units. (When the Modocs first saw the army's flag signals, they were amused and imitated them, waving their arms and pretending they were signaling back.) In the fog the flags were useless. Commanders resorted to communicating with messengers, and Captain Bernard at one point was informed of a change in plans from a messenger shouting across an arm of the lake. Midway through the day, the mist lifted momentarily, but before signalmen could again send or receive, "the mist settled down thicker and darker than before."[16]

The army, attacking from extended lines on both sides of the Stronghold's long outer perimeter, assumed that it would be easy to overwhelm the Modocs' vastly inferior manpower and antiquated guns. But inside the Stronghold, the Modocs masterfully shuttled warriors from place to place as the attackers appeared. Modoc snipers fired unseen from cracks, fissures, and gaps in the Lava Beds. A single Modoc rifleman could pin down a company of soldiers. Captain Jackson, who had conducted the ill-fated attack on Captain Jack's village, described the scene in a military magazine nineteen years later: "Stripped to the buff and of the same color as the rocks, [the Indians] glided stealthily from cover to cover through the intricate passages and could not be seen . . . [T]he fog and the exceedingly difficult nature of the country baffled all efforts." He said he never saw a Modoc warrior during the battle, only the muzzle flashes when they fired.[17] All accounts of the battle describe eerie shadows and deceptive shapes in the mist that made their advance terrifying.

Approaching before dawn from the east was the smaller force commanded by Captain Bernard and his First Cavalry. Bernard's troops made a winding sixteen-mile march in the dark of night, scrambling through lava and broken rock to get into their assigned position before dawn. Visibility limited to only a few yards, the enveloping mist wiped out landmarks, and Bernard unknowingly got much closer to Modoc positions than intended. Advancing in a skirmish line with troops spread out to probe enemy positions, his men were detected and greeted by a sudden fusillade from the Modoc warriors. When Bernard realized his error, he retreated with his wounded, but the Modocs followed with withering fire. Bernard backed up 50 yards, and his crouching men assembled small piles of stones as fortifications near a rock formation called Hospital Rock.

"Out of sight, Modoc snipers fired from hidden walkways, caves, and convenient apertures. There was no way for an enemy to approach the Stronghold unseen." *Photo by Bill Stafford.*

By engaging the Modocs, Bernard destroyed the element of surprise. He was later harshly criticized by Lieutenant William Boyle, an officer in charge of supplies at Van Brimmer's, who said Bernard had relied on his instincts rather than trust his Indian guide, effectively upsetting Wheaton's entire plan. Boyle called it "a sad blunder, for had the troops taken their position at night and without the knowledge of the Indians, how different might have been the outcome of . . . the fight."[18]

The cannons that Wheaton expected to terrify the Modocs were in place, but they proved useless. He had been sent two twelve-pound howitzers, the familiar high-wheeled bronze workhorse of the Civil War that could fire a cannonball a thousand yards.[19] The morning of the attack the guns arrived and were quickly assembled. The artillerymen were instructed to fire three rounds to signal the beginning of the attack and to alert Bernard on the east. The howitzer was a dubious choice for the Lava Beds, as they were notoriously ineffective in frontal attacks on rock fortifications. But in any event, the army never knew if their exploding shells would awe the Indians, because it was impossible to tell where the rounds were landing. Artillerymen could not shoot blindly into the mist; fearing they would hit their own troops approaching from the other direction in their pincer formation, the guns were silenced.[20]

Despite the difficult terrain and lack of visibility, Green's troops advanced from the west. The soldiers formed a line, more than two miles long, swinging in an arc toward the north. Officers, who could not see more than a handful of their troops at any time, experienced a nightmare trying to issue commands. They came under intense fire from Modocs in the rocks. Private J. N. Terwilliger wrote that several in Green's force on the west were wounded as the line advanced: "Guttermuth and Hollis, close to myself, were victims. We took Hollis under cover, took off his belts, gave him a drink, and as he was badly wounded we signaled the hospital corps, and two men were shot in attempting to reach him."[21]

As Green's long line swept north, the troops encountered "a very deep chasm, beyond which no advance could be made without great sacrifice of life."[22] Wheaton and Green agreed that it would be suicidal to cross the fogbound gully under Modoc fire. The chance of surrounding the Modocs from the south was quickly disappearing. Bernard's troops, advancing slowly on the eastern side of the battlefield, were again met with a hail of gunfire. He ordered a charge, but the rough terrain halted his men, who were "stopped by a steep gorge," so they fell back and piled rocks to form a defensive position. The attack was stymied on two fronts.

It was decided to change direction: the new strategy was to join the columns on the north, seize the shoreline of the lake, and deny the Modocs access to water. Three companies, led by Green, Mason, and Perry, began their way along the lake. But the Oregon Volunteers did not move forward, later claiming they were blocked by a ravine. The most deadly moments of the battle followed. As the troops tried to shelter behind boulders along the lakefront, they were raked by Modoc fire. Perry described the scene: "It was at this point that our greatest number of casualties occurred. I was wounded about four P.M., having raised myself on my left elbow to look at a man who had just been killed."[23] When Perry, shot through the arm and the breast, cried out in pain, Modocs hidden in the rocks ridiculed him. A woman cried out, "You come here to fight Indians and you make a noise like that! You no man, you squaw!"[24]

Oliver Applegate said he heard the voice of Hooker Jim shouting orders to the Modocs. Applegate witnessed the death of one of his men: "Franklin Trimble, a young man about 17 years of age, was shot in the left breast. He straightened to his full height, threw up his left hand, cried out and fell heavily backward and crawled past me a few feet towards the rear. Going to him, I saw him draw his breath with difficulty, and soon expire."[25] Green next made a brave (and foolhardy) attempt to rally his troops. He stood up and ran forward. "With a gauntlet in his hand [he] used language scarcely fit for a parlor," encouraging his men to attack.[26] Miraculously, he escaped being shot down. The Modocs apparently thought his gauntlet—a heavy glove—had magic powers and they shot at it repeatedly as he waved it about.[27]

Several accounts convey the soldiers' frustration and fear. Those fighting their way along the lake were trapped by the Modoc crossfire, and they could only lie behind rocks for shelter. The troops on the west were ordered to stay in place until darkness when they finally found safety with Bernard's troops on the east. Modoc signal fires were lighting up in the Stronghold, and someone could be heard shouting orders. As things worsened for the army, Wheaton, stranded with troops on the west, asked the advice of General Ross of the Oregon Volunteers. "We'd better get out of here, by God!" replied Ross. So Wheaton dismissed the Oregon Volunteers, who rapidly retreated up the bluff, "a wild free for all," in the words of one observer.[28]

Some of the army officers judged the Oregonians harshly. Lieutenant Boyle wrote, "Had the volunteers maintained their line and not fallen back . . . we might have succeeded in killing some Modocs."[29] But the Oregonian Volunteers boasted they could have carried the day if only they had been allowed to fight. They had a champion in Colonel William Thompson, an irascible California journalist and an officer in the militia. Thompson later wrote that the volunteers had actually fought their way right into the Modoc fortifications before being recalled. "We were within 50 yards of the scalp pole over Captain Jack's cave which was the center of the stronghold. The volunteers were anxious to charge."[30] Bancroft, who was often sympathetic to the Applegate family, said Oliver Applegate "was preparing to charge the stronghold" at the other end of the line when he was ordered to withdraw, losing two of his men.[31] Applegate's own account says his volunteers were still advancing under heavy fire, charging the deep ravine, when the order came to retreat. Applegate claimed (incorrectly) that his Oregon Volunteers had already killed three Modocs.[32]

At 5 p.m. the fog began to lift and Wheaton decided to recall his battered regulars from the field. The Modocs had thrashed a better-armed, better-trained force that was six times their size, without the loss of a single man. The full extent of the army's defeat became clear during the retreat. There was no provision for litters, so the wounded were carried in blankets with a man at each corner. One of the California militia was gravely wounded: "Lt. Roberts, of Fairchild's Company, received a terrible wound in the head, which will undoubtedly prove fatal, as the brains protrude."[33] Another volunteer suffered terribly: "One of Fairchild's men, Jerry Crook, whose thighbone was shattered, rode the whole distance [on horseback] with his leg dangling. His comrades tied a rope to it by which it could be lifted out of the way of obstacles; but nothing could prevent frequent rude shocks from the rocks and bushes."[34]

The troops retreating to the west made a disorderly climb up the eight-hundred-foot bluff, with more than two dozen wounded. A false rumor circulated that the Indians had captured the summit of the bluff, and the column stopped moving up the steep slope. Thompson claimed that he found "Indians [Klamath mercenaries], volunteers, and officers all jumbled together without semblance of order." He crept up the slope, and found no Indians. He passed the word back, and the retreat resumed. "Then began a scramble to reach the top. It was everybody for himself, as it was too dark to even attempt to preserve a semblance of order, or discipline."[35]

In their hasty retreat, the troops left the dead and some of the wounded on the field. The Modoc warriors continued firing, jumping from rock to rock, "picking off every soldier that they could see."[36]

They even killed some of the fallen soldiers who had not yet died, as recorded in a Modoc account of the battle from ethnographer Albert S. Gatschet.[37]

The army's defeat was humiliating. Three officers had been seriously wounded in the attempt to cross the ravine on the west side. The army reported six dead had been left behind, each recorded as "immediate death." When the army finally announced its casualties, they were stunning—over 10 percent of their force. Among the regular army troops, nineteen were wounded and seven killed. One of these wounded later died. Among the Oregon Volunteers, five were wounded and two killed. The California Volunteers had four wounded, of whom two later died.[38]

Wheaton wrote to Canby that "it was only with the greatest difficulty that our wounded could be removed, and it was found utterly impossible to remove our dead."[39] Colonel Thompson—often given to self-promotion—claimed that he sat with Wheaton in his tent the morning after the battle and recorded Wheaton's lament: "I have seen something of war, and know something of fortifications. I commanded 19,000 men at the battle of the Wilderness, and saw many of the great engineering works of the Civil War, but I do not believe that a hundred thousand men, in a hundred thousand years could construct such fortifications."[40]

The attack became known as the First Battle of the Stronghold, although Wheaton didn't honor it with the word "battle." He wrote to Canby two days after the fighting that "under the circumstances, it was utterly impossible to accomplish more than make a forced reconnaissance."[41] The Modocs had no casualties. None. The army had finally tested the Modocs, and found them formidable.

19

The Army Licks Its Wounds

The morning after the battle, the Modocs reaped a rich harvest. Combing the battlefield, they found a bounty of arms, getting the latest models of carbines and rifles, and enough ammunition to withstand another siege. As usual, the Modocs on the fields stripped the dead. There is no credible evidence the Modocs scalped the dead, but reporter Bogart claimed in the *Chronicle* that following the attack on the supply train one soldier was scalped and mutilated.[1]

The army was reeling from its losses. The little cabin at Dan Van Brimmer's ranch, which had been reserved for officers, was now used to accommodate the wounded. Officers slept on the frozen ground "with two thicknesses of blanket beneath us, when we slept at all."[2] The troops had been in the field without rest or food for more than twenty-four hours. Soldiers gathered at Van Brimmer's to bury Patrick Maher, a young private in the First Cavalry. The casualty report said he was killed while "crawling on his belly when shot with a round ball, in the left groin." Jerry Crook, the gravely injured California volunteer, held on for nearly three weeks before dying. Major Bernard described his shattered cavalry unit: "The troops [came] out of the fight, so badly demoralized, that they could hear the whizzing of balls, and the War-whoop of Indians, for the next twenty-four hours; besides, two thirds of the command was so badly bruised and used up, that they are limping about yet."[3]

A newspaperman wrote: "At one time I feared the larger half of the army would desert, so badly were the troops demoralized."[4] Later in the year, when he took command over the forces fighting the Modocs, General Jefferson C. Davis (no relation to the Confederate president) was struck at the "considerable humiliation felt by the troops." In his annual report of military operations, he wrote: "I found them laboring under great depression of spirits; their cheerless winter camps, heavy losses, and repeated failures, had doubtless diminished their zeal and confidence."[5]

As officers penned their final reports, the casualty figures shocked the public. Among the military—regular troops and volunteers—there were thirty-seven casualties, eleven dead. The army left six of its dead behind on the battlefield.

The dramatic humiliation of the U.S. Army in remote northern California became a newspaper sensation "We have horrible news from the Modoc country," shouted the *Napa Valley Register*. "The troops under General Wheaton attacked the Modoc camp in the Lava Beds and lost FORTY MEN KILLED AND WOUNDED! The Indians have whipped Army!"[6] San Francisco dailies rushed reporters to the front, where they filed stories for the next nine months. The Modoc victory solidified the public's view of them as wild desperadoes terrorizing innocent settlers in the remote west. San Francisco papers painted an Armageddon in the Lava Beds, and eastern newspapers soon picked up the theme. The *San Francisco Bulletin* shrieked that Indian war was spreading and quadrupled the number of Modocs involved: "There are at least 200 Indians in the field, and they are constantly drilled by leaders well acquainted with military tactics, and especially ambushing."[7]

Garish battle accounts were printed: "The Indians fought with desperation. . . as was their custom, naked, with nothing but an ammunition sack hung to the shoulder." One reporter wrote: "Jack has the strongest natural fortification in the country."[8] New York papers moved the sensational Boss Tweed corruption story aside to put the Modocs on the front page. The *New York Times* published its first full account on January 21: "The troops fought an unseen foe from 8 o'clock in the morning to dark, under a terrific fire, during which not one Indian was seen." The *Times* reported forty dead and wounded.[9]

General Canby, from his headquarters in Portland, wrote: "I have been very solicitous that these Indians should be fairly treated . . . I think they should now be treated as any other criminals. And that there be no peace in that part of the frontier until they are subdued and punished."[10] In mid-February, a Grand Jury in nearby Jackson County, Oregon, indicted for murder Scarface Charley, Hooker Jim, and the other killers of the settlers.[11] The California newspapers were skeptical.

"This mode of procedures," wrote the *Sacramento Daily Union*, "is, to say the least, in contempt of the Government of the United States."[12]

General William Tecumseh Sherman (ranking officer in the U.S. Army) ordered every available resource shifted to the front on the California-Oregon boundary. Sherman briefed the war secretary, William Worth Belknap, who took the issue to President Grant's cabinet. Wheaton, after retreating to Van Brimmer's, claimed he had fought no fewer than 150 Indians and the Modocs had recruited some of the neighboring Pit River tribe to fight with them.[13] He asked for three hundred more troops and four mortars immediately and pointedly suggested the governor of California be importuned to provide troops for protection of his own state.[14]

California Governor Newton Booth, perhaps contrite after refusing to provide volunteers a month earlier, offered "three companies of sharp-shooters" to be recruited in nearby Siskiyou County. He told California's Senator Cornelius Cole that the Californians would be ready immediately, but Cole reported back that Grant—after meeting with his cabinet—had declined the offer of volunteers from California. The *Bulletin* remarked that Grant's decision was judicious: Volunteers have been "the cause of much cruelty and jobbery. The government ought to deal with the present difficulty without such assistance."[15]

Captain Bernard, who fought in the January 17 battle, was left disillusioned and embittered with the Modoc's situation. Bernard wrote to a superior officer in San Francisco that the Modoc action had accomplished nothing, caused serious casualties, and was a blow to the confidence of those he commanded. More than anyone who fought the Indians in battle, Bernard voiced his belief in the pointless cruelty of the war against the Modocs: "These Indians have acted more humanely, in every instance, than we have." Faced with the loss of their homeland, Bernard thought the Modocs were justified to resist: "They have fought like men fighting for their rights, and the Modocs are more than entitled to what they claim." The government had squandered lives and treasure for the benefit of settlers. "But for the gratification of a few cattlemen, land-grabbers etc.," he wrote, "the Modocs must be compelled to kill and wound soldiers and citizens to twice their numbers, costing the Government and private parties hundreds and thousands of dollars."[16]

Bernard's sympathy for the Modocs, however, was not widely shared. The army was immediately mobilized all across the West. Troops traveled in punishing winter weather to get to the Modoc front. On January 27, 1873, an artillery company under Colonel Charles Beaujolais Throckmorton marched north from San Francisco, arriving at Portuguese Flat, a mining town near Mount Shasta, during a blizzard. Company E of the Twelfth Infantry, commanded by Lieutenant Thomas Wright, arrived from Fort Gaston, a tiny post on the Trinity River in California, where troops had been guarding Hoopa Indians. It was "a severe march of 15 days," and it snowed or rained every day. Another artillery company arrived from Portland on February 4, "footsore and jaded." A "fearful snowstorm" pinned down a group marching from Boise. Snow delayed orders to Fort Warner. "I don't know if the road is blocked, or the rider scared too badly. I presume the latter," wrote Lieutenant John Quincy Adams from Lost River.[17]

Materiel poured north from California. Troops made their way north burdened with 40,000 pounds of provisions, camp equipment, and clothing. Their wagons were mired in mud but the supplies arrived in spite of the "wretched condition" of the roads.[18] War profiteers soon arrived. Two Yreka businessmen established a sutler's store at Van Brimmer's, and complaints of swindling began. An unprecedented price rise within one twenty-four hour period led to grain prices shooting up over seven times the original price.[19] Saddles bought for the army were forty dollars, but the same saddles could be bought by individuals for twenty.[20] Tobacco was $1.50 a pound. Colonel Thompson wrote that when an army surgeon asked him to get eggs for a wounded man, the Van Brimers charged 50 cents each in cash. "From that time forward," wrote Thompson, "I spent a considerable portion of my time studying human villainy with the Van Brimers as a model."[21]

Wheaton wanted to get his battered troops farther from the scene of battle, so on January 21, 1873, he moved his forces from Van Brimmer's ranch to a site known as Stukel Ford on Lost River. They made the twenty-five-mile march in one day, and Wheaton threw himself into preparing for a fresh attack. He decided to approach by water in his next siege of the Lava Beds and ordered four flat-bottomed boats built, two to carry supplies, and another two as platforms for artillery and mortars. He hoped to use the vessels to position his guns on the shore of Tule Lake to shell the Modoc positions.[22]

But before he could carry out his strategy, on January 23 Canby abruptly replaced the industrious Wheaton with General Alvan Cullem

Gillem.[23] Not even a week had passed since the army's humiliation at the Stronghold. Although Gillem, as commander of cavalry in the region, outranked Wheaton, the change of command was a clear slap at Wheaton's handling of the disastrous January 17 attack.

Gillem assumed command on February 8, 1873, and he put his stamp on the Modoc expedition immediately. He reported to Canby, who was in Portland, that the Indians numbered no more than fifty to seventy-five—the first accurate estimate of Modoc strength. He also correctly reported that despite the war hysteria, none of the neighboring tribes—Paiutes, Pit Rivers, Achomawis, Klamaths, or Rogue Rivers—were aiding or joining forces with the Modocs, although he could not convince the settlers. Gillem was outraged at the rates being charged to bring freight to the front, and he fired some of the offending teamsters. With his force growing to seven hundred men, Gillem began to reposition units for attack. He decided not to mobilize volunteers "without absolute necessity."[24] Volunteers were in bad odor with the regular army, as President Grant had indicated: not reliable in battle, and sometimes disruptive with both civilians and Indians.

Gillem, a West Pointer, was from Tennessee and had fought for the Union in the Civil War. He was a friend of former President Andrew Johnson and thought by some to have risen in the ranks through connections and patronage. Gillem's health began to fail after he arrived on the Modoc front, and illness confined him to camp several times during the remaining months of the war. Army records show he died just two years later of unknown causes.[25]

Gillem did not hesitate to veto parts of Wheaton's plan. He did not favor the idea of using boats—he feared that strategy would split forces and not achieve any tactical advantage. He thought boats were more exposed to attack by Modocs along the shore. But he agreed enthusiastically that the use of mortars to lob shells into the Modoc camp "would materially reduce the loss of life."[26] Two weeks after arriving, Gillem decided it was time for the army's recuperation to end and to resume pressure on the Indians. He began to move his men closer to the Lava Beds. On February 17, 1873, Gillem took his forces twenty-five miles from Lost River and established them at John Fairchild's snowbound ranch. Conditions were terrible: "Lake country is covered with snow 1 to 2 feet deep. The Weather is very stormy," said one reporter.[27]

Fairchild's little ranch on Cottonwood Creek became a sprawling army post. Three hundred new soldiers had arrived from barracks up and down the coast.

This was a ragtag army. Decorum in military dress disappeared. Soldiers were allowed to improvise their own garb for all except formal muster. Most of the standard issue clothing was of Civil War vintage, cheap and poorly made, so soldiers substituted canvas pants and flannel shirts for Union blue. Some had been issued Civil War surplus shoes that were at least a decade old, and the sutlers were there to sell them decent footwear. "Luxuries" like soap, cards, and tobacco were bought on credit, and many privates had spent their thirty-one-dollars a month salary before they were paid.

Several hundred soldiers were living nearby in a crowded and chaotic camp at Van Bremer's. "It was a confusion of teamsters, packers, scouts, stockmen, and settlers, and even a few squaw men were here," wrote Sergeant Maurice Fitzgerald.[28] Troops were detailed to cut firewood from the sparse juniper groves on the nearby hills. Fitzgerald, in his 1927 memoir, said there were several hundred soldiers and at least two hundred civilians: "It was a motley crowd, and all had money. A saturnalia of gambling naturally followed. It would have done the heart of a forty-niner good to behold the layouts for the accommodation of those sportingly inclined and brought back to his mind, 'the days of old and the days of gold.' Monte seemed to be the favorite game, while chuck-a-luck, Honest John and twenty-one had their votaries."[29]

Drinking was often out of control, and the commanding officer at Fort Klamath wrote a stern note to one trader: "You are hereby informed that the sale of Liquor to enlisted men and citizen employees is limited to two drinks per man, per diem and only one drink at a time, with an interval of two hours between each drink."[30] Some soldiers were temporarily broke, because the paymaster came late. He explained that because of "high water rendering it impossible to pass the many streams on the route without rafting materials," payment for February would be delayed until April.[31] Regardless, the sutlers operated on credit, and soldiers ran up bills for drink without cash.

Troops from Fort Bidwell, California, were assembled at the desolate ranch of Louis Land east of the Lava Beds. Land was a settler who had "fled from the wrath of redskins to some safer locality." Fodder for the animals was almost nonexistent, and grass was "snowed under." Others troops marched to Applegate's ranch on Clear Lake along the rough Indian trail skirting the Lava Beds to the south. Sergeant Fitzgerald was astonished at the landscape, "winding through endless defiles, or narrow passages, between immense quantities of basaltic rock, scattered in great confusion over the extensive area." They encountered mountain sheep that "ran with the greatest fleetness over the tract of crags and rocks, across yawning piles of boulders." They were sternly admonished not to fire upon or molest Indians as they traveled, except in self-defense.[32]

Troops of the era carried "shelter halves," pieces of white duck canvas that could be buttoned together at the peak to form a cramped shelter for two, and rows of the tents were pitched for enlisted men. A sympathetic newspaperman observed that in a heavy snowstorm, "the shelter tents furnish but slight protection from the rigorous blast."[33] The men were "especially in need of shoes and boots."[34] Officers lived in "Sibley tents," large round tipi-shaped canvas tents—eighteen feet in diameter—that could sleep a dozen men. The soldiers maintained a fire inside the tents, and smoke exited at the peak. Cooks concocted meals using cast-iron pots hanging on iron tripods that straddled campfires. Second Lieutenant Harry DeWitt Moore from Pennsylvania wrote he lived in "a den of rocks" with a canvas cover. He had enough blankets, but he "frequently awoke with an unpleasant sensation of having a rattlesnake or a scorpion for a bed-fellow."[35]

Some officers were extremely worried about the Modocs hanging around camp. Shacknasty Jim, Hooker Jim, and Curley Haired Jack often visited Fairchild's to talk.[36] Lieutenant Moore thought these visits put the officers in danger because the visits from the Modocs allowed them to identify the officers. In a fight, he wrote, "they will pick off the officers first." To prevent identification by the Modocs, officers adopted a disguise. Moore wrote to his wife: "We have all adopted the precaution of discarding all insignia of rank and it would be a difficult matter to tell us from enlisted men. I wear a private's uniforms [*sic*] no straps or stripes, and white broad-brimmed hat. I have discarded boots and taken to government gun boats. Altogether, I feel ragged and happy. [But] I doubt if you would consent to dance the German with me in my present garb or even to admit me into your house."[37]

Gillem kept his forces in constant action all across the area, and some found the military exercises punishing. Moore's anguished letter home shows life in the Modoc campaign. He told of marching thirty-three hours without food: "I have slept in a dirty little log cabin in the heart of the Modoc country with nothing to cover me but my overcoat, afraid to build a fire on account of the Indians. . . I nearly froze to death. . . In the middle of the night I was awakened by what I supposed to be Indians at the door. . . It was a few sneaking coyotes, which I drove away without difficulty, for they are the most cowardly animals on earth."[38]

William Murray, a private or corporal in Company G of the Twelfth Infantry, was stationed at Benicia, near San Francisco, when his unit was suddenly ordered north to the Modoc front. He was "rudely wakened" from his cot in Benicia at 4 A.M., and Company G was ordered to pack their knapsacks immediately. General Wilcox of the Fourth Artillery admonished the men "to preserve the reputation of the regiment in the coming campaign against the Modocs." They then marched—preceded by a band—to the Oakland Depot to await a boat that would take them north. Murray said the whistle of the steamer *SS McPherson* "gave a demonic shriek" as it approached the wharf in the predawn darkness to collect them for the first leg of their five-hundred-mile trip. During the following months of monotony and cold, Murray would witness horrors he could not imagine.[39]

Another soldier, Gilbert F. Davis (probably a corporal), kept a meager and near-illegible record of his time fighting the Modocs. His terse and often apathetic entries reflect the monotony of camp life, and his longing for his "gentle Annie." For six long weeks he pined for her while the Modocs were trapped in the Stronghold, and the army was stalled on the frozen plain at the Fairchild and Van Brimmer ranches. The stalemate continued until the day in April when the Modocs killed Gilbert Davis's commanding officer and unleashed a maelstrom of violence. In his diary, Davis foresaw how monotony would turn to terror and the effusion of blood: "April 11 Friday. Some of us will meet our deaths tomorrow/ in hopes it will not be me. God Protect me."[40]

20

Trouble in the Stronghold

Following their January 17, 1873, victory in the Lava Beds, the Modocs were jubilant. There were bonfires in the Stronghold, and singing and dancing went on all night. But the joy was fleeting; a power struggle began among the Modocs that would last for months. Even before the attack on the Stronghold, there had been hints of strife among Modoc factions, but tensions now flared openly. Captain Jack saw their overwhelming victory as a chance to sue for peace. He knew the army would launch another assault, probably massive and overpowering. To avert disaster, Captain Jack believed the Modocs had to agree to terms.

But the picture was different for the war faction led by Hooker Jim and Curley-Headed Doctor. These were the men who had participated in the murder of fourteen settlers, and they faced the wrath of the white man's law. The Modocs knew they would have to surrender to state authorities in any peace deal, and they would certainly be tried for murder. Some of the Modocs were genuinely convinced their victory in the January 17 battle at the Stronghold proved they could defeat the entire U.S. Army. Many credited the medicine of Curley-Headed Doctor for turning back bullets and believed his power was so potent that the Modocs were invincible.

The army first recognized the divisions in the Modoc camp when Captain Jack reached out to negotiate in early February 1873. A Modoc woman named One-Eyed Dixie, who often served as an emissary from the Modoc camp, showed up at Fairchild's ranch carrying a message from Captain Jack. The chief refused to come out of the Lava Beds, but he sent an invitation to Fairchild to come to his camp in the Stronghold.[1] General Wheaton heard Captain Jack was "tired of fighting," so he sent First Lieutenant John Quincy Adams to see if negotiation was possible. But Wheaton's position was rigid: he wanted no less than a full surrender and Captain Jack's return to the reservation. Adams ventured close to the Lava Beds, sending in a Modoc messenger, who returned with no message but important intelligence.[2]

Ugly infighting erupted in the Stronghold. Adams learned there had been an all-night wrangle in the Modoc camp. Captain Jack and Scarface Charley had a "long and stormy discussion" with Curley-Headed Doctor and Shacknasty Jim about whether the Modocs should approach John Fairchild, whom the tribe still viewed as a friend. Captain Jack was convinced he would be killed if he tried to visit Fairchild. The war faction rejected the idea of settlement and threatened the lives of Jack's supporters.

Artinie Choakus, Queen Mary (Captain Jack's sister), and One-Eyed Dixie. "These Modoc women were translators and messengers for the Modocs, the army, and the peace commissioners." *Courtesy Cheewa James.*

Adams learned that the entire "peace faction" under Captain Jack—including Scarface Charley, Black Jim, Big Dick, and eight other "prominent Modocs"—was eager to settle because they believed the army would kill them if they continued to resist. But Curley-Headed Doctor, who had led the Hot Creek band that killed the fourteen settlers, was in favor of continuing to fight because "they might as well die in arms as to give themselves up and be hanged for murder." The war faction included Shacknasty Jim, Bogus Charley, Ellen's Man Frank, and about 35 supporters. The messenger told Adams the Modocs were near blows, and he expected a fight soon. Adams came away "convinced that Jack is so anxious to stop fighting that he will eagerly seek [to bargain]."[3]

Throughout the weeks that followed, the bickering within the Stronghold escalated, the divisions among the Modocs deepened, and the power of the Modoc peace faction waned. Life became dangerous for Captain Jack.

21

The Reporters

By the beginning of 1873 half a dozen reporters had made their way to the army front from San Francisco, Sacramento, and New York. At first, the fighting in the remote Modoc country of northern California and southern Oregon had been given little attention. When accounts of the Modocs' resistance against the army attack at Lost River reached San Francisco, there was disbelief. How could a ragtag band of rebels mount serious resistance against the U.S. Army, much less successfully wage a war? When news came of the killing of the fourteen settlers two days later, newspapers rushed correspondents to the field. When Modoc warriors defending the Stronghold humiliated the army on January 17, 1873, the Modoc conflict became a national sensation. Intense competition for coverage began among newspapers to cover what was now trumpeted as the "Modoc War."[1]

In 1873 reporting from the front presented great logistical challenges. Reporters could not telegraph news directly; couriers had to carry dispatches by horseback to Yreka, eighty-one miles to the west, or travel to the more distant town of Jacksonville, Oregon, more than one hundred miles away. Before the war was over, correspondents skillfully employed relay riders to race their stories to the telegraph, sometimes bribing telegraph operators and resorting to various stratagems to hoodwink their competitors. One paper boasted that their dispatch was brought by express to Yreka from where it was telegraphed to San Francisco "being by far the longest message ever sent over California."[2]

Some excellent reporting and writing emerged from the Modoc conflict, and the press accounts (sometimes inaccurate or exaggerated) are nevertheless rich raw material for historians. Unfortunately, correspondents often focused on describing their own personal experiences to create a story line, add atmosphere, and bring "self-glorification through hardship."[3] First at the scene was Robert D. Bogart of the *San Francisco Chronicle*, who braved primitive transportation by rail, stagecoach, wagon, and ultimately on foot to get to Yreka, California, on December 8, 1872. Bogart reported Yreka was in chaos, awash with rumors and terrorized by Indians. (Actually, the closest Modocs were eighty-one miles away.) Bogart then went to "the seat of war" in an area a dozen miles west of the Lava Beds, grandly filing reports from "The Chronicle Expedition" (which was Bogart alone), doing his best to inflame the public. Bogart's initial reports were wildly inaccurate. He wrote stories datelined "From 'Captain Jack's cave'" long before he was even close to the Lava Beds.

After the army's stunning defeat in the January battle at the Stronghold, other reporters rushed *en masse* to join Bogart in the army camps near the Lava Beds. Officers and troops were camped at the farmhouse of John Fairchild, fifteen miles west of Captain Jack's stronghold, licking their wounds. First to arrive after Bogart was Edward Fox, a lanky longhaired Englishman and adventurer dispatched by the *New York Herald*. He crossed the continent by rail to San Francisco, suffered a seventeen-hour rail trip north to Redding, California, during a blizzard, and endured the bruising eight-hour stagecoach ride to Yreka. Once there, Fox was still eighty-one grueling miles from the combatants. [4]

Fox was an improbable war correspondent. He served in the British army and had fought several duels in Europe. He was perfectly suited for the pursuit of splashy exclusives by *Herald* publisher James Gordon Bennett Jr., who had famously dispatched the reporter Henry Morton Stanley on the seven-thousand-mile expedition to the Congo in 1871, where Stanley found the missing David Livingston. The stunt had won a huge increase in *Herald* circulation, and Bennett wanted another editorial coup, so six months after the Stanley caper he sent Fox west to cover the Modoc War. [5] Fox's audacious reporting did not become as legendary as Stanley's, but he wrote perceptive and thrilling accounts of the war. Fox's daredevil reporting often put him at considerable risk, but he regularly scooped his competitors.

Arriving in Yreka, Fox reported that the rough mining town of fifteen hundred was cleaning up financially on the Modoc War. Fox wrote "the business portion of the residents were rather jubilant, as trade was good." Contemporary photographs depict a picturesque but ramshackle town with a single muddy street full of saloons. Its brothels were notable. Fox interviewed everyone in sight but couldn't get a straight story on the war from anyone. Unwilling to be "steamboated," as he put it, Fox hired a wagon to go to the front, taking blankets and "a rubber sheet" to sleep on. Fox's wagon was mired in mud to its axles during most of the trip. He met several army deserters going in the other direction, running away from the war.[6]

Shortly after Fox arrived, two competing reporters joined the press corps covering the war: H. Wallace Atwell, a veteran of decades of newspapering in California, who called himself "Bill Dadd the Scribe," reporting for the *Sacramento Union;* and Alex McKay, writing for the *San Francisco Evening Bulletin* and the *Yreka Union.* By the end of February, the newspapermen found themselves stuck in cramped quarters outside the army camp with no news to cover. They expected to be covering a war and were disappointed to learn the Grant administration was delaying hostilities to parlay for peace.

When former Indian Superintendent Alfred Meacham returned to Modoc country in February 1873 as part of a peace delegation sent by President Grant, the reporters expected finally to get a story. But the peacemakers were holding "mysterious talks together," and the reporters could not pick up any news. When settler Bob Whittle returned from a meeting in the Lava Beds with news of the peace talks, the newsmen wanted to hear his report to the peace commissioners. But Meacham, in his high imperious tone, announced that reporters were excluded from all discussions about the peace negotiations and he alone would control the release of information.[7]

Fox particularly disliked Meacham and his treatment of the reporters. "This war was a godsend to this Micawber politician," he wrote. "Words fell from his silvery tongue like peas rolling off a hot platter."[8] Fox called the peace meetings the "Star Chamber" and Meacham "the Grand Inquisitor."[9] Meacham's blackout on news continued for weeks; journalists were "religiously excluded" from information. Meacham rejected any suggestion they might appoint one of their number as observer or "pool" reporter.

But the enterprising reporters found ways to get information in spite of Meacham's news blackout. The reporting coup everyone coveted was an interview with Captain Jack, and Fox finally devised his own strategy. In mid-February a peace delegation was formed—John Fairchild, Bob and Matilda Whittle, and One-Eyed Dixie—to visit Captain Jack in the Stronghold. Meacham forbade Fox to accompany them, but he decided to go anyway: "I finally concluded that Mr. Meacham had no authority to govern my going and coming in this section of the country and therefore determined to make an attempt to go on my own responsibility."[10]

Fox knew the army was watching him, so he found out what time the delegates were leaving and rode ahead early to the nearby Van Brimmer ranch to sleep. The group was set to depart at 7 A.M., so Fox bought two pounds of tobacco, "filled his flask," and left at dawn to intercept them several miles from camp. When Bob Whittle saw Fox, he refused to let him come along, so Fox rode back as if returning to camp. After a half hour, he reversed direction, following their tracks in the three inches of new-fallen snow all the way into the Lava Beds. It was an act of considerable risk, if not folly, as the Modocs would have no idea who the lone horseman was.

Two hours later, Fox caught up with the peace party just as they reached the perimeter of the Modoc camp. Whittle was annoyed but realized he could not safely send Fox back now that they were being watched by the Modocs. Whittle lit a sagebrush fire to signal their arrival, and a mounted Modoc escort came to take the delegation, with Fox, into the Stronghold.

Fox's article on the peace conference ran to about fifteen thousand words. Capturing the resentment and bitterness among the Modocs, the story reported that provocation of the Modocs had begun twenty years earlier when Ben Wright ruthlessly killed four dozen Modocs after failing to poison them under the guise of peace. Fox was the only reporter to note (1) the Modocs wanted the same law for Ben Wright and white murderers as the law for the Modocs; (2) they had the right to resist a surprise attack made while they slept in their homes on the Lost River; and (3) the killing of settlers was justified as retaliation for an act of war. Fox's report filled two full pages of the *Herald*. The story had an immense headline and a four-column map of the battlefield. Fox's telegraph bill alone was five hundred dollars.

22

The Applegates Meet the Press

Bad pressed dogged the Applegate family. California papers railed relentlessly against the Applegates, accusing them of graft in their administration of the Klamath reservation. The *Daily Alta California* charged the Applegates and the "Oregon Hay and Grain Ring" with price gouging.[1] The *San Francisco Chronicle* accused the Applegates of giving out "half blankets" to the Modocs and blamed them for destroying all the wocus, dried fish, and other food the Modocs brought to the Klamath reservation, leaving the Modocs without enough to eat.[2] The *Chronicle* accused Ivan Applegate of delivering and charging for yearling calves said to weigh one thousand pounds, which—depending on the breed or sex—probably weighed several hundred pounds less. "Both the Government and the Indians seem to have been swindled in the most ingenious manner."[3]

California Judge Elijah Steele told the *Chronicle* that Meacham, Ivan Applegate, and others had "concluded a contract with themselves for supply of beef to the Indians." He said they charged eleven cents a pound, "when any settler on Lost River and for miles around would have been glad to provide it for five cents a pound." But, he added, "Not one ox in ten of Applegate's beef finds its way into Indian bellies." Steele's theory was that the Applegates wanted the Modocs back on the Klamath reservation just to increase the government's purchase of beef: "The more Indians, the more mouths to feed, and the more mouths the more beef at eleven cents a pound."[4]

Even Oliver Applegate, not usually a prime target of the reporters, was accused of malfeasance and cowardice. The *Chronicle* reported that Oliver—who led the Oregon Volunteers in the battle at the Stronghold—threw away his rifle "with not a charge missing. . . The regular cavalry poke heaps of fun on him."[5] Oliver, the paper said, was "one of those persons who can never rest until they have a raw Modoc stewed on toast for breakfast, and stand ready, silver tankard in hand, to drink Captain Jack's blood for dinner."[6]

When the Applegates later got involved in peace negotiations with the Modocs, the California papers kept the family in their cross hairs. The *Daily Alta California* wrote on February 19 that the Indians held the Applegates in detestation, especially Jesse Applegate, and their involvement doomed the future of the peace commission.

An indignant but unsigned defense of the Applegates was published the next day in a letter to the editors of the *Daily Alta California,* defending Jesse and distinguishing his role from that of the other Applegates on the scene: "[Jesse] had nothing whatsoever to do with the origin of the Modoc War, and had no business connection with the Applegates referred to as causing the troubles. He had nothing to do with the issuance to the Indians of 1,000-pound yearlings, quarter blankets, putrid bacon, or any other supplies."[7]

But a few days later, the *Daily Alta California* wrote again: "We owe the Modoc outbreak to the deception and thievery on the part of those who should have been honest. No possible good can come of a peace conference conducted by the very men who by their rascality have precipitated the war. . . For every one of the miserable blankets furnished by the agents, Government will have to pay dearly in money and in the life-blood of her soldiers."[8] Other San Francisco papers joined the charge, and controversy over the Applegates' role reverberated up and down the coast.

The *San Francisco Chronicle*'s Robert Bogart, whose affection for the truth was sometimes questionable, reveled in rumors that the Applegates were behind the Modoc War. He picked up the claim that the Applegates were cheating the Modocs in their contract to supply the reservation with beef. In a story headlined "Applegate's Credit Mobilier" (a reference to the infamous railroad stock scandal in the Grant administration), Bogart quoted Steele: "Every word about the Applegates and that crowd of coin-thirsty cormorants was strictly true."[9] Bogart charged the Applegates with delaying peace with the Modocs until "the last pound of grain in Southern Oregon is sold for its weight in gold. . . The Oregon War Ring, with the Applegates at its head, will take good care that peace is not brought about too hastily."[10] Bogart was relentless: "This Indian business up here is a good deal like a decayed egg. Puncture the shell anywhere and you will find an Applegate."[11]

The *Chronicle* reporter particularly infuriated the Applegates and their allies. Ivan Applegate wrote to the *Oregon Sentinel* on March 27, condemning the press for "prostituting itself to the vile wishes of cowardly and reckless liars like Bogart."[12] Other family members and friends echoed the charges and warned of reprisals. Indeed, the troublesome Bogart left the Modoc front suddenly, reputedly induced by a bribe from the Applegates.[13]

Oliver Applegate did his best to tell the family's side of the story. "The *San Francisco Bulletin* man is O. K. and gets his information from us," Oliver reported to his brother. "His Statement of the History of the Modoc Difficulty is my own composition."[14] Indeed, a few days earlier the *Bulletin* had printed an unsigned story headlined: "MODOC INDIANS: An Interesting Review of their Depredations," a three-hundred-word item that bore Oliver's fingerprints. It alleged a history of "depredations and massacres" starting in 1847, including several incidents not mentioned elsewhere.[15]

Oliver made progress promoting the Applegate viewpoint in the press. On February 25, a family friend wrote to Oliver: "The Chronicle has had nothing in it now for two numbers!! About the Applegates or the Modocs!!"[16] Oliver wrote to his father, "The most influential of the California papers are gradually getting right and we stand with the whole people of Oregon on the same platform."[17] He even got the *San Francisco Chronicle* to print "Oliver Applegate's Statement," a lengthy account justifying the food and supplies given to the Modocs at the Klamath reservation. The Modocs' "native provisions," he said, were collected from Lost River and delivered to the reservation. Reporting Modoc lawlessness and defiance of the Oregon treaty, the story blamed the Modocs for firing the first shot of the war. Applegate ended by claiming the Modocs were now "under the sway of the murderers of the settlers, undoubtedly the most potent power in the tribe at this time."[18]

The Applegates and their allies continued to counterpunch vigorously. Elisha Applegate (Lindsay's son) made a statement in the *San Diego Union*, and Lindsay placed a letter in the *Oregon Statesman*—a Salem paper whose masthead listed Jesse, Lucien, and Ivan Applegate as its "agents." The letter was copied to all the papers in Washington, D.C.[19] Apparently prodded by the Applegates, the *Oregon Statesman* complained that the California papers were filled with "ridiculous stuff" and "malignant abuse of the Oregonians."[20] In a letter to the *Oregon*

Bulletin, Jesse Applegate—dubbed the "Sage of Yoncalla"—delivered an explanation of the topography of the Lava Beds. "There is no name more honored among the list of early pioneers of Oregon," opined the *Bulletin*, "than that of Jesse Applegate."[21] But in a private letter, Lindsay Applegate warned the Californians were "getting up sympathy for the modocks." He added bluntly, "There is no danger of any thing Being done in favor of the modocks only to kill them."[22]

23

The Peace Commission

News of the Modoc victory in the first battle in the Lava Beds electrified the nation. The U.S. Army was ready for a second assault on the Stronghold, and the public was clamoring for retribution. But President Grant decided to give peace a chance.

Grant announced his controversial Peace Policy shortly after his first inauguration in 1869 to manage Indian affairs by "conquering with kindness." The Peace Policy (called "Quaker Policy" by some critics) sought to reform the notoriously corrupt Indian service by allowing Christian denominations to appoint Indian Agents to run reservations. Grant appointed Ely Parker, an educated Seneca Indian who had been his military aide, as commissioner of Indian Affairs.[1]

In January 1873 President Grant met quietly at the White House with Secretary of War William Belknap and Interior Secretary Columbus Delano to discuss the Modoc hostilities. The men reached "an understanding" that military operations against the Modocs would cease "with a view of stopping, if possible, the further effusion of blood."[2] Peace negotiations would begin, and while talks went on, the army's duty would be only to protect white settlers.[3] Disgruntled General William Tecumseh Sherman, head of the U.S. Army, wrote Canby: "The President seems disposed to allow the peace men to try their hand on Captain Jack."[4]

Several strands of the distant Modoc struggle came together in Washington, D.C., in early 1873. The city was crowded for the meeting of the Electoral College and formal reelection of President Grant. Alfred Meacham, a prominent and active Republican, was there as an elector to cast Oregon's vote for Grant, and he was busy parlaying himself into a new job. As a Grant delegate in 1869, he had received a patronage appointment as Oregon Indian Superintendent—but now had been fired from that job. He had fresh chips to cash in, and arrived in Washington at least three weeks before the scheduled meeting of the Electoral College on February 5.

Elisha Applegate—Jesse's nephew—and several other prominent Oregonians were also in Washington on various missions.[5] The Oregon group caucused several times to discuss what to do about the Modocs, and Elisha suggested they propose a "peace commission" to talk sense into the Indians and avoid further bloodshed. The Applegates, of course, wanted to get the Modocs out of the Lost River area, and Elisha went on a mission to accomplish this aim. "I went right off and seen the War Office and the other offices," Elisha wrote to his brothers. "Have impressed the idea that it will not do to allow that band to escape and they must not be allowed to remain in that country atall [*sic*]."[6]

The Oregonians wasted no time in going right to the top. Elisha wrote to the Secretary of Interior outlining the plan. In addition to urging a peace commission, the Oregonians recommended military operations be suspended immediately and that the Klamaths, "Yai-nax," and Modoc tribes all be removed to a reservation on the Oregon coast.[7] Everyone agreed Meacham should run such a commission. Above all, they wanted the Modocs out of the Lost River area, but urged against sending them back to the Klamath reservation to live with the Klamaths, which they saw as "a most irritating cause of discontent with the Modocs." Attorney General Williams liked the scheme, and he got the Oregonians an appointment with Secretary of the Interior Delano.

Whatever influence or patronage was involved, Secretary Delano accepted the idea, got it approved by President Grant, and gave Meacham the job as head of the new commission. Meacham later took pains to insist the commission was not his idea. "I was not consulted," he said.[8] He benefitted financially, however, getting a salary of $3 a day plus $1,000 in expenses for his work.[9]

The Peace Commission appointed by Delano nearly died stillborn, as the Interior Secretary proceeded to organize the group in complete ignorance of Oregon politics. His appointments included Alfred Meacham's archrival Thomas Odeneal, who had taken Meacham's job only a year earlier, and as well Father Wilbur, a Methodist Indian Agent in Yakima, Washington, with whom Meacham had tangled politically in 1869. Meacham refused to serve with either of the men. Delano then substituted Jesse Applegate and Samuel Case, supervisor of the Alsea Reservation on the Oregon coast, to represent the Indian service.[10]

A flurry of correspondence among the Applegates suggests their strategy was to take off the table any consideration of a Modoc reservation at Lost River. They wanted unconditional surrender of Captain Jack and his people, execution for the killers of the settlers, and transportation of the other Modoc to some "distant location." They called it "The Oregon Platform" or "Modoc Platform" in their letters.[11] The Applegates also feared anything that might jeopardize their lucrative management of the Klamath reservation: "The proposition to break up the Klamath Reservation has not yet manifested itself, but if it should we will be prepared to fight it to the 'bitter end,'" Oliver wrote.[12] "Sink or Swim," he wrote to his brother Lucien. "Ivon [*sic*] and I stand square on the Modoc Platform and propose to fight it out on that line."[13]

Oliver Applegate received a letter marked *"Confidential"* from his friend and family ally Quincy Brooks, an officer of the Oregon Volunteer Militia in Ashland. Brooks said if peace was to be made with the Modocs, it must be based on "our platform." Any other outcome "would be tantamount to an acknowledgement of the truth of the charges brought against your family by the California Press." Brooks advised Oliver to get a number of top southern Oregon figures from politics and military to endorse their position.[14] However, the Applegates were concerned that the family not be seen as meddling in commission affairs, and Oliver told his father Lindsay to stay away: "There are Applegates enough now at the front to make it seem like [we] are trying to 'run' the thing."[15]

By mid-February, the Peace Commission was organized. Among other duties, the Commission was charged with reporting on "the causes of the existing difficulties with the Modoc Indians."[16] Oliver Applegate, secretary of the peace commission and privy to its proceedings, wrote his father on February 26: "(Confidential) The Peace Commission has already prepared its report on the causes which led to the Modoc War and that exhibits the actual causes, and of course exempts us from blame."[17]

Assured the family would not be blamed for starting the war, Jesse Applegate resigned from the Commission with a flourish of high principle. He said he could not in conscience rule on the reasons for war, given the family's wide involvement in Klamath country: "As two of my nephews have been employed in subordinate places on the Klamath Reservation for the last five years, and the press has charged them of having a personal interest in securing the return of the rebel Modocs to the reservation, as their near relative, I am not the proper person to sit in judgment upon their conduct, or to be a member of a tribunal charged to make investigations that might impugne it."[18]

Applegate's resignation was accepted, and a month later Eleazar Thomas, a Methodist minister, was appointed to take his place.[19] Although Jesse blamed his nephews' employment on the reservation for the conflict of interest, he failed to mention that his brother Lindsay had been the principal Indian Agent for several years. And he did not mention his own much larger ethical problem: his involvement in the purchase of lands around Captain Jack's village and the scheme of the "Two Jesses" to dam Lost River and cut off its flow to the Modocs. As newsman Edward Fox pointed out, Meacham—the head of the Commission—knew about the Applegate conflict of interest, but never raised the issue: "Meacham knew Uncle Jesse and his partner (another man by the name of Jesse) had a little interest in certain swamplands in which he might be able to lend assistance."[20]

When the time came for the Commission to submit its report on the causes of the war, Oliver Applegate, as promised, made sure the Applegates were not blamed. "Malicious falsifiers," he wrote to a friend, were trying to "saddle on them the whole blame of the war." To stop this, Oliver was taking statements to prove the Modocs were supplied with abundant food and clothing on the reservation.[21] Jesse Applegate submitted the Commission's report on March 9, 1873, blaming Captain Jack for all the trouble: "The cause leading to war was the dissatisfaction of Captain Jack's band of Modocs with the provisions and execution of the treaty of October 14, 1864, and refusal to abide thereby." The Peace Commission, Applegate concluded, was an "expensive blunder."[22]

But the Peace Commission helped solve President Grant's growing problem with the Modocs. The national mood against the Modocs had turned bloody and vengeful after the army's trouncing on January 17. But the president was also being bombarded with letters from prominent pacifists about "the frauds and injuries suffered upon [the

Modocs]."[23] Quakers, in particular, who were deeply involved in Grant's Peace Policy, began to deluge the White House with "memorials"— petitions for nonviolent and moral treatment of the Modocs.[24]

It is debatable whether President Grant had a deep or genuine appreciation of national Indian issues. His primary goal, he told General Sherman, was to wrest control of Indian affairs from the Interior Department and place Indian reservations under military management. One historian labeled the Grant administration's Indian policy "a mixture of wars, frauds, and blunders."[25]

Sherman succeeded Grant as the commanding general of the U. S. Army upon Grant's election as president. Sherman brought a harsh and uncompromising view of Indian tribes, whom he saw as an obstacle to expansion in the West. He communicated privately to General Canby that he didn't have much use for the peace commission idea. In a chilling telegram, Sherman said he had no compunction about making an example of the Modocs: "If peaceful measures fail . . . I trust you will make such use of the military force that no other Indian tribe will imitate their example, and that no other reservation for [the Modocs] will be necessary except graves among their chosen lava beds."[26]

Canby replied to Sherman with a diplomatically worded telegram assuring that "the utmost patience and forbearance has been exercised toward the Modocs."[27] Two days later, he informed Sherman he was tightening his encirclement of the Modocs and closing off escape routes so the Modocs will see "the hopelessness of any further resistance."[28] In fact, Canby's patience and forbearance toward the Modocs soon reaped a bloody and fatal outcome.

24

Talking Peace

The newly appointed Peace Commissioners were directed to meet with Canby in Linkville on February 15, 1873. Meacham left Washington, D.C., for Oregon in such haste he appears to have skipped the meeting of the Electoral College. It took him nearly two weeks to cross the continent, and he arrived two days late for the initial meeting. He didn't like what he found when he passed through Yreka. His first telegram assessed the mood: "Things very much mixed. Everything said since my arrival has been discouraging. Evil prophecy."[1]

Meacham soon learned that appointment of the Peace Commission had inflamed the Oregon public. A grand jury in Jackson County, Oregon, indicted the Modocs who had murdered the fourteen settlers.[2] Oregon Governor Grover launched an all-out campaign in letters and newspapers to prevent a peace settlement with the Modocs. He wrote a formal letter to the Commissioners announcing: "The people of Oregon desire that the murderers [of the fourteen settlers] shall be given up and be delivered over to the civil authorities for trial and punishment." Grover warned the Commissioners that territory on the Lost River could not be given to the Modocs because the 1864 Oregon Treaty extinguished Indian title to those lands. Those lands, he pronounced, were "now occupied by *bona fide* settlers under the homestead and pre-emption laws of the United States."[3] When Jesse and Oliver Applegate learned of Grover's ultimatum, they were "flabbergasted" and "[made] some remarks respecting the sanity of the aforesaid governor."[4]

The Modocs were also not happy about the Peace Commission. Captain Jack mistrusted the commission in part because of the involvement of the Applegates. Captain Jack blamed the Applegates for shooting into his sleeping village on the Lost River. "It was the lies of [Ivan] Applegate and the Klamath Lake Indians that brought this trouble upon me," he said. "I want nothing to do with him. Want nothing to do with Applegate, and will not talk to him."[5] Reporter Edward Fox wrote that the war party Modocs "do not entertain the most kindly feelings toward [Jesse] Applegate, and are reported to have expressed an extreme interest as to the length of his hair, with a view to adorning their wigwam with those revered grey hairs."[6]

The Modocs also were shocked the Peace Commission did not include any of the Californians they considered friends. The Modocs asked that the sympathetic Judges Steele and Roseborough of Yreka be added to the commission, and Canby sent for them. Two new members now also joined the commission—Reverend Thomas and L. S. Dyar, the Indian Agent assigned to the Klamath reservation.

The Modocs—who had freely roamed their own lands for millennia—did not care about the artificial border between California and Oregon. But the split between the Californians and Oregonians bedeviled the peace talks from the beginning. The Californians bore no animus toward the Modocs, who stayed peaceably in the rancheros outside of Yreka and worked as laborers and mineworkers and did business in Yreka. But the Oregonians were settlers and ranchers, greedy for land. The Californians did not begrudge the Modocs a piece of their traditional territory, but the Oregonians wanted the Indians moved completely away. Portland papers mercilessly lashed out against Judge Elijah Steele and the Californians, and the California press railed against the Oregonians and blamed them for causing a war.

Peace talks began in mid-February 1873. The Peace Commissioners and representatives of the Indian Agency—including Oliver, Ivan, and Jesse Applegate along with General Canby and the reporters—were initially billeted at Fairchild's ranch. The accommodations, reporter Fox noted ironically, were "rather limited." Fox brought mail to the army and was welcomed to bed down with the officers in a two-room farmhouse. But, Fox reported: "[A]bout fourteen [officers] occupy a floor of one room fifteen feet square; seven sleep in an adjoining apartment, nine feet by fifteen and General Canby and staff have an adjoining shed about eight feet square." Fox was also displeased with the food: "We have two meals per diem, one at 8:00 a.m. and the other at 4:00 p.m. . . . served with a fair allowance of dirt. The staple article of food at both meals is beef, fried in grease in the morning, and boiled in fat in the afternoon." Nevertheless, Fox was stoical. "A man might make a campaign under worse auspices," he said.[7]

On February 18, 1873, the Peace Commission made its first over-
ture to the Modocs, recruiting Bob Whittle and his Modoc wife Matilda
to act as interpreters and intermediaries. Matilda was sent off to the
Modoc camp, accompanied by Artinie, who was dressed with war paint
and a white bandana over her head. Matilda, wearing "a neat fitting red
dress, with a white cloth tied around her chest," was nervous about the
mission, but she was "gifted with the indomitable Indian pluck."[8] The
three carried to the Modocs a rather patronizing message—said to be
directly from President Grant but undoubtedly drafted by Meacham.
"The President of the United States was very sorry his children were
fighting," the message stated, "and he did not want them to spill each
other's blood." But the message warned the Modocs: "[The President]
never failed to win in war."[9]

When Matilda returned to the army camp the following day, she
reported she was surprised at having been received "kindly" by the
Modocs. But Meacham—the "grand inquisitor," as Fox called him—
refused to allow the reporters to sit in on Matilda's account of the
meeting. Instead, Meacham issued a prepared statement for the press.
The published stories include identical quotations, suggesting a military
stenographer provided the text. It made a vivid tale (as embellished
by the newsmen). The Modocs, according to the story, told Matilda
they were out of clothes, out of provisions, and "ready to wash their
hands of blood." Captain Jack said he was still angry about the attack
on Lost River when the army "pitched into us when [we were] asleep,"
and he spoke bitterly about the killing of the woman and two babies.
But Captain Jack gave the first hope the Modocs might negotiate. He
wanted to be the peacemaker "breaking the trouble as he would a string
in the middle." He told the messengers: "I am ready to talk, and I want
to talk with those men that come from a long way off." Captain Jack
also repeated his request to talk to Elijah Steele or Judge Roseborough,
his California friends. Captain Jack also said that in the event peace was
concluded, he would insist upon having "his place on Lost River."[10]

Matilda reported that Schonchin John also spoke, saying his heart
was wild during the fighting, but now peace talks "sent out [calmed] his
wild spirit." He expressed a lasting distrust of whites: "I can control
my people, but I am afraid you cannot control your people." Matilda
said she thought Captain Jack was losing his influence, and that Schon-

chin John's faction was ascendant, now supported by a majority of the
Modocs. But even Schonchin John seemed to soften slightly: "Send
more talk; we will send more back."[11]

Bob and Matilda Whittle were then dispatched back to the Lava
Beds to set up a meeting with the Peace Commissioners. On their
return, Bob Whittle reported shaking hands with the Modoc warriors
Long Jim and Steamboat Frank. Captain Jack and his party rode up,
and Bob shook hands with them, too, and assured the warriors Meacham was trying to get them back their land on the Lost River. Captain
Jack remembered meeting with Jesse Applegate and their talk about the
Lost River land. The Modocs said they were willing to meet with the
Peace Commissioners, but demanded again to talk with Judge Steele
and Judge Roseborough and the rancher John Fairchild, all white men
whom they trusted.[12]

The Peace Commissioners sent Bob Whittle, Artinie, and Matilda
back to Lava Beds for another meeting, this time accompanied by John
Fairchild. Their trip was the occasion for the great journalistic escapade
by the *New York Herald's* Edward Fox, who traveled with the party as
they rode past several Modoc camps into the Lava Beds. Fox described
fifty men and women "in costume of a very heterogeneous nature,"
many of the men in military overcoats, and they went by foot into the
rocks of the Stronghold.[13]

The droll reporter wrote: "I had the pleasure of an introduction to
Hooker Jim, Modoc Dave, and Steamboat Frank. [T]hose three men
were armed to the teeth." The escort led the white delegation along a
difficult trail through the broken rocks to a group of Modoc warriors
warming themselves around a fire. Fox described the scene: "They were
all painted. . . . The entire lower part of the face was smeared with a
brownish or black composition of a greasy nature. It gave them a very
hideous appearance, and coming upon this group standing round the
blazing fire, each with a musket in his hand, and revolver and knife in
the belt, [was] not calculated to reassure visitors of the pacific nature of
the inhabitants of the Lava Beds."

When Fox and the others managed to get inside the Stronghold,
he saw several "rancherias." Captain Jack's was the innermost of the
encampments. The Modocs argued about whether the party should be
admitted and, if so, whether Fox, the "paper man," should be allowed

to enter. Heated arguments broke out in the Modoc language about the presence of the whites, and the visitors feared things were becoming dangerous. Scarface Charley, who usually sided with Captain Jack, played a role in pacifying Hooker Jim and the hotheads and he escorted the visitors deep inside the lava fortress.

Finally the group reached Captain Jack's cave. Then began a good deal of argument among the Modocs about where the visitors would sleep. "If [these] gentlemen came to blows over this little question of etiquette," Fox observed dryly, "the guest would probably fare worst of all." The Modocs then argued over whether he should be allowed to witness the council with Captain Jack, but Fox quipped, "I am happy to say that friends of literature predominated."

Overnighting in the Lava Beds as the guest of Wild Girl, Fox met Captain Jack. Fox reported that "[Captain Jack] looked very sick, and was sitting with a blanket around his limbs and supporting himself by resting his hands on the handle of one of their root diggers, which was stuck in the ground before him." Fox then saw a medicine man (probably Curley-Headed Doctor) perform a healing ceremony on Captain Jack. Although Fox did not understand what he saw, he was witnessing a traditional Modoc healing ritual. Late that night in Captain Jack's cave, he saw two Modoc men "jumping up and down on the ground and singing some kind of unintelligible words to a meaningless kind of tune." The cave was crowded; Captain Jack was lying beside the fire. The Doctor then lay Captain Jack on the ground, jumped on his back, and bit him: "[He] put his teeth into Captain Jack's shoulder blade. He held on there for a couple of minutes, writhing and twisting his body about, the men kept up their dancing and howling." The Doctor then rose and going to a corner of the room, vomited. All the Modocs ran up after him "to see what the healer had sucked out of the sick man."[14]

By the next morning, Fox was surprised Captain Jack had recovered and looked better, "as if the treatment he received had really done him good." The group then assembled "[at] a large cave, thronged with fifty or sixty Modocs, around a blazing fire." Fox and the others elbowed their way through the crowd to sit next to Captain Jack and Scarface Charley. Bob Whittle, Fox, Bogus Charley, Captain Jack, Schonchin John, and Shacknasty Jim sat in a semicircle, and Whittle's Modoc wife, Matilda, translated. Fox's presence was explained: "He came from afar, from Boston Illahee [White Country] and he came to hear their story even though the commissioners forbid it." The assembled Indians were impressed that the "paper men" had come from afar off. "Their approbation was expressed in a perfect chorus of 'A's'," Fox said.

After being presented with a peace proposal, the Modocs began several hours of speeches, in which they revisited their bitter grievances. Several Modocs recalled the professional Indian hunter Ben Wright had slaughtered their family members in 1852. Captain Jack was furious above all at the unprovoked attack on his village. He had thought negotiations were still under way. Captain Jack asked repeatedly if the soldiers who killed Indians would be put on trial, as Modocs would be tried for killing of the settlers. "[Ben Wright] killed nearly fifty of my people. Among the killed was my father. He was holding a peace council with them. Was he or any of his men punished? No, not one."[15]

The peace talk had a momentous result: Captain Jack agreed to hold more face-to-face meetings with the peace commissioners. He said he was willing to meet Meacham, Canby, Case, Applegate, and Steele and Roseborough from Yreka. He also wanted the "paper men" to be present. "No gassing, want them to come." But Captain Jack said he would not meet if the commissioners insisted on bringing a military escort. Schonchin John agreed. "Soldiers no good for peace," he said.

Shortly after the meeting, two of the leaders of the militant faction—Hooker Jim and Curley-Headed Doctor—visited the army camp to negotiate the return of forty horses captured by the army before the January battle. During the visit, the Modoc warriors got a good look at General Canby's growing force, now over five hundred troops, posted at three locations surrounding the Stronghold. On February 27 Elijah Steele and A.M. Roseborough arrived at "The Modoc Expedition" at Van Brimmer's, where the Peace Commissioners were now staying. Meacham thought the idea was folly, but Steele nevertheless was chosen to go into the Modoc camp and present a peace proposal to the Modocs. A few days later, in a blinding late winter snowstorm, Steele led a caravan of negotiators into the Lava Beds. His party included John Fairchild, Frank Riddle and Winema as interpreters, and several newsmen—Atwell for the *Sacramento Record*, Fox for the *New York Herald*, Alex McKay of the *San Francisco Evening Bulletin*, and Bogart for the

San Francisco Chronicle.[16] (Meacham had by this time lifted his futile press ban.)

Once again, Captain Jack was "very sick," but he welcomed the party to his cave for a talk. The first night Steele slept in Captain Jack's cave with Scarface Charley and Queen Mary, Jack's sister, standing guard. Captain Jack himself slept at their feet. The next morning talks resumed, but the Modocs were "excited and insolent."[17] After the delegation slept overnight in the Modoc camp, Steele presented the peace proposal, promising that if the Modocs would surrender, the Modocs could move out of the Lava Beds to a warm country in the south and the government would protect them. After a full day of speeches and negotiation, Steele concluded—mistakenly as it turned out—that the Modocs were favorable to the peace proposal. On the second day, they jawboned again until noon, and things seemed so friendly that Steele thought he had a deal. The *New York Herald* reported, "It is now safe to say there will be no more trouble with the Modoc Indians."[18] "The Dawn of Peace," announced the *Chronicle*.[19]

When Steele's column emerged from the rocks and appeared at the army camp, he triumphantly waved his hat. "They accept peace!" he shouted.[20] Steele brought with him a party of leading Modocs, including Hooker Jim, Queen Mary, Bogus Charley, Boston Charley, Long Jim, Shacknasty Jim, Duffy, William, and Curley-Headed Jack. Captain Jack was "too sick" to join the group.[21] Couriers were sent off with the good news. "We felt a great victory had been won over blood and carnage," Meacham later wrote, "and that our hazardous labors were nearly over."[22] Canby telegraphed Sherman: "The terms proposed will be accepted by the Modocs."[23]

It soon became evident, however, that something was very wrong with the Steele "agreement." The Modocs who returned to the camp with Steele's party demurred when asked to describe the deal, and John Fairchild recognized there had been a dangerous misunderstanding: "They do not understand that they have agreed to *surrender yet, on any terms*."[24]

The Modocs, it turned out, feared the peace talks were a ruse to kill them. A few days earlier at the army camp several Modocs were approached by the troublemaking settler Charlie Blair, who told them he had a warrant for their arrest and that they were being tricked into surrendering. Blair told the Modocs they would be burned alive or hanged if they surrendered. Alarmed, the Modoc delegation hurried back to the Lava Beds and reported that it was unsafe for the Modocs to step outside the Stronghold.[25]

But the ever-idealistic Steele insisted the Modocs agreed to peace and proposed to go back to the Stronghold to confirm his impression. Atwell, the reporter, would accompany him. Fairchild warned they would be in great danger and refused to participate. Fairchild "declined with a peculiarly slow swinging of his head, which said a great deal . . . especially when he closed his eyes in doing so."[26] Steel persisted and a few days later undertook the new peace mission to Captain Jack.

It would be a frightening trip. The Modocs believed Blair's rumor, and when Steele arrived he found the assembled group rude and surly. He heard loud arguments going on. Steele, who had dealt with Indians for a decade, said he counted sixty-nine warriors. Most of the Modocs believed Steele was trying to draw them into a lethal trap, and they were now in a bloody mood. They thought Steele had offered a deal that would leave the Modocs in peace by Lost River. In fact, Steele was only authorized to propose that the Modocs surrender to the military and remove to a new home on a distant reservation (probably in Arizona). The Modocs understandably thought Steele had betrayed them.[27]

Accusing Steele of duplicity, Captain Jack said he had never sold his land and would never leave it. Fox (who evidently got the story from Atwell) reported Captain Jack was raging furiously, "[speaking] in a wild strain . . . [to] his savage auditors, and their eyes sparkled and told a tale of blood that their fingers itched to shed." Schonchin John announced he was tired of talking. "I want everything wiped out and to live as we used to," he said. "That is the way I want to settle this matter."

Captain Jack then said all he wanted was to stay in the country where he had been born and always lived. He offered to let the settlers have the far side of Tule Lake while his people kept the side where they lived. The conversation ended with Schonchin John warning, "You talk now of the soldiers coming. I don't want much more talk about it. I want these men to come and fix this trouble right and straight."

That night Scarface Charley probably saved Steele's and Atwell's lives by inviting them to sleep in his own cave, where he guarded them, sleeping next to them with Captain Jack at their feet.[28] The next morning Steele assured the Modocs that the drunken men in Linkville had started the false rumor. He told them that if he and Atwell were released, he would return with all the Peace Commissioners to negotiate. In response, Captain Jack told Steele to make sure Meacham and Applegate were included in the delegation—the two whom the Modocs now hated especially. "The Modocs appeared to be anxious for a lock of Meacham's hair," wrote Fox.[29] The peace envoys hurried home happy that they were not sent off "to the other side of that dark river."[30] Steele was followed by several "Modoc squaws," who warned Fox the negotiators should not return, "as the bucks are mad and want more blood." Steele said no amount of money would induce him to enter the Lava Beds ever again.[31]

Disappointed, Meacham telegraphed the bad news to Washington: there was no peace deal, and the Commissioners believed "treachery was intended."[32] Interior Secretary Delano telegraphed a surprising response: "I do not believe Modocs mean treachery . . . Continue negotiations."[33]

The episode did nothing to increase the Modocs' trust of the peace process. Jack later said he had wanted to take his band out of the Lava Beds peacefully, but he heard that a man by the name of Nate Berwick had said the Peace Commissioners had "pile of wood ready built up," and they were going to burn him there if he came out of the Lava Beds.[34]

On March 7 Captain Jack sent a trusted envoy, his sister Queen Mary, with an escort of warriors to the army camp to talk with General Canby. Canby, tired of quarreling, told Queen Mary that unless Captain Jack or his principal men came out to negotiate in person, all talks would end. He threatened an immediate attack if there was no movement toward peace. Queen Mary went back to report to Captain Jack, but no one held out much hope.

To everyone's surprise, Boston Charley, "a squaw named Limpy," Queen Mary, and other Modocs returned to the army camp the next day with a message saying the Modocs would come out of the Lava Beds and surrender. Boston Charley said Captain Jack had requested three wagons be sent to evacuate his people. Boston Charley was insolent to the commissioners, boasting that he was the equivalent of twenty soldiers in a fight. Before he returned to Captain Jack's camp, he stole a case of gunpowder from John Fairchild's ranch.

The Peace Commissioners quarreled about how to react, but finally accepted Captain Jack's terms of surrender after a two-to-one vote (Meacham voting no). Wagons were to be sent to Captain Jack's Stronghold to bring his people out. On Monday, Canby ordered out four wagons and a detail of troops. They set up tents and provided firewood, food, and many "actual luxuries for the headmen."[35] Their optimism was misplaced, however. The day before the date set for the surrender, another messenger arrived from the Lava Beds to say that the Modocs could not come for two more days because they were cremating some of their dead.

The Peace Commission struggled to reach an agreement with no success. There were more charges of treachery. An Oregon newspaper called the peace process a "farce" and urged mass meetings in every town and hamlet against "any further temporizing with these murdering red devils."[36] Even General Canby was growing exasperated. In early April he wrote to his wife, Louisa: "[The Modoc leaders] are the strangest mixture of insolence and arrogance, ignorance and superstition I have ever seen, even among Indians, and from this cause results the great difficulty in dealing with them in any way but force. Treacherous themselves, they suspect treachery in everything."[37]

But the impasse in the Lava Beds would soon to be overshadowed by an event that rattled the entire nation.

25

A Lethal Decision

By the middle of March the peace talks had produced little hope and abundant frustration. Various Modocs had emerged to negotiate, but it was unclear whom they represented or who was in charge in the Stronghold. Inside the Lava Beds, the militant faction threatened Captain Jack's life if he ventured out to talk with his friend John Fairchild. Captain Jack's party was losing control, but the Modocs agreed on one thing: they wanted the soldiers to go home and give them back Lost River, and they demanded amnesty for the Modocs who had murdered settlers.

General Canby resolved to personally intervene in the Modoc peace talks. "I propose to open communication with them again in the course of two or three days," he wrote to General Sherman on March 17. Observing that the Modocs would not consent to return to the Klamath reservation where they had been mistreated, he recommended, "With a little patience I believe that a better arrangement can be effected."[1] At the same time, Canby planned to continue the army's strategy of encirclement and compression to contain the embattled Modocs.

On March 21 Canby had an unintended—and dramatic—face-to-face encounter with Captain Jack. Canby, who had intended to make no contact with the Modocs until his troops were in place, went into the field with General Gillem to examine the terrain and choose a site for a camp from which to launch an attack. Canby and Gillem rode with a force of about one hundred men, including sixteen officers and the indefatigable Edward Fox. The soldiers rode to the bluff overlooking the Lava Beds and dismounted. As Canby and Gillem surveyed the landscape with their field glasses, they saw Modocs on a ledge of rock at the foot of the bluff. The Modocs shouted for someone to "come down." When Fox and army surgeon Thomas Cabaniss went down, a meeting was arranged for Canby and Gillem to talk with the Modocs at a lone juniper tree about halfway down the bluff. Canby agreed, went to the meeting point, and waited for Captain Jack.[2]

Two warriors suddenly emerged from the rocks: Boston Charley and Bogus Charley. Then Captain Jack's sister Queen Mary appeared, along with the woman known as Wild Girl. They approached the soldiers, impressing Gillem with their conciliatory talk and their stated desire to stop fighting. What the officers did not realize was that this group represented only the smaller Modoc peace faction associated with Captain Jack.

When Captain Jack arrived an hour later, he was escorted by several of the war faction Modocs, including Curley-Headed Doctor, Steamboat Frank, and about a dozen more. Canby immediately recognized they were there to monitor what Captain Jack said, to see "he did not commit himself to their prejudice." After this encounter, Canby cabled Sherman: "[The meeting] confirmed the impression previously reported, that the war faction is still predominant. Captain Jack's demeanor was that of a man under duress and afraid to exhibit his real feelings. Important questions were evaded, or not answered at all." He said that with the troops moving into position, communication could again be opened with the Modocs "with the hope of better results." Canby added he did not think Captain Jack would accept any peace unless he got back "his home on Lost River."[3]

Surprisingly, the idea of a reservation on Lost River was still in the air. Interior Secretary Delano instructed Canby to "consult the wishes of the Indians" in regard to location of a new reservation. "Lost River was suggested," he wrote.[4] In early March, however, Delano wired much harsher instructions to Meacham, who was still quartered at Fairchild's ranch. "This is important," he wrote. "If Modocs leave Pacific coast, remove them to Indian Territory." Although Delano also instructed Meacham to continue negotiations, his wire was the first indication the Modocs might be exiled from the far west.[5]

Gillem, wanting to impress the Modocs with the hopelessness of resistance, moved his camp closer to the Stronghold. His troops at Fairchild's ranch marched down the steep mule path to the foot of the bluff and established a base on the west side of the Lava Beds (known today as Gillem's Camp). He also moved other troops closer to the Modocs, to a point just three miles east of the Stronghold. Canby's slow compression strategy continued as the troops closed in on the Modocs. "Troops are being moved into positions that will make it difficult for [the Modocs] to egress for raiding purposes," he wrote to Sherman.[6] If Canby could not succeed with persuasion, he would attack.

Captain Jack asked for another meeting, and on April 2, 1873, he met for the first time with the three peace commissioners and Canby together. They gathered at a point halfway between Gillem's large new camp and the Stronghold, smoked pipes, and talked. There was a fierce wind and rainstorm, and Captain Jack boasted that weather didn't bother Modocs. Everyone was drenched, and they agreed to erect a "peace tent" for future meetings. Two more meetings were scheduled, but the Modocs didn't show up for the first. A few Modocs, including Hooker Jim, visited the army camp and saw the new weapons and much-expanded force. When they heard what the signalmen were doing with their flags, they protested it was not sportsmanlike to talk over the heads of the Modocs.[7]

On April 5 Captain Jack arrived for a meeting with Canby, Gillem, Thomas, Meacham, and Dyar—the two commanding generals and the three peace commissioners. Captain Jack had grown more conciliatory and expressed his fear of a powerful general and a religious man—Reverend Thomas—whose magic might be stronger than his. He made his usual demand that the Modocs be given back their home at Lost River, but then surprised the whites by saying he might be willing to accept a reservation in the Lava Beds. Meacham thought it might be the needed breakthrough that could lead to a settlement. He told the Modocs if they surrendered, they would have to turn over the murderers for trial. Captain Jack asked who would be the judges and was told they would be "white men, of course." Captain Jack asked if the settlers who killed the Modoc babies at Lost River would be given to the Indians to try for murder, a question he later repeated at his trial.[8]

Canby seized on the idea of a Lava Beds reservation, and he sent Winema to assure Captain Jack that anyone (including the killers of the settlers) who surrendered would have the army's complete protection. Unfortunately, this proposal caused a new quarrel among the Modocs. Captain Jack and his eleven followers would take a peace deal, but the larger war party—three or four times the number of Captain Jack's faction—threatened to kill anyone who defected.[9]

A man called Weium (or William), a member of Captain Jack's faction, warned Winema the militant Modocs planned treachery and the whites should not agree to any further meetings.[10] Winema was shocked to learn an assassination plan had been hatched, and when she reported to husband Frank Riddle what she had heard, he immediately alerted Canby, Gillem, and the Commissioners. Reaction was divided: Gillem didn't believe the story, and Canby was skeptical. Reverend Thomas said, "God will not let them do such a thing. I trust in God to protect us."[11] Meacham and Dyar were deeply worried.

Despite their doubts, the Commissioners agreed to meet the next day at the peace tent and parley. Canby sent the Riddles to the Modocs to try to schedule the meeting. He suggested both sides bring armed guards, but the Modocs rejected the idea. The Riddles reported the Modocs were piling rocks and slaughtering beef as if readying for war. The Modocs had heard Winema had warned the white men they were planning treachery, and they upbraided her violently, demanding to know where she got the information. Unwilling to identify Weium, she told them she had dreamed the story, a claim the Modocs could not challenge.[12]

Inside the Lava Beds a meeting was held in a rocky depression, a kind of steep amphitheater near Captain Jack's cave. On Thursday night, April 10, 1873, the eve of Good Friday, all the Modocs—women and children included—gathered around a fire at the bottom of the bowl. A large rock served as a rostrum.

Schonchin John and Black Jim led the talk.[13] They argued that if they could entice the commissioners and Canby to meet with them, they would kill them and win a decisive victory that would cause the white soldiers to go away. Schonchin John said he was fed up with negotiation and Black Jim spoke of murder. Captain Jack told the assembly that only a peace settlement could save his people. He announced he was willing to take his band to the hamlet of Yainax on the Klamath reservation to live among the other Modocs on the reservation. Captain Jack warned that the Oregonians were vengeful, and the killers of the settlers would face certain retribution; they would inevitably be captured and hanged. Captain Jack felt they should not all die for the crimes of the few murderers. Black Jim, notoriously anti-settler, argued fiercely that a large army with dangerous artillery surrounded the Modocs. Capitulation was no choice, he argued; killing the commissioners was their best hope. On this fateful night, thirteen Modocs sided with Captain Jack, and thirty wanted war.[14]

When Captain Jack rose again to speak, the war party challenged his authority as leader by portraying him as a coward, a move deeply rooted in the Modoc's traditional culture. War leaders such as Captain Jack were chosen for their courage, prestige, and effectiveness as fighters—but their post was only temporary. They served only when needed, only as long as they had the confidence of the band.[15]

When Captain Jack spoke, several men seized him and pinioned him against the rostrum. They forced a woman's shawl over his shoulders and put a woman's hat on his head. Hooker Jim said: "You are like an old squaw, you have never done any fighting yet; we have done the fighting, and you are our chief. You are not fit to be a chief." [16] Captain Jack's authority and honor were at stake. If he refused to kill Canby, he faced humiliation and loss of authority. But he also knew he faced certain death if he killed the general. Enraged and humiliated, Captain Jack leapt up and agreed to spill the white man's blood. "If Canby refuses to give us a home in our country," he said. "I will ask him many times. If he won't agree to do what I want, then, only then, will I commit the bad act."[17]

If they wanted murder, Captain Jack said, he would give it to them—and they would all die. The Modocs decided they would not just kill the Commissioners; they would attempt to draw officers out from Mason's Camp three miles east and slay them as well. The warriors clamored to choose their victims. As chief, Captain Jack said Canby would be his prize, and Ellen's Man George would assist him. Schonchin John claimed the right to kill Meacham, with Hooker Jim as his second. They awarded the "Sunday Doctor" (Reverend Thomas) to Boston Charley and Bogus Charley. Dyar, apparently considered a lesser trophy, was assigned to Shacknasty Jim and Barncho. Black Jim and Slolux were to assassinate Gillem, who would be sick in his tent and not attend the meeting.[18]

There was jubilation in the Modoc camp as the Modocs celebrated their bold decision. The Doctor led a dance that lasted all night. The army could hear the noise from three miles away at Gillem's Camp. But no one—in the army camp or in Stronghold—knew that the warriors who had shamed him would soon betray Captain Jack.

26

The Fateful Meeting

The night before the meeting at the peace tent, members of the Peace Commission were still deeply divided. Canby, veteran of previous Indian wars, doubted the Modocs would harm them. Reverend Thomas trusted in God's protection. Indian Agent Dyar was fearful, and Alfred Meacham expected treachery.

Reverend Thomas—not sure he would return from another peace meeting alive—welcomed martyrdom. He paid off his account at the sutler's store, saying he did not want to die with bills unpaid. He told Canby: "If [God] requires my life, I am ready for the sacrifice," then he spent hours praying alone in the rocks.[1] Matthew Deady later commented drolly that "[Thomas] was afflicted by a kind of serene idiocy . . . that God would allow no harm to befall a party setting forth on so good a mission."[2] Meacham felt he should go because the meeting would have no legitimacy if he were absent, but he was plainly terrified. He made rancher John Fairchild promise to dispose of his remains: "If my body is brought in mutilated and cut to pieces, you will bury me here, so that my family shall never be tortured by the sight."[3]

Canby had several visitors to his tent who pleaded with him not to meet with the Modocs. Frank Riddle asked to meet Canby to "offer a proposition" that the general hide twenty-five or thirty men at the meeting site to "catch them if they done something wrong." But Canby was suspicious of Riddle because his wife was Modoc, and felt posting guards would be an insult to Captain Jack. Field glasses were protection enough. "I have dealt with Indians for thirty years, and I have never deceived an Indian," he said. "I will not consent to it—to any promise that cannot be fulfilled."[4] Optimistically, Canby wrote his wife Louisa: "Don't be discouraged or gloomy, darling. I will take good care of myself and return home as soon as possible."[5] Riddle and Winema then went to Meacham to warn him the Modocs intended to kill him. "My woman went and took ahold of Mr. Meacham and told him not to go, and held on to him and cried," Frank Riddle recalled later. "She said, 'Meacham, don't you go! For they might kill you today, they might kill all of you today!'"[6]

Winema.
"Winema became one of the heroines of the Modoc story. Her name lives on, including at Winema High School, Winema National Forest, Wi-Ni-Ma Family Camp, and Winema Lodge."
Courtesy Author's collection.

Boston Charley, who had overnighted in the army camp, was scurrying around trying to make sure the meeting wasn't canceled. The army had grown accustomed to his presence. Boston was a diminutive figure, about five feet tall, scarcely in his twenties, and shabbily dressed. Reverend Thomas gave him a new shirt and pants and invited him to breakfast. When Boston Charley saw Meacham changing to his old boots, he urged him to wear his new twenty-dollar ones to the meeting. He circulated around the camp, assuring soldiers peace was nigh. Ominously, he carried a loaded rifle as he strode among the tents.

Bogus Charley was also in the camp, and he too had received new clothes. He had become Canby and Gillem's favorite translator.

When Good Friday, April 11, dawned, the commissioners gathered in Gillem's tent. They were surprised the general was not dressed. Gillem's health had been fragile since he arrived at the front, and he said he was too sick to go with them to the "peace tent." Meacham proposed again to cancel the meeting, saying it was problematic if Gillem were absent. At least, Meacham said, they should all go armed. But Reverend Thomas thought it would be a breach of trust to take weapons to a peace negotiation.

Eventually, the reluctant Meacham succumbed to group pressure and decided to join the group, saying, "I *must go* if the general and [Reverend Thomas] do."[7] Convinced he would die, he returned to his tent, sat on a roll of blankets, and wrote an emotional note to his wife at home:

Souvenir card of Boston Charley.
Courtesy author's collection.

> You may be a widow tonight; you shall not be a coward's wife. I go to save my honor. John A. Fairchild will forward my valise and valuables. The chances are all against us. I have done my best to prevent this meeting. I am in no wise to blame.
>
> Yours to the end, ALFRED
>
> P.S. I give Fairchild six hundred and fifty dollars, currency, for you. A.B.M.[8]

Fairchild sat nearby whittling. Meacham had given him a package containing the money, his gold rings, and his watch.[9]

Leroy Dyar, the third commissioner in addition to Meacham and Thomas, thought the meeting was hazardous, if not suicidal, and later admitted he went along for fear of being considered a coward.[10] Dyar was told he was under no obligation to go, but he too refused to change his mind. He also gave his money to Fairchild for safekeeping. Oliver Applegate, who had just arrived in camp, approached Dyar quietly before the party left and convinced him to take Oliver's "little two-barreled derringer and cartridges" in his pocket. Meacham, it turned out, had also provided himself with a pocket pistol.[11] The men kept their guns secret from the others. In the end, five men—Canby, Meacham, Thomas, Frank Riddle, and Dyar—agreed to attend the peace conference, along with Winema as translator.

Spring brought brilliant cold weather to northern California, and the morning was bright and clear. Most snow had melted from the hills. The cavalryman Maurice Fitzgerald said the lake was like glass, and the April air was filled with the scent of wild flowers. Gone was the fog that had bedeviled the army in the January attack, and the signal station halfway up the bluff could easily communicate by flag with Colonel Mason's camp almost three miles east.

Meacham recalled he made a final appeal to Canby and Thomas: "Gentlemen, my cool, deliberate opinion is that, if we go to the council tent to-day, we will be carried home to-night on the stretchers, all cut to pieces." Still hoping for some way to protect himself, Meacham said that if they found they faced certain death, they should make any promise in the world, "rather than that they should have my life or [yours]." Thomas replied sternly: "I will be party to no deception." As Canby and Thomas turned to leave, Meacham had a plaintive final word: "Gentlemen, I beg you not to go. I have too much to live for now; too many are depending on me; I do not want to die. [But] if you go, I must go to save my name from dishonor."[12]

Canby, Thomas, and Meacham left together at about 9 A.M. Canby and Thomas were on foot, Meacham on horseback. Canby wore the epaulettes and full-dress blue uniform of a Major General with two rows of nine brass buttons down the breast and his high felt hat with the gold cord. He took his gold watch. His sword scabbard was symbolically empty, and he carried a box of cigars under his arm. He penciled a brief note to his wife Louisa. Thomas had dressed in a light grey tweed suit, but Meacham, Dyar, and Riddle wore old clothes, which they believed would be less tempting to the Indians. Dyar ambled toward the meeting place tent on his horse named Old Blue. Boston Charley and the Riddle couple followed in the rear. Winema, who had tried to keep Meacham from mounting his horse when he left, rode a pony. She was crying.

The peace tent had been erected about a mile from Gillem's Camp. Captain Jack had demanded the meeting be held at another site a mile closer to his camp in a bowl or depression not visible from the bluff. Gunmen could be hidden around its rim, so Canby refused. Some of the troops hiked up to the signal station at a high point on the bluff to watch events a mile below. Signalmen were poised with binoculars, even though they could not see inside the peace tent.

Meanwhile, unknown to them, the Modocs inside the Stronghold were arguing again about assassinating the commissioners. Bogus Charley was convinced that killing these men would make the army withdraw. Ellen's Man George taunted Captain Jack, saying Captain Jack lacked courage. Ellen's Man George should be allowed to fire the first shot at Canby. But Captain Jack stood his ground, saying it was his right as chief to kill the general. The argument ended when the Modocs saw the commissioners approaching, led by Canby.

As they arrived, Canby and the commissioners saw the Modocs had built two sagebrush fires. Captain Jack and his men gathered around the fire on the east side of the tent, which put the tent between them and the binoculars of the signalmen watching from the bluff. The understanding was that each side would send five people, but the Modocs brought six. Bogus Charley and Boston Charley made it eight. Everyone noticed there were bulges beneath Modoc shirts and blankets, which they took to be pistols. The war faction outnumbered Captain Jack seven to one. The commissioners huddled quietly, and Dyar and Riddle said they would run if there were an attack. Meacham said that was hopeless; they should fight back as a group.[13]

There was a sudden disruption. A stranger was seen trudging along the trail toward the tent. The Modocs suspected the whites were trying to reinforce their numbers. Canby told Dyar to ride back and send the man home. It turned out he was a civilian named Smith, looking for his horse.

Captain Jack wore a "slouched hat" and a worn grey jacket. Meacham thought he looked moody and "not at ease in his mind." Hooker Jim paced back and forth behind Captain Jack. "His face tells you he is a cut-throat," remembered Meacham, "tall, stout-built, very muscular, an ugly customer in a fight." Black Jim was there, half-brother to Captain Jack, tall and striking, his jet-black hair parted in the middle. Ellen's Man George looked pudgy and benign, but the whites had heard he was ruthless in a fight.

Unseen by the delegation, two younger Modocs, Barncho and Slolux, were hidden in the rocks. They had snuck up during the night, their arms full of rifles. Also watching from the rocks was Scarface Charley, armed with a pistol. His mission was not to kill commissioners, but to protect Frank and Winema and avenge them if they were attacked. Meacham struggled with his fears to the final moment, and he was the last man to dismount. He did not tie his horse but left the reins on the ground, hoping the horse would escape if there were trouble. Meacham felt high tension in the air, all eyes darting nervously and watching for trouble.

General Canby, a tall man, sat down on a rock facing Captain Jack and passed out cigars, which were lit with coals from the fire. Reverend Thomas did not smoke. Meacham sat down beside Canby, facing Schonchin John. He said the Modocs' welcome seemed "suspiciously cordial." It was now late morning, and the sun was high in the clear sky. Meacham started with a long statement of the good will of the white men and all they hoped to do for the Indians. He tried to be intentionally nonchalant, but the Modocs said later he was speaking very loudly, perhaps from nerves. In his lecturing mode, Meacham said, "Let us talk like men, and not talk like children." Schonchin John "told him to shush in Indian," but Captain Jack said to let him talk.[14] Meacham reminded the Modocs the meeting was at their request, and he hoped to hear new proposals for a settlement from them. Talking was slow because Winema's husband first translated the English to the Chinook trade dialect, then Winema translated the Chinook into Modoc.

Captain Jack was invited to reply first, but the meeting was interrupted when Hooker Jim strode boldly over to Meacham's horse and took Meacham's coat down from the saddle. It was a charade, intended to disrupt the meeting, and everything stopped. Hooker Jim slowly donned the coat and strutted around, calling out, "Bogus, you think me look like Old Man Meacham? Me Old Man Meacham now." Meacham cheerfully offered to let Hooker Jim take his hat, too. "Don't worry old man," Hooker Jim said. "I will by and by." Meacham claims he understood Hooker Jim's action as a chilling sign that murder was ahead.[15]

Canby talked next. He told the Modocs that the president of the United States had sent him to protect the Indians, and they could not be moved without the president's consent. He related his dealings with other tribes, who, he said, respected him greatly. He even claimed that one tribe made him a chief and gave him an Indian name. A time would come, Canby explained, when the Modocs would give similar respect. He invited Reverend Thomas to speak, but Captain Jack caused a delay when he jumped suddenly to his feet and announced in a loud voice that he had to obey a call to nature.[16]

When Captain Jack returned, Reverend Thomas spoke. He dropped to his knees, delivering a kind of sermon. He said God was in the heart of President Grant, and the president sent them to make peace. The white men came with good hearts, he said, and God would hold them responsible for everything they did. Captain Jack spoke next. He sat with his hands on his knees, staring at Meacham. His mood was agitated, perhaps because he was surrounded by his Modoc political foes, watching his every move. Captain Jack began with his standard demand that the soldiers leave and give them back their land. Schonchin John stood and interrupted, demanding loudly that the Modocs be allowed to live at Hot Creek. "Take away your soldiers and give us Hot Creek, or quit talking. I am tired of talking. I talk no more."[17]

As the Riddles began to translate the speech, Captain Jack, now standing, gave a signal and the Modocs together made a war whoop. Drawing a revolver from his coat, Captain Jack shouted, "Ot-we-kau-tux!" ("All ready!").[18] He cocked his revolver, aimed at Canby from about four feet, away, and pulled the trigger. The gun failed to fire, but Canby was momentarily transfixed. The cap, the tiny copper cylinder of gunpowder used to ignite the main charge, had not exploded.

In the second or two that followed, Canby—rather than run or protect himself when Captain Jack's gun misfired—inexplicably stared at the Modoc long enough for Captain Jack to cock the gun again. The second shot struck Canby in the left eye, a fatal wound. But it did not kill the fifty-five-year-old general immediately, and he staggered away into the low sagebrush. Captain Jack and Ellen's Man George pursued Canby, and when he stumbled and fell, Ellen's Man George cut Canby's throat and fired a second bullet into Canby's head. Together, they stripped his clothing and left his naked corpse lying face up, a few yards from the peace tent. Ellen's Man George took his gold watch.[19]

Boston Charley, who had earlier shared breakfast with Reverend Thomas, used the rifle he carried to the peace conference to shoot Thomas in the chest. Thomas pleaded with Boston not to shoot again, crying out that his wound was fatal. Thomas ran, but Bogus Charley and Boston Charley followed and tripped Thomas, ridiculing his religion. "Why don't you turn the bullets?" they shouted. "Your medicine is not strong!" The youth Slolux brought Bogus Charley a rifle, and Bogus shot Thomas, this time in the head. All three Modocs went to work stripping Thomas's clothing from his body.

The Modocs had previously agreed Schonchin John would kill Meacham. Schonchin John, standing nearly beside him, drew a pistol and a knife. Meacham attempted to defend himself with his secret derringer but could not make it fire (it was not cocked properly). Schonchin John fired at point-blank range, sending a bullet through Meacham's collar and coat, so close that the powder scorched the white man's beard. There was now general firing by the Modocs. Meacham fled into the sagebrush but was knocked unconscious by the next shot. Its source was unclear—perhaps from Schonchin John or Shacknasty Jim. Meacham fell on the rocks, stunned. The bullet, probably ricocheting from a rock, struck him a glancing blow between the eyes, passed on over his left eyebrow, and knocked him out. Meacham was also shot in the shoulder and wrist, and a part of his right ear was shot off. Winema rushed to protect him, but Shacknasty Jim swung a rifle and knocked her down.

Meacham was unconscious for some time. Slolux approached and offered to dispatch him, but Shacknasty said it was not necessary; he didn't want to bloody or damage the clothes. Boston Charley commenced to scalp him. Meacham, who was nearly bald, had only a fringe of hair. He later quoted Hooker Jim, saying, "He had no scalp, or I would have had it myself." But Boston Charley, holding Meacham's scant hair, cut a curving gash on the left side of his head with a clasp knife, trying to remove the lock of hair and the ear.[20] (Unconscious, it is not clear how Meacham was later able to give direct quotes from Hooker Jim, Boston Charley, and Shacknasty Jim.)

Dyar, who had been so afraid to attend the meeting, had sensed trouble from the start and had moved to a safer place, standing behind his horse, ready to run. At the first shot, he fled west on foot toward the army camp as fast as he could, abandoning his horse. Frank Riddle also ran, and just behind him, Hooker Jim was in hot pursuit. Dyar probably saved his life by stopping to draw the secret derringer from his boot. He pointed it at Hooker Jim, who stopped and then ran the other way. Black Jim gave up his pursuit of Frank Riddle and returned to help the others strip Meacham. Both Riddle and Dyar escaped unscathed, although Dyar lost his horse.[21]

The frenzied attack stopped suddenly when Winema cried out in Modoc, "Shŭ'ldhăsh gépka!" "The soldiers are coming!"[22] There were no soldiers, but Captain Jack ordered an immediate retreat to the lava rocks. The war party was now transcendent; Captain Jack had kept his place as chief, but he had doomed himself to the noose.

Unknown to the Modocs and whites at the peace tent, another fateful murder was unfolding. The sentries at Mason's Camp, three miles to the east, were surprised to see Modocs approaching, indicating they wanted to talk. The outpost had seen little Modoc activity, and the officer of the day was summoned. Three Modocs (probably Curley Haired Jack, Miller's Charley, and Rock Dave) came forward slowly. The officer of the day, Lieutenant William Sherwood, enlisted Lieutenant W. H. Boyle, an officer who could speak Chinook, to accompany him, and they went forward to investigate. They were under standing orders to say that Major Mason would parley at the sentry post if Modocs approached.

Curley Haired Jack lured Boyle and Sherwood beyond their sentry post by claiming he could not hear them. The officers were unarmed and well beyond the camp's safe perimeter and the protection of the sentries' rifles. The Modocs chattered aimlessly, and sensing trouble, the officers decided to return. Immediately, one of the Modocs seized a rifle from the grass and fired at Boyle and Sherwood. The officers ran, separating to help their chances of survival, but Sherwood was hit by rifle fire before he could travel thirty yards. Mortally wounded, he lived for three days.

The attack on Boyle and Sherwood slightly preceded the attack on Canby, and was actually the army's first sign of trouble. Flaggers sent a hasty message from Mason's camp to the signal officer, Lieutenant John Quincy Adams, who was watching from the bluff at the army base, alerting him to the shooting. As Adams started to scribble a note to General Gillem, lying sick in his tent in the camp below, the shooting began at the council tent. Adams rushed down the slope, shouting the news that the commissioners and Canby were under fire.

Chaos ensued. Although army discipline required that men not advance without orders, some sprinted toward the peace tent, but they were called back. Sergeant Maurice Fitzgerald later reported his frustration: "Puffs of smoke arose from the tent, followed by the rapid report of several shots. . . . Each man grabbed his gun and ran at top speed toward the council tent; but before we had gone many steps, the command 'fall in' rang out clear and strong, and the military instinct of obedience prevailed."[23] Bugles sounded the call for assembly. The troops quickly lined up in formation, but stood at attention for several minutes. Gillem wasted precious time, stopping to write a note to warn Canby.[24] Another signal officer, Major Biddle, shouted, "I saw Canby fall!" Finally stirred to act, Gillem ordered the assembled troops to advance at double time in a skirmish line. Soldiers met the nearly hysterical Leroy Dyar running in the opposite direction, shouting, "They are all killed but me!"[25] Frank Riddle, just behind him, told a reporter, "Oh the Devils! It has turned out just as I thought it would and now I guess they will believe [us] when we say there is danger."[26]

The reporters moved quickly. The *New York Herald's* Fox was sulking in his tent, having been denied permission to attend the talks. When he heard the alarm, he put on his boots and strapped on his revolver.[27] Quickest to move, however, was reporter Atwell ("Bill Dadd the Scribe"), who dashed out with the first rescue party. The scene at the peace tent was appalling. Atwell described the bloodied and half-scalped Meacham as a "terrible looking object." He had been stripped of everything except his red-flannel drawers, so drenched with blood as to be unrecognizable. A trooper mistook Meacham for a Modoc and had to be restrained from shooting him. Meacham later reported he was convinced his wounds were mortal, but Dr. Thomas Cabaniss felt the bullet wounds with his finger and said Meacham would probably survive. He knelt beside Meacham and tried to administer brandy, but Meacham, now fully awake, said, "Good God, I am a temperance man!" Cabaniss retorted, "Stop your nonsense! There is no time for temperance talk now! Down with it!"[28] The enterprising Atwell managed to get "a few words" from Meacham before he was carried off on a stretcher. Meacham was transported north across Tule Lake in one of the army's newly acquired boats, accompanied by Cabaniss.[29]

Clouds appeared, and a light snow began to fall. Canby's aide-de-camp, Lieutenant Scott, who served Canby throughout the Civil War, was so distraught when he saw the general's naked body that he threw himself across the corpse and sobbed. Reporter Atwell pulled him back and covered Canby with his coat. Later, Atwell cut a piece of canvas from the tent to cover the body.[30] A surviving photograph, taken by Eadweard Muybridge, shows the little peaked tent standing alone on the rocky plateau, a wide swath of material cut from its front flap, a forlorn and haunting image of the war.

Reporters dashed off stories and bargained with couriers to deliver their dispatches to the telegraph in Yreka eighty miles away. Atwell offered a fifty-dollar bonus if his story was first; another reporter offered one hundred dollars. The horses dashed up the bluff on the steep trail with their scribbled dispatches. Fox's bulletin anticipated

The Peace Tent. "The little peaked tent stood alone on the rocky plateau, a swath of material cut from its front flap." *Courtesy author's collection.*

the public outrage after the fruitless months of talking peace with the Modocs: "Peace Policy and the Indian Bureau have accomplished the bitter end, and offered as martyrs to the cause the lives of Brigadier General E. R. S. Canby, commanding the Department of the Columbia, and the Reverend Mr. Thomas."[31]

The next day lurid headlines announced the tragedy. "MASSACRE: Bloody Treachery of the Lava Beds Indians!" screamed one paper. "The Red Judas," read another. "The Red Devils!" "MODOC Treachery and Massacre!" "Modoc Plot Revealed!"[32] The *San Francisco Chronicle*—which immediately put out an extra edition—reported that when readers saw the "startling news," "People seemed to discredit their own eyes and acted as though dumb-founded."[33] The correspondents finally had a war to cover.

27

Outrage!

The killing of Canby outraged the white community. General Sherman wasted no time in advising General Gillem, "Your dispatch announcing the terrible loss to the country of General Canby by the perfidy of the Modoc band of Indians has been shown to the president, who authorizes me to instruct you to make the attack so strong and persistent that their fate may be commensurate with the crime. You will be fully justified in their utter extermination."[1] He advised the Secretary of War that the Modoc leaders should be shot and the remainder of the tribe sent to distant locations so "the tribe of Modocs would disappear."[2] General Wheaton wrote to Oliver Applegate: "[The Modocs'] utter extermination is a necessity."[3]

At the army camp on Easter morning, there was a funeral for Canby and Thomas. Coffins had been improvised from wooden ammunition boxes. Six officers of Canby's staff were pallbearers, and there were gun salutes and muffled drums. In the afternoon a detail of soldiers carried the coffins on their shoulders up the steep mule trail to the top of the bluff, where they were loaded on a wagon for Yreka. Two days later, Canby and Thomas lay in state in Yreka's Masonic Hall, where over a thousand people, "nearly the whole population," visited their remains. Public schools were closed, and three hundred students marched past the caskets.[4]

Canby's body was sent north to Portland by stagecoach and train. The army directed that "every honor consistent with law and usage" be paid to his remains.[5] The body was "placed in a large zinc coffin . . . and securely packed in ice to slow the process of decomposition." His remains were found in "a remarkably good state of preservation" when he was transferred to a large metal casket in Portland.[6] There was an outpouring of grief across the nation. The army declared, "The record of his fame is resplendent with noble deeds well done."[7]

Sixteen honorary pallbearers were chosen for a service in Portland, including the state's most eminent figures from Governor Grover and Chief Justice Matthew Deady to the railroad baron Ben Holladay.[8] Mrs. Louisa Canby asked that there be no excessive demonstration or military display, but nevertheless a group of citizens formed a special committee to receive the remains in Portland, flags flew at half mast, the general's remains lay in state there, and the City Council passed a resolution declaring Canby "a brave and true soldier."[9]

Canby's coffin was shipped south to San Francisco. There the body lay in state in a room draped in mourning.[10] At least a thousand troops and various dignitaries, including the governor of California, escorted the cortege through the city. The sidewalks were lined with a "dense mass of people" watching the procession, said to be "one of the finest and most impressive that ever marched through the streets of San Francisco." The coffin was brought to the Oakland wharf where it was loaded onto a special train for its journey to Canby's final resting place in the east.[11] Sheet music for the newly composed "General Canby Funeral March" along with a "beautiful picture of the brave General" promptly went on sale in San Francisco.[12]

Within the Stronghold, the Modocs rejoiced, dancing for three days and three nights, with roaring fires and chanting. They quarreled over the division of clothing stripped from the victims. Captain Jack got Canby's uniform, which he reportedly wore in a later battle. Ellen's Man George kept Canby's watch; Boston Charley and Bogus Charley shared Thomas's clothes; and the others divided Meacham's clothing. Hooker Jim was denied a share of the loot because Indian Agent Dyar, his assigned victim, got away alive. In keeping with their belief that the army would disband if the chief were killed, the Modoc war party was convinced the killing of General Canby would force the army to withdraw. When the army did not mount an immediate counterattack, it was taken as a sign that the strong medicine of the shaman Curley-Headed Doctor was protecting them.[13]

The immediate fear across the Northwest was that other tribes would be emboldened to join in a widespread Indian revolt. Rumors flared. The *San Francisco Chronicle* headlined "Fear of a General Uprising of all the Indians of Frontier Oregon and Northern California."[14] Another newspaper reported Modoc runners had visited all the tribes in northern California and southern Oregon.[15] Yakama Indians three hundred miles north were said to be "arrayed in war paint."[16] "Indian trouble" was expected at Fort Hall, Idaho, where the Indians were "well posted on Captain Jack's movements" and were supplying him with blankets.[17] There was fear that the Paiutes would join the Modocs, and the prominent Paiute woman Sarah Winnemucca confirmed that "quite a number" of her relatives had gone to Oregon to the Modocs.[18] The army was concerned about "well-authenticated information" of disturbances among the Quinaults, "hostile demonstrations" among the Yakamas, and "unease and excitement" among the Indians north of Vancouver.[19]

The commanding officer warned that the army could not defend Fort Klamath against a Modoc seige.[20] The Applegates feared an attack at Yainax. Ivan advised "great *caution.*" He warned his brother that news came from the Lava Beds daily, the Modocs were still in the rocks, and he should be "terable [sic] careful."[21]

The Modocs on the Klamath reservation living in the village of Yainax feared Captain Jack's men would return to attack them. Oliver had stockpiled weapons and ammunition, and he now fortified his cabin and kept sentries on duty. Meacham, despite his numerous wounds, was pronounced out of danger, and he went to recuperate at the farm of his sister on Upper Klamath Lake. A medical bulletin reported the wound on his head from the attempted scalping was only six inches long. Meacham's most serious injuries were a bullet wound to his right forearm and a fractured finger.[22] Within ten days Meacham sent off memos to officials in Salem and Washington with his recollection of the killings at the peace tent, and he suggested further peace talks would be hopeless. "We believe complete subjugation by the military is the only method to deal with [the Modocs]."[23]

President Grant's Peace Policy was the immediate casualty of the events in northern California. Interior Secretary Delano was hanged in effigy in Yreka, and papers across the country relentlessly attacked Grant's policy of compassion toward Native peoples. The *Daily Rocky Mountain Gazette,* believing Meacham had died, wrote: "Indians have been swindled and otherwise under the cloak of this peace policy, and its authors are responsible for the lives of Canby, Meacham, Thomas, and hundreds of others."[24]

Secretary Delano wrote a long apologia in the *New York Times* explaining that Grant's policy was to mix education, religious instruction, and material support for Indians, together with strong efforts to get them on reservations as soon as possible.[25] Vice President Wilson told a reporter the administration would not abandon the Peace Policy, although the Modocs should be hastily exterminated at any cost.[26] The *Daily Rocky Mountain Gazette* raised the issue of the cost of the war: "It is computed that each of these Modocs—dead or alive at the end of the war—will have cost the government about seventy-three thousand dollars."[27]

As people throughout the nation tried to make sense of the carnage, the Modocs still had their defenders. In the *New York Times* an unnamed "occasional correspondent" attributed the war to the Ben Wright Massacre of Modocs in 1852, and the "despotic arrogance of Indian agents." The writer admired their resistance: "Captain Jack and his savages show, in my opinion, excellent judgment in their determination to die in one act, like Samson, instead of ekeing [*sic*] out the miserable existence that some agents have forced them to endure."[28]

There were also voices from California urging the government to go slowly in avenging the deaths. J. K. Luttrell, a congressman from Siskiyou County in northern California, visited the Lava Beds and concluded the Indian Service was to blame: "I believe there never was a time since the organization of the government, that there was as much corruption and swindling—not only of the government, and people, but the Indians as is today being practiced on Indian Reservations on this Coast." Luttrell opined that no Indians should be executed until the roles of settlers and federal officials were established.[29] An undated clipping from a Philadelphia newspaper, probably published in April, said, "It is folly and madness to [demand] rigid accountability for their misconduct, and then to neglect to punish our own citizens for the same crimes."[30] The *New York Times* printed a letter asking, "Mr. Editor, we may as well honestly admit it, that our whole conduct toward the Indians has been most infamous, and if they occasionally retaliate, is it to be wondered at?"[31]

General Sherman's call for extermination of the Modocs drew swift condemnation from religious and pacifist groups in the Northeast. In June, public meetings to discuss the Modoc situation were convened at Cooper's Union in New York. Lucretia Mott and members of the Universal Peace Union urged President Grant to continue "any and all peace measures" and not to execute the Modocs. They pointed out that the white men had repeatedly broken promises to the Modocs and had treacherously murdered the father of Captain Jack. The killing of Canby and Thomas—in the eyes of the Modocs—was just retribution. "There was no alternative for them to kill or be killed." They urged the issues with the Modocs be resolved through peace.[32]

In the West, however, a consensus emerged that negotiating with Indians had become pointless. Although there were quite credible charges that some Klamath Indians had secretly assisted the Modocs, the Klamaths demanded compensation for helping the army and staying peacefully on their reservation. Klamath chief Allen David claimed he had prevented meddling by other tribes and kept troublemakers "under surveillance." David said his work attending to tribal matters had kept him from his farming, and as *de facto* justice of the peace on the reservation, he should be paid three hundred dollars annually. (The chief had consulted chiefs of other tribes regarding the amount they had received for aiding the army.) The commanding officer at Fort Klamath, Captain Rob Pollock, recommended Chief David be paid to keep peace on the reservation.[33]

Photo by Bill Stafford.

Part Three
A Shooting Star

After death the soul travels the path traveled by the sun, which is the westward path. There it joins in the spirit-land (ĕ' ni) the innumerable souls which have gone the same way before. If the deceased was a chief, his "heart" can be seen going west in the form of a shooting star.

—Gatschet, *Klamath Indians*

Lava Beds Army Camp, an image from *Illustrated London News* (May 21, 1873).
Courtesy author's collection.

28

Second Attack on the Stronghold

Never before had any Indians killed a regularly commissioned general of the U.S. Army, and the troops massed at the Lava Beds knew the long-awaited attack on the Stronghold would soon begin. "Some of us will meet our deaths tomorrow, [hope] it will not be me," wrote artilleryman Gilbert Davis.[1] If troops blamed Canby for months of pointless talking and agonized waiting in punishing weather, they wanted even more to avenge his brutal murder by the Modocs. General Gillem assumed command when Canby was killed. Gillem never moved quickly, and now, physically sick and demoralized, he dallied. After the assassinations, Gillem had called back the troops who had gone in hot pursuit of the fleeing Modocs and kept them waiting in camp for two days.[2] Some of the troops were furious, but Sergeant Maurice Fitzgerald agreed with Gillem's judgment: "Had we advanced into the Lava Beds, there would have been few, if any, to tell the tale of the disastrous adventure."[3]

Gillem, who had never been inside the Modocs' fortifications, angered his officers by boasting that "a half dozen men could take the Stronghold," and he ridiculed their caution.[4] Newspaperman S. A. Clarke wrote: "The most of them who served under him had lost all confidence in his ability to compete with Captain Jack's strategy." The common soldiers were "terribly demoralized." Gillem began positioning his forces for a three-pronged assault, virtually the same battle plan developed by General Wheaton in January. An impressive force of about 675 troops assembled, nearly three times what Wheaton had commanded.[5] Wheaton had predicted a thousand men would be required to take the Stronghold. After subtracting for troops who were sick or did not fight, such as cooks and blacksmiths, Gillem had easily ten times more troops than the Modocs had warriors.

Gillem's two large, roughly equal squadrons were camped on the east and west of Captain Jack's Stronghold. Much-decorated Civil War veteran Major Edwin Mason of the Twenty-first Infantry led the east-ern force of about 300 men: two cavalry troops and three companies of infantry. Major Green was in command on the west side of the Lava Beds. Green's force was slightly larger than Mason's—about 375 men, consisting of three cavalry troops, four artillery batteries, and two com-panies of infantry.

Gillem knew Wheaton's January 17 assault had failed because his troops had been forced to advance in a heavy fog, making them prey for Modoc snipers, and because Wheaton had greatly underestimated the impregnability of the Modocs' citadel of twisted rock. But Gillem had a much larger force, better weather, and better knowledge of the terrain. Where Wheaton had been unable to safely aim the howitzers in the fog without danger of hitting his own troops, Gillem now had both artillery and mortar batteries, as well as abundant ammunition. Perhaps most importantly, Gillem was prepared to fight for longer than one day. He did not intend to overrun the rocky positions all at once; he planned to encircle the Indians and force surrender through attrition.

Gillem planned to harass the Modocs with the newly arrived Coe-horn mortars, then march on their position from the south, east, and west. Reversing his previous decision, he ordered boats built to shuttle troops between the camps on Tule Lake and to move heavy howitzers and mortars into position. Gillem's mortars were crude but effective weapons.[6] Gillem said their light weight and mobility—two or three men can carry one—made them perfect for his needs. "The hiding places of the Indians can be reached, and in addition to the *physical*, they exercise a considerable *moral* effect."[7]

Gillem's confidence that the Coehorns would terrify the Indi-ans proved well-founded. He had requested four mortars and three hundred shells, but Canby had decided two mortars and seventy-five rounds were plenty. Thinking hand grenades would be equally effective, Canby had requested a supply. Five hundred grenades were found and shipped north, but they didn't arrive in time to be used.

The army was uncertain about how many Modocs now faced them. Gillem thought they numbered between 55 and 75 warriors.[8] During one of his trips into the Lava Beds, Judge Elijah Steele counted sixty-nine, twenty of them "strangers" or warriors from other tribes.

Some were wearing moustaches, and Steele though they belonged to the Snake band.[9] But if reinforcements arrived from other tribes, they did not fight in the next battle.

The Modocs had substantially increased their firepower. They would not again have the advantage conferred by fighting in the fog, but the guns they collected from dead soldiers after the January 17 fight gave them weapons that matched the army's in quality and number. Jeff Riddle wrote that the Modoc braves were "overjoyed" when they found Spencer sporting rifles, old patent Henry rifles, Remington rifles, Ballard rifles, and ammunition "scattered all over the ground."[10] The Modoc warriors were now able to replace most of their guns, including antiquated muzzle-loading muskets, with modern weapons of various types. Many of those captured on the battlefield, being Army-issue, may have been Springfields—a weapon known for its power and accuracy, the powerful breech-loading Sharps carbine, and at least four Spencer repeating carbines.[11]

General Canby had ordered a party of Indian scouts recruited from the Warm Springs reservation in northern Oregon. A few hours after Canby's coffin disappeared over the bluff on its way to Yreka, the seventy mercenaries arrived. The Warm Springs scouts were led by a colorful and rather disreputable character named Donald McKay. The Warm Springs didn't much like him, believing he had swindled them out of pay during a campaign against the Snake Indians, and they said they wouldn't serve under McKay. Canby told them they would have to accept McKay or he would hire other Indians, so they signed up.[12]

Gillem announced the major assault on the Stronghold would begin on Tuesday, April 15, 1873, four days after Canby's assassination. At 2 A.M. that morning, he ordered a force of about 300 dismounted cavalry to move silently out to Hovey Point, a small peninsula that juts into Tule Lake north of the Lava Beds. Silently, the troops moved into position to stand by and ambush any Modocs who tried to move north toward the main column of troops. "There was no moonlight," Sergeant Fitzgerald wrote, "but a star-bespangled sky afforded us enough light to enable us to pick our footsteps over the jagged rocks."[13] Suddenly the silence was broken when a soldier accidently fired his weapon, and a Modoc picket cried out an alarm, "wow-ow-ow!"[14]

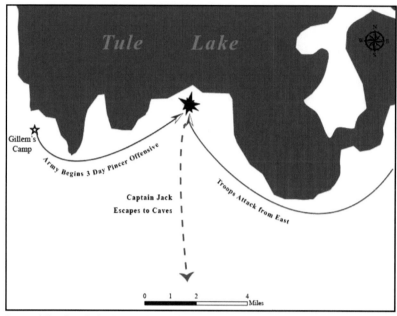

Second Battle of the Stronghold, April 1873

As morning broke, buglers wakened the remaining forces at the western camp before dawn; and after a hurried breakfast, they mustered before their officers. A company of artillerymen acting as foot soldiers was first to march out at 8 A.M. About a mile from camp, they were deployed as skirmishers—an irregular line advancing with soldiers spaced a few yards apart.

Inside the Lava Beds the Modocs readied for battle. They stripped their clothes and painted their faces. They faced a daunting challenge—defending a perimeter several miles long against a force ten times their number. But Captain Jack's strategy was to move the warriors constantly and fire from different points, disguising their positions to make their force seem larger than it was. The Modocs began the battle by peppering the advancing troops with sporadic fire all morning, greatly slowing the army's advance. At 1:30 P.M. Green's forces began a major charge from the west, driving the Modocs back several hundred yards toward their central fortifications. Correspondent Edward Fox witnessed the attack, calling it "one of the most dashing charges of the day." He saw an infantry corporal shot dead during the charge.[15]

At first, the Modocs were able to repel the attack with sniper fire; but by late afternoon, troops were compressing the Modoc warriors into the heart of the Stronghold. As his force advanced from the west, Green was able to bring up howitzers and mortars within range of the Stronghold. The mortars, which had arrived disassembled on a string of mules, were put together at the rear of the army's lines. The first mortar round was a misfire that nearly decimated the army's own ranks. The squat brass gun was loaded, aimed, and "touched off," but Fitzgerald said its shell fell in the midst of Troop K of the First Cavalry "about 15 feet in front of our line, and spun around, hissing and sputtering like a thing of life . . . [Some] seemed too dazed to move, and looked upon the antics of the shell as if they were charmed by it. An officer, who took in the situation and imminent danger to which the men were exposed, shouted, 'Everyone lie close to the ground!' He was instantly obeyed, and then the thing exploded, scattering fragments through the air in every direction; no one was hurt, but everyone was badly scared."[16]

Civil War veteran William Murray, the infantryman who had earlier lamented the boredom of Indian war, said he was reinvigorated by the "sharp work" of fighting the Modocs. Murray was exhilarated by "the whiz of bullets" and "lead spattering on rock just inches from my head." His diary captures the frenzied fighting during the siege of the Modoc positions, and he admires the skill of the Modoc fighters: " I began to have an inclination for a smoke, and taking my pipe from my pocket as I lay partly on my side, I struck a light, and the next instant a bullet entered the ground, not more than a foot from my body."[17]

The Modoc fire spared no one. Murray said that as bullets spattered on the rocks, Company G of the Twelfth Infantry was ordered to charge. Led by Lieutenant Charles Patrick Egan, soldiers ran pell-mell, firing back at the "small puffs of smoke that curled up over the black forbidden cliffs ahead." The infantry company arrived at the base of the Stronghold, yelling and firing. Lieutenant Egan fell with a painful flesh wound to his thigh, and "Sergeant [Herman] Gude fell desperately wounded, a ball having shattered the bone of his right leg."[18] Hours later, Egan and Gude were evacuated. Egan's wound was serious, but he returned to service a week later. Gude's leg, the tibia shattered, was amputated, encased in a small wooden box, and buried in "Gillem's

Graveyard" at the foot of the bluff. At day's end, five army men had been killed and ten wounded, fewer casualties than in the previous assault on the Stronghold. After the war, the army dead were relocated to military cemeteries, but Sergeant Gude's leg was never found.

Gillem's Graveyard. *Photo by Bill Stafford*

As darkness fell, Major Green held his forces in place, but Modoc fire did not cease and the army continued to take casualties. Gillem's grand plan unraveled in part when Major Mason, commander on the east, disobeyed orders. Although Mason had specific instructions to send the Warm Springs scouts south to meet forces advancing from the west, he did not dispatch them. Instead, he used artillery to shell the Modoc positions, but from too great a range to inflict damage. Mason's failure to follow orders left an unsecured narrow route out of the Lava Beds, allowing the Modocs to escape the army's pincer move.

When Gillem learned his orders had been disobeyed, he was enraged. He ordered the officers to rush south and cut off the escape route, but they too ignored his command and joined forces north of the Lava Beds. The Modocs were now cut off from their water source at Tule Lake, but Mason's error allowed an escape route.

A curious civilian who blundered onto the battlefield narrowly escaped death. The sutler Pat McManus, "filled to the brim with his own bad whiskey and the Dutch courage," rode his mule out to the front to see some fighting. He unwittingly placed himself in the gun sights of Steamboat Frank, who shot the mule out from under him. The unfortunate sightseer sheltered behind a rock, but Steamboat Frank sniped at him until sundown when McManus finally "crawled on his hands and knees in hot haste to the rear." McManus was infuriated when sentries challenged him, and he called out, "Don't you know a white man on his knees from an Indian on his belly?"[19]

Mortars boomed every fifteen minutes through the night, "the blazing fuze describing a curve of fire." Civil War veteran Murray said they were hailed with a cheer: "It was the only touch of real war we had seen or heard for years, and I for one, felt my heart rebound at each report, the peculiar noise of a Shell passing through the air, and the Stunning explosion that follows, which was a relief to a war-worn veteran in these dreary lava beds."[20]

Late in the evening the Modocs began to holler and banter from the rocks. Army and Modoc lines were so close that both sides shouted insults "in plain, but not classical English" as they fired during the night.[21] One Modoc was infuriated at a mortar round that came close, and he rose to fling oaths at the army. "Although they were few, it would be hard to excel them in vulgarity and profanity," wrote correspondent Fox.[22] Another Modoc said, "How long you soldiers stay here? Why you no go home, get something to eat?"[23]

Throughout the next day the forces commanded by Green and Mason—now merged on the north—moved south toward the Modoc Stronghold. As the troops advanced, they occupied the small, fortified positions recently abandoned by the Modocs. There was a deadly surprise: "Behind a barrier which three or four of us reached at the same moment, a Modoc had the termerity [sic] to remain until one of our party [Private Charles Johnson] looked over it and received a bullet through the head, killing him instantly."[24] The army attracted less Modoc fire as they advanced. When darkness fell on the second day, the soldiers believed they were close to overrunning the Stronghold itself. The Modocs, with two forces advancing from the north, could no longer reach Tule Lake and they were desperate for water. Their attempts to break through to the lake during the night were repulsed. Jesse Applegate, who had arrived on the scene by boat, saw one shell "fall directly into a big crevice where the Modoc camps were." The mortars continued to lob shells into the Stronghold in the darkness.[25]

A few Modocs led by Hooker Jim sought to outflank the army by sneaking back toward Gillem's Camp two miles west and attacking there. It caused mild panic, as the camp had few fighting men available. "[We] broke open boxes of Ammunition and Arms," wrote Corporal Pentz in his diary, "and made all the Camp Followers, sutlers, teamsters, and also the sick and wounded that were able, take a gun and throw themselves out as Pickets, to keep the Enemy from firing into camp."[26] Hooker Jim gave up the attack, but the army found later that his raiding party had come across a young civilian packer named Eugene Hovey with his mule. Hovey had been killed cruelly: the Indians had "flattened the packer's head between two rocks to almost the thickness of a hand."[27]

By the morning of the third day, the Modocs were gone from the Stronghold. For 149 days they had sheltered in one of the most inhospitable places in North America, enduring a harsh winter and extreme hunger. Now, with the U.S. Army at their threshold, Modoc families gathered their children and what possessions they could and left in the darkness, retreating down a twisted lava corridor leading to the south. Their pathway is today called Schonchin Flow. Probably numbering about 135 men, women, and children, the Modocs walked deep into the Lava Beds. A few Modoc snipers stayed behind to give the impression the camp was still occupied. A campfire was seen later far to the south, "and it was correctly conjectured that Captain Jack was there."[28] The soldiers thought they were burning their dead.

But the war was far from over. The fight now moved across the desolate countryside in a ferocious guerrilla war. On the morning of April 17, 1873, Green and Mason slowly advanced their combined forces, their line now three miles long, encircling much of the Stronghold. There was occasional sniper fire, and it soon became evident the Modocs had fled. By afternoon, soldiers stood on the rocks of the Stronghold, "men cheering and tossing their hats in the air and howling their delight."[29] Wild misinformation began to spread. It was reported that the body of Scarface Charley had been found and scalped, and the scalp cut in pieces and distributed among the Warm Springs scouts.[30] But Scarface Charley was very much alive, joining the Modoc retreat to the south. Within a few days he would lead the devastating ambush of an army patrol.

Soldiers occupying the Modoc Stronghold, from *Harper's Weekly* (June 14, 1873). *Courtesy author's collection.*

Soldiers were shocked at what they found in the Modoc fastness. William Murray's party arrived just before sunset and was astonished at "the horrid den": "Black rugged cliffs, holes and Crevices reeking with human filth, and swarming with disgusting vermin; the putrid carcasses of beeves and horses, old decaying and decayed bones of every Kind of animal Known in the surrounding country; pieces of old, tattered blankets, worn out army coats, blouses, caps and uniform hats of the existing pattern, with their brass ornaments Stuck all around them in the most fantastical array possible; besides fragments of old Indian matting, and broken vessels were seen on every hand; the whole constituting and emitting the most foul, deadly and unnatural Stench I ever experienced."[31]

An elderly woman had been found left behind, cowering in a cave, too frail to join the others in their hurried flight. She begged them not to hurt her. The cavalryman Sergeant Fitzgerald described her as eighty or ninety years old: "Her gray hair was hanging in disorder over her wizened and wrinkled countenance; her long and emaciated arms were bare; and her skinny hands, with fingernails like the talons of some bird of prey, rested on either knee."[32]

There are differing accounts of what happened next. Murray said she begged the soldiers for water. Just as Baldy Walsh, a soldier from G Company of the Twelfth Infantry offered her his canteen, Murray says, a Warm Springs scout appeared, gave a war whoop, shot her dead, and then scalped her.[33] Fitzgerald, however, blamed Lieutenant George R. Bacon, a West Point graduate commanding a cavalry company: "Turning his cold blue eye upon her, Lieutenant said 'Is there anyone who will put that old hag out of the way?' A Pennsylvania Dutchman stepped from the ranks . . . deliberately placed his carbine against her head, and blew out her brains." Fitzgerald said everyone present was profoundly shocked, and the thoughts of soldiers "dared not find utterance."[34]

The soldiers searched the Modoc camp for souvenirs, but there were few left behind of any value. They marveled at Captain Jack's cave, littered with fish and animal bones and bits of hide. The place was a "foul-smelling and nauseous hole."[35]

It was impossible to calculate the number of Modoc dead. One newspaper reported sixteen Modoc dead were found in the Lava Beds, their bodies "horribly mutilated by shells." The same paper announced: "The death of the chief Schonchin is fully confirmed."[36] But Lieutenant Boyle later wrote there were only three Modoc men and two women killed, and one old man taken prisoner.[37] William Simpson also counted only four bodies, and saw three prisoners.[38]

There are several reports of soldiers committing mutilations and atrocities. Modoc author Jeff Riddle said the soldiers killed four old or helpless Modocs, and "God will truly punish such heartless people."[39] Two witnesses reported soldiers kicking around decapitated Indian heads. William Murray also reported seeing desecration of Modoc bodies: "The gory heads of two Modoc braves were Kicked about like footballs by Soldiers, citizens, newspaper reporters, etc., along the main passage of the Stronghold." Surgeon Edwin Bentley collected the skulls later and sent them back to camp.[40]

The Indians had left behind some macabre trophies of their own. William Simpson found "a string of scalps, noses, and fingers," which he assumed were trophies taken by the Modocs.[41]

A cavalry lieutenant discovered the symbolic pole made by a Modoc medicine man—probably Curley-Headed Doctor—that had stood at the southwest corner of the Stronghold since the January attack. The artist for the *London Daily News* drew a sketch, describing it as "a mink's skin and hawk's feather with medicine bead, attached to a pole four feet long, standing on a heap of stones."[42] The pole was standing on a "medicine rock," which is still identifiable today on the northeastern end of the Stronghold.[43] The Modocs had left the medicine man's staff behind when they departed from the Stronghold, but—as the army would soon discover—its powerful spirits were still on the side of the Modoc warriors.

29

The Thomas-Wright Battle

Under relentless siege, the Modoc families had gathered their meager possessions and fled miles south from the Stronghold into the volcanic plateau, a hundred square miles of arid wasteland, crisscrossed with lava ridges, waterless except for the ice in a few caves. They were protected mainly by the vastness of the rocky wilderness that stretched all the way from the Stronghold to Goose Lake forty miles to the east. For millennia this had been traditional Modoc territory; they knew every secret cave and hidden route, although they seldom visited except to hunt bighorn sheep, deer, and antelope.

On April 26, 1873, General Gillem dispatched a large party of cavalry led by Captain Perry to circle the Lava Beds, taking the easiest terrain. They found no trace of Captain Jack's people. Gillem then sent out twenty-four Warm Springs scouts, who within a day found about forty of Captain Jack's people, camped twelve miles south of the army camp on the frozen river of black stone now known as Schonchin Flow. Gillem then sent another patrol, this time to find a location to position howitzers to shell Captain Jack's camp.[1] Why he was scouting artillery positions is unclear—howitzers are cumbersome to maneuver, take days to move, and would have little use against the fluid movements of the fugitive Modocs. Gillem assigned Major John Green of the First Cavalry to organize the reconnaissance, and Green assembled a squadron of sixty-five men—five officers, fifty-nine enlisted men, and an army surgeon.[2] Henry Tickner and Louis Weber, two civilians well acquainted with the area, came along as packers. They had a string of six mules, later used to carry home the dead. The large patrol marched past the last pickets of the army camp at 7 A.M.

Major Green stayed behind. The five officers chosen to lead the scouting operation were sons of three generals and two West Point graduates. Captain Evan Thomas led the patrol. Thomas, promoted in the field during the Civil War battles at Fredericksburg and Gettysburg, was the son of Lorenzo Thomas, much-decorated Union Army major.[3]

184

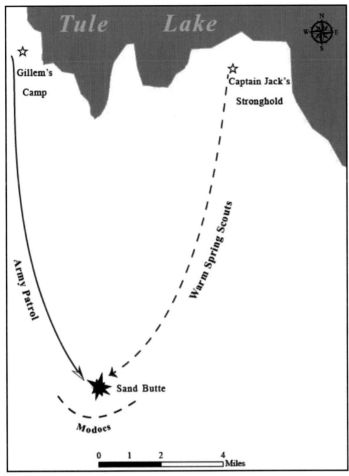

Thomas-Wright Battle, April 26, 1873.

Green also selected First Lieutenant Thomas Wright for the patrol. He was a West Pointer (who did not graduate) and the son of General George Wright, late commander of the army forces for the entire Pacific Coast. Green assigned Second Lieutenant Albion Howe, decorated at the Civil War battles at Cold Harbor and Petersburg, to command another artillery company. Green added First Lieutenant Arthur Cranston, an academy graduate, a ruggedly handsome Civil War veteran and artilleryman who brought mortar experience, and the much younger Second Lieutenant George M. Harris, an artillery officer who graduated from the military academy in 1863.[4]

Donald McKay and his Warm Springs scouts, posted at the base on the east side of the Lava Beds, were ordered to march south on a parallel course and join the army column en route. His orders were to "cooperate with Thomas' left"—that is, to move parallel to the path of the army patrol. The Warm Springs had seen nightly fires where they believed the Modocs were camped, and marched directly toward where they thought the Modocs were hiding. But McKay's scouts, not slowed by skirmishers or mule packers, moved with inexplicable slowness.

The sixty-five-man army troop soon disappeared behind the lava formations, hidden from spyglasses on the high bluff at Gillem's camp. Nevertheless, it was not considered a hazardous operation: three companies of soldiers, well armed and officered, with civilian packers carrying supplies. The ground was broken and undulating, but devoid of the treacherous chasms and contorted rock masses found in the Stronghold. When they could be seen, signalmen reported no Modocs had been found.

Lieutenant Wright order Company E to form "skirmish lines," standard practice for a column moving through dangerous territory. Skirmishers were loose rows of men advancing in a line stretching out to either side of the main troop to protect the flanks and to detect any potential ambush. The column steered itself over the terrain that was the easiest walking, rather than taking a route amid the scorched rocks that would have better protected them from attack. As the party neared a sandy hill three miles south, the footing became easier.[5]

Unknown to the soldiers, the Modocs had quietly followed them from the time the patrol departed Gillem's Camp. Twenty-four Modoc warriors moved noiselessly behind the rocks as the troops marched toward the sandy butte. Scarface Charley led them. When they realized the army patrol was headed through a depression (now called Semig Basin), the Modocs moved ahead, surrounding the soldiers' likely stopping place. They hid in the rocks and waited for the army to stop for lunch.

Mountain mahogany offered some shade in the still air. Thomas decided to wait for the Warm Springs scouts. But the site was a virtual fishbowl from which the soldiers could not flee. The Modocs, crouching in wait behind the surrounding rocks, went undetected. Thomas placed no sentries and ignored the usual practice of spreading his troops out for safety. "They were bunched together like children at a church picnic," wrote historian Keith Murray.[6] Some even had their shoes off. As the troops relaxed, Thomas, Harris, and two signalmen began to plod up the sandy hill ahead to send a semaphore message back to camp. "When the halt was called and every man had sat down," wrote reporter William Simpson, "each Indian crawled, in silence and invisibly, to a point where his rifle could be pointed at a victim, and with fatal certainty, at a given signal, fired at once."[7]

A hellish barrage of rifle fire rained down on the hapless soldiers. The first shots from the rocks directly ahead, where Captain Jack was one of those lying in wait, did little harm. But then came a fusillade from behind at fifty to sixty yard range. The troops in their cul-de-sac, surrounded by rock with no shelter but sagebrush, were at the mercy of the Modoc warriors. Perhaps a third of the patrol died in the early salvoes. Some hysterical soldiers fled rather than fight. Several were later charged with desertion and cowardice.

It was a perfect ambush. Because of the heavy fire from their rear, there was no way to retreat. Captain Thomas, who had fought at Gettysburg, did not shrink from the gunfire and tried to calm his panicked men. Modoc warriors circled to Thomas's south and southeast, moving ever closer, firing down on the army from near-perfect cover. Thomas and his officers mounted several counterattacks hoping to gain higher ground, but the Modocs in the rocks easily repulsed the men. Wright ordered four men to advance northeast to gain a ridge fifty yards away. They unwittingly ran toward another group of hidden Modocs, who attacked them as they approached. The men retreated in panic.

Officers were the first targets; Modocs always aimed to kill the chief. The Modocs who had visited camp were well acquainted with the officers and shot at them first whenever they could. In the end, every officer in the Thomas-Wright battle was killed. The desperate Thomas tried to send a message to the army camp four miles north. Lieutenant Arthur Cranston volunteered to lead a group to a point from which they could signal. Their destination was a thousand yards distant, and they had to sprint through the sagebrush, dodging Modoc fire. It was a suicide mission and the men certainly knew it. A signalman did succeed in climbing atop a red cinder boulder, where he frantically signaled a ten-word message: "We have found the Indians; they are behind the bluff."[8] But the signal ended, and all six men in Cranston's party were killed. Their bodies were not found for almost two weeks. Later, when many of the Modocs surrendered, Boston Charley was wearing Cranston's hat, "at a jaunty angle on his head."

Thomas then ordered Wright to make another charge with a larger party of infantrymen to gain a ridge on the west and outflank the Modocs. Had he succeeded, the patrol might have been saved, but many of the men panicked under fire and deserted. Thomas was left with only seven men. "The Modocs fired with greater fury." Wright was shot in the groin; knowing he would not survive, he buried his watch. "And his company, with one or two exceptions, fled him like a pack of sheep."[9] Wright died when a second bullet pierced his heart. Thomas tried to counterattack again, and led twenty-five or thirty of the remaining men from the artillery batteries (the rest had fled) on a fresh charge to the northwest. His men built low walls for protection as they moved, but the rocks were pitiful protection against the galling fire from the Modocs. Casualties mounted, but the Modocs were unharmed.

Erwin Thompson, in his detailed study of the engagement, reported that all semblance of order disintegrated. More deserters ran north toward Gillem's Camp. A small party of the remaining patrol battled together to the end, including Thomas, Harris, Howe, the doctor Bernard G. Semig, and twenty other men. But their situation was hopeless; they were fighting from a small hollow with no protection except a few rocks and sagebrush. All three of the generals' sons—Thomas, Howe, and Wright—were dead. A witness said, "Lt. Howe had his skull crushed frightfully."[10] Dozens of enlisted men fell. The whole encounter lasted only twenty minutes.

Where were the Warm Springs scouts? They had a much shorter distance to travel, over easier terrain. They claimed they had arrived within one hundred yards when the shooting began but were unable to help in the fight because the army, thinking they were Modocs, fired on them. But the scouts were wearing army uniforms and high-topped hats, and one respected local historian was convinced that they had struck a deal with the Modocs and were guilty of sabotage and treason. "Someone sold the secret of the sand butte," wrote Van Landrum.[11]

Gillem did not believe the story told by the first man who rushed back into his camp. Only later, when the mangled and bloody wounded began to arrive, did he begin to understand. A terrified bugler and an artillery sergeant staggered into camp at dusk and described the attack.[12] Lieutenant Boyle, in a later memoir, was scathing: "Gillem, as usual, lost all control of himself and would not act, nor let others."[13] When he realized that flag signals had ceased, Gillem grasped what had happened: more than half the force he had dispatched was dead or wounded. It was after dark—several hours later—when Gillem finally sent a relief party. The rescue squadron was assembled from tattered remnants of units who fought in the second assault on the Stronghold, led by Major Green. Their effort was pathetic: as darkness fell, men were afraid to advance for fear of a fresh Modoc attack, and it was thirty-two hours before rescuers returned with the first of the wounded.

Dr. Henry McElderry, the army's ranking medical officer, thought he should stay in camp with Gillem and treat the wounded as they returned, rather than hurry to the battlefield. Gillem agreed, and the three surgeons from Mason's command three miles east at the other end of the Stronghold were also held back and not dispatched. The sole doctor accompanying the patrol, Bernard G. Semig, was lying beside a corpse at the site of the ambush. He had been shot in the shoulder and ankle; his leg was later amputated at the knee. McElderry would face intense criticism for sending insufficient medical personnel. Corporal Pentz, the young signalman on the ill-fated expedition, wrote in his journal, "Col. Green gave [Dr. McElderry] a great blowing up, on account of their being no one out before to attend to the wounded."[14]

Daylight was gone. The rescue party took six hours, stumbling south in the dark, to travel the four miles to the battlefield. The weather turned windy and cold. It began to rain, the temperature plunged, and the rain turned to snow. Late in the day Gillem ordered a second party to march south under Mason's command, which was occupying Captain Jack's Stronghold three miles to the east. Mason rushed south, and his column soon converged with the other rescue party of sixty-five sent out by Gillem. They became hopelessly lost and could not find the site of the ambush. They camped in freezing cold.

When the party finally reached the site at dawn, they realized the horror of what had happened. "We came upon the most heartbreaking sight it has been my fate to behold," wrote Lieutenant Boutelle.[15] Captain Trimble said the dead seemed frozen in postures in which they died, "presenting different forms of anguish and distortion, some in position of desperate defense, others prostrate in figures of dire hopelessness, and quite a number still alive, but in the agony of painful wounds."[16] "[There] were Major Thomas, dead, Lieutenant Howe, dead, Lieutenant Harris, mortally wounded, and Acting-Assistant Surgeon Semig dangerously wounded," Boutelle wrote, "together with a number of enlisted men, all dead or wounded."[17] All had been stripped, and some scalped. Nearby was Lieutenant Wright with a few of his men. Wright "had been pierced by several balls, and he lay dead still grasping the weapon in the act of firing, with the body of a dead sergeant lying across his body."[18] Some of those still living who had abdominal wounds began to suffer peritonitis. They pleaded for water. A few Modocs were still nearby, in plain sight, but they thought better of engaging the rescue party.

Lieutenant Cranston could not be found. Although his body was nearby, it was not located until thirteen days later. He had been scalped, "hair and whiskers." When they were finally located, the bodies of the eight men with him were so decomposed that they were buried where they fell. Boutelle, who had seen many dead and wounded in the Civil War, wrote to his fiancee, "I have witnessed one of the most horrible scenes ever witnessed. [It] is enough to make our heart sick."[19]

The wounded had lain all night with no food and water, fearing that the Modocs would come back to finish them off. "It was almost impossible to find the wounded," wrote Boyle, "as they were afraid to answer when called to, thinking it was some device of the Modocs to get them out and massacre them." He continued: "Never did men suffer as did the officers and soldiers that night, hearing the wails of the dying . . . It was a picture too fearful to contemplate."[20] A few men, terribly wounded, managed to stagger home on their own feet: "One splendid specimen of physical manhood made his way to camp over that awful trail (a truly wonderful feat) with more than twenty bullet wounds in his body, and lived about thirty-six hours thereafter. It might truly be said he was 'shot to pieces.'"[21]

As stretcher-bearers began their trek north in the dark carrying the wounded, the snow turned to freezing sleet. "The night was as black as a wolf's mouth," Boutelle wrote.[22] Leaving at seven in the evening, the rescuers took twelve hours to return the four miles to camp. It was so dark that men had to hold the shoulder of the soldier ahead to avoid losing their way in the rough landscape. Trimble said they "suffered in the Inferno, substituting the misery of cold for the torture of heat." Snow collected on their heads and shoulders. Trimble related that when two pack mules began to bray and "disclosed our position to the wily Modocs," the Indians fired a volley into the column, but no one was hit.[23]

Harris, gravely wounded, finally reached camp on his stretcher. When his mother in Philadelphia was notified by telegraph that he was wounded but still alive, she rushed across the continent to be at his side. She traveled to San Francisco by rail, rode north by stagecoach to Redding, and took a wagon to Yreka. After a week of travel, a mule brought her down the bluff to the camp where her son lay in a hospital tent. "She was thus enabled to soothe his dying moments," Trimble wrote of this maternal devotion, "to be recognized by him and remain by his cot side until the last." He died just twenty-four hours after she arrived, and she accompanied his coffin back to Philadelphia.[24]

Could the carnage have been avoided? Many observers felt that the wrong officer was in charge. Boyle said that Thomas, newly arrived from the East, had never seen Indian fighting duty and should not be blamed. But his errors were fatal. "Had he sent out flankers, and made the proper disposition of troops, when he came to a halt, the surprise could not have happened . . . He should have at once charged the enemy and drove them from their position. He would have lost some men . . . [instead of] falling back to an open country and allowing the enemy to shoot down his men without retaliating."[25] Boutelle thought the same, saying that although Thomas was a distinguished veteran of the Civil War, he should never have commanded the patrol with no Indian experience. "He died," Boutelle wrote, "as did many other brave fellows, sacrificed to the blunders of [Indian Agent] Odeneal and others."[26]

An avalanche of criticism fell on General Gillem—who had authorized the reconnaissance—but Gillem refused to take any responsibility. Instead he blamed Major Green for ordering the reconnaissance and the officers in command for becoming "panic-stricken" when the Modocs attacked.[27] But Colonel Thompson thought that Gillem's insecurity was at fault. He wrote in his memoirs: "Instead of sending out competent men, these men were sent out to be slaughtered . . . Gillem was not only incompetent personally, but was jealous of every man, civilian or regular, who was competent."[28] The influential but rarely outspoken *Army and Navy Journal* rebuked Gillem: "We need a fuller explanation than is contained in the report of General Gillem . . . as to the reasons that prompted him to send Captain Thomas on so delicate a mission as that of hunting for Indians among the lava rocks, and leaving him entirely to his own resources and unsupported."[29] When he arrived on the front a few days later, General Jefferson Davis blamed the tragic outcome on the enlisted men for their "conspicuous cowardice." They were unfit for Indian fighting, he said, "being only cowardly beef eaters."[30]

But for Gillem it was a career-ending disaster. He had lost everyone's confidence, and would have to go. Five officers had perished, together with twenty enlisted men. Sixteen other enlisted men were wounded, many seriously. An early report to army headquarters said five Modoc bodies were found, but after the war the Modocs said they had lost only a single fighter. The Modocs had now been fighting the army for five months and, according to their later accounts, they had lost only two or three warriors.

Boutelle, the young cavalry officer who fought in every battle of the Modoc War, recalled in 1907: "I have always considered the disaster to Major Thomas' command as one of the saddest in our military history. It was a small affair, but so senseless and unnecessary, and such a waste of good life."[31] But for the Modocs, the ambush was part of the ongoing battle, a continuation of the army assault on the Stronghold a few days earlier. The Thomas-Wright battle has been regarded as a significant episode in the Indian wars, not just because of the tragic casualties, but also because of the brilliance of the Indian strategy. Historian Francis Paul Prucha pointed out that "Indian warfare was guerilla war—stealth, cunning, and ambush in small parties were the rule."[32] To the Modocs, the battle was not "senseless and unnecessary," but a brilliant victory in the war the army had started months earlier at the sleeping Modoc village at Lost River.[33]

30

The Battle of Sorass Lake

The Modocs had not yet lost a fight, and the Thomas-Wright battle was the army's greatest humiliation yet. By May 1873 the Modocs were no longer just a group of warriors but a collection of families— about 165 men, women, and children—fleeing into the lava wilderness. Walking south from Tule Lake, the Modocs left their water supply, and the parched stone plateau did not offer a drop. All they found was some ice accumulated in the lava caves. Over eons, seepage and condensation had left floors of ice that looked like tiny skating rinks. By chipping at the ice with an ax, the Modocs collected enough to melt for drinking water. They camped for a few days beside one ice cave, then moved on to another called Frozen River Cave, and from there to Caldwell's Ice Cave. Ice that had taken millennia to accumulate was soon gone and thirst ended their sojourn in the badlands directly south of the Lava Beds.

When Canby was slain, an outraged General Sherman had sought a tough officer to end the army's humiliation by the Modocs. He chose General Jefferson C. Davis (no relation to the Confederate president), a controversial officer whose conduct under General Sherman during the notorious "March to the Sea" during the Civil War had tainted his reputation as a racist. Davis' major footnote in history, however, was his murder of another Union general in an affair of honor in which Davis shot and killed Major General William "Bull" Nelson. Davis was charged with manslaughter and jailed, but in the end the charges were set aside in the face of demand for general officers during the war, and Davis returned to the battlefront.[1]

Called to the Modoc conflict from home leave in Indiana, Davis took two weeks to get across the continent. Arriving May 2, 1873, he didn't like what he found. He wrote that although the troops were in decent physical health, "there is a very perceptible feeling of despondency in this whole command." The battered veterans were in no condition for combat, so Davis set out to restore their training and effectiveness.[2] He took over all operations, calling back General Frank Wheaton from his exile in California and restoring his command.

The energetic Davis toured the area on horseback to survey the terrain. He reported that the Lava Beds were "not insurmountable," and his men were drilled vigorously to prepare them for fresh combat. Davis's force grew in size as well as strength as the army moved even more troops to the Lava Beds, the army brass finally acknowledging that General Wheaton's request for a thousand troops was merited. The panicky War Department also authorized the hiring of four hundred additional Indian scouts, which never happened.[3]

The Modocs were on the move. The majority of the band headed east, crossing twenty miles of waterless badlands toward Clear Lake. The Modocs proved hard to follow; they now had a new advantage—the vastness of the land. They traveled light; and when the cavalry followed them, the dust column rising from the marching soldiers warned the Modocs hours before the army could arrive. As the Modocs made their way east, they left the desert environment and moved into a landscape of canyons and timber. They began to split up and live off the land, making the army pursue a dozen bands instead of one. Spring was arriving. Snow had served to reveal the tracks of the Modocs during winter, and Canby had warned against fighting Modocs in warm weather for that reason.

The equation was beginning to tip in the army's favor, but the Modocs had a few more surprises to offer. As if to remind the soldiers that hostilities had not ended, the Modocs attacked again at Scorpion Point. Twenty warriors ventured north and ambushed a supply convoy. The wagons were plodding down a dusty road near Tule Lake with an escort of twenty cavalrymen when the Modoc warriors attacked. The surprised soldiers fled rather than fight; and the Modocs captured four wagons, six mules, and three horses. This fresh embarrassment generated only a scant report in the official documents. Davis wrote tersely: "Escort whipped, with three wounded, no Indians known to be killed."[4]

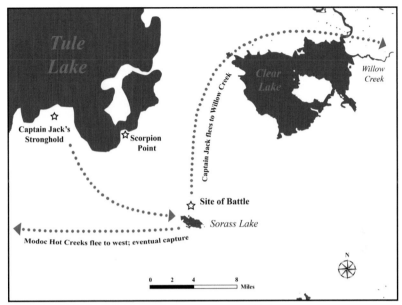

Battles of Sorass Lake and Scorpion Point, May 1873.

The Modocs continued to light fires in the Lava Beds, "evidently by way of braggadocio with a view to letting [the army] know they were rejoicing over temporary victory."[5] Davis borrowed a page from Canby and sent out as scouts the two Modoc women Artinie Choakus and One-Eyed Dixie. The women walked south into the lava wilderness but found nothing, returning eighteen hours later, exhausted, their water used up.[6] Davis still couldn't find where the Modocs were hiding.

The Warm Springs scouts were then sent to find the Modoc band. As they searched, they found the remains of Lieutenant Cranston and other missing troops, victims of the Thomas-Wright disaster. Davis dispatched a patrol to recover the decomposed bodies. The men covered the bodies with rocks and marked the site with boards.

On May 10, 1873, scouts located the Modocs, who had been forced by shortage of water to move farther to the southeast. Davis, hoping to prevent their escape, sent a large patrol under the newly arrived Captain Henry Hasbrouck. He led two cavalry companies—an artillery company mounted on horseback, and a group of Warm Springs scouts. They rode fifteen miles into the rocky plateau south and east of Tule Lake, but found no signs of the Modocs except for a few tracks of a mule and a pony. When they reached Sorass Lake (today known as Dry Lake), they found it entirely devoid of water. It was a miserable site, a sandy depression surrounded by small stone ledges and a few junipers. Soldiers were ordered to dig into the lakebed to find water, but they finally stopped when their excavations were dangerously close to caving in. The patrol was now paralyzed without water, and Hasbrouck decided to send a party at dawn to ride seventeen miles north to Tule Lake. The men camped, thirsty and exhausted, their horses without water.[7]

What the patrol did not know was that a band of Modocs—led by Captain Jack—was stalking them. In a familiar strategy the Modoc warriors moved to attack the vulnerable and unsuspecting army from well-protected positions. During the night the Modocs sneaked past the outer sentries and took positions on rocky ledges overlooking the army camp. Captain Jack deployed his men before dawn. The only signal of danger was when packer Charlie Langell's dog "began growling deep down in his throat." When Langell tried to warn a sentry, he was laughed at. The sleeping soldiers were startled from their bedrolls before dawn by a commotion of shouts and rifle fire. As in earlier attacks, there was immediate confusion and panic.[8]

The first volley from the Modocs killed two cavalrymen and seriously wounded several others.[9] Horses stampeded and men groped for weapons. The attack looked like a repeat of the bloody ambush of Captain Thomas's patrol. But this time Hasbrouck took charge. "The men who were asleep in their blankets got their arms with steadiness and alacrity," he later wrote. His first concern was the stampeding horses, and he sent Lieutenant John Kyle with a group to corral them. He barked orders at Captain James Jackson and Lieutenant Henry Moss to attack the Modocs from the left and right. Warm Springs scouts were sent to outflank the Modocs on both sides. A later account said the enlisted men were hesitant to run into the teeth of Modoc fire until quartermaster sergeant Thomas Kelly "sprang up and shouted, 'God damn it, let's charge!'"[10]

It took only a few minutes for the soldiers to mount the ridge and drive out the Modocs, who fled on horseback. Cavalrymen pursued them for four miles before they escaped. The Warm Springs scouts under Donald McKay could not overtake them, and the Modocs disappeared west into the sagebrush. The chase ended for want of water. "I had but twenty gallons," Hasbrouck said, "and that was reserved for the wounded, of which there were twelve."[11]

Sorass Lake. "The Battle of Sorass Lake was the first time the Modocs had been routed in a head-to-head fight." *Photo by Bill Stafford.*

The Modoc warrior Ellen's Man George died in the fighting at Sorass Lake. According to Cheewa James, the body of Ellen's Man George was taken about three and a half miles away from the battlefield. In a clearing there, a pit was hollowed out and the body placed on top of a pile of brush and logs. In the age-old tradition of the Modocs, the body of the warrior was cremated.[12]

He was a prominent fighter in Captain Jack's force, and it was a serious and demoralizing loss for the Modocs. The army suffered serious casualties in the brief encounter: three soldiers dead, five men wounded, and two Warm Springs scouts dead. However, they captured twenty-one of the Modocs' ponies and three mules "laden with ammunition." The Modocs had collected rifles and ammunition after the Thomas-Wright battle, and Hasbrouck's men recaptured most of it. So much ammunition was found at Sorass Lake that there was speculation that Captain Jack must have had a secret supplier. One reporter wrote: "It appeared strange how he got 6 boxes of our center-primed carbine cartridges [at Sorass Lake], as he did not capture any from our forces."[13] All the captured weapons were given to the Warm Springs scouts.

The Battle of Sorass Lake was a turning point in the Modoc War. In the five months since the war began, it was the first time the Modocs had been routed in a head-to-head fight. Modoc resources were degraded, and a prominent Modoc fighter was dead. It was the beginning of the end for the Modocs.

31

The Bloodhounds

The victory at Sorass Lake greatly buoyed the army's morale and shattered Modoc unity. When the Modocs stopped to camp on the night of May 10, 1873, a few miles west of the battleground, they began again to quarrel among themselves. While they repeatedly whipped the army, Modoc spirits had soared. The defeat at Sorass Lake crushed their brittle morale and revived the divisions between Captain Jack's band and the Hot Creeks. Captain Jack was accused of causing the death of Ellen's Man George in the battle, and he reacted furiously. Ironically, the same militant Modocs who had harangued and shamed Captain Jack into assassinating General Canby were now repudiating his leadership. "You men are the very men that led me to kill General Canby," he told them, "and now you want to blame me."[1]

The factions were irreconcilable; and after a night of wrangling, the Modocs split up. Before dawn, Captain Jack packed his ponies, gathered his family, and headed east, leaving the Hot Creeks to ride in the opposite direction. The majority of the Modocs went with Captain Jack, including Schonchin John and his family, as well as Boston Charley. Captain Jack's group headed toward the clean water of Clear Lake and its tributary Willow Creek. He had with him both his wives, his four-year-old daughter Rosie, his half-brother Humpy Joe, and about twenty-five of the men who had fought with him, along with their families. As the tattered band trudged east, some began to leave the column and split into smaller groups, some as small as one or two families. Their horses were emaciated; their clothes in rags. Many were on foot. They had lost much of their ammunition and several rifles to the army in the Battle of Sorass Lake, and their ability to fight was seriously diminished.

Meanwhile, the smaller Hot Creek faction rode twenty miles west. They knew Captain Jack was a man marked for the rope, and they wanted to distance themselves. The militant Hot Creeks—among them the killers of the settlers, including Curley-Headed Doctor and Hooker Jim—took their families and sought succor with the Hot Creek band's old friend, John Fairchild.

Soon after the Sorass Lake battle, the Warm Spring scouts spotted the high sandy butte where Captain Jack's group camped. Davis dispatched a large force toward the location. Troops approached carefully, stretched in a line three quarters of a mile long to avoid an ambush like the one that befell the Thomas patrol. They drew close, built a long perimeter of small rock fortifications facing the Modoc position, and waited. Captain Hasbrouck and Major Mason, in an excess of caution, spent a full day planning an attack, and the Modocs were gone before their attack began. Army frustration was high; the Modocs had been virtually surrounded, but they slipped away again. The soldiers did not realize they were now pursuing two groups of Modocs traveling in different directions.

Captain Hasbrouck—guessing some of the Modocs would head to Fairchild's ranch—began scouring the area to the west with a large mounted patrol. He sent scouts riding ahead, and late the next day they spotted the Hot Creeks eighteen miles west. A galloping seven-mile cross-country chase began. The Hot Creeks, who had a head start, raced into the timber on the slope of Mahogany Mountain and disappeared. It was a costly escape; the army killed five (two men and three women) and captured several men, women, and children, plus a number of horses. Hasbrouck thought he was breaking their will: "The Indians were now so much scattered and the horses so exhausted," he wrote, "that the pursuit was stopped."[2]

General Davis—who did not realize his troops had found only one of the two Modoc groups—thought the war was over and hurried west to Fairchild's ranch to join in the pursuit. His troops camped overnight, and at dawn they were mounted and about to leave when a Modoc woman appeared, announcing that the Modocs were ready to surrender. Davis decided a peaceful surrender was better than another running gunfight, and he called off the pursuit. Davis then ordered the reluctant One-Eyed Dixie to go directly and inform the Modocs of his terms of surrender. She was told the government "did not intend to trifle any longer."[3]

She returned and reported the Modocs agreed to come in, but it was too great an indignity to arrive with military escort. They wanted no soldiers to accompany them, just John Fairchild and his wife. Dixie told Davis "the Modocs feared the soldiers would kill them the instant they entered the camp." Davis thought he had all the Modocs, and their surrender would be an historic moment. He assembled five troops of cavalry, one troop of infantry, one battery of artillery, and the Warm Springs scouts. He waited to accept the surrender, and a gaggle of camp followers showed up to watch. Donald McKay, head of the Warm Springs scouts, was pledged not to harm the Modocs when they arrived. Assembled on the patch of prairie next to Fairchild's cabin, five hundred people awaited the Indians. Someone finally cried, "Here they come!"[4]

It was a huge anticlimax. Fairchild came from the woods leading a sullen column of sixty-nine Modocs, sixteen of them warriors. "They entered the camp at a funeral pace, and all the noise and bustle among the soldiers was hushed." Second Lieutenant Kingsbury was shocked at their pitiful condition. The starving horses "were scarcely able to bear the women and children who were literally heaped up on them," he wrote. Many of the Modoc prisoners wore articles of soldiers' clothing which had been stripped from the dead soldiers. One woman was wearing the jacket of Corporal Mooney, Fourth Artillery. "We recognized it from the chevrons still being on it," said one soldier.[5]

The Modocs were extremely fearful of what would happen to them. Bogus Charley, the leader of the procession, came forward to General Davis. As reported in the *Daily Rocky Mountain Gazette*: "He smiled sweetly on the general, shook his hand, and then all the leading warriors came forward, and every [warrior] laid down his gun beside him and awaited orders." General Davis demanded their pistols and all other arms, but each warrior said he no longer had any arms.[6] The Modocs—including the children—had blackened their faces with pitch, the traditional Modoc sign of grief. "It gave them a hideous appearance," wrote Kingsbury to his hometown paper in Vermont. Many of the Modocs wore nothing but rags, and it was evident to Kingsbury that Captain Jack had lost "his best fighting warriors."[7]

Davis told the Modocs where to sleep and warned if they tried to escape they would be shot dead. That evening, the Warm Springs scouts mounted their horses in a line facing the surrendered Modocs and ceremoniously mocked them. "[They] chanted a melodious war song preparatory to go on the warpath. They were mounted on their Indian ponies, which were gorgeously decorated with every art of the Indian warrior. The exercises were mostly . . . a series of yells and suggestive gesticulations where not only every part of the Indian's body but also that of his pony was made to 'keep time to the music.'"[8]

Surrendering Modocs continued to straggle into Fairchild's ranch for days. Nevertheless, more than half the Modocs were still at large—those who had fled east, including Captain Jack and Schonchin John. Davis mistakenly thought Captain Jack was somewhere to his south, beyond Mahogany Mountain. And two of the leading Modocs were missing—Boston Charley and Hooker Jim. The Modocs said they were dead. Davis invited three of the leading Modocs to his tent to be questioned; and while they were talking, there was a commotion in the camp. The flap to Davis's tent was thrown open, and an exhausted Modoc threw himself at his feet. It was Hooker Jim. When he saw the others had not been killed, he decided to give himself up. He dashed past the sentries and into the general's tent, fearing he would be shot on sight.[9]

The Hot Creek leaders—those who had humiliated and harangued Captain Jack into killing General Canby—now betrayed Captain Jack. Meeting with General Davis, Bogus Charley, Steamboat Frank, Shacknasty Jim, and the newly arrived Hooker Jim offered to lead the army to Captain Jack's hiding place. "The Modocs were deceived by Captain Jack at every stage of the war," Bogus Charley said, "and were thoroughly disgusted with him. He had a lying tongue in his head."[10] They told Davis that Captain Jack and the others were probably somewhere near Willow Creek, Clear Lake, or Coyote springs, forty miles east. And they said (correctly, it turned out) the remote Willow Creek Canyon was Captain Jack's most likely hideout.

These Modocs later became known as "the Bloodhounds." Davis abhorred their treachery, calling them "cutthroats," but he agreed to hire them as scouts and send them to hunt for Captain Jack. On My 27, the Modoc search party was given four days' rations and horses. Samuel

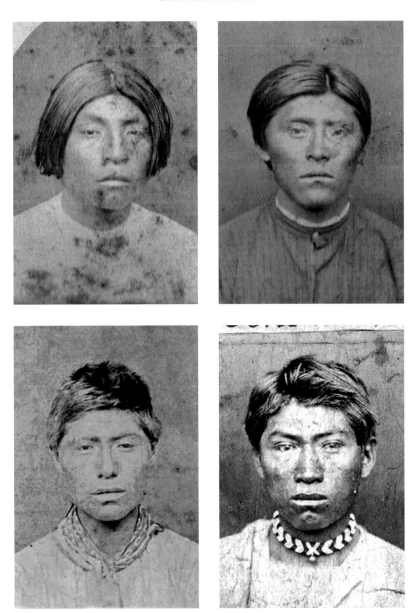

Shacknasty Jim, Steamboat Frank, Bogus Charley, Hooker Jim.
Courtesy author's collection.

Gatschet, the Swiss ethnographer, recorded in the Modoc language why Steamboat Frank joined the Bloodhounds: the officers promised not to execute him if hunted down the Modoc Chief. Gatschet saw their bargain as despicable: "An Indian who has fought with the most decided bravery against the enemy of his tribe, is ready, as soon as the chances of war run against his chief, to sell himself for a few coins to the enemy, body and soul, and then commit on his own chief the blackest kind of treason."[11]

Riding east to search for Captain Jack, the four Bloodhounds got to Clear Lake on the second day, and then rode up Willow Creek Canyon. It is a narrow defile—a little wider than fifty yards across—bordered by vertical black stone walls, about sixty feet high. The miniature canyon, carved into the volcanic rock by centuries of water erosion, meanders east into the rocky plateau. A few small caves provide some shelter. The stream is nearly dry at times, but it rushes with snowmelt in the spring.

On this day in late May 1873, an unseasonal snowstorm was on its way when the Bloodhounds encountered four of Captain Jack's sentries. They were allowed to enter the camp and were met by Captain Jack and his comrades, all armed. The warriors had not spoken since their angry breakup ten days earlier, and Captain Jack was bristling with anger. In a "stormy interview," he demanded the Bloodhounds give up their arms, but they refused. Hooker Jim told Captain Jack they had surrendered to the army and thought he should do the same.

These were the same men who a few weeks before had dressed Captain Jack in woman's clothing, called him a coward, and shamed him into killing General Canby. Now they wanted him to surrender. Infuriated, Captain Jack told the Bloodhounds he would die if he surrendered or die if he fought, and he preferred to die with a gun in his hands. He ordered the Bloodhounds out of his camp, telling them they could live like dogs with the white men, but if he ever saw them again, he would kill them on the spot.

But the Bloodhounds would not leave, and the wrangling continued. Scarface Charley, traveling with Captain Jack, stepped aside to talk with Bogus Charley, who advised him that the majority of Captain Jack's tattered followers—now just twenty-four warriors and their families—were hungry and exhausted, ready to give up. Bogus Charley told him soldiers were already on their way with the Warm Springs scouts.

The Bloodhounds, having located Captain Jack and planted fear among his followers, now rode back toward General Davis and the advancing army. They carried vital intelligence—the location and number of fighters and the demoralized mood of Captain Jack's contingent. The majority of Davis's forces now gathered at the Applegate ranch on Clear Lake, within eight miles of Captain Jack's fugitive band.

General Wheaton, restored to the command he had lost after the January battle, hurried to be present for this last act of the war. Davis smelled victory and wrote in his report: "The pursuit from this time on, until the final captures . . . partook more of a chase after wild beasts than army action; each [army] detachment vying with each other as to which should be the first at the finish."[12] Excitement mounted that Captain Jack would soon be captured. A reporter telegraphed, "Many officers predict a speedy settlement of the war. We sleep among the junipers to-night and expect a snow-storm before morning."[13]

The next morning Hasbrouck marched three squadrons toward the Modoc hideout. One went up the north side of Willow Creek Canyon, led by Hasbrouck and guided by Hooker Jim. On the south, Green took the majority of the troops, guided by Steamboat Frank. A smaller force, including John Fairchild and the Warm Springs scouts, guided by Shacknasty Jim and Bogus Charley, warily moved up the canyon, approaching within a mile of the Modoc camp when they saw the fugitives.

Boston Charley, one of the Modoc warriors the army most wanted to capture, stepped dramatically from the woods and announced he wanted to talk. He was immediately "covered by a dozen rifles." The killer of Reverend Thomas threw down his gun. He held out his hand to shake, and the Warm Springs scouts in the party stepped forward to greet him.

More Modocs appeared and drifted toward the army, and a complete surrender seemed within reach when Steamboat Frank accidently discharged his rifle. The jumpy Modocs ran for cover and the ones waiting in the woods, about to surrender, fled from what looked like an army ambush. Boston Charley was enlisted to round them up again; his gun was returned and he was sent off. But when he headed out of the canyon to follow the fleeing Modocs, he was intercepted by Hasbrouck's troops and detained. They thought he was lying about his mission, and he was arrested and held at the army camp. It took hours before Donald McKay discovered the error, and got Boston Charley released.[14]

Meanwhile, Captain Jack's sister Queen Mary and five Modoc women "from 9 to 90 years of age," and seven ponies and mules came in and surrendered.[15] But the mistaken discharge of Steamboat Frank's gun had derailed a major surrender, and they would have to start over. It began to snow. General Davis telegraphed his headquarters: "I hope to end the Modoc War soon."[16]

The next day the scouts followed a dim trail out of the canyon north toward the reservation town of Yainax, over extremely rough terrain. Hasbrouck followed with a large squadron of 230 troops for the capture. The tired and hungry Modocs had scattered into the remote hills that rise north from Clear Lake, but the Warm Springs trackers were able to follow their faint traces over a ridge into Langell Valley. When the army spotted the Modoc warriors at midday, the Modocs aimed some sporadic gunfire toward the troops, but without effect. Captain Jack shouted to an army surgeon, Dr. Cabaniss, asking what the terms of surrender would be. Captain Jack pleaded for food and clothing and agreed that if the army pulled back a few miles, his people would surrender the next morning.

Cabaniss said Captain Jack appeared shattered: "He presented a most woebegone appearance. The wily warrior sat upon a rock in the center of a little lava bed, twenty yards back from the crest of a bluff, and seemed as lonely as his surroundings. He was wrapped in a faded army blanket, and his head was buried in his hands." His sister Queen Mary, captured at Willow Creek the day before, talked to him "with tears in her eyes."[17]

The army was delighted with their bounty of captives. They now had most of the warriors and they thought they had the ultimate prize, Captain Jack himself. A San Francisco paper headlined: "The Modoc Captives! 34 Men, Women and Children Corralled! Captain Jack Not in Good Spirits! 12 Modocs still at Large! Appearance of the Leading Warriors!"[18] But Captain Jack would escape again. As agreed, most of the Modocs waited overnight to give themselves up. Dr. Cabaniss brought them army bread and even slept in their camp. Most were still there at dawn, but Captain Jack slipped away during the night with his family and a few loyal followers.

In the morning, Scarface Charley gave up, and he was treated with respect. He had been in the vanguard of every battle since the ambush on Lost River almost six months earlier, when he and Lieutenant Boutelle exchanged the first shots of the war. Scarface Charley, the mastermind of the Thomas-Wright battle that took twenty-seven army lives, was respected because he had not betrayed Captain Jack. He was treated as a soldier who had fought effectively for his cause, "the boldest warrior in the band."[19] Scarface Charley would escape prosecution, and within months, he would lead the Modocs when they were sent into exile two thousand miles away in Oklahoma.

Scarface Charley was followed by Schonchin John, whose loathing for his captors was palpable. The *New York Times* reporter Sam Clarke said Schonchin John still appeared ferocious, and dangerous: "The old villain, who drove the tribe to war . . . laid down his repeating rifle with a look of the most profound and savage mistrust and gloomy sorrow." He had "much to dread, and all his fears and half his hate of white men were visible in his sullen manner."[20] Schonchin John, a key conspirator in the killing of the peace commissioners, was sure to hang.

By the end of the day fourteen Modoc men, ten Modoc women, and nine Modoc children gave themselves up to the cavalry. The bedraggled prisoners were marched west to a temporary camp on Lost River. "All of them gave evidence of gloomy terror," reported Clarke.[21] The next day they were marched to General Davis's camp at the Applegate ranch on Clear Lake where the army was concentrated. By now, 131 of the Modocs had been captured from two different bands.

But Captain Jack was still at large. The army did not know Captain Jack and his family had walked through the night and returned to Willow Creek, the meandering stream flowing through a steep canyon eleven miles south. Davis telegraphed army headquarters in San Francisco: "Jack and three men escaped in one direction, 9 others escaped in other directions, 12 still out. Will push them lively till caught."[22]

32

The Capture of Captain Jack

East of Clear Lake rugged Willow Creek Canyon ascends between steep basalt cliffs and dusty hills. The large Carr Butte looms just to the northwest. From the north rim of the canyon a few miles east of the lake the view reveals a private Eden, carved into the black rock by the meandering stream. The canyon, barely fifty yards wide, is lush with green. Willow Creek is nearly dry in hot weather, but in the spring it surges and sparkles over its bed of boulders, its banks covered with bright grass and blanketed with wild flowers. A few junipers and some twisted mountain mahogany—more bushes than trees—cling to the scarce soil near the rim. Archeologists have found ancient petroglyphs carved into the stone cliffs. There is a small cave behind a huge lava obelisk on the east bank of the creek, not a comfortable place, but

"Willow Creek Canyon is a private Eden, carved into the black rock by a meandering stream." *Photo by Jim Compton.*

nicely concealed. This cave offered a cramped shelter for Captain Jack, his young wife Lizzie, his old wife Rebecca, and four-year-old Rosie. Captain Jack's half-brother Humpy Joe, with his twisted body, was also with them. It was June 1, 1873.

Clear Lake and its tributary, Willow Creek, were familiar to the Modocs. There were two large permanent villages on the north shore of the lake that had been occupied until about 1865. They were winter villages, each with about seven of the traditional earth-covered lodges, each lodge housing one or two families. Each of the villages had a crematory adjacent where the Modocs burned their dead.[1] Clear Lake offered bird hunting and egg gathering, and provided "an excellent summer resources of roots and seeds." In spring there were abundant ipos in Willow Creek Canyon, to be eaten or preserved. Just south of Clear Lake was a summer village that was a base for hunting and the gathering of ipos.[2] All this was part of the Modoc land purportedly relinquished in the Oregon treaty of October 1864.

Captain Jack had gained one more day of freedom by slipping away at night and returning to Willow Creek. The majority of the Modocs were in custody, and the few holdouts were drifting in to give themselves up. The army believed there were twelve Modoc warriors still at large, including several with Captain Jack. There may have been two warriors camped nearby, but Captain Jack was now alone in the cave with his family. There is a lichen-spattered shelf of volcanic tuff that juts out from the rim. They did not dare light a fire. Captain Jack posted his half-brother Humpy Joe as sentinel.

Captain Jack's hideaway was just twelve miles east of Jesse Applegate's ranch at Fiddler's Green where a large army now camped alongside Jesse's house and stables. By 1873 there were five Applegate claims on the north rim of Clear Lake on plots previously surveyed and laid out by Jesse in 1871. Jesse's forty-one-year-old daughter, Rozelle, lived nearby with her husband, Charlie Putnam, and their son, Charlie Jr. Next door, another of Jesse's children, Henry, had built a two-story house in 1870. Jesse's daughters, Sallie and Flora, and his son, Daniel Webster Applegate, owned plots just to the west.

Davis, Wheaton, twenty officers, and more than two hundred troops were headquartered at the Applegate ranch. Davis accepted the offer of the Bloodhounds—Hooker Jim, Bogus Charley, Shacknasty

Jim, and Steamboat Frank—to guide the army to Captain Jack. Davis said, with apparent chagrin, "They were promised no rewards for this service whatever. Believing the end justified the means, I sent them, thoroughly armed [as scouts]."[3] A newspaperman said the turncoats "followed the trail as unerringly as hounds after game."[4]

Davis ordered troops to Applegate's ranch with rations for three days and pack mules with ten days' supplies. Iron tripods were set up to boil beans over the fires, and horses grazed on the lush grass bordering Clear Lake. With hundreds of troops available, it was only a matter of time before the army would overtake Captain Jack, and a methodical search began. Twenty-two Warm Springs scouts, in their blue Union Army uniforms and high-topped hats, milled around, waiting for orders. General Davis had told his superiors that the end of the war was near, but he had to capture Captain Jack to close the account. The thirty-plus Modocs just captured were now confined in a corral belonging to the Applegate ranch. Indian scouts were crisscrossing the area, sometimes finding they were following the same tracks.

The governor of Oregon, fearing the roving Modocs would attack settlers, mobilized three companies of the Oregon volunteer militia, who arrived at Clear Lake from Jacksonville. General Davis pressed the search. On June 1 two squadrons, led by members of the Applegate clan, made their way up Willow Creek. Jesse Applegate's grandson Charlie Putnam led a patrol, commanded by Captain Trimble, along the south bank of the canyon. Henry Applegate, Jesse's son, guided the party commanded by Captain Perry on the north bank. Warm Springs mercenaries accompanied each party as trackers.

That afternoon the scouts caught a trail. One of the scouts showed young Applegate the print of a moccasin in the pulverized lava.[6] Captain Perry says the searchers saw footprints of a tiny moccasin, "pattered on the earth" by Captain Jack's little daughter. Following the moccasin tracks, they found places of broken earth in the riverbank where the Indians had stopped to dig ipos to eat. Two miles from Clear Lake, where the stream turned sharply to the left at the point today called Sagebrush Butte, Perry caught a glimpse of movement on the opposite bank of the canyon: "I saw an Indian dog suddenly appear at the top of the ravine, and just as suddenly an arm appeared and snatched the dog out of sight. I then knew the coveted prize was mine."[7]

An old soldier named Jim Shay was first to see Humpy Joe, so intent on watching the soldiers moving up the opposite bank that he was easily surprised and surrounded. The excited cavalrymen dismounted, intending to charge the site, but the Indian scouts told them to be patient. The Warm Springs scouts disarmed Humpy Joe, and Charlie Putnam descended with him to speak with Captain Jack. They could only communicate by using the Chinook trade jargon. Humpy Joe asked for three days to bring Captain Jack in, but Putnam said, "Hell no, we want him now."[8]

There are several accounts of the moment of Captain Jack's surrender. Humpy Joe called out in Modoc to Captain Jack that he had to give up, but there was no reply. He called again, and all waited. The *New York Times'* Samuel Clarke described what happened next: "The famous chief then stepped boldly out on a shelf of rock, with his gun in his hand. He showed no timid fear or trepidation, and his conduct commanded the admiration of those who were his captors for a certain sort of native dignity was apparent, and even in defeat, and at the moment of his surrender, the great Modoc chief was self-possessed, and acted a manly part."[9]

Sergeant McCarthy, who was with the search party, saw Captain Jack emerge "with his little girl about 5 years old in his arms." McCarthy thought he "appeared very affectionate to the little one."[10] McCarthy added, "After some parley Jack came up on our side [of the canyon] and handed his gun to Jim Shay, shook hands with him and surrendered himself."[11] It was a solemn moment. The Warm Springs scouts put down their rifles and stood in a circle as Captain Jack shook their hands one by one. Captain Jack was calm. He asked to be allowed to return to the cave for clothes, and he donned a clean striped calico shirt. He was wearing denim trousers with the bottoms turned up several inches, and a sort of cap fashioned from a felt hat with most of the brim cut off. "He told me his legs had given out," wrote General Davis in his report of the capture.[12]

Captain Jack's wives and daughter emerged. Lizzie, his young wife—who was "rather pretty"—changed her clothes. Captain Jack's little child appeared, clean and washed, also looking "very pretty."[13] The prisoners were assembled on the canyon rim, and each mounted behind one of the Indian scouts to ride back to the army base. Captain Jack apparently suffered from a broken arm, perhaps shot in a battle.[14] But those who saw him said "he bore himself with dignity, and sat there like a Roman hero. He never moved a muscle, or bore evidence that he felt humiliated."[15]

Captain Trimble and Captain Jack shook hands and chatted. Then Trimble shouted out the news to the troops around him. All "cheered lustly [sic] and the cheer was reported by the main body on the other side."[16] Charlie Putnam believed there were three other Modocs hiding near Captain Jack who escaped up Willow Creek.[17] Putnam asked Captain Jack how many of his men had been killed. Captain Jack consulted with his wives, counted on his fingers, and said about ten.[18]

It was a three-hour ride back to the Applegate ranch. Captain Jack and his wife Lizzie rode together on a spotted Cayuse.[19] As they neared the camp, the Warm Springs scouts lined up single file and began "a strange wild chant, ringing in the air," galloping the last mile. Reporter Clarke wrote that Captain Jack "gave no token, by look, or word, or act that would have shown he resented the rejoicing over his defeat."[20]

Officers and enlisted men were having an idle afternoon at the Applegate camp, many napping, when "prolonged yells and cheers aroused this camp from a pleasant siesta." The camp erupted. They saw "a grand cavalcade of mounted horsemen [and] steeds rushed forward at a furious rate." "Captain Jack is captured!" shouted a sturdy sergeant.[21] There would be decades of claims about which officers and men had actually taken the greatest trophy of the war, but credit was probably due to Captain Perry and the First Cavalry. "It amuses a civilian," one newsman observed, "to see the jealousy manifested by some of the officers regarding the distribution of the little honor won in this farcical campaign."[22]

At the Applegate ranch the Modoc captives were given tents, the men on one side of the prison and the women on the other. Only Captain Jack's wife Lizzie was allowed to sit beside him and "lay her head upon his breast." Captain Jack's little girl "had the freedom of the tent."[23]

McCarthy said the capture party was careful to preserve the possessions of Captain Jack and his family intact, and they took no souvenirs. But when Captain Jack was delivered to the camp, troops fell on the their effects. "A squad of idle men . . . took everything of value, several articles belonging to the dead officers and soldiers were found in the baggage and a small sum of money."[24]

Everyone wanted to gaze upon the chief of the Modocs. As reported in the *Daily Alta California*: "Jack is about forty. He is five feet eight inches in height, and compactly built. He has a large and well-formed head, and a face full of individuality. Although dressed in old clothes, he looks every inch a chief. He does not speak to anyone."[25] The other Modocs respected him: "Those who have seen him do not wonder that he is the leader of the Modocs."[26]

General Davis immediately sent a courier to Yreka with a telegram that reached San Francisco and Portland the next morning. "Jack, two warriors and their families have been run down, captured and brought in by Colonel Perry's Command," he wrote. "I am happy to announce the termination of the Modoc difficulties."[27]

In early evening an armed escort of six came to take Captain Jack and Schonchin John to the blacksmith to be "ironed" (put in shackles). Scarface Charley was summoned to act as translator and explain to Captain Jack and Schonchin John what was happening. Captain Jack was indignant, saying he had surrendered in good faith and had no desire to get away.

Nevertheless, iron shackles were placed on their ankles and closed with a rivet pounded into place. The two men were then joined by a two-foot chain, which would not be removed until they were in the army guardhouse in Fort Klamath. They wore these iron anklets until the hour before they were hanged. The principal Modoc figures, including Captain Jack and Schonchin John, were held overnight in a small building adjoining Jesse Applegate's house under strong guard. Captain Jack would discuss nothing with his captors, "making no explanation or revelations, but to die and make no sign."[28]

Schonchin John and Captain Jack in Chains. *Courtesy author's collection*

33

Captain Jack Will Be Tried

On the evening of Captain Jack's capture, two dozen Warm Springs Indian scouts built a huge fire and staged a raucous victory celebration at Applegate's ranch. Since it was Sunday, the scouts—who had converted to Methodism—first held a Christian religious service. They then began drumming and dancing, long past midnight, acting out the events of the war.[1]

The next day a reporter for the *San Francisco Bulletin* was allowed to visit Captain Jack. One of the Modoc prisoners had overnight filed his shackles almost in two, nearly escaping, and guards were on high alert. Captain Jack, who had said little since his capture, erupted in a fiery oration. He was angry that none of the whites who had killed innocent Indians would be punished.[2] A few days later, a California newspaper reported, "Confinement is beginning to wear him away. The restriction of his liberty has a greater effect on him than suspense about his future fate." He told an officer that his "Indian heart was dead." All he asked was for Lizzie to sit beside him.[3]

In the days following Captain Jack's capture, the Oregon Volunteers continued to mass at the Applegate ranch. Scouring the hills, they captured a few more warriors and families, most importantly Black Jim, a stalwart of the Lava Beds resistance and a major participant in the killing of the commissioners. Modoc prisoners of war were now split between army camps to the east and west of the Lava Beds. Three days after Captain Jack's capture, General Davis consolidated all his forces and their prisoners at a large camp on the southeast corner of Tule Lake, known as Peninsula Camp (or Boyles' Camp in some accounts). Peninsula Camp was located on a sandy isthmus connecting the mainland with a towering rocky peninsula that juts into the southeast corner of Tule Lake.[4]

General Davis ordered Colonel Hasbrouck to bring his five companies of infantry and Modoc prisoners from Fairchild's ranch to the Peninsula Camp. A long column made the thirty-nine-mile march, escorting about seventy-five Modocs and their meager possessions, along with all the army's equipment and livestock. The military force still stationed at Applegate's ranch—six cavalry companies, seventy Warm Springs scouts, and all their ferriers, cooks, and mule drivers, numbering about two hundred and forty—also marched to the Peninsula Camp with their seventy or so Modoc hostages, including Captain Jack, Schonchin John, Black Jim, and Boston Charley. For the first time since the beginning of the war the army forces were gathered at one camp.

The wagon train carrying the Modoc families from Clear Lake was a melancholy sight. Seven large freight wagons were devoted to the captives, one occupied by deserters, and seven wagons were loaded with equipment and general stores.[5] The column of prisoners was flanked by Battery G of the Fourth Artillery, twenty-five mounted enlisted men, with their firearms. The Warm Springs scouts followed the wagons, chanting as they rode. A crowd of civilians had gathered to see the Modoc prisoners. "'Where is Captain Jack? Where is Captain Jack?' was the cry among the spectators. None had the pleasure, however, of seeing the chief's face. He had anticipated the excitement . . . and was concealed in the wagon, completely in a blanket."[6]

At the Peninsula Camp the army confined the Modocs in two large tents, "pent up in rather narrow quarters."[7] The men and women were segregated, although Captain Jack's young wife Lizzie and four-year-old Rosie were allowed to share his tent. "The Modoc women and children are contented, in one sense at least," Meacham later wrote. "They are well fed, and have rest."[8]

The recently arrived Oregon Volunteers soon committed an atrocity against the captive Modocs that sickened the nation and discredited the Oregon Volunteers for decades. When a group of four Modoc men and their families showed up at Fairchild's ranch to surrender, Fairchild decided to turn them over to the army. He sent the seventeen Modocs with his brother James Fairchild and a four-mule wagon on a fifteen-mile trek to join the other prisoners at General Davis's headquarters at the Peninsula Camp.

A contingent of sixty-three Oregon militiamen, commanded by Captain Joseph Hyzer from Jacksonville, heard the Modocs were being transferred and intercepted them near the Lost River ford. They interrogated James Fairchild, and the wagon was allowed to pass. But seven miles down the road Fairchild and the Modocs were again stopped by two men in masks. Fairchild gave a vivid account of what happened next. He pleaded for the Modocs' lives, "but the cowardly hounds were not to be balked." Fairchild's mules were cut loose and the masked men began firing. They shot and killed four Modoc men—Tee-Hee Jack, Little John, Pony, and Mooch—and then seriously wounded Little John's wife. An artillery sergeant named Murphy appeared unexpectedly with a patrol of ten men and gave pursuit, but the killers escaped. The Modoc men died immediately, but the woman survived.[9]

Colonel Thompson, a California Volunteer, arrived on the scene the next morning. In his reminiscences, Thompson painted a horrifying picture. "The women and children were still in the wagon with their dead, not one of them having moved during the night," he wrote. "It was a most ghastly site, the blood from the dead Indians had run through the wagon bed, and made a broad, red streak for twenty yards down the road." Even many years later, Thompson could not forget the horror of the moment.[10]

When the Modocs arrived at Peninsula Camp, General Davis had intended to hang their principal leaders immediately without trial. He ordered a gallows be built. He telegrammed the Assistant Adjutant General on June 5, saying scaffolds and ropes were being prepared, and he intended "to execute eight or ten ringleaders at sun set tomorrow."[11] Davis drew up a "declaration of charges" to be read to Captain Jack—more of a broadside than an indictment. He accused the Modocs with as many as "three hundred murders" recalled by old settlers, although none were named. It alleged that Modocs "strewd [*sic*] the shores of Tule Lake with the victims of [their] bloody band" and placed themselves "outside the bounds of civilized warfare."[12]

On June 6 Davis invited civilian witnesses to come to the camp to identify which Modocs had killed settlers during the November rampage. Two of the women widowed by the Modocs, Mrs. Louisa Boddy and her daughter-in-law Mrs. Nicholas Shira, came from their home nine miles north on Tule Lake to identify their husband's killers. Hooker Jim and Steamboat Frank were taken to the tent occupied by the women. Davis was astonished when the women drew weapons and charged the men, trying to conduct their own summary execution.

"[Mrs. Schira] drew a pistol and started for Steamboat Frank, and Mrs. Boddy drew a knife and dashed at Hooka Jim." Davis had to hurl himself between the Modocs and the women to prevent the killing. He managed to disarm them, but Davis received a gash to his hand from Mrs. Boddy's knife.[13]

It was not Davis' plan to hang all the perpetrators. Whatever contempt Davis may have had for the Bloodhounds, he did not intend to execute them. He said that without their help, Captain Jack and his band would not have been captured. He genuinely detested the Bloodhounds, not only as murderers of defenseless civilians, but also as men in arms who gave up their leader to the enemy. He was uneasy with the appearance of his decision: "Two of them, Hooka Jim and [Steamboat] Frank are among the worst of the band." Nevertheless, Davis wrote to his commander in San Francisco, "Hooka Jim, Shacknasty Jim, Steamboat Frank and Bogus Charley offered important services." He added, "Honor on my part requires me to urge their exemption."[14] In the end, the Bloodhounds would live to watch the army hang Captain Jack, Schonchin John, Black Jim, and Boston Charley.

The impromptu gallows was ready for immediate use. Davis had decided he would leave immediately after the hangings to visit with other chiefs in northern Oregon to impress on them the swiftness of military punishment. Davis told a reporter: "I procured lumber, chains, ropes, tackles, and all the other phariphernalia [*sic*] of an execution, and had selected Friday last [June 6] as doomsday."[15] As he prepared for the hangings, Davis received a telegram ordering him to halt the executions. General Sherman now instructed Davis to hold the prisoners in military custody until their fate was decided.[16] Davis was furious. He wired back that he regretted the "long delay of cases of these red-devils." Delay, he urged, would "destroy the moral effect which their prompt execution would have upon other tribes." He added: "Have no doubt of the propriety and had none of my authority as *Department Commander* in the field to execute a band of outlaws, robbers and murderers."[17]

Davis was swimming against the tide. By 1873 the army was applying the laws of war that were codified and published by President Lincoln during the Civil War.[18] On June 7, 1873, U.S. Attorney General George Henry Williams (a former U. S. Senator from Oregon) issued an opinion authorizing a military commission to try and sentence the

Modocs who were charged with offenses against "the recognized laws of war."[19] Williams determined the Modocs, acting during a temporary armistice, had committed acts of violence too odious to tolerate—even in wartime—and these acts required punishment. Specifically, the Modocs would be charged with transgressing the common law of war by treacherously assassinating an American commander under a flag of truce. The Attorney General opined: "The circumstances attending the assassination of Canby and [Reverend] Thomas are such as to make their murder as much a violation of the Laws of savage as well as civilized warfare, and the Indians concerned in it fully understood the baseness and treachery of their act."[20]

Once they were deemed foreign belligerents, the Modocs were exempted from prosecution by Oregon courts, which had issued several writs for their arrest. Oregon newspapers were outraged. "It is right that the prisoners be executed immediately. They have sinned against humanity, and the world has recorded its verdict against them."[21] But Davis obeyed the federal decision.

Loud voices were soon raised in California urging the government to go slowly in avenging the killing of the white settlers. A California congressman, J. K. Luttrell of Siskiyou County, surprised Davis by arriving in person at Peninsula Camp with Judge Steele, the public figure most sympathetic to the Modoc cause. Lutrell said they had come to investigate the causes of the war. He concluded: "the War was caused by the wrongful acts of bad white men." Luttrell then added the following inflammatory remark: "Not since the organization of the [U.S.] government had there been so much corruption and swindling of the government and Indians of the Pacific Coast."[22]

On the evening of June 10, a large party of Modoc prisoners—Captain Jack, his sister Queen Mary and wife Lizzie, Scarface Charley, Boston Charley, Schonchin John, One-Eyed Mose, and William—was assembled by the army in "the office tent," probably one of the large round high-peaked tents used by senior officers, to meet with Steele. Captain Jack and Schonchin John, along with Boston Charley and Black Jim, were shackled together at the ankle. The Modocs sat in a semicircle for a kind of deposition. Captain Jack and Schonchin John sat on a dry goods box. Captain Jack was wrapped in a dingy blanket, wearing "a sullen look all the time." No one but Captain Jack removed his hat. He wanted Lizzie near him, and she crouched at his feet.

Steele quizzed them vigorously about the personal property of their victims. What had happened to Reverend Thomas's watch and Lieutenant Cranston's ring? The captives pleaded ignorance but then blamed Hooker Jim, Shacknasty Jim, and Steamboat Frank. Boston Charley finally averred that the missing watch had been "placed under a rock" by someone, and the ring was with Ellen's Man George when he was cremated after the Battle of Sorass Lake. Steele told them sternly that he wanted better answers, and he also wanted to know where their rifles were cached or he would turn them over to the mercies of "Tyee Davis." He gave the Indians one day to reply, and then Steele and Luttrell left for Yreka without waiting for an answer.[23]

The most lasting and famous images of the war were made at Peninsula Camp when the German-born photographer Louis Heller arrived.[24] Heller had previously visited the warfront from Yreka in April, when he made a series of twenty-four landscape views of the Lava Beds and army camps. He had used his chemical skills (he was also a pharmacist) to embalm a dead infantryman. At the Peninsula Camp in June, he made the portraits of the key Modoc figures that have become lasting icons of the conflict. Like the great Civil War photographers, he was undaunted by challenges in the field. He set up a blanket to create a neutral background. The scattered rocks in the foreground of some of the portraits reveal that it was at best a crudely improvised studio in which to expose his cumbersome glass plates. The result of Heller's work was a series of twenty-four cartes de visite, 2¼- by 4-inch cards sold by a San Francisco photo studio (which later claimed authorship of the photographs). Each picture carried a certification by General Davis that it was an authentic image.[25]

The unwilling and skeptical Modocs were escorted to Heller's impromptu studio by army guards. All the Modocs were said to be "greatly adverse" to the photo session. Captain Jack refused to be photographed until Hooker Jim first had his image captured. Heller photographed each of the most well known leaders alone—Captain Jack, Hooker Jim, Scarface Charley, and Schonchin John. Others were depicted in twos and threes, some seated on a box, others standing.[26]

Heller captured Captain Jack's steady gaze and enigmatic hint of a smile in what has become the most evocative image of the Modoc War. Heller's telling photo of Schonchin John portrays a graying man who looks surly. The individual portraits of the Bloodhounds make them seem like a dangerous gang. There is also an interesting full-length photo of Captain Jack and Schonchin John, looking disgruntled, showing the chains joining them at the ankle, and the odd caps they had fashioned by cutting off the brim of hats. The *New York Times* reported that "even the dignity of Capt. Jack yielded to the claims of art."[27]

General Davis continued to fume at the decision overriding his authority to hang the prisoners, which he felt delayed unnecessarily the execution of the "red devils." He gave a lengthy interview to a reporter, saying it would now take at least six months to try the ringleaders and he should have shot them while he had a chance.[28] That remark was rebuked by General Sherman a week later in New York, who said it would have been permissible to shoot the Modocs as they fled the army, but not after their capture. Sherman added, "We all know they are murderers. . . . It was a pity the Modocs were not shot at first; then all this commission business and expense would have been avoided."[29]

Preparations were made to move the Modoc prisoners from the Peninsula Camp to Fort Klamath for trial. As the camp readied for the move, there was the report of a firearm and a great commotion. Soldiers raced to the scene and found that Curley Haired Jack, one of the Hot Creeks who had surrendered to John Fairchild, had shot himself dead. The army could not explain how he obtained a pistol. Curley Haired Jack thought "it was better for him to die with his own hand, than to give the soldiers the satisfaction of seeing him swinging in the air, with a rope around his neck."[30]

34

The Trial of Captain Jack

Everyone—Modocs and army alike—knew Captain Jack and others would hang. The U.S. Army had won the war and would now impose its own justice. The generals, all the way to the top, agreed that the Modocs had wronged the U.S. government by breaching a treaty, victimizing white settlers, and impudently resisting white authority. Now not only would the Modoc rebels be executed, but the Modoc nation itself would be extinguished. General Sherman wrote that the Modocs should be scattered around the country, "so the name of Modoc should cease."[1]

But first, the Modoc leaders had to be tried. Although it would be a charade whose outcome was foretold, the government wanted the appearance of fairness and respect for the law. When the Attorney General halted the summary hanging planned by General Davis and ordered a trial by military commission, he set in motion a proceeding that would take place in a Fort Klamath courtroom far outside the experience or understanding of the Modocs.

Seven wagons with a cavalry escort rumbled north, taking the Modoc warriors and their families as prisoners of war fifty-five miles from Peninsula Camp to Fort Klamath. They rolled past the point on Tule Lake that they believed was the center of the universe, and the hub of their spiritual world. They traveled past the ranches of Henry Miller, William Boddy, and Rufus Brotherton, among the fourteen men killed by the Hot Creek Modocs on the first and second days of the war. Captain Jack, who had no part in those killings, sat in a wagon, chained at the ankle to Schonchin John. Passing Upper Klamath Lake, the party stopped to camp overnight at Modoc Point, where three years earlier the Modocs had been harassed and humiliated by the Klamaths.

The hot summer of 1873 was spent assembling the necessary machinery of a military commission to conduct a trial: officers were assigned, a courtroom designated, and translators hired. At first, it was unclear who would be put on trial. And what would happen to the refugees from the war, the 153 men, women, and children now in army custody? Two cavalry companies had gone ahead to build a stockade, a large pen where all the Modoc families would be held. An internal wall within the stockade segregated Captain Jack's band of Lost River Modocs from the Hot Creeks to keep the bands from fighting.[2]

The stockade was extremely crowded. One news report noted that the captives "chafe under restraint." The prisoners who spoke a little English "inquire anxiously when they will be given their liberty." The captives believed the Modocs who were not hanged would be sent to San Francisco and "confined on a little island." Rations and firewood were issued once a day, the families cooking over little fires. They were guarded day and night by sentries at the gates and on each corner of the compound.[3]

The Modoc leaders, Captain Jack's lieutenants and the others considered most dangerous and likely to escape, were confined in the post guardhouse, chained in heavy shackles. The guardhouse was really a jail, a whitewashed log building with a high-shingled roof and a generous porch that stood on the southern verge of the army post.[4] It was divided into three cells, one for Captain Jack and Schonchin John; another for Black Jim, Rock Dave, Boston Charley, One-Eyed Mose, Pete, and Curley-Headed Doctor's son. In the third were Buckskin Doctor, Curley-Headed Doctor, and Ike.[5]

The cells were dim and claustrophobic, illuminated only by air vents with bars at the top of the walls. All the prisoners were shackled at the ankle, some chained pairs. There was no ventilation and the prisoners could see nothing outside their cells. Two or three times a week they were taken to the stockade for visits to their families. They suffered from the lack of fresh air and "there was sickness among the prisoners." As the days wore on, Captain Jack became "gaunt and weak by reason of close confinement." The cell doors were occasionally opened when requested by visitors to the post who wanted to gaze on the famous killers.

But it was spring at Fort Klamath for the battle-worn troops, and the soldiers enjoyed a taste of relaxation. The physical setting was enchanting, but rations were short, and some troops longed for their home base at Camp Harney. Enlisted men grumbled that the officers spent all their time "enjoying the hospitality of the fort, the post traders, etc." Those soldiers for whom there was no room in the barracks were confined to tents and campfires around the perimeter. Sergeant McCarthy had to deal with drunken soldiers and break up occasional fisticuffs.[6]

The post swarmed with Klamath Indians, and McCarthy was surprised by the extent to which the Klamaths had adopted white ways: "They were a bright intelligent host of people, and had about discarded anything in their dress that savored of the wild Indian. The men affected a military dress, and all who could get them, wore chevrons as an ornament. Even the small boys wore chevrons. The women were neatly dressed in colored goods, calicos I guess . . . and red or colored handkerchiefs on their heads. They seemed prosperous and happy."[7]

The Warm Springs Indian scouts were still at Fort Klamath with their leader Donald McKay, waiting to be dismissed and return home. The mercenaries were an irritation to army regulars, and Sergeant McCarthy had nothing but contempt for them.[8]

It was more than two weeks before the charges against the Modocs were announced. Only the killers of General Canby and the peace commissioners, and those who assisted them, would be prosecuted. The six—Captain Jack, Schonchin John, Black Jim, Boston Charley, and the younger men, Barncho and Slolux—would be tried for murder and assault with intent to kill in violation of the laws of war.[9] Major H. P. Curtis, the Judge Advocate acting as prosecutor, made the decision not to proceed with criminal charges against the Bloodhounds—Steamboat Frank, Hooker Jim, Bogus Charley, and Shacknasty Jim—the turncoats who had assisted the army in capturing Captain Jack. The Bloodhounds, he explained, should become an example to other tribes that "treachery to their race would earn a sure reward." With no apparent irony, Curtis said that one of the Bloodhounds—Hooker Jim, "the worse by far"— might be useful as a witness if Curtis decided to prosecute the killers of the fourteen settlers.[10] Meacham was appalled at the decision not to prosecute the Bloodhounds: "To pardon these men as an encouragement to other Indians to betray their people is not good logic, when it is understood that they were the real instigators of the treacherous deeds of the Modocs."[11]

Curtis also decided not to proceed against the killers of Lieutenant Sherwood, who was slain the same day as the peace commissioners. This decision was a practical one: none of the suspects were in custody.

Curley Haired Jack had killed himself with a stolen revolver. Miller's Charley was still at large, although he gave himself up shortly after Curtis's decision not to charge him with a crime. It was never established that Comstock Dave was the third killer.[12]

The trial was set to begin on Tuesday July 1, 1873, at 10 A.M. Captain Jack despaired of having a fair trial in white man's court. "Will you give up the men who killed the Indian woman and children on Lost River, to be tried by the Modocs?" he asked Meacham. "Will you try the white men who fired on my people . . . by your own law?" Meacham told him that was impossible. "Oh, yes, I see," Captain Jack replied, sarcastically. "The white man's laws are good for the white man, but they are made so as to leave the Indians out."[13]

General Davis, as commanding officer, appointed the military tribunal, supposedly selecting officers "who had no connection with the Modoc difficulty," but in fact the panel of officers he appointed was heavy with veterans of the recent war.[14] Davis chose Lieutenant Colonel Washington Eliot, a much-decorated Civil War officer based in California, as the senior and presiding member. He also selected Captain John Mendenhall of the Fourth Artillery, who had recently commanded troops in the Second Battle of the Stronghold, and Captain Robert Pollock, the post quartermaster during the Modoc War. Captain Henry Hasbrouck, who had defeated the Modocs in the battle of Sorass Lake and led the hunt for Captain Jack, was chosen along with Second Lieutenant George Kingsbury—the officer from Vermont and correspondent to his hometown newspaper—who had fought in several engagements. Major Curtis, the judge advocate who had written the eleven page brief explaining the authority to try the Modocs by military commission, was to be the prosecutor.

On the morning of July 1, 1873, the six prisoners were marched into the courtroom. The Fort Klamath adjutant's office was chosen for the proceedings. A whitewashed clapboard building at the end of the large parade ground, it was a short walk from the guardhouse, about a hundred yards past an abandoned stable. The defendants walked in their chains with an escort of six infantrymen.

In the makeshift courtroom the five officers who made up the military commission sat along one side of a long narrow table in the middle of the room, the chairman at one end, with the judge advocate (prosecutor) sitting at the other. All six officers wore their dress blue uniforms with brass buttons and braid. The six defendants sat on a bench at one side. They wore the same shabby clothing in which they had been captured, old denim work pants or cast-off army pants, ragged shirts, and work shoes. Four of the six accused defendants were shackled together—Captain Jack chained to Schonchin John, and Black Jim to Boston Charley.

Major Curtis wrote later that the young men Barncho and young Slolux took no interest in the trial and lay on the floor during most of the proceedings. "Slolux [sometimes] sat holding his face in his hands, and much of the time on the floor, apparently asleep. He is quite a boy in looks." Curtis regarded them as "merely tools in the hands of other and abler men." He thought they were only acting "in obedience to orders" and had no adequate understanding of the magnitude of their crime. "It would be an unnecessary outlay of national vengeance to put [them] to death," he wrote.[15] He later requested that President Grant reduce their sentences.

The Modocs had no legal representation. During the first session of the proceedings Major Curtis asked the defendants if they wanted to be represented by a lawyer; they replied they were "unable to procure" representation.[16]

The trial might have gone differently if the Modocs had legal counsel. A lawyer most certainly would have challenged the impartiality of the grossly biased military commission. Four of the five officers on the panel had fought against the Modocs in the war; three of those had members of their units killed by the Modocs. Military rules of the era guaranteed defendants the "right of challenge" to the make-up of the military commission for bias. The Modocs could have requested removal of members of the panel and demanded an unbiased commission, but Major Curtis failed to advise the defendants of those options.[17]

Some observers from California raised objections to the proceedings. California congressman J. K. Luttrell wrote to the Secretary of the Interior saying he wanted to attend the trial and offering to pursue evidence, including sworn statements, to present to the "Court Martial, or board, who may be designated to try the prisoners at Fort Klamath."[18] There is no record of a reply. Yreka Judge Elijah Steele finally recruited Colonel E. J. Lewis to act as lawyer for the Modocs. Lewis, an attorney from Colusa, a small railroad town near Red Bluff in northern California, hurried north to Fort Klamath. It was reported he reached Yreka in early July and left on the night of July 5 for Fort Klamath. Unfortunately, Lewis arrived too late; he was "much chagrined to find the trial over."[19]

Did Meacham offer to act as counsel for the four Indians? Writing two years later in *Wigwam and Warpath*, he claimed that after the Commission had adjourned for the day, he urged the court's presiding officer to allow the Modocs representation. According to Meacham, Elliott quickly agreed and suggested that Meacham himself serve, saying, "It would be an act of magnanimity on your part that is without precedent." But Meacham had no legal training or experience. He said he was dissuaded from serving as counsel because of his frail health; friends warned the strain "would cost him his life."[20]

The trial proceedings took five days. It took a half-day to read and translate the lengthy charges. Each prisoner heard the details of the charges repeated and translated. Each was asked individually to enter a plea, and each pleaded not guilty. E. S. Belden, a shorthand reporter, did the remarkable verbatim transcript of the trial. When questions were put to the Modoc witnesses, Frank Riddle or Winema translated them. The process was laborious and time-consuming, but Belden pared out all the pauses and interruptions and produced a record of the proceedings filled with drama. Even the meticulous and sometimes tedious questioning by Judge Advocate Curtis came to life when witnesses recounted the chaotic events of the assassinations.

First to testify was Frank Riddle. He (and later, Winema) interrupted their work as translators and stepped to the witness table in the center of the room. Their conflict was glaringly obvious. Frank was an employee of the court, receiving ten dollars a day translating for the commission, and his wife was a cousin of the principal defendant. *New York Times* correspondent H. Wallace Atwell—who sought an investigation of the "great wrongs" committed by the whites against the Modocs—did not shrink from challenging the testimony of both Frank and Winema. He wrote they not only had a serious conflict of interest, but were incompetent. "We know the interpreter employed [Frank Riddle] is unworthy of credence. We know he is illiterate, can neither read nor write, cannot translate the idioms of our tongue, cannot even understand good English. We know the squaw [Winema] with whom he cohabits has shielded her relatives in her interpreting at the expense of others."[21]

But Frank and Winema had become favorites of the army, and their lengthy eyewitness testimony, rich in detail, was powerful and damaging to the Modocs. Remarkably for an era when Indians generally were not considered competent to testify at all, they were star witnesses. Frank testified how he was chagrined when his warnings of danger to the peace commissioners were discounted on the day of the killings. He reminded the commission he had pleaded with General Canby not to attend the peace tent meeting.[22] Winema followed her husband. Her testimony was rather stilted, but her description gave vivid details—the frantic firing of pistols, and how Steamboat Frank appeared from the rocks, stripped Reverend Thomas, donned Thomas's coat, and walked back to the Stronghold. Steamboat Frank himself, one of the Bloodhounds who had assisted in Captain Jack's capture, sat listening in the courtroom.

Leroy Dyar, the hapless Indian Agent who saved his own life by running from the shooting, took the stand next. He said he had heard the warnings and was terrified of attending the peace conference. "[But] I thought that if I didn't go, and there was trouble, I would be blamed, and perhaps considered a coward, and I had rather take the chances with the rest of them." Dyar confirmed there was a cease-fire and the parties agreed to attend unarmed. Dyar neglected to mention that O. C. Applegate had slipped him a derringer, which Dyar carried in his boot. Neither was it mentioned during the trial that Meacham also had a small gun hidden under his coat.

Captain Jack and his co-defendants were then faced with the testimony of their betrayers, the Bloodhounds. The four men, all involved in killing the fourteen settlers, listened in the courtroom before they took the stand. There is no record of how Captain Jack and the three others reacted as they silently listened to the Bloodhounds testify. One after another, they related the events of the killings and candidly admitted their role in them. Shacknasty Jim, testifying for the prosecution, sat at the witness table. He admitted he was among the Modocs attending the peace meeting. He described in explicit terms how General Canby was shot in the face and how Ellen's Man George dispatched him with another shot to the head. Shacknasty admitted he had pursued and attempted to kill Indian Agent Dyar.

Steamboat Frank, a small dark-skinned man with an odd deformity to his face alongside his nose, was interrogated next. He too admitted chasing Indian agent Dyar, shooting at him as he fled. He claimed it was Captain Jack's idea to slay the commissioners and that he heard him plot the murders with Schonchin John. He said he was hiding about four hundred yards away when the firing began, and rushed up to witness the killings. Hooker Jim, the notorious killer, testified he had been at the peace tent on the day of the assassinations and he too ran after Agent Dyar, firing at him. He said he had wanted to kill Canby, but Captain Jack kept the honor for himself. Probably because he had been granted immunity, he freely admitted his part in planning the killings and testified he went to the peace tent expecting to take part in the murders. "I said I would kill one if I could." Some of his replies seem heavy with irony:

QUESTION: Are you now a friend to Captain Jack?

HOOKER: I have been a friend of Captain Jack, but I didn't know what he got mad at me for.

Bogus Charley, the fourth Bloodhound to testify, denied knowing the killings were planned, saying he "heard very little about it." He was known, however, to have been one of those who bullied and shamed Captain Jack into killing General Canby. Bogus was in the army camp the morning of the killings, cajoling the commissioners to make sure they attended the meeting. Fearing the assassination plan would fall through, he followed the white men on his horse to make sure none turned back. Asked if he liked or disliked Captain Jack, he said, "I don't like him very well now."

Alfred Meacham, just arrived at Fort Klamath, was called on the third day. After being sworn and seated, he poignantly related Canby's assurances that they were in no danger from the Modocs: "General Canby, to allay my fears, said 'I have more confidence in these Indians than you have; I think them capable of [violence] but they dare not do it; it is not in their interest.'" Meacham said he advised Canby that they should all arm themselves, but Canby refused and said indignantly, "I have never deceived an Indian, and I will not consent to it."

Meacham's account of the events at the peace tent was vivid. He described the rising tension as the Peace Commissioners realized the great danger. He testified he tried to catch Canby's eye to convey his alarm. Meacham's report of the first minute or two of the shooting was detailed up to the point when he was struck unconscious by a bullet.

Chief army surgeon Dr. Henry McElderry then took the stand. He testified he was present at every fight of the Modoc War, and he attended the dead and wounded at the peace tent. McElderry said when he first saw Canby and Thomas in death, they had been stripped naked. In stark medical terms, he described their wounds. "[Canby] had three wounds on his body, and several abrasions of the face. One of the wounds, apparently made by a ball, was the inner canthus [corner] of the left eye. I think the gunshot wound of his head caused his death; this ball, which entered in the eye and came up in the head, and fractured the left parietal bone and went through the brain." McElderry said Reverend Thomas had multiple gunshot wounds, but it was a bullet to the heart that killed him.

On the fourth day, the Modocs called witnesses for their defense. Captain Jack, dressed in his collarless flannel shirt and filthy trousers, did most of the questioning and speaking. He clearly did not understand the nature of a legal defense; he apparently thought he would be exonerated if he could show the Klamaths also played a role in the war. Captain Jack called Scarface Charley as his first witness, and put questions to him designed to implicate the Klamaths. Scarface's responses, probably spoken in English, were quite revealing, but useless as a defense for the murder charges.

Scarface Charley, who exchanged the first shots of the war, was the best known of the Modoc warriors except Captain Jack. Under Captain Jack's questioning, he detailed how the Klamath mercenaries hired by the army had promised the Modocs they would not shoot at them, but would discharge their guns in the air. He said Allen David, the principal Klamath chief, had asked the Modocs not to shoot at them, either. Said Scarface Charley, "[The Klamaths] wanted to make the soldiers believe they were our enemies, but they were our friends."

He also testified the Klamaths had supplied the Modocs with ammunition. During the first month of the war, he said, a party of ten Klamaths visited the Lava Beds and gave them all their ammunition.

Link River Jack, a Klamath, snuck into the Lava Beds in January to give Scarface Charley eighty caps (small explosive cylinders or detonators used to ignite the powder charge in pistols and rifles). He also offered Captain Jack twenty caps, and gave the contents of his powder horn to Indian George. Although Scarface Charley established Klamath treachery toward the army, his testimony did nothing to provide a defense for the four defendants.

Captain Jack then called Dave, a Modoc who fought with Captain Jack in the Lava Beds, to the witness stand. Dave continued the description of Klamath double-dealing. He said Klamath chief Allen David had encouraged the Modocs to fight, and promised to help them. One-Eyed Mose, another Modoc warrior, also testified that Link River Jack had come to their camp and had given them caps and all the powder they had.

Captain Jack finally made a statement in his own defense. "I hardly know how to talk here," he began. "I don't know how white people talk in such a place as this." Judge Advocate Curtis reassured him: "Talk exactly as if you were at home, in a council." If Captain Jack had been represented, he might have been advised not to testify. But Captain Jack's soliloquy lasted at least three hours—over an afternoon and morning session. He was usually taciturn in talking with whites, but now he engaged a lengthy defense.

Captain Jack spoke with great sincerity, conveying his bewilderment at the way the war began. Samuel Clarke, writing for the *New York Times*, admired his understanding and intelligence. "His power," Clarke wrote, "comes from the possession of more than average intellect and force of mind."[23] Captain Jack's eyes "fairly snapped when he spoke."[24] He argued strenuously that he was always peaceful toward whites ("You men here don't know what I have been heretofore") and that he had good relations with many of them. "I considered myself as a white man; I didn't want to have an Indian heart any longer," he said. "I always tried to live peaceably and never asked any man for anything. I would like to see the man who started all this fuss, and caused me to be in the trouble I am in now." Captain Jack said emphatically that he did not start the war. He claimed he had encouraged whites to settle on land near his village on Lost River and never bothered them. He said the homesteaders found his Modocs welcoming and employed them as farm hands.

Captain Jack testified he thought negotiations were set to resume when the army attacked on November 29, 1872. He admitted he had defied orders to return to the Klamath reservation, but he and Schonchin John said Ivan Applegate had promised negotiations would continue the next day. "It was my understanding that [Ivan] Applegate was to come and have a talk with me, and not to bring any soldiers." Captain Jack said he had hoped to call a meeting that would include Henry Miller, a nearby farmer, and the settler Dennis Crawley, who lived closest to the Indians. Captain Jack and Schonchin John both expected two or three men would return to their village to talk. When the army arrived at dawn, Captain Jack said he had no idea he would be attacked, and thus did not post sentries.

Captain Jack testified he was fast asleep when the army appeared at his village at dawn. He was given no chance to negotiate, and was angered when "Major Jackson commenced on me; I didn't know why they were mad at me." He said he had so few warriors it was useless for him to retaliate. "I run off, I didn't fight any." Captain Jack said that after taking sanctuary in the Lava Beds, he went to friendly ranchers and tried to settle things. He was deeply angered when Hooker Jim and the men who killed the settlers arrived at his camp and demanded to stay, implicating him in their crimes. At this point Captain Jack turned dramatically to Hooker Jim, who was standing in the crowd. Captain Jack asked, "What did you kill those people for? I never wanted you to kill my friends." When Captain Jack was told of the killings, he recounted, he tried to send Hooker Jim and his accomplices out of the Lava Beds. "I didn't want them to stay with me. I don't know who told them to kill the settlers. I always advised them not to kill white people."

The Modoc chief said it was the Bloodhounds who had pushed him to kill Canby: "Them four scouts knew all about it. . . . They were in our councils, and they all wanted to kill the peace commissioners; they all advised me to do it." He lamented his loss of control over the Modocs gathered in the Stronghold. He recounted the tumultuous meetings, his dwindling authority, and the ascendancy of Hooker Jim and the war faction. "When I got to talking, they would tell me to hush!" He said Hooker Jim told him: "You are like an old squaw; you have never done any fighting yet; we have the fighting and you have never done any fighting yet; you are not fit to be a chief."

Captain Jack argued that all the men involved in planning the murders should share responsibility, and particularly those who forced him to kill Canby. "Hooker Jim was the one that agitated the fighting, that wanted to fight all of the time. I was by myself with my few men and did not say anything about fighting. Now I have to bear the blame for him and the rest of them."[25]

The five officers of the military commission went into private session on the afternoon of the fourth day of testimony and returned quickly with their verdicts. Lieutenant Colonel Elliot read Captain Jack's verdict first: "On Charge 1, Guilty; on Charge 2, Guilty; on Charge 3, Guilty." Elliot then intoned identical judgments for each of the five remaining defendants. Then Captain Jack heard the sentence he knew would come: "And the commission does therefore sentence him, Captain Jack, to be hanged by the neck until he be dead, at such time and place as the proper authority shall direct; two-thirds of the members of the commission concurring therein." The others would hang with him on October 3, 1873.[26]

35

The Execution

The weather in August and September was sultry and oppressive, and the barracks at Fort Klamath were stifling. Some troops slept outdoors in tents. Frazier Boutelle said in his weekly letter to Dolly that he went fishing most days or "just lounged around from morning until night."[1] Post commander General Frank Wheaton was deemed champion at catching "abundant fat trout." Troops, though rarely furloughed, were allowed visits to Linkville, and the town teemed with soldiers in pursuit of drink and scented ladies.

The 153 Modoc prisoners, confined in their log stockade, waited to learn what would happen to them. Tensions between the Lost River and Hot Creek bands subsided as the hangings neared. "The Modocs are united in sympathy and friendship once more."[2] The condemned men confined in the guardhouse two hundred yards away were allowed occasional visits from wives and children. Modoc women smeared their faces with pitch and ashes as a symbol of grief. The imprisoned warriors, including Captain Jack and the five others condemned to death, were not faring well in their sweltering cells. A reporter for the *San Francisco Bulletin* wrote: "There is sickness among the prisoners in the guardhouse, and in less than three months we shall hear of deaths by disease in that locality."[3]

The families in the stockade were wearing rags when captured, and General Wheaton thought "humanity seemed to require that blankets and other covering be issued to them at once." He knew the bureaucratic wrangle that would ensue, so he went ahead without authorization from the secretary of war. Three weeks of correspondence followed about whether the provision of clothing and blankets could be approved, and if so, which department of government would pay. The Office of Indian Affairs, a division of the Interior Department, said it was not their mission to clothe prisoners of war. The War Department finally accepted the charges, but stipulated that, if possible, Indians would receive only damaged or used clothing.[4]

Captain Jack's health declined rapidly during his four months in shackles. Visitors to his cell reported he was thin and lethargic, with jailhouse pallor. His lustrous black hair, which he previously wore just below his ears, now fell to his shoulders. Sharing his cell with Schonchin John, he slept sullenly on the plank floor, in a corner, wrapped in a grey blanket. He spoke rarely. He ate little and complained of pain in his hip and left arm, broken years ago in a fall from a horse.[5]

Captain Jack's suffering may have stemmed in part from humiliation. He had been betrayed by his former comrades in arms, endured a humiliating defeat and capture by the enemy army, and he and Schonchin John were heavily "ironed" with shackles riveted around their ankles. Even the manner of his execution was shameful. "The notorious chief expressed his deep humiliation at being hanged, preferring to be shot, as a warrior should."[6]

The approach of Captain Jack's hanging aroused a moral furor across America. Humanitarian groups were clamoring for changes in Indian policy, and the Modoc War was a fresh lightening rod. The Quaker Society of Friends and the Universal Peace Union met in New York and Philadelphia, demanding leniency toward the Modocs. The American Indian Aid Association deplored the "ridiculous farce of erecting the gallows . . . before the trial begins [it was actually erected nearly three months after the trial] . . . and the unprecedented reading to the accused Modocs their indictment and sentence of death from the same paper [which did not occur]."[7]

Not long before the scheduled time for the hangings, the sheriff of Jackson County, Oregon, presented arrest warrants demanding General Wheaton turn over the prisoners and other alleged killers for civil trials in state courts.[8] Governor Grover asked that the execution be delayed until "final action" on the warrants.[9] Davis told Wheaton to decline to obey because the Modocs were federal prisoners of war and not subject to state law.[10]

As September progressed, sunsets came earlier and evening weather became brisk. With execution day approaching, spectators began to arrive at Fort Klamath to see the public hangings. Klamath Indians made the five-mile trip from their villages on the Williamson River to look at the Modocs in their pen and see the gallows erected. Food vendors set up tents, and cook fires filled the air with smoke. The four Bloodhounds requested General Wheaton reserve them a position from which they could watch Captain Jack hang.[11] "An enterprising embalmer named Sherwood arrived," reported the *New York Times*, "and claimed he had reached a bargain with Captain Jack by which the body of the chief was to become his property after death. When he was told the body became federal property, he said he would appeal to the Secretary of War."[12]

On October 2, 1873, soldiers were ordered to dig six graves alongside the guardhouse where they could be seen by the condemned men. A private marked the outlines with stakes, and troops excavated the rich earth of the meadow. "What a contemplation for a sentient being," wrote Alfred Meacham, "watching the grave digger hollowing out his own charnel-house!" He joked tastelessly that Captain Jack was "waiting for Uncle Sam to arrange for him his neck-tie." There was sadness among the condemned men.[13]

The afternoon before his hanging, Captain Jack's family was allowed to leave the stockade and pay him one last visit. A reporter described the family meeting as "an affecting incident." Captain Jack met his wives and sister Queen Mary in the stockade. Scarface Charley brought a box for him to sit on, his wife Lizzie covered the box with her shawl, and Captain Jack seated himself. At this time Rosie, then about four years of age, ran toward her father, rending the air with "frantic screams." Captain Jack extended both his arms to receive his daughter and at the same time turned his head aside. Lizzie wept. Jack held this position for several minutes, not moving. The members of the tribe looked on, in "stoical silence." Finally an old Modoc man crept up with a lighted pipe, which he "gently and almost reverently placed in the chieftain's mouth."[14]

General Wheaton visited the condemned men the evening of October 2 to inform them they would be hanged the next day. Captain Jack continued to blame others for shedding the first blood in the war, and forcing him to kill Canby. He reviled the Bloodhounds, saying, "I believe that [as long as] these four men—Bogus, Shacknasty Jim, Hooker, and Steamboat—are free, they have triumphed over me." Asked who should care for his family after his death, he said, "I cannot trust even Scarface Charley."[15] A chaplain said a prayer for the Modocs, which was translated. The clergyman burst into tears when he finished.[16]

Ever cocky, Boston Charley, just twenty-one, lashed out at the other condemned men, calling them cowards. "When I look on each side of me," he said, "I think of these other men as women. I do not fear death. I am the only man in this room." Schonchin John worried for his son, Peter, and asked that he be sent to live with his uncle Old Schonchin at Yainax. He blamed Indian agent Odeneal for "the war, the murder of Canby, the blood on the Lava Beds, and the chains on my feet."[17]

That evening, the condemned Modocs were permitted a last visit with their families. "Slowly and painfully" the four prisoners made their way from the guardhouse to the stockade. "Not a countenance of the four betokened fear." The women, dressed in black as a sign of grief, "rocked back and forth and wailed a dismal chorus." The warriors stood erect and calm. Then "the chieftain [Captain Jack] shook hands with one and all, and his companions followed suit." The last sounds were the "mingled shrieks of Lizzie, Rosie, and Captain Jack's sister Mary."[18]

A wagon with a four-horse team arrived at the guardhouse at 9:30 the next morning. All six men were instructed to sit on the coffins in the wagon, which took them to the huge scaffold. Although there were six men condemned to hang, there were only four coffins. Just before the executions, it was announced that President Grant had commuted the sentences of the boys Barncho and Slolux; they were to be sent to Alcatraz to serve life sentences.[19] As the wagon approached the gallows, the condemned men could see that three hundred of the rival Klamath Indians had arrived on ponies and on foot, arraying themselves to watch the hanging. The Bloodhounds asked to be seated where they could watch the execution.[20] The Modoc families, confined to their log stockade, were not allowed to attend, but caught glimpses of the execution by looking between the logs of their enclosure. Scarface Charley refused to watch the hangings, but he sat on a bench next to the guardhouse and wept.[21]

Captain Jack's death was mercifully quick. He and Boston Charley died instantaneously. Schonchin John and Black Jim convulsed for several minutes, their legs writhing. There is no record of how long they struggled. All four men were checked for a pulse after twenty minutes and declared dead by army doctor Henry McElderry.

36

Exile

The surviving Modoc prisoners of war had been penned in their crowded log stockade for 117 days—almost four months—with no word of their future. Many of the Indians had feared from the day of their capture that they would all be killed. Now Captain Jack and his lieutenants had been hanged and cut down from the scaffold.

Unknown to the captive Modocs, a decision about their future had been reached months earlier, but was kept secret by the Interior Department and the army. In June 1873 General Sherman, who had once called for their extermination, requested to Secretary of War Belknap that the Modocs be transported east and "distributed among a tribe easily guarded, such as the Winnebagos of Lake Superior." His goal was clear: "Thus the tribe of Modocs would disappear, and the example would be salutary in dealing with other Indians similarly disposed."[1]

When President Grant met with a Quaker peace delegation about the Modocs in August 1873, he announced his intention to break up the tribe, placing some east of the mountains and leaving others in the west. He wanted them to live with peaceful tribes. The Quakers applauded his "judicious and beneficent action" and suggested some of the Modocs might be relocated among the Quakers in Pennsylvania. They also asked Grant to provide rail transportation for a Quaker delegation to go west to investigate and "carry out this plan of action."[2] Grant declined.

The Interior Department began discussing what to do with the tribe in mid-summer of 1873, even before the military commission had tried Captain Jack and the others for murder. It was decided that the 150 "peaceful" Modocs (that is, the followers of Old Schonchin) who were not involved in the war would be allowed to remain in Oregon on the Klamath reservation. But Interior Secretary Columbus Delano later made it clear that as a matter of policy, the government intended to destroy the Modocs as a tribe. Forcing the followers of Captain Jack to live far from their ancestral land among other tribes was "the severest penalty" that could be inflicted upon the Modocs.[3]

In Washington, D.C., the Commissioner of Indian Affairs put out word that a location was being sought. Enoch Hoag, a Quaker superintendent of several reservations in Indian Territory and Kansas, offered to receive the Modocs and locate them in the northeast corner of Indian Territory—the future state of Oklahoma—thousands of miles from the Modoc homeland. The Modocs would be in the care of Hogue's brother-in-law, Hiram Jones, Quaker Indian Agent on the Quapaw Agency.

On September 13, 1873, the War Department, on orders from President Grant, announced the Modocs (except those sentenced to execution) were to be removed to Fort D. A. Russell in Wyoming Territory as prisoners of war.[4] The destination of the Modocs was not to be made public "any sooner than necessary."[5] The prisoners themselves were to be kept "in ignorance." There was some worry the Modocs would resist removal to the East, or that outsiders might try to "rescue" them. There was special concern that the Bloodhounds—the four who had betrayed Captain Jack—might try to escape.[6] But Wheaton said he "found no foundation for the dread entertained very generally that an attempt will be made to rescue the Modocs during their removal to Wyoming."[7]

Finally it was suggested the Modocs be sent instead to Fort McPherson in Nebraska Territory on the Platte River. General Sherman agreed, and decided that they be temporarily confined there on Brady's Island where they could more easily be kept from escaping, and where they could fish and forage for food.[8]

On October 12, 1873, a cavalcade of twenty-five wagons left Fort Klamath and rumbled away with 153 Modoc men, women, and children, still prisoners of war. Captain Henry Hasbrouck (first officer to win a battle against the Modocs in the war) and a platoon of twenty men from the Fourth Artillery and Twelfth Infantry escorted them. When they reached the town of Shasta, California, a group of twenty-five schoolboys met their caravan of wagons and escorted the Modocs into town.[9]

It took a week for the wagons to reach Redding, averaging twenty miles a day. When they arrived, the Modocs began their 1,930 mile trip by rail to their new home. Barncho and Slolux—the two whose death sentences were commuted by President Grant—were separated and sent south under guard to serve life sentences at Alcatraz. Reporter H. W. Atwell boarded the train when it reached Sacramento and described the scene: "With three or four exceptions, men, women, and children had striped their faces with a black and shiny paint, in mourning for the ill-fated Captain Jack." He saw some of the Modocs "cluster and crouch together" while others lay prone on the floor, "their heads wrapped in blankets, refusing to speak or rise." Atwell said the men were in leg irons, joined together in pairs. He met Captain Jack's young wife Lizzie, with her "sad and pretty eyes, swollen with weeping."[10]

They traveled by train across California, continuing through Nevada and Utah toward Wyoming. Although it is sometimes claimed the Modocs traveled in boxcars, they were put in three wooden passenger coaches, their army escorts traveling in the cars ahead and behind. They reached Fort McPherson on October 29, 1873. The captives still did not know their final destination.

Hasbrouck surrendered custody to Colonel J. J. Reynolds, commanding officer at Fort McPherson.[11] Two days later, the War Department turned the Modocs over to an Infantry officer, Lieutenant Melville C. Wilkinson. From there, they were to go on to the Quapaw Agency in Indian Territory.[12] By the middle of November Wilkinson had moved the Modocs to Baxter Springs, Kansas, a tough cattle town near the Quapaw Agency that was notorious for its saloons and dance halls. Wilkinson recommended the Modocs be removed because "it was a notorious place for corrupting Indians."[13]

Hiram Jones, Quaker agent at the agency, assumed custody of the Modocs in Baxter Springs on November 22, 1873. The Interior Department thought the Modocs would benefit from "the personal attention of a Christian agent."[14] Ironically, Jones would turn out to be the corrupt leader of a criminal "Quaker Indian Ring," which he and his extended family used ruthlessly to exploit the Modocs for the next six years. Jones immediately put the refugee Modocs at Seneca Springs, on Shawnee tribal land. Jones hired his son Endsley Jones at a salary of fifty dollars per month and claimed he would "shield [the Modocs] from certain whites, care for their aged, and at the earliest possible moment place them in schools." Their new home was in the extreme northeast corner of Indian Territory, where Missouri and Kansas meet. It was heavily timbered, and Jones thought it was excellent for farming.[15]

When they arrived, Jones ordered the Modocs to construct a barracks for themselves just two hundred yards from his home. The Modoc women and children were housed temporarily in the W. Hyland Hotel in Baxter Springs, while the able-bodied men (with Scarface Charley in charge) constructed the barracks in just one week.[16] The Modocs moved into their new home on Thanksgiving, November 27, 1873, just two days short of a year after the Modoc War had begun alongside Lost River.[17]

Jones received $8,660 annually to operate the Quapaw Agency, with which he employed 18 assorted teachers, blacksmiths, carpenters, and Indian "apprentices." But by time the Modocs arrived towards the end of 1873, Jones had expended his annual stipend for the year. Only one hundred dollars remained for food, clothing, and medicine to sustain the ninety-three Modoc adults and sixty children through the winter. A Quaker organization contributed winter clothes. The American Indian Aid Association in Philadelphia sent them seeds for spring planting, and provided Jones with cash to buy shoes and stockings. The Modocs fed themselves during the first winter in part by hunting.[18]

In June 1874 an agreement was made with the Eastern Shawnee tribe to cede four thousand acres to the United States as a permanent home for the Modocs. They were to be paid six thousand dollars. The Shawnee wanted money up front and would not agree to the sale until they saw "the first installment of the purchase money." The Indian Department would not approve the expenditure, so land was leased from the Shawnee for five years at three thousand dollars a year.[19]

The land set aside for the Modocs was described in several reports as ideal for agriculture, but by 1880 the Commissioner of Indian Affairs stated: "Less than one quarter of their land is good for anything but grazing."[20] The land farmed by the Modocs was in one large undivided field, resulting in turf wars among them, "yearly feuds of more or less consequence, frequently ending in broken bones and bruised bodies."[21]

For a time, Indian officials considered sending the Modocs still in Oregon to Oklahoma. Indian Commissioner F. H. Smith felt the 150 or so Modocs on the Klamath reservation at Yainax were making lit tle progress toward learning cultivation or industrial pursuits. Among the Modocs in Indian Territory, "great solicitude was expressed for the removal of their Oregon brethren to this Territory." It was estimated the cost of moving them would be about twelve thousand dollars, and an additional eight thousand dollars would be required for subsistence.[22]

The Modocs in Oregon would have no part of it. The chief Old Schonchin—whom Dyer called "a terrible and bloody warrior in his day"—was determined to live and die on the reservation in Oregon. Old Schonchin had received letters and encouragement from the Modocs in Oklahoma "extolling that country and the advantages there," but the chief feared trickery and had no intention of moving.[23]

Initial reports from Oklahoma were filled with praise for the Modocs' energy and industry. In 1874 Commissioner Smith visited the Modocs, and found them thriving, "willing and energetic in the discharge of every duty." He assembled all of the Modocs, adults and children, for a talk on the morning of September 23, 1874. He summarized the meeting with his unlikely conclusion that "[The Modocs] expressed their satisfaction in their present location, their determination to go to work immediately on their new reservation . . . and to become like white men as rapidly as possible."[24]

Indian Agent Jones said the main problem among the Modocs was gambling. Failing to understand the role of gaming in Modoc culture, Jones labeled it immoral. He said some Modocs were willing to gamble away all their possessions. Scarface Charley, the acting chief, refused to intervene, and "was deposed and Bogus Charley appointed." The Commissioner reported: "The change proved acceptable to the band, and its moral effect was excellent."[25]

In spite of the sanguine reports, corruption was rampant on the Quapaw reservation, as it was all across the Indian Service in the 1870s. Interior Secretary Columbus Delano, who played such a large role in the Modoc War, was removed for corruption in 1875. It was thought that religious people, like the unassailable Quakers, were best to run the reservations as they would be less likely to steal money allocated for the tribes. In fact, Jones (a Quaker himself) was running a skillful and efficient ring that was systematically defrauding the Modocs and the six other tribes he supervised. It was a family business; eleven of the twelve agency employees were relatives of Hoag or Jones.[26]

Jones and Hoag devised a myriad of schemes to defraud the Indians. The agency school charged "exorbitant" fees to the government, and the ring inflated the price of beef and foodstuffs. Jones had a kickback arrangement giving all Indian business to one store. Merchants in nearby Seneca challenged the activities of Hiram Jones's son, but Hoag appointed a family friend to investigate, and Endsley was exonerated. Questions about the Quakers and the Quapaw reservation continued to mount.[27] An inspector was sent in January 1878 to check out the Quapaw agency. The investigation found bookkeeping irregularities as well as Jones' fraudulent cattle-buying business that inflated the price of livestock by 25 percent and delivered near-inedible meat.[28]

In a sworn statement, Bogus Charley described the horrific management of their affairs. "My people die eighty-six since we come here. We were one hundred and fifty seven when we came. I have been to [Jones] and told him my people are sick, my people are going to die, and he told me, 'I've got no medicine for you.' He said he was sorry but he had got no money; the government didn't allow money for us. I think Jones has our money; he didn't give my people any money." Bogus Charley described how cheap and inferior flour and rotten meat were given the Modocs. He alleged that Jones turned over a twelve-year-old wagon to them and charged the government $125. Jones told him to "hush."[29]

Commissioner of Indian Affairs E. A. Hayt seemed unconcerned when he received the report of graft in Oklahoma. When he visited the Quapaw Agency that same year, he did not even mention the charges against Jones. Instead he praised the Modocs for their industry and their "great progress in civilization." The Commissioner met Bogus Charley, whom he called "a bright, intelligent man; he is, however, suffering from a pulmonary disease which threatens to terminate his life at an early day."[30]

A congressional investigation in October 1878 finally caught up with the Quaker ring. In testimony taken at the Quapaw Agency, a string of witnesses condemned the fraudulent regime of Jones and Hoag. Bogus Charley testified again: "We die; we lose a good many in this country; this land don't suit them. I tell you what I feel now. We die out; my people. We don't like that. I wonder what makes me talk. We want health. Our people lose a good deal. That is what makes me talk."[31] Pressure became so great that Hayt removed Hiram Jones in April 1879. Hayt himself resigned later over charges (which he disputed) he had used his influence so his son could buy a silver mine in Arizona.[32]

The Modocs' health tragically declined from their arrival in Oklahoma. Ten times more Modocs perished of disease in exile than died in the Modoc War. In little more than a decade the Modocs' numbers were reduced from 153 to 90.[33] Saddest of all, the Modoc children were dying. In 1884 an Indian Agent reported: "The Modocs especially complain that they can raise no babies here."[34] Three years later, the reservation physician reported that "owing to prevailing syphilitic diseases among the Modocs, many of their children die quite young, and only a few families succeed in raising any children."[35] Three years after that, the doctor wrote, "At this late date little can be hoped for more than to make life more comfortable and save the younger ones from premature death."[36]

In 1887 the agency physician reported that because of nearby river bottoms, "Malarial fevers are very numerous. . . . Many of these Indians are afflicted with phthisis [pulmonary tuberculosis]. In some of its stages, pneumonia and bronchitis are quite serious and often fatal."[37]

In mid-1890 John S. Lindsay, physician for the Quapaw Indian Agency who then oversaw the Modocs, filed his annual report. He seemed horrified at how many Modocs had died from scrofula (a tuberculosis of the neck) and forms of pulmonary trouble, and was concerned with "the great decrease of the Modoc Tribe." He reported that during the first seventeen years the Modocs had been in Oklahoma, there had been 170 deaths and only about 100 births.[38]

Lindsay feared that without additional means, "the tribe will be almost wiped from existence within the next ten years." Lindsay gave perhaps the first true report of the Modocs' terrible living conditions in the 1880s and 1890s: "They live in cabins with dirt floors, and often with walls plastered until airtight. If light is admitted, it is only through a single window, without any means of ventilation whatever. Many of these consist of but a single room, and this is crowded to many times its capacity. In winter these are kept at a high temperature, and are practically dry at all times."[39] Lindsay then described the horrifying conditions inside these Modoc homes: "Exhalations from dogs and persons, with sputa from consumptives and pus from scrofulous sores, are allowed to lodge in walls and floors. These are rapidly dried in the high temperature, and suspended in the already unpure air of the room, and is breathed over and over again by the inmates, thereby transmitting the germ of disease."[40]

In 1901 an Oregon newspaper reported the "ancient Modoc tribe has dwindled to 77 members, mostly women and diseased or sick children." From "the most savage and indomitable fighters, only thirteen able-bodied warriors were left. The spirit of the old days has gone, and nobody will ever hear of a story about 'the last of the Modocs.'"[41] In 1904 a census of the Oklahoma Modocs found there were only fifty-four alive.[42]

In 1937 an Oklahoma historian interviewed a woman who had been among the original Modocs to arrive in Indian Territory. She recalled the graveyard planted with flowers and rosebushes, but lamented the number of unmarked graves. Sixty-seven-year-old Cora Hayman said, "The greater number of graves were made there in the first few years after the Modocs came when so many of the tribe sickened and died and [were] buried in a row or rather two rows marked by native rocks but today no one knows one grave from another."[43] The first to die, in April 1874, was Captain Jack's four-year-old, Rosie. She is in the grave numbered 33.

37

The Skull of Captain Jack

In January 1949 an employee of the Lava Beds National Monument, acting on a hunch, wrote to the Smithsonian Institute in Washington, D.C., asking if the museum held any Indian remains from the Modoc War. The inquiry, by Ken McCleod, a feisty descendent of a southern Oregon pioneer family, threw open a door on a great deal of shocking and previously unreported information. Captain Jack's skull—and those of his lieutenants—had not been in their graves for three quarters of a century.[1]

Not only had Captain Jack and the other executed men been

Captain Jack's Tombstone.
Photo by Bill Stafford.

denied a dignified cremation and burial according to sacred Modoc tradition, but the corpses of those hanged at Fort Klamath in October 1873 had been decapitated and scalped. The severed heads were most likely boiled and immersed in a solution of lime to separate the flesh from the bone. Then army doctor Henry J. McElderry sent the skulls to a museum in Washington, D.C. More than a century would pass before the skulls of Captain Jack and the other Modoc warriors would come home.

McCleod learned that an old catalog of specimens in the collection of the Army Medical Museum recorded seven Modoc skulls, of which four were received at the time of the executions—those of Captain Jack, Schonchin John, Boston Charley, and Black Jim.[2] Dr. M. T. Newman of the Department of Physical Anthropology told McCleod there were no records of full skeletons of Modocs in their inventory, just skulls, and that "in all probability, the bodies were buried, possibly at the fort after the execution, and only the skulls sent to the museum."[3]

Dr. Newman was right. After the execution, coffins containing the four torsos were buried alongside the guardhouse where they had been jailed, and the graves marked with whitewashed wooden boards. But the heads were never there. What happened on that cold fall night in October 1873 was witnessed by Colonel H. S. Shaw, the city editor of the *San Francisco Chronicle*. Shaw, who had come to Fort Klamath to report on the hangings, saw a lantern burning late into the night in the crude mortuary tent. A black India rubber sheet was spread out and a barrel stood in the corner. He saw "a case of surgical instruments and apparatus necessary for some anatomical disintegration." A surgical procedure was under way.[4]

Unknown to Shaw, McElderry, the army surgeon, was removing the heads of the four Modoc warriors. Three weeks after the hangings, McElderry packed the skulls in a barrel and shipped them to Dr. George Alexander Otis, a colleague and the curator of the Army Medical Museum in Washington, D.C. The shipping receipt noted the contents of McElderry's submission: "(1) One Barrel—specimens of natural history." In a letter to Otis a few days later, McElderry blandly provided the details: "The barrel contains the heads of the four Modoc Indians, No. 1018 Captain Jack, No. 1019 Schonchin, No. 1020 Boston Charlie, and No. 1021 Black Jim, executed on the 3rd Instant [October 3] at this post for the murder of Maj. General Canby and the Reverend Thomas, Peace Commissioners. The heads are labeled with the respective names of each."[5]

McElderry had been collecting Indian skulls for years, as did military surgeons throughout the country.[6] Earlier that summer he had promised to send the skulls in a letter dated July 13, 1873, to Otis.[7] A few months earlier, Dr. Skinner, another army doctor at Fort Klamath, had shipped the skull of a Modoc woman to the museum. The Modoc woman died on November 28, 1872, supposedly "of some unknown disease." In all likelihood, the woman was the one killed by the soldiers and burned following the attack at the Lost River village.[8]

But when he shipped the skulls, McElderry withheld another macabre collection he had made—the scalps of all four of the executed

Modocs. On the night of the execution, McElderry not only severed the Modoc heads from their bodies, but apparently scalped them. Nearly two decades later, the scalps showed up at the Army Medical Museum with a record indicating they belonged with the skulls of Captain Jack, Schonchin John, Boston Charley, and Black Jim.[9]

The desecration of Native American corpses and collection of skulls was widely practiced by the U.S. Army in the decades following the Civil War. In 1867 Surgeon General Barnes sent a "circular letter" to army medical officers in the field calling upon them to collect "Indian crania," together with artifacts such as weapons, dress, implements, diet samples, and medicines.[10] To support the surgeon general's directive, the army collected Indian skulls regularly during the Modoc War.[11] In May 1873 a reporter for the *Sacramento Union* observed that, "Four or five [Indian] heads have been forwarded to the War Department Museum from the Modoc headquarters and we learn that some more curiosities of the same kind are to be sent shortly."[12] Army surgeon Dr. Edwin Bentley collected the heads of the two Modoc braves that were being kicked around by soldiers and citizens who entered the Stronghold after the Indians abandoned it on April 17, 1873.[13]

The skulls of the four hanged Modocs were among the few whose names were known and recorded in records of the Army Medical Museum. Most of the Native American specimens were nameless, identified only by the name of the collector, the place collected, and usually the tribe. There was no distinction between bones taken from a grave or from the recently dead. In May 1898 the Army Medical Museum transferred 2,206 skulls to the Smithsonian Institution.[14] The skulls of the four Modocs were among them.

In 1975 a group of Indians claiming descent from Captain Jack, his immediate relatives, and other executed warriors petitioned the Smithsonian for return of the four crania. After lengthy negotiation, the institution agreed to surrender the skulls to tribal members who could show direct descent from the victims. In January 1976 a tribal delegation of four, led by Donald "Duck" Schonchin, went from Klamath Falls to Washington, D.C., to collect the skulls. But Schonchin died suddenly of a heart attack in his motel, and the transfer was canceled.[15]

In November 1979, Lee Juillerat, a reporter for the Klamath Falls *Herald and News*, visited the Smithsonian and snapped a black and white photograph of the four skulls—the negative of which is now in the Klamath County Museum. Published on the newspaper's front page, the picture shows the skulls in a row, their perfect teeth an eerie rictus. As McElderry reported, the skulls' identifying numbers were inked on their foreheads.[16]

Interest in the skulls waned for several years, until a determined Modoc woman, Debra Riddle, took up the cause. Riddle, a great-great-granddaughter of Winema and a collateral descendent of Schonchin John, has a degree in museology from the Institute of American Indian Arts of New Mexico and a vast knowledge of the complexities of Modoc genealogy. Tracing ancestry is vital to establishing eligibility for tribal enrollment, and Riddle periodically ventures to the massive federal archives in Seattle to study the records.

Riddle was the one who recovered the skulls. In August 1983 Douglas Ubelaker, chairman of the Smithsonian Department of Anthropology, approved Riddle's standing to receive the skulls and assume responsibility for their burial.[17] She met with Ubelaker and Lawrence Angel, curator of Physical Anthropology. Following their meeting, Riddle flew home to Klamath Falls with the four skulls, packed two to a box, plus one additional of a Modoc woman.[18] That was the last public trace of the Modoc skulls. Riddle has refused to reveal what happened to them, saying only that she did not dishonor them. In 1996, she told a reporter simply: "They're home."[19]

In 2012, Debra Riddle escorted author Jim Compton to view the gravesites of her great-great-grandmother Winema and her husband, the miner and translator Frank Riddle. Their son Jefferson Davis (Jeff) Riddle, is buried alongside. The privacy evinced by Riddle and others regarding their ancestors is less about secrecy than a deep respect for the tribal dead and the sense of gravity and reverence Modocs feel for tribal remains. But the author couldn't help but wonder if the missing skulls of Captain Jack and the others might be buried in the cemetery.

"Debbie," the author later asked, "Did you bury the skulls?" She replied, "I brought them home, Jim." The author tried again, hoping for a clue. But she only repeated, "I brought them home."[20]

Epilogue: The Aftermath

When he had finished everything, Kumush [the creator of the Modoc world] took his daughter and went to the edge of the world, to the place where the sun rises. He travelled on the sun's road till he came to the middle of the sky. There he stopped and built his house, and there he lives now.

—Jeremiah Curtin, *Myths of the Modocs*

Memories of the Modoc War dwindled quickly. The nation, once inflamed by exciting news reports, soon forgot about the events that took place in the Lava Beds. But when the costs of the Modoc War were calculated based on the number of enemy combatants, it became the most expensive Indian War in American history. The Secretary of War informed Congress in June 1874 that the total cost of the Modoc War was $411,068.[1] Other estimates that included property damage, loss of life, and participation of the California militia range as high as a million dollars in the currency of the day.[2]

There were wild overestimates of the number of Modoc combatants and Modoc dead. However, most agree that about 60 Modoc warriors fought in the Lava Beds, including Captain Jack, and of those, five died in battle. There were several Modoc noncombatants killed, probably about eight. On the U. S. Army side, Davis had over one thousand troops under command by the end of the War. There were 143 casualties and 68 soldiers dead.[3]

THE OKLAHOMA MODOCS

The Modoc population in Oklahoma plummeted sharply in the 1890s, mostly from the devastating health conditions. Their numbers were further reduced when some of the exiles drifted back to Oregon. When the twentieth century dawned, there were only 49 Modocs remaining out of the original 153 who had been exiled there.[4]

Curley-Headed Doctor died in Oklahoma in 1890. The aging Jennie Clinton said in 1910 that the night he expired, there was a wild and frightening storm all night, but the sun burst out in the morning at the moment of his death. She said a large flock of pigeons alighted in a tree and sang.[5] Scarface Charley, who was removed as chief in Oklahoma after he declined to crack down on gambling, died of tuberculosis in 1896. Steamboat Frank changed his name to Frank Modoc and was recognized as a minister by the Society of Friends. Slolux, whose sentence had been commuted to life imprisonment by President Grant, was released from Alcatraz after five years. He traveled to Oklahoma and changed his name to George Denny. He died of tuberculosis in 1896.

In 1909 Congress gave the remaining Modocs in Oklahoma the opportunity to return to Oregon, and a number of them went west where they were enrolled in the Klamath Tribes.

The Modoc Tribe of Oklahoma was federally recognized as an independent tribe in May 1978, and today the Oklahoma Modocs operate several successful tribal businesses. At the original tribal graveyard in Oklahoma a small sign that reads "Modoc Cemetery" marks a dusty red-dirt road off the county road. The site is dominated by the towering Quaker church, clad in weathered gray clapboards, shaded by a bower of seventy-foot trees. A low metal fence surrounds the graveyard. Although many of the men, women, and children who rest there are unknown, a few of the graves have been identified. George Denny (Slolux) is in the grave marked 20. Captain Jack's four-year-old child Rosie lies in the grave numbered 33. James Long (Long Jim), the ancestor of Chief Follis, is in grave 31, the headstone inscribed: "Youngest Warrior in the Modoc War."

JESSE APPLEGATE

Jesse Applegate's fortunes declined sharply after the Modoc War. In 1874 he lost 1,800 sheep in freezing weather.[6] In yet another attempt to win profit and influence, he and a friend signed a ten-thousand-dollar security bond for Thomas May, elected Oregon secretary of state in 1862 and in 1866. Jesse considered May, a Republican, a close friend and had nominated him for election. But May led an "extravagant and luxurious lifestyle," embezzled state funds, and absconded to Utah.

The May affair was ruinous to Jesse Applegate financially and emotionally. He was subsequently found guilty of fraudulently conveying land to his children to avoid paying $5000 on the forfeited security bond.[7] Jesse's property and his renowned house in Yoncalla were auctioned off (although his wife was allowed to keep forty acres). The purchaser found the grand Applegate house too big, so he tore it down and "sold it for the valuable wood and stained glass windows." Jesse wrote, "For another man's sins I have been deprived of all my earthly possessions. I have . . . not even a spot to hide away my body."[8]

After the death of his wife Cynthia, Applegate's mental health further deteriorated. "God has called her to her rest," he wrote to his son in 1881, "and I am left behind without an occupation, without an earthly ambition, and without an obligation to any human being. Expecting to follow speedily."[9] In 1886 a Jackson County judge ordered him to the Oregon State Mental Hospital. The commitment papers said he suffered from dementia and was "insane and unsafe to be at large." The doctor thought the causes of his insanity were "old age, physical debilities, but chiefly worry over financial reverses." Applegate was released after twelve months to live with his family. He died in April 1888 at age seventy-seven.[10]

WINEMA

Winema remained on the Klamath reservation in Oregon. After the war, Alfred Meacham recruited Winema and husband Frank Riddle for his lecture tour, "The Tragedy of the Lava Beds." Winema was featured as the "Little Woman Chief," and Meacham wrote a biography of her, *Wi-Ne-Ma and Her People*, in gratitude for having saved his life.[11]

When Meacham's lecture show disbanded in April 1875, Winema returned from the East Coast to the Oregon reservation, where she became a revered personage. In 1891 Congress granted her an unusual military pension of twenty-five dollars a month.[12] Winema died at Yainax in 1920 and is buried in the Chief Schonchin Cemetery near Sprague River, Oregon.

Winema's reputation is somewhat tarnished among some Modocs because she provided intelligence to the army about what she saw and heard in the Lava Beds. Cheewa James, a fourth-generation Modoc descended from Shacknasty Jim, wrote, "Toby was a woman torn between two loyalties. Cousin to Captain Jack, she understood the pain they suffered in being forced from their homeland . . . But Toby was married to a white man, and lived in [his] world."[13]

Alfred Meacham

Meacham did not stay in Fort Klamath for the hangings, but went to San Francisco and launched a traveling lecture show, touring the United States for several years. To prepare, he asked Oliver Applegate to provide him accounts of atrocities against Modocs. He also wanted the Indian words for "I am for peace! I am for war! Hooray!"—words he promised to "use cleverly."[14] Meacham lectured in San Francisco on October 2, 1873, the eve of the hangings. The show got a tepid review from the *Alta California*: "His poor delivery of this very interesting subject failed to give general satisfaction." The reviewer thought the public was tired of the Modoc issue.[15] Meacham later went to Indian Territory and recruited three of the exiled Modocs for his troupe—Scarface Charley, Steamboat Frank, and Shacknasty Jim; the traveling show crisscrossed the nation.

Meacham's magnum opus, *Wigwam and Warpath,* was published in Boston in 1875 and sold by subscription. But it was so large (seven hundred pages) and expensive (four dollars) that it sold poorly. *Wi-ne-ma,* his encomium to her, appeared in 1876, but the slim volume also had weak sales. Meacham defaulted on $1,675 owed the Oregon Indian Superintendancy, and he spent the final years of his life in debt. Meacham took a brief appointment on the Ute Commission in 1880 where he was assigned to the White River Utes and worked on the ratification of an agreement with the Colorado Utes.[16] Deeply sympathetic to the tribe, Meacham was charged as an accessory to murder when some Utes killed a white freight hauler.[17] He was finally exonerated and returned to Washington, D.C., but his health continued to decline.

Meacham was sitting at the editor's desk of the pro-Indian magazine *Council Fire* when he died suddenly on February 16, 1882.[18] Congress awarded his wife a fifty-dollar monthly pension after his death, more than he provided her in life.[19]

The Klamath Tribes

The Klamath and Modoc tribes and the Yahooskin band of Snake Indians—the signatories to the 1864 Oregon treaty—are now known as the Klamath Tribes. In the first half of the twentieth century, the combined Klamath Tribes were prosperous due to the sales of tribal timber, and its members enjoyed relative economic comfort.

But their prosperity would not last. In 1953 the U.S. Congress enacted House Concurrent Resolution 108, which declared the policy of Congress to terminate the federal relationship with recognized Indian tribes. In 1954 Congress terminated the Klamath tribes, ending federal control over them, and abolished all offices of the Bureau of Indians Affairs that served the Klamaths. One historian concluded, "The Klamath Indian Reservation was gone and the Klamath Tribe effectively destroyed."[20] The Klamath reservation land base of approximately 1.8 million acres was taken by condemnation, leaving total tribal land of only 308 acres. Tribal members were offered a one-time lump sum payment of about $43,500 per person, but that windfall soon evaporated, and there were "grave consequences" for the tribes as a result of termination.[21]

Congress later reversed course, and the Klamath Tribes were restored by an act of Congress in 1986. Today the Klamath Tribes are travelling the long road toward resurrecting their tribal identity. The tribe has built a handsome tribal headquarters building outside Chiloquin, Oregon, and a nearby casino has realized modest earnings that are distributed to enrolled members on a *pro rata* basis.[22]

THE KLAMATH WATER WARS

The irrigation scheme hatched by Jesse Applegate and Jesse Carr was eventually accomplished, but not until decades later. When Theodore Roosevelt was president, the Two Jesses' plan to replumb the water system of the entire Modoc plateau became the blueprint for an immense project by the U.S. Bureau of Reclamation. The "Klamath Project," built between 1906 and 1922, was a complex drainage and irrigation undertaking that radically modified the natural water systems of the area.

The old fault lines between Indians and whites split open again in 2001, when federal authorities ordered the cut-off of irrigation water to hundreds of farmers and ranchers in the Klamath Basin area of southern Oregon. The region was threatened with severe drought, and the Klamath Tribes argued that continued diversion of water from lakes and rivers posed a threat to their traditional fish resources (the native suckerfish and Coho salmon). A federal judge agreed that the Endangered Species Act did not permit water to be reserved for irrigation at the expense of fish. The so-called Klamath Water Wars got extensive national media coverage—focusing on whether environmental regulation had gone too far and the cost to farmers of saving the suckerfish.

In 2011 farmers, ranchers, Indian tribes, the state, and the federal government negotiated an historic settlement. The settlement provided for removal of four hydroelectric dams on the Klamath River, assuring water supply for farmers, protecting fish, and giving economic compensation to the tribe. In an ironic aftermath, in 2013 the state recognized—after decades of argument—that the tribe did indeed have a "superior water right dating from time immemorial," giving the tribe the dominant position in water disputes and the ability to withhold water to save fish. A legal scholar observed: "Native peoples and species are [finally] seeking an even break."[23] Unfortunately, approval of the settlement was stalled for years in the U.S. Congress.[24]

Captain Jack's Lingering Legend

Interest in the Modoc War continued in the late nineteenth century. In 1873, Seth Hardinge published *Modoc Jack: or the Lion of the Lava Beds*. Part fiction—Hardinge invents an early life for Captain Jack (and his mother) in Santa Barbara before the Modoc War—the imaginary Captain Jack calls out imprecations like "Yes, vengeance, we will have vengeance, and nothing else but vengeance."[25]

Curiosity about Captain Jack and the Modoc War languished in the twentieth century until Charles Bronson played Captain Jack in *Drum Beat*, a 1954 Warner Brothers potboiler about the Modoc War. In the B-movie, Bronson dressed like an Apache and looked like Geronimo with his signature headband. "You think I have chicken heart? I kill plenty soldiers! I no afraid of brass buttons!" says the Captain Jack character. "Lost River mine! I kill to keep it mine!" Dell later released a comic book based on the movie.[26]

The Modoc War later inspired at least a dozen novels and several plays.[27] At least two of the plays have been produced. *Lost River: The Story of the Modoc War*, by Ben Van Meter (1998) enjoyed thirty-two amateur performances over four years in Alturas, California. *Captain Jack's Revenge*, by Michael Townsend Smith (1970), set in New York's Greenwich Village, was performed at the Café La Mama experimental theater. A favorable review from *Village Voice* reviewer Arthur Sainer found it "freakily enchanting."[28]

THE LAVA BEDS TODAY

In 1925 a national monument was established at the site of the Modoc War. At Lava Beds National Monument, the Modoc War battlefields sometimes attract groups of Civil War re-enactors, who stake tents at Gillem's Camp and simulate soldiers and Modocs in battle. In April 1998 the author watched their noisy skirmishes and the firing of a twelve-pound howitzer. The Modocs have no interest in participating; and the reenactments, at the site of the Modoc War, have little or no connection with the Modoc War or Modoc history. The re-enactors sit around campfires, eat hardtack with boiled beans, and drink black coffee. A young man says, "Beans are timeless." Two Indians, Bill and Rachel Duffy, were among the crowd of about 150 who had come to watch. Bill, then sixty-nine, was dressed in impeccable faded blue jeans, a windbreaker, and black cowboy hat. He said, "It just seems like the war goes on and on, we never get any closure." Duffy says the Modocs are "enduring people."[29]

DESCENDANTS OF TOBY RIDDLE

Christine Riddle Allen, the charming granddaughter of Jeff Riddle—the son of Winema and Frank Riddle—lives quietly in Klamath Falls with her daughter Debra Riddle.[30] Christine recently issued a new edition of Jeff Riddle's invaluable 1914 *Indian History of the Modoc War,* with an added useful introduction.

Proud of her Modoc pedigree and unique Modoc heritage, Debra Riddle believes that those who ignore history deprive themselves of the strength of their ethnic past. She recently appeared on the TV program *History Detectives*, where she offered expert opinion on the authenticity of a Modoc basket woven by her ancestor, Winema. She participated briefly in a desultory and short-lived Modoc movement to secede from the Klamath Tribes and form a Confederated Modoc and Yahooskin Tribe. The secession movement died quickly when it could not attract members willing to "disenroll" from the main tribe. Nevertheless, Debra Riddle remains among the small cadre of tribal members who fiercely assert their Modoc identity. When she attends pow-wows on other reservations, she is irritated when she is identified as Klamath rather than Modoc. She enjoys T-shirts with mottos like "Modoc 4 Life!"

In 2013 Christine and Debra Riddle invited the author and his wife on a tour of their family's former lands on the Klamath reservation. In the 1920s, when the reservation was still intact, the Riddle family owned hundreds of acres of timbered land dotted with sparkling springs and enclosed meadows. Christine took us up dirt roads to point out where as a child she and her friends rode bareback across the idyllic landscape. She stoically pointed out the landmarks of her memory: "Dad had a pretty good house over there and did OK with cattle."

Debra and Christine try to venture annually to the bay at Rocky Point on Upper Klamath Lake to gather wocus. Debra sometimes prepares wocus muffins and wocus mush for visitors. And they return every year to the Modoc cemetery, where they rake up leaves and pine needles. The graves stand as a lasting narrative of the Riddle family and the Modoc tribe. Debra and Christine proudly tell visitors who the Modocs were and how they died.

Afterword
by Boyd Cothran

The Klamath Basin is a land of abundant water and little rainfall. Known in the nineteenth century as the "District of the Lakes," its rich liquid resources led one early visitor to exclaim, "The Country as far as the eye can reach [is] one continuous Swamp and Lakes."[1] Located in the moderate rain shadow east of the Cascades, spring-fed creeks spread out to form the Klamath Lake complex, the largest lake by area west of the Rocky Mountains. From these

Photo by Christy Kirwan

reservoirs flows the Klamath River, California's second-longest river. Although blessed by nature, the region has nonetheless been marked by fierce conflicts over access to water, land, and other resources. As Jim Compton demonstrates with grace and skill, these battles over the region's vital resources stretch back to the beginning of American settlement. The story of the Klamath Basin is the story of the American West. And the Modoc War—long forgotten by history but enjoying a kind of renaissance in recent years—is rich soil for understanding the causes, costs, and consequences of American settler colonialism.

Spirit in the Rock accomplishes many things and contributes in vital ways to the historical record on the Modoc War. Deeply researched and written with an eye toward detail and accuracy, Compton expertly weaves a multitude of narrative strands and divergent perspectives. He balances evidence, sifting through a complex and contradictory historical record to arrive at measured and considered conclusions. In this way, he has left us with a historically accurate yet still passionate narrative of one of the most significant events in American history. But Compton's work is more than just good history. It is a story that connects the past to the present. And in doing so, he leaves us with many lessons to ponder.

The Modoc War was fundamentally a struggle over who would control the land and resources of the Klamath Basin. With forensic precision, Compton uncovers the economic forces that shaped the course of the conflict and led to its tragic, lethal conclusion. Previous historians, most notably Andrew Isenberg but others as well, have emphasized the centrality of Indigenous labor, its control and exploitation by ranchers and miners, to the eventual conflict.[2] But Compton's research reveals that it was not solely the formation of large tracts of private ranching haciendas through the enclosure of the commons and the proletarization of Indigenous workers—their transformation from communities that derived their livelihood from the land to communities dependent upon wage labor—but also the expropriation of the land for regional infrastructure and development that spurred on the conflict. In his narrative, Ben Holliday and Jesse Applegate's scheme to construct a railroad through the region combined public and private interests to enrich settlers and create infrastructure for future settlement, but at tremendous cost for the Klamath Basin's Indigenous people. The scheme ultimately failed and the region would not enjoy the benefits of railroad transportation for another generation, as the Southern Pacific Railroad finally connected the Klamath Basin to the regional hubs of Portland and San Francisco in 1909.[3] For the Klamath, Modoc, and Yahooskin Paiute peoples, however, the costs were catastrophic.

Environmental justice, then, is a central theme of Jim Compton's work. He tells a story about the costs and consequences of progress. Development is necessary. Roads must be built, infrastructure must be developed, resources must be extracted. But one of the enduring challenges of American history, if not human society more broadly, has been the question of how to balance the costs against the benefits. Who benefits from these projects and who must bear their costs and destructive effects? Far too often in the story of American settler colonialism, this equation has remained out of balance. Time and time again, Indigenous people have been required to bear disproportionally the costs of development while receiving few if any of the benefits. This was true for the Modoc and Klamath people in the 1870s and it is true for many communities around the world today. And, if the contemporary protests against the tar sands in Alberta, against oil development in Venezuela, or against the Dakota Access Pipeline near the Standing Rock Indian Reservation are any indication, the importance of Compton's story will continue to resonate with readers for generations.

If the Modoc War contains lessons for all of us about the long history of environmental injustice in America, it also reminds us of the disproportionate power wielded by politicians and the media when they use their positions to stoke the passions of an aggrieved and enraged populace. The Modoc War was exceptional among the nineteenth century Indian wars for its length, intensity, and the duration of media coverage it received. It lasted for months. The principal participants remained relatively immobile. And it unfolded during a pivotal moment in U.S.–Indian policy when the federal government sought, briefly, to negotiate nonviolent resolutions to their disagreements with Indian nations without resorting to new treaties. This approach ultimately failed. The death on April 11, 1873, of Major General Edward R. S. Canby, the highest-ranking general officer to die in any Indian war, transformed the Modoc War into an international sensation. Political and military leaders responded to the crisis by answering the public's cry for vengeance. And the media amplified the racial animus of the day by reproducing, circulating, and endorsing genocidal responses. One of the fundamental tensions in any democratic society is always how to balance the will of the majority against the rights of minorities. The genocidal policies of the federal government in the nineteenth century toward North America's Indigenous peoples, what others have called the ethnic cleansing of the American Indian, remains a black mark against the Republic.[4] The Modoc War was a significant moment in our nation's dark history. The racial rhetoric of the day together with the popular appetite for vengeance displayed during the Modoc War should give pause to Americans today as we struggle to balance our own fears of insecurity against the rights of potentially vulnerable minorities.

But while the Modoc War might offer us sweeping lessons about the history of economic inequality and resource exploitation in the American West or about the shortcomings and failures of the Republic towards its most vulnerable members, it is also, ultimately, a story of survival, renewal, and even hope. One of the most enduring aspects of

Compton's book is his desire to bring this tragic story into the present and to include the voices of the Indigenous descendants of the Klamath Tribes today. The Modoc War claimed many lives, not just in the battle-fields of the Lava Beds but also among the survivors who were forced from homeland and who struggled to recreate their lives and their communities in the Indian Territory on the southern plains. The violence and destruction of the Modoc War is still felt deeply, especially by those who grew up enduring its consequences. Reparations, repatriation, and historical justice may never be entirely possible. We should, however, always strive toward a more just society. The dead can never be made whole. But they can, as Debra Riddle reminds us, be brought home.

May Jim Compton's book give you a truer and fuller picture of the Modoc War, its causes and consequences. May you drink deeply from its stories. And may its many lessons enrich your understanding of the past and its bearing on our present and future world.

Boyd Cothran
Associate Professor of History
at York University
Toronto, January 31, 2017

Author's Acknowledgments

They made this book possible:

Among sources, the the late Francis "Van" Landrum, extraordinary local historian in Klamath Falls, gave me invaluable guidance and factual support that were the basis of all my research, and I utilized several of the documents he had uncovered. Van steered me toward investigating the railroad and land activities of Jesse Applegate and Jesse Carr that were keys to understanding causes of the Modoc War. Van did decades of research and had a near-photographic knowledge of the facts of the war that will never be equaled. He was first president of the Shaw Historical Library in Klamath Falls, which has an excellent collection of Modoc War materials and preserves his holdings.

Debra Riddle is in many ways the hero of the book, the lone force in rescuing the skulls of Captain Jack and his lieutenants, and relentless champion of Modoc tribal history and rights. She guided me and my wife Carol on visits to little-known reservation locations, and the companionship of her mother Christine was a joy. I give them both my affectionate thanks.

I had considerable help from local historians and journalists in Klamath Falls, Oregon. The estimable and charming Lee Juillerat of the *Herald and News* has served his community for decades and is an unrivaled scholar of recent local history. Todd Kepple has transformed the County Historical Museums into a rich and accessible trove of community treasures. Ryan Bartholomew is an industrious and effective student of the area and chronicler of his hometown of Malin. The hard working staff of the Shaw Historical Library at Oregon Institute of Technology proved invaluable. Steve Kandra provided unexpectedly important deeds and maps from his family collection.

The custodians of the precious materials at the University of Oregon Knight Library in Eugene and the Oregon Historical Society in Portland were endlessly patient and helpful. My work required repeated visits to both collections, and each new tour of the documents yielded new insights. The libraries and their staffs are doing an invaluable service to historians.

No one has been more important to the writing of this book than my wife Carol Arnold. She served as cheerleader and editor for more than three years, bringing her legal and historical training to help me shape the work as it progressed. (She became a knowledgeable student of the Modoc War in the process.) When the final draft was finished, she undertook the laborious formatting and checking, a massive contribution to the project. I can't adequately express my affection or gratitude.

The Modocs—a tribe that once seemed to disappear in name and influence—still survive today in the persistence and courage of the living descendants of the Modoc War. This book is written in their honor.

Jim Compton

Notes

Author's Preface: The Modoc Story

1. Limerick, *The Legacy of Conquest*, 190.
2. Paige Raibmon,"Unmaking Native Space: A Genealogy of Indian Policy, Settler Practice, and the Microtechniques of Dispossession," in Alexandra Harmon, ed. *The Power of Promises: Rethinking Indian Treaties in the Pacific Northwest* (Seattle: University of Washington Press, 2008), 66.
3. Limerick, *The Legacy of Conquest*, 30.

Prologue: The Hanging

1. Leonard Case Jr. "Diary," 3 October 1873.
2. *The New York Times*, 5 October 1873.
3. George Hoge to Friend Fraser, 4 October 1873. Cornell University, Special Collections, Ithaca, NY.
4. George Kingsbury, *Bellows Falls* [Vermont] *Times*, 24 October 1873. Lieutenant Kingsbury played several roles in the Modoc War. He served as a camp commander at Fort Klamath, fought in several battles, was a reporter for his hometown newspaper, the *Bellows Falls* [Vermont] *Times*, and was a member of the military commission that tried and sentence Captain Jack to death.
5. *Yreka Journal*, 7 January 1874.
6. Case, "Diary."
7. *San Francisco Evening Bulletin*, 30 June 1873.
8. F. [Frazier] to My Beloved Dolly, 22 June 1873, Special Collections, University of Oregon.
9. *San Francisco Chronicle*, 3 October 1873.
10. Reported in *San Francisco Evening Bulletin*, 5 July 1873.
11. Case, "Diary."
12. *Bellows Falls Times*, 25 July 1873.
13. Details of activity in the camp at Fort Klamath are from Case, "Diary," 1 October 1873.
14. *San Francisco Bulletin,* 4 October 1873.
15. Hoge Letter, 4 October 1873. The other details are reported in the *San Francisco Chronicle*, 5 October 1873.
16. *San Francisco Chronicle,* 5 October 1873.
17. Ibid.
18. *San Francisco Chronicle*, 12 October 1873.
19. Riddle, *Indian History*, 198.

Chapter 1: A Harmonious World

1. Ray, *Primitive Pragmatists*, 24, 117, 119. Originally published in 1946, the book is based on interviews conducted with elders at the Klamath reservation in 1934.
2. Riddle, *Indian History*, 187.
3. The great diversity of Indian cultures in the Pacific Northwest is the subject of Ruth Kirk and Richard D. Daugherty's *Archeology in Washington* (Seattle: University of Washington Press, 2007). Garth Simpson, "Nightfire Island: Later Holocene Lakemarsh Adaptation on the Western Edge of the Great Basin," *University of Oregon Anthropological Papers*, No. 33 (1985), 33.
4. Odie B. Faulk, *The Modoc People* (Phoenix: Indian Tribal Series, 1976), 7. According to Modoc oral tradition, Kumash—the Creator of the human race—told the Modocs they will

be warriors, the "bravest of all," but to the Klamaths, he said, "You will be like women, easy to frighten." Curtin, "Kumash and His Daughter," *Myths of the Modocs*, 45.

5. John R. Swanton, *Smithsonian Institution Bureau of American Ethnology Bulletin 145: The Indian Tribes of North America* (Washington, D.C.: Smithsonian Institution Press, 1952), 464-65. Swanton concludes the Modoc language is a Lutuamian division of the Shapwailutan linguistic stock.

6. Cheewa James, "Modoc: An American Indian Saga," in *Roundup!* Ed. Paul Andrew Hutton (Cheyenne, WY: La Frontera Publishing, 2010), 95.

7. Swanton, *Indian Tribes of North America*, 461-65.

8. Haynal, "Sacred Rock," 174.

9. Gatchet, *Klamath Indians*, lxxxi-lxxxii. Gatchet spells the spirit's name "K'mùkamtch.".

10. Ray, *Primitive Pragmatists*, 23.

11. Upon reaching the age of marriage girls had their own quests and rituals. Numerous taboos surrounded puberty for girls and menstruation; and dreams or violations of these taboos were dangerous and the spirits would retaliate. Ray, *Primitive Pragmatists*, 71-81.

12. Haynal, "Sacred Rock Cairns," 172, 178.

13. David, "The Landscape of Klamath Basin Rock Art."

14. Curtin, "The Stone People," *Myths of the Modocs*, 314-317; "Latkakawas," 7.

15. Gatschet, *Klamath Indians*, 179. Despite its title, this work is rich in information about the Modocs as well as the Klamaths. Gatschet's dictionary of the Klamath-Modoc texts and language consists of two massive volumes each weighing 15 pounds

16. Haynal, "Sacred Rock Cairns," 178. Robert David's study of the pictographs in the Tule Lake area was limited because the tribe declined to give him access to photographs or to show his own images of the pictographs in this area. David, "Landscape of Klamath Basin Rock Art," 116.

17. Ray, *Primitive Pragmatists*, 146-59. Ray offers a detailed description of Modoc earthen houses used in winter and mat houses for summer.

18. Kroeber describes the Modoc boats in detail and describes their use in gathering wocus. Kroeber, *Indians of California*, 329-31.

19. Meacham, *Wigwam and War-Path*, 284.

20. Kroeber, *Indians of California*, 323, 331.

21. Ray, *Primitive Pragmatists*, 129-31.

22. Ray, *Primitive Pragmatists*, xi, 5-6, 135.

23. Spier, *Klamath Ethnography*), 35.

24. Ray, *Primitive Pragmatists*, 31-41.

25. Ibid., 37.

26. Ibid., 63.

27. Kroeber, *Indians of California*, 853.

28. Ibid., 20-21.

29. Powers, *Tribes of California*, 257-58. University of California ethnologist Alfred Kroeber criticized Powers for inaccuracies, but "with all its flimsy texture and slovenly edges, it will always remain the best introduction to the subject." Kroeber, *Indians of California*, ix.

30. Quoted in Ray, *Primitive Pragmatists*, 29.

31. An alternative story of Captain Jack's origins says he was a Rogue River Indian raised by Joseph Knott and his wife, who gave him the name "Jack." *New York Herald*, 1 October 1873; *The New York Times*, 5 October 1873. Yet another version of the story claimed he was the son of a Kentucky man who came west and married the daughter of a Modoc chief. *Oregon Statesman*, 10 June 1873. These stories are most likely fiction. Elijah Steele said he personally gave him the name "Jack"; the name Keintpoos is widely accepted as his Modoc name; and Jack did not speak any English. The *San Francisco Bulletin*, 4 October 1873,

reported, probably correctly, that Captain Jack was born at the mouth of the Lost River. "He has remained there his whole life and any reports to the effect that he was raised in a white family, or even resided among the whites, are false and groundless."

32. Kroeber identifies five old Modoc villages, one of which—Wachamshawash—was located a few miles up Lost River. *Indians of California*, 319.

33. According to one of Ray's sources, Keintpoos may have had a third wife, who hanged herself with a buckskin rope. Interviewed in 1938, Modoc elder Usee George said "she was jealous about a man." Quoted in Ray, *Primitive Pragmatists*, 94.

34. Ray, *Primitive Pragmatists*, 103, 107.

Chapter 2: The White World Arrives

1. Applegate, "South Road Expedition," 20–22. Levi Scott, a member of the expedition, confirmed the Modocs had likely not seen many whites. Descending from the prominitory, Scott saw a "small party of Indians [who] ran like wild beasts, and concel[ed] themselves in the woods." Hazelett, ed., *Wagons to the Willamette*, 71.

2. J. A. Myers, "Finan McDonald—Explorer, Fur Trader, and Legislator," *Washington Historical Quarterly* 13, no. 3 (July 1922): 196–208.

3. Archie Binns, *Peter Skene Ogden, Fur Trader* (Portland: Binford and Mort, 1967), 196–98.

4. The designation "Applegate Trail" will be used in this book, but the name has been controversial. In his *Reminiscences*, Lindsay Applegate referred to the route as the "South Road." Descendents of Levi Scott, one of the leaders of the 1846 expedition, have argued the route should be called "Scott-Applegate Trail." Charles George Davis, *Scott-Applegate Trail 1846-1847 Atlas and Gazetteer* (North Plains, OR: Soap Creek Enterprises, 1995), 6. Following more than a century of disagreement over the name, Congress officially designated the trail as the "Applegate Trail." Today it is part of the National Historic Trails system.

5. The Oregon territorial government, needing to establish American ownership of lands rapidly being colonized, bought vast tracts of Indian land for ten cents an acre. The *arriviste* Americans negotiated stunning purchases and negotiated treaties allowing development and settlement. Bancroft, *History of Oregon*, 2: 210-12.

6. The Oregon Donation Land Act of 1850 provided that white U.S. citizens and American "half-breed Indians" over the age of 18 could claim 320 acres of Oregon land for each man and 640 acres for each married man. The donee was required to reside on and cultivate the land for four years. 9 Stat. 496 (1850).

7. E.R.S. Canby to Commanding Officer, District of the Lakes, 17 February 1872, *House Document 122*, 213.

8. Jeff LaLande, "Dixie of the Northwest: Southern Oregon's Civil War," *Oregon Historical Quarterly* 100, no. 1 (1999): 39. Hereafter cited as *OHQ*.

9. Reed to General Clarke, 29 September 1859, quoted in "Piper's Reports and Journal," 231.

10. A. Piper to Major W. W. Mackall, 12 August 1860, in "Piper's Reports and Journal," 250.

11. "Proceedings of a Military Commission Convened at Fort Klamath, Oregon, for the Trial of Modoc Prisoners (July, 1873)," in *House Document 122*, 173. Hereinafter "Trial Transcript."

12. Abraham Henry Garrison, "Reminiscences of Abraham Henry Garrison—Over the Oregon Trail in 1846," *Overland Journal* 2, no. 2 (1993), 25.

13. As quoted in Gatschet, *Klamath Indians*, 13. Winema, known during the Modoc War as Toby, married an eighteen-year-old miner from Yreka by the name of Frank Tazwell Riddle. One of the heroines of the Modoc story, her name lives on in southern Oregon, including at Winema High School, Winema National Forest, Wi-Ni-Ma Family Camp, and Winema Lodge.

14. Meacham, *Wigman and Warpath*, 299-300.

15. The following account of the Ben Wright massacre and the quotations are from Gatschet, *Klamath Indians,* 13-15; Wells, *History of Siskiyou County,* 129-33; Thompson, *Reminisences,* 82; William M. Turner, "Scraps of Modoc History," *Overland Monthly and Out West* 2, no. 1 (July 1873), 21-25; Riddle, *Indian History,* 27-30. The Gatschet account in the Modoc language reports Wright's attempt to poison the Modocs, but Harry Wells says the story is not true.

16. Gatschet, *Klamath Indians,* 13-15.

17. A recent study estimates 15 to 64 dead from pistol shooting or drowning. Benjamin Madley, *An American Genocide* (New Haven: Yale University Press, 2016), 213.

18. Wells, *History of Siskiyou County,* 133.

19. E. Steele to Dear Brother (n.d.), *House Document 122,* 303.

20. Wright's Indian wife, named Jenny Chetco, "betrayed him to his death and afterward ate a part of his heart." Bancroft, *History of Oregon,* 2: 394n45.

21. "The meaning of a white flag was forever changed in the eyes of the Modocs." James, *Modoc: The Tribe That Wouldn't Die,* 26.

22. John Keast Lord, *The Naturalist in Vancouver and British Columbia* (London: Richard Bentley, 1866), 1:277.

23. Piper, "Reports and Journal," 225.

24. Joseph H. Chaffee, *SemiWeekly Independent,* 20 May 1862, quoted in Stern, *The Klamath Tribe,* 253.

25. Piper, "Reports and Journal," 249.

26. Francis "Van" Landrum, "Part of the Modoc Tragedy," 32, unpublished manuscript in possession of the author.

Chapter 3: The Applegate Factor

1. Victor was a widowed Portland writer and suffrage crusader who worked for several years in H. H. Bancroft's "History Factory" in San Francisco, a virtual sweatshop where several writers ground out a thirty-seven-volume history of the West produced under Bancroft's name. When he hired Victor at $23.10 a week, she had to surrender all of her collected writings and notes to him for publication. It is generally acknowledged she wrote most, if not all, of the two-volume *History of Oregon,* published in 1886 and 1888. She also wrote most or all of the Modoc War chapter of *California Inter Pocula* (1888), 446–560. William Alfred Morris, "The Origin and Authorship of the Bancroft Pacific States Publications: A History of a History," *Oregon Historical Quarterly* 4, no. 4 (1903): 287–364.

2. Bancroft, *History of Oregon,* 1: 393-94.

3. Applegate, "Recollections of My Boyhood," in *Westward Journeys,* ed. Martin Ridge (Chicago: R.R. Donnelly & Sons, 1989), 101.

4. Applegate, "The South Road Expedition," 22.

5. Ibid., 21.

6. Hazelett, ed., *Wagons to the Willamette,* 78.

7. Bancroft, *History of Oregon,* 2:61n3.

8. Neiderheiser, *Jesse Applegate,* 155.

9. Abernathy's "Advice to Emigrants of 1847" appears in Hazelett, ed., *Wagons to the Willamette,* 227-28.

10. Stafford Hazelett, "'To the World!!': The Story Behind the Virtriol," *OHQ* 116, no. 2 (2016):196-219.

11. Phileo Nash states that the white intrusion into Modoc land caused a "serious disruption of their economic live." Nash, "Religious Revivalism," 384.

12. U.S. House of Representatives, "Statement of Disbursements for the Indian Service." In *Letter from the Secretary of Treasury Transmitting Estimate of Appropriations—Paymaster General,* 40th Cong., 2nd Sess., Ex. Doc. 69, 149.

13. List of expenses certified by "Commissary," 30 September 1872, Fisher Papers, 2:275. The "Fisher Papers" were compiled in the late 1930s by Don Fisher, first superintendent at the Lava Beds National Monument. The compilation consists of hundreds of transcriptions of Modoc War papers from documents in the National Archives, the War Department, the Presidio in San Francisco, the University of California (Berekely) Library, and the Applegate Collections. The source of each document is indicated on the document. The Klamath County Museum scanned the papers in 2012 and they are available on the Klamath County Museum website at http://klamathcountymuseum.squarespace.com/fisher-papers.

14. Oliver Applegate to Lucien Applegate, 21 August 1869, Applegate Collection. The massive Applegate family papers at University of Oregon Special Collections include the Lindsey Applegate Papers and the Oliver Cromwell Applegate Papers.

15. Bancroft, *Inter Pocula*, 458.

16. Jesse Applegate to Elwood Evans, 13 October 1867, Applegate Collection. Also quoted in Neiderheiser, *Jesse Applegate*, 287.

17. Hazel Emery Mills, "The Emergence of Francis Fuller Victor—Historian," *OHQ* 62, no. 4 (1961): 309–36.

18. Bancroft, *History of Oregon*, 2:559n4.

19. Frances Fuller Victor to Dear Bliwas ["Eagle"], 17 September 1876, Applegate Collection. The first three and a half pages of this seven page handwritten manuscript are a kind of ode to Oliver Applegate and their mutual affection.

20. Victor, quoted in Alfred Powers, "Scrapbook of a Historian: Frances Fuller Victor," *OHQ* 42, no. 4 (1941), 329.

21. Bancroft, *History of Oregon*, 2:394.

Chapter 4: Dueling Treaties

1. *San Francisco Chronicle*, 3 February 1873.

2. E. Steele to Dear Brother, in *House Document 122*, 303-5.

3. Ibid., 305. The passes were highly prized, especially by Captain Jack.

4. Ibid., 297, 299.

5. Old Schonchin as quoted in Meacham, *Wigwam and Warpath*, 297.

6. No one had expected to see Old Schonchin's authority as the premier Modoc challenged. He was an imposing, and apparently engaging, seventy–year–old liked by the whites for his tractability. A photo from the era shows him as an ancient grizzled character in a shabby deerskin jacket and pants, with an immense quiver of arrows over his shoulder and a tomahawk in his hand.

7. E. Steele to Commanding Officer Fort Klamath, 28 August 1865, Fisher Papers, 1: 1-2.

8. *Annual Report* (1864), 120.

9. Boyd Cothran, "The Valentine's Day Treaty," *New York Times*, 14 February 2014.

10. Wheeler–Voegelin, "The Northern Paiute of Central Oregon," 120n16.

11. Testimony of Monchnkasgit, *Report of the Klamath Boundary Commission,* Sen. Exec. Doc. 93 (1896–97), quoted by Stern, *Klamath Tribe*, 40. Wheeler-Voegelin spells his name "Moshenkosket." He is sometimes misidentified as a Yahooskin, but later scholarship concluded he was a Klamath from Sprague River.

12. The treaty was signed by Modocs, Klamaths, and Yahooskins. According to the anthropologist Ermine Wheeler–Voegelin, the Yahooskins were "a score or so of Great Basin Northern Paiute, deriving from the Surprise Valley–Warner Valley region in northeastern California and south–central Oregon." They lived in the Sprague River area. Wheeler–Voegelin, *Ethnohistory,* 106. See also Gatchett, "Ethnographic Sketch," *Klamath Indians*, xxxv.

13. Captain Jack later repudiated his signature on the Oregon treaty, but there is no doubt he was there and signed. "Treaty with the Klamath, Etc., 1864," *Indian Affairs Laws and Treaties*, compiled and edited Charles J. Kappler (Washington, D. C.: Government Printing Office, 1904). However, Captain Jack's authority to sign any treaty on behalf of other bands of Modocs is questionable. Identifying a "chief" to sign for his "tribe" was a widely practiced technique for dispossessing Indian lands. Russell Lawrence Barsh, "Ethnogenesis and Ethnonationalism from Competing Treaty Claims," *The Power of Promise: Rethinking Indian Treaties in the Pacific Northwest*, ed. by Alexandra Harmon (Seattle: University of Washington Press, 2008), 217.

14. Lindsay Applegate, Applegate Collection.

15. Calculations differ as to the amount of land relinquished by the 1864 Oregon treaty. The consensus is the tribes ceded 23 million acres (about 35,937 square miles). Ermine Wheeler–Voegelin examined the Klamath tribe's 1908 petition to the Indian Lands Commission, in which they claimed the tribe ceded 13.7 million acres (21,406 square miles), of which 1.65 million acres (2,578 square miles) were reserved for a reservation. See "Amended Petition, Docket Number 100, before the Indian Lands Commission," cited in Wheeler–Voegelin, *Ethnohistory*, 120, note 13. The Court of Appeals for the Ninth Circuit, in its historic ruling regarding water rights stated the tribe had given up twelve million acres. *U.S. v. Adair*, 723 F. 2d 1394 (9th Cir. 1983), cert. denied, 467 U.S. 1252 (1984).

16. Murray, *Modocs and Their War*, 38.

17. Stern, *Klamath Tribe*, 169.

18. Ibid., 166.

19. Due to the rush to get title to Indian lands, there were nineteen other Oregon Indian treaties signed, but never ratified. Howard McKinley Corning, Ed., *Dictionary of Oregon History* (Portland: Binford & Morts, 1956), 122.

20. E. Steele to Dear Brother, no date, in *House Document 122*, 304-5.

Chapter 5: Captain Jack Flees

1. Meacham, *Wigwam and Warpath*, 248.

2. Ibid., 304.

3. E[lijah] Steele to Commanding Officer at Fort Klamath, 28 August 1865, Fisher Papers, 1:1-2.

4. Riddle, *Indian History*, 32–33.

5. John H. Reed to General Clarke, 29 September 1859, quoted in Piper "Reports and Journal," 226-7.

6. *Daily Alta California*, 21 December 1872. Though Artinie spoke English, the reporter's transcription follows the caricature of Indian idiom. This problem plagues the effort to accurately tell the Modocs' side of the story, because their words are filtered through the ears of a white writer.

7. Dillon, *Burnt-Out Fires*, 93-5.

8. Applegate to J.W. Perit Huntington, 20 January 1865, Applegate Collection.

9. Applegate to Huntington, 20 January 1865, Applegate Collection.

Chapter 6: Jesse Applegate Meets Captain Jack

1. DeVere Helfrich, "Railroads to Klamath," 17-18. The story of Jesse's railroad survey and meeting with Jack was discovered by DeVere Helfrich, a remarkable local historian. He and his wife, Helen, published a series of sixteen magazines called *Klamath Echoes* from 1964 to 1978. They are rich with local lore and overlooked information.

2. Ibid., 18.

3. Applegate's rail ambitions and connections with Holladay have gone essentially unnoticed in most other books about the Modoc War.

4. Larry Mullaly, "The Ashland Golden Spike: Part I: The Railroad comes to Oregon," Private Papers, 18 December 2012. Mullaly's assistance to the author in sorting out the intricacies of rail politics has been invaluable.

5. Johansen, *Empire of the Columbia*, 371.

6. Neiderheiser, *Jesse Applegate*, 233.

7. Helfrich, "Railroads to Klamath," 17–18.

8. Neiderheisser, *Jesse Applegate*, 222–3.

9. Jesse Applegate to Ainsworth, 17 September 1869, reprinted in Glen Thomas Edwards, ed., *Call Number*, vol. 30, no. 1 (Spring 1969), 6-7.

10. Henry McAllister Jr. to Judge W. L. Celb, 24 November 1870, Landrum Collection.

11. Jesse promised to support the senatorial candidate who favored a railroad from Portland to southern Oregon. Jesse Applegate to B F. Dowell, 8 May 1864, Landrum Collection.

12. Leslie M. Scott, "History of Astoria Railroad," *OHQ*, 15, No. 4 (1914), 221-40.

13. "Articles of Incorporation of the Oregon Branch Pacific Railroad Company," filed at Jacksonville, OR, 25 August 1870. Capital stock of five million dollars, with shares one hundred dollars. Including Jesse, there were thirty signers, all from Ashland or Jacksonville except the prominent banker C. C. Beekman of Portland, and Nat Langell, who lived near Lost River. Beekman, coincidently, was the financier who handled all the Modoc War bonds.

14. A railroad of the same name—Oregon Branch Pacific—had been incorporated earlier by B. J. Pengra. Pengra's scheme appeared so promising that the California rail baron C. P. Huntington agreed to finance it. It would have rendered all Jesse's work in vain and bankrupted Holladay. But Jesse perhaps sensed that the rival railroad would fail, and he could assume its name—the very name used in the congressional resolution.

15. Jos. S. Wilson, *Railroad Lands in Western Oregon*, (San Francisco: Edward Bosque, 1872), 9-10. Johansen said the land company "acted as a colonizing agent." Johansen, *Empire of the Columbia*, 375.

16. Jesse Applegate (?), no date, Applegate Collection.

17. Major Elmer Otis, 29 July 1872. Otis requested that a tracing of his map be returned to him on 20 September 1872. "Modoc War correspondence." The map on which Otis made his marks was probably the one produced by the Army Engineer Corps and forwarded to Fort Klamath in April 1871. See G. A. Goodale to Headquarters Fort Klamath, 26 April 1871, Fisher Papers, 1:31.

18. *Morning Oregonian* [Portland], 24 February 1871.

19. White, *Railroaded* (New York: Norton, 2011), 117.

Chapter 7: Alfred Meacham

1. Clarke's report as quoted in "The Last Conflict Between the Races" unpublished typescript, Special Collections, University of Oregon Libraries, Eugene, Oregon. "The Last Conflict Between the Races" is an unsigned compilation of letters and documents from the Modoc War written in the first person. The introduction states: "I am telling my story in a series of letters and interviews written while the events were in progress—a contemporary view, no doubt biased, as contemporary views are likely to be, but possessing the freshness only contemporary views can have." The writer says the events occurred "nearly seventy years before." Jim Compton believed the author was Oliver C. Applegate, who died in 1938. Authorship has not been confirmed.

2. S. A. Clarke, "Scenes on the Reservation," from "A History of the Modocs," Samuel A. Clarke Papers, Special Collections and University Archives, University of Oregon Libraries, Eugene Oregon, chap. 15.

3. Meacham, *Wigwam and Warpath*, 339-441. These events are described with Meacham's usual lavish embroidery.

4. Ibid., 330-31.

5. T. W. Davenport, "Recollections of an Indian Agent," *OHQ* 8, no. 3 (September 1907): 344.

6. Bancroft, *History of Oregon*, 2:559–60.

7. Meacham did a booming liquor business at first, although he was a "temperance man" and was contemptuous of whites who sold liquor to Indians. He took the pledge never to drink and then destroyed the bar in his hotel. Phinney, "Meacham," 50, 75.

8. Phinney, "Meacham," 78. In 1869, the year he became Indian Superintendent, Meacham also became active in the Masonic Order, which brought him wide connections in business and politics. In 1870 he was initiated as a Master Mason, and he later joined a lodge in Salem, Oregon.

9. Meacham, *Wigwam and Warpath*, 161–62.

10. Ibid., 162, 254. Meacham's views toward the Indians were consistent with Grant's Peace Policy. For a detailed discussion of that policy and its impact, see Prucha, *The Great Father*.

11. L. C. Merriam Jr., "The First Oregon Central Military Road Survey of 1865," *OHQ* 60, no. 1 (1959): 89–124.

12. Meacham, *Wigwam and Warpath*, 244.

13. Applegate to T. B. Odeneal, 8 May 1872, *House Document 122*, 226.

14. Meacham, *Wigwam and Warpath*, 311-29.

15. Applegate to "My Dear Brother," 25 December 1869, Fisher Papers, 1:13-14.

16. Meacham, *Wigwam and Warpath*, 328-34.

17. Telegram to Lindsay Applegate, 4 January 1873, Applegate Collection.

18. Meacham, *Wigwam and Warpath*, 334, 336.

19. Ibid., 229-30.

20. O. C. Applegate to "Friend Woodworth," 16 March 1870, Applegate Collection.

21. Meacham, *Wigwam and Warpath*, 333-34. Meacham took pains to defend his own fair distribution of goods to the tribe. He claims he gathered the Modocs to the "Peace Tree" on the Klamath reservation on a hill overlooking Captain Jack's camp and in a lavish ceremony distributed grand federal largesse. Meacham thought the Modocs were happy with their bounty.

22. Gatschet, *Klamath Indians*, lxx.

23. Captain Jack quoted in *San Francisco Chronicle*, 27 February 1873.

24. Dillon, *Burnt-Out Fires*, 107.

25. Riddle, *Indian History*, 34-5.

26. Stephen Powers, "The California Indians—the Modocs," *Overland Monthly* 10, no. 6 (1873): 543.

27. Riddle, *Indian History*, 37, offers an account of the confrontation, including created dialogue.

Chapter 8: General E. R. S. Canby

1. Heyman, *Prudent Soldier*, 384.

2. Heyman, *Prudent Soldier*, 116-36.

3. Paul Andrew Hutton, *Phil Sheridan and His Army* (Norman: University of Oklahoma Press, 1999), 185.

4. G. A. Goodale to Asst. Adj. General, Department of the Columbia, Fisher Papers, 16-17.

5. Heyman, *Prudent Soldier*, 350-351n4.

6. Ed. R. S. Canby to Commanding Officer, District of the Lakes, *House Document 122*, 213.

Chapter 9: Storm Clouds for Captain Jack

1. Perry Chocktoot, culture and heritage director for the Klamath Tribes, claimed the Indians would drive a wagon into the center of the river, fill it with fish, and then drive back onto the land. Interview with the author in 2013.

2. Foster, "Refugees and Reclamation," 150–87.

3. *Yreka Union,* 15 October 1864.

4. "Report of Conversation," Fisher Papers, 1:162.

5. C. Blair to Captain Knapp, 26 April 1870, Applegate Collection. Blair most likely observed the Modocs' celebration of the first sucker fish of the season. The first fish taken in the spring was cast into the fire and the entrails were returned to the water. Such a ritual was not an expression of hostility. Theodore Stern, "Klamath and Modoc," in Deward E. Walker Jr., ed., *Handbook of North American Indians,* vol. 12 *Plateau* (Washington, D.C.: Smithsonian Institute, 1998), 12:449.

6. "Report of Conversation," Fisher Papers, 1:172-73; 2:177-78.

7. Wells, *History of Siskiyou County,* 146.

8. Jackson to Acting Adjutant Attorney General, 29 August 1871; John Meacham to A.B. Meacham, 21 August 1871, Fisher Papers, 1:58, 64.

9. U.S. Senate, *Letter from the Acting Secretary of the Interior accompanying Information called for by the Senate resolution of January 8, 1873, relative to the Modoc and other Indian tribes in Northern California.* 42nd Cong., 2nd Sess., Ex. Doc. 29, 6.

10. Unsigned letter to A. B. Meacham, 25 June 1871. The writer says the killing occurred on June 9. Meacham Papers.

11. Applegate to Sheriff of Siskiyou County, Oregon, 5 July 1871, Fisher Papers, 1:38.

12. E. Steele, 28 June 1871, Fisher Papers, 1:37. Bancroft identifies the document as "a paper carried around by Jack." *History of Oregon,* 2:563n 12.

13. A. M. Roseborough, 13 May 1870, Fisher Papers, 1:18.

14. Untitled Document, 5 July 1871, Fisher Papers, 1:39. The account of the fire is from Murray, *Modocs and Their War,* 65-66.

15. Pencil note on a two- by three-inch scrap of paper, Applegate Collection. It is worth noting that Jack's village was on the west side of Lost River, and he may have wanted his village and the east side as well.

Chapter 10: A Lost River Reservation

1. Jesse Applegate to A. B. Meacham, 27 July 1871, Fisher Papers, 1:40-45. The account and all quotations are from Jesse Applegate's letter.

2. Ibid.

3. Meacham to Jesse Applegate, 2 August 1871, Meacham Collection.

4. Meeting reported in Neiderheiser, *Jesse Applegate,* 263.

5. Meacham, *Wigwam and Warpath,* 350. Meacham somewhat overstated Jesse Applegate's enthusiasm for the reservation. While sympathetic, Applegate pointed out that a Modoc reservation on the Lost River would not satisfy the whites and might be too small for proper administration. Applegate to Meacham, 27 July 1871, Fisher Papers, 1:40-45.

6. Jesse Applegate to Meacham, 1 February 1872, *House Document 122,* 13.

7. Elijah Steele to Commanding Officer at Fort Klamath, 28 August 1865, Applegate Collection.

8. *San Francisco Chronicle,* 9 February 1873; E. Steele to Dear Sir, 19 September 1872.

9. Meacham, *Wigwam and Warpath,* 350-51.

10. "Annual Report" (1871), 305-6.

11. Meacham to I. D. [Ivan] Applegate, 11 November 1871, Meacham Papers.

12. *San Francisco Sunday Chronicle,* 5 January 1873.

13. *Sacramento Union,* 7 January 1873.

14. Canby to Assistant Adjutant-General, 7 February 1872, *House Document 122,* 6.

15. Canby to Assistant Adjutant General, San Francisco, 13 April 1872, *House Document 122,* 19-20.

16. Lieutenant Louis Caziarc to Commanding Officer, District of the Lakes, 16 February 1872, *House Document 122,* 10-11. Caziarc was Canby's adjutant and often issued letters and commands in Canby's name.

17. R. F. Bernard to Major Saml Breck, 26 January 1873, Fisher Papers, 4:586-92.
18. "Report of Conversation, between Colonel Otis, Mr. J. N. High sub agent Klamath Indian agency and Mr. J. D. Applegate Commissary, Yainax Agency, Oregon, at the Gap on Lost-River Oregon on the 3d of April 1872, with Captain Jack the Chief of the Modoc Indians and about Thirty five of his Indians," Fisher Papers, 1:161-179; 2:174-81. The details of the meeting, including the direct quotations, are taken from this report.
19. Ivan Applegate to T. B. Odeneal, 8 May 1872, Applegate Collection.
20. Canby to Assistant Adjutant General, 17 April 1872, *House Document 122,* 20-21.

Chapter 11: Captain Jack Must Go

1. Jessie Applegate to Meacham, 1 February 1872, *House Document 122,* 13–14.
2. The contract for surveying was executed sometime between late June and September-October of 1871. Johnston, "The Two Jesses," 23-24.
3. Interview by the author with Ryan Bartholomew [Klamath Falls, Oregon, June 6, 2011]. Bartholomew has meticulously traced how Carr assembled property around Tule Lake. Bartholomew, "Jesse Carr's Cattle Empire," 25–34. Local historian Francis Landrum of Klamath Falls was early to recognize the Carr/Applegate water strategy. Letter from Landrum to George Burrell of Medford, 2 April 1977, in the author's possession.
4. The Lost River system began in Clear Lake, where Jesse Carr and the Applegate family acquired property. Lost River looped sixty miles north, then back south to drain into Tule Lake. Foster, "Refuges and Reclamation," 152.
5. Johnston, "The Two Jesses," 23 (emphasis added).
6. Johnston, "The Two Jesses," 23-4.
7. An 1889 criminal prosecution against Carr alleging he fenced off 38,000 acres of public land to deny access to Tule Lake was avoided only when Carr agreed to open up seven miles of waterfront. *Sacramento Daily Union,* 10 April 1889. Another California publication said, "Carr's rancho near Clear and Rhett Lake, in Modoc County, has 15,000 acres of patented land, is so situated with reference to water that his herds have the exclusive pasturage of 150,000 acres more." J. S. Hittel, *Commerce and Industries of the Pacific Coast* (San Francisco: A. L. Bancroft, 1882), 260. Quote from *San Francisco Call,* 19 July 1903.
8. F. G. Young, "The Financial History of the State of Oregon, Part II," *OHQ* 10, no. 4 (1909): 378–83. Young has fascinating explanations of the various ways the state was defrauded. Robert Johnston compiled the following list of swamp lands: Clear Lake, 12,728 acres; "Horse Pasture" east of Clear Lake, 2,620 acres; "California Field" adjoining Tule Lake, 3,670 acres. These numbers do not reflect land held for Applegate in other names or properties east of Tule Lake. Johnston, "The Two Jesses," 24.
9. Bill Johnson, "Cattle Kingdoms in the High Desert, 1869-1900," in *Buckaroos & Barons: Cattle Ranching in the Land of the Lakes* (Klamath Falls: Shaw Historical Library, 2011), 6.
10. "Quitclaim Deed," Sallie Applegate to Jesse D. Carr (February 27, 1872); "State Deed," State of Oregon to Sallie Applegate (March 4, 1872); "Quitclaim Deed," Dan W. Applegate to Jesse D. Carr (February 27, 1872); "State Deed," State of Oregon to D.W. Applegate (March 4, 1872). Copies of the deeds are in possession of Steve Kandra, Merrill, Oregon. The author is grateful to Kandra for bringing this to his attention.
11. Johnston, "The Two Jesses," 42n127.
12. Johnston, "The Two Jesses," 25.
13. Ryan Bartholomew uncovered much of this remarkable information about Carr's activities. See Bartholomew, "Jesse Carr's Cattle Empire," 27-29.
14. There were two Modoc villages on the north side of Clear Lake. Applegate's ranch was at or near a village called Ste-Okas, "important because it was in a desirable location for winter housing. Ray, *Pragmatists,* 206–9.

15. "Articles of Incorporation of the Link and Lost River Irrigating Manufacturing and Navigation Company," County Clerk's Office, Jackson County, Oregon (filed 16 October 1871). No less than three similar irrigation schemes were proposed in 1871. First to be filed in the Jackson County Courthouse was the "Klamath Lake Irrigating and Manufacturing Company" incorporated by Miller, Gilfry, and Jackson on September 13, 1871. Next was Applegate and Carr's company. The third, the "Klamath Lake Draining Company," was incorporated on December 13, 1871 by Miller, Brooks, and [illegible—Waldon?], but not registered with the county.

16. *New Northwest* [Portland, OR], 15 September 1871; 6 October 1871.

17. Applegate and Carr's announcement was premature. Klamath Falls historians DeVere and Helen Helfrich researched the issue and concluded that no work was ever commenced. Personal memo from DeVere and Helen Helfrich to Francis Landrum, in the possession of the author, n.d.

18. Bogart, *San Francisco Chronicle*, 1 March 1873. Meanwhile, Oliver Applegate was defending charges about the "amount of swamp land claimed by the Applegate family." O. C. Applegate to Colonel T. H. Cann, 20 March 1876, Applegate Collection. Interestingly, Oliver made a point to separate his own interests from that of Jesse Applegate.

19. The two partners once ran into a buzz saw when Carr tried to bribe several officials with fifty thousand dollars to get Applegate appointed to survey the so-called "swamp land" near Rhett (Tule) lake. According to his testimony, the Surveyor of California told Carr to "go to hell" and refused the bribe. "Testimony of J.E. Hardenbergh, *Appendix to the Journals of the Senate and Assembly of the Twentieth Session, Legislature of the State of California*, 5: 208-09 (Sacramento: G. H. Springer, 1874).

    Carr relentlessly acquired land for his Modoc Ranch until the turn of the century. In 1903 at age eighty-nine he finally cut a deal to acquire the last ten thousand acres of Modoc land to complete his sprawling cattle ranch. "Wonderful Career of a Ninety Year Old Cattle King," *San Francisco Call*, 19 July 1903, 13. See also Bartholomew, "Jesse Carr's Cattle Empire."

20. Applegate in 1875 prepared a map of Carr's holdings. For a detailed description of the map, see Johnston, "The Two Jesses," 34. The map is in the Robert Johnston Collection on Jesse D. Carr at the Shaw Historical Library, Klamath Falls, Oregon.

21. *Kansas City Gazette,* 5 September 1901.

22. For information on Steve Kandra and his family, see "Growing Up Boomer," *Journal of the Shaw Historical Library* 28 (2016): 97-112.

23. Interview, 1 November 2012.

24. Ibid.

25. Canby to Superintendent of Indian Affairs, 17 February 1872, *House Document 122*, 15.

26. Quoted in James, *Modoc*, 121.

Chapter 12: Meacham Is Fired

1. "J.E.P." to Editor *Oregonian*, 22 February 1872, Fisher Papers, 1:145-7. The identity of J.E.P. is unknown.

2. Meacham to M.P. Berry, 25 January 1872, *Meacham Papers.*

3. Meacham to My Dear Friend I.D. [Ivan] Applegate, 27 January 1872, Meacham Papers.

4. Meacham to Thos. K. Cree, 19 January 1872, Meacham Papers.

5. These terms are found in Meacham's correspondence from February 13 to March 14, 1872, in the Meacham Papers.

6. Loring Benson Priest, *Uncle Sams's Stepchildren* (NJ, 1942), 60, cited in Phinney, "Meacham," 133.

7. *New York Herald,* 17 February 1873, in Cozzens, *Wars for the Pacific Northwest*, 75.

8. The Portland *Gazette* was founded by the flamboyant railroad magnate Ben Holladay in 1870.

9. A. B. Meacham to Thos. K. Cree, 19 January 1872, Meacham Papers.

10. Jesse Applegate to Meacham, 1 February 1872, *House Document 122*, 13-14. Applegate's letter is addressed to Meacham as "Superintendent of Indian Affairs." News that Meacham had been fired was slow to reach Oregon, and apparently Applegate had not heard the news when he addressed his letter.

11. Meacham to Canby, 8 February 1872, *House Document 122*, 12.

12. Odeneal to Office Superintendent Indian Affairs, 17 June 1872, *House Document 122*, 224.

13. F. A. Walker, Commissioner of Indian Affairs, to T. B. Odeneal, 6 July 1872, *House Document 122*, 237–38. The language of the order is sometimes incorrectly quoted without the word "possibly." In fact, Walker cautioned strongly that arrest of the Modoc leaders "avoid any unnecessary violence or resort to extreme measures."

Chapter 13: A Grave Mistake

1. G. G. Hunt to Headquarters, 18 February 1872, Fisher Papers, 1:123.

2. Canby to Oregon Superintendent of Indian Affairs, 17 February 1872, *House Document 122*, 14-15.

3. Applegate to Meacham, 1 February 1872, *House Document* 122, 13-14.

4. J. N. Shook and others to Meacham and Canby, forwarded J. M. Schofield to Headquarters Military Division of the Pacific, 7 February 1872, *House Document 122*, 8-9.

5. Elmer Otis to Assistant Adjutant-General, 18 April 1872, *House Document 122*, 229.

6. I. D. Applegate to T. B. Odeneal, 8 May 1872, Fisher Papers, 1:222. The letter also appears in *House Document 122*, 225-26, where the author is incorrectly identified as "J.D. Applegate." This transcription is clearly in error as the letter was signed by the "Commissary in Charge," i.e., Ivan Applegate. Most likely the error was caused because the "I" in the written document was confused with the letter "J."

7. Odeneal to F. A. Walker, 17 June 1872, *House Document 122*, 223-24.

8. Odeneal to F. A. Walker, 21 December 1872, Fisher Papers, 3:445-46.

9. Louis V. Caziarc to Commanding Officer District of the Lakes, 30 October 1872, *House Document 122*, 27. Canby frequently conveyed his orders through messages signed by Caziarc.

10. "Buckaroos" were cattlemen known for their distinctive style, rawhide gear, and language in Oregon's Great Basin desert country. Carole Fisher, "Introduction," *Buckaroos & Barons: Cattle Ranching in the Land of the Lakes* (Shaw Historical Library: Klamath Falls, OR, 2011), 1.

11. Odeneal to Wheaton, 25 November 1872, *House Document 122*, 38.

12. Odeneal to John Green, 27 November 1872, *House Document 122*, 84.

13. Schonchin as quoted in *New York Herald,* 17 March 1873, quoted in Cozzens, *Wars for the Pacific Northwest*, 206.

14. Ibid., 207.

15. "Trial Transcript," *House Document 122*, 173.

16. Odeneal to Oregon Superintency, 27 November 1872, *House Document 122*, 84. The Commissioner of Indian Affairs, and Indian agents and subagents, were in fact authorized to "remove from the Indian country all persons found therein contrary to law," and the President was authorized to direct the military to be employed in the removal. Rev. Stat. sec. 2147 (1873).

17. Judge Elisha Steele to his brother I. Steele, 26 May 1873, *House Document 122*, 297-308, at 307. This is one of the most extraordinary surviving documents of the period, an eighteen-page letter responding to demands by Thomas Odeneal and other Oregonians that Judge Elijah Steele be criminally prosecuted for starting the war.

18. Odeneal to John Green, 27 November 1872, *House Document 122*, 84.

19. Boutelle, "Duel," in Brady, *Fights and Fighters*, 264-65. Historian Erwin Thompson notes that Boutelle, writing about the Modoc War many years later, "tended to sound as if his were the one cool brain present. Such are the advantages of hindsight." Thompson, *The Modoc War*, 144n4.

20. John Green to Odeneal, 28 November 1872, Fisher Papers, 11:1880.

21. Quoted by Boutelle, "Duel," in Brady, *Fights and Fighters,* 265, parentheses in the original.

22. Wheaton to Canby, 26 December 1872, *House Document 122,* 49, emphasis in the original.

23. Ed. R. S. Canby to Assist Adjutant General, 20 January 1873, *House Document 122,* 447.

Chapter 14: Attack on Lost River Village

1. Captain Jack's village is sometimes called the "south-side camp," because of the curve in the river at that point.

2. List of Modoc names from Meacham, *Wigwam and Warpath,* 367.

3. [O. C. Applegate?], "The Battle on the East Side." A note at the top of the manuscript says "O. C. Applegate furnished me with the following interesting account," and the manuscript continues in the same hand, suggesting that Applegate is the author and that the document is a copy. Applegate's account also appears in [Applegate?], "The Last Conflict Between the Races," Applegate Collection, 19-22.

4. Ivan Applegate, "The Initial Shot," in Brady, *Fights and Fighters*, 274.

5. Boutelle, "Duel," in Brady, *Fights and Fighters*, 266. Jackson was a cavalry captain at the time of the ambush at Lost River. Thompson, *Modoc War*, 176. Jackson was later given the rank of Major, and Boutelle refers to him that way in his account.

6. Meacham, *Wigwam and Warpath,* 368-69.

7. Applegate, "The Initial Shot," in Brady, *Fights and Fighters,* 275.

8. Captain Jack as quoted in "Trial Transcript," 173.

9. Applegate," The Initial Shot," in Brady, *Fights and Fighters,* 275.

10. Boutelle, "Duel," in Brady, *Fights and Fighters*, 266–67.

11. Riddle, *Indian History*, 45.

12. Applegate, "The Initial Shot," in Brady, *Fights and Fighters*, 273-76.

13. [Applegate?], "The Battle on the East Side."

14. Jackson to John Green, 2 December 1872, *House Document 122,* 42-3.

15. [O.C. Applegate?], "The Battle on the East Side"; Murray, *Modocs and Their War,* 21. In all their engagements the army exaggerated how many Modocs they killed, numbers usually corrected later.

16. Boutelle confided to Dolly, his fiance, that Green told him the wounded men said the troops would have been defeated but for Boutelle's actions. F. [Frazier] to My dear little girl, 21 December 1872, Boutelle, "Letters," Special Collections, University of Oregon.

17. Murray, *Modocs and Their War*, 88-89.

18. Riddle, *Indian History*, 48.

19. Fox, *New York Herald*, 8 March 1873, in Cozzens, *Wars for the Pacific Northwest*, 183. Gatschet also reported that soldiers "fired upon the uprotected women and children of another Modoc camp." *Klamath Indians*, lxxi.

Chapter 15: Revenge: Fourteen Settlers Murdered!

1. Lucien Applegate (brother of Jesse, Ivan, and Oliver Applegate) blamed the failure to warn the settlers on the California men who were "at the bottom of this whole business." L. Applegate to Capt. Cromwell, 19 December 1873, Applegate Collection.

2. The events described here are from Putnam, "Incidents," 1-15. Putnam's account is vivid and appears reliable.

3. Meacham, *Wigwam and Warpath*, 378.

4. *Jacksonville* [OR] *Sentinel*, 28 December 1872.

5. Based on a war chronicle obtained from the Riddle family in the Modoc language, Gatchet reported that the killings were retaliation for the slaughter of the unprotected Modoc women and children. Gatchet, *Klamath Indians*, lxxi.

6. In addition to the Boddys, the Brothertons, and Miller, the Modocs killed Christopher Erasmus, Robert Alexander, John Tober, and a man named Follins. A bronze monument with the fourteen victims' names has been erected in a park in Malin, Oregon.

7. *Marysville Daily Appeal*, 6 December 1872; *San Francisco Evening Bulletin*, 9 December 1872; unidentified newspaper clipping date lined San Francisco 3 December 1872, in Fisher Papers, 3:374; *Russian River Flag*, 12 December 1872.

8. Meacham, *Wigwam and Warpath*, 372-74.

Chapter 16: Captain Jack's Stronghold

1. Murray, *Modocs and Their War*, 122.

2. Wheaton to Canby, forwarded by Wheaton to E.D. Townsend, 5 May 1873, in *House Document 122*, 55.

3. Quoted in *Army and Navy Journal* 10, no. 16 (19 April 1873):565.

4. Wheaton to Canby, 19 January 1873, *House Document 122*, 50-51.

5. James, *Modocs*, 11.

6. Simpson, *Meeting the Sun*, 380.

Chapter 17: Ready for War

1. Grover to Canby, 2 December 1872, *House Document 122*, 28.

2. Canby to Grover, 3 December 1872, *House Document 122*, 29.

3. *Sacramento Daily Union*, 27 December 1872.

4. Bancroft, *Inter Pocula*, 486. The California rifles could have been muskets that had not been converted by boring out the .58-caliber barrel to accept a rifled .50-caliber liner tube. *See* McChristian, *The U.S. Army in the West, 1870-1800*, 30.

5. Canby to H. Clay Wood, 15 January 1873, in *House Document 122*, 47-8.

6. Boyle, *Personal Observations*, 19.

7. Wheaton to Canby, 28 December 1873, Fisher Papers, 3:457.

8. Robert Pollock to Canby, 20 February 1873, in "Modoc War correspondence and documents."

9. Wheaton to Canby, 26 December 1872, in *House Document 122*, 48.

10. Wheaton to Canby, 13 January 1872, in *House Document 122*, 50.

11. Rickey, *Forty Miles a Day on Beans and Hay*, 127.

12. Riddle, *Indian History*, 52. Jeff Riddle claimed that a panicked soldier shot at his reflection in the lake, throwing the volunteer camp into chaos, and some Volunteers fled to the hills.

13. *Army and Navy Journal* 10, no. 22 (28 December 1872): 313.

14. J.G. Trimble, "The Country They Marched and Fought Over," in Brady, *Fights and Fighters*, 280-85.

15. Bernard had enlisted as a blacksmith in 1855 and rose through the ranks during the Civil War, twice decorated for gallant and meritorious service. An experienced Indian fighter, having fought the Chiricahua Apaches in Arizona in 1869, Bernard had been in 103 military operations by his retirement.

16. Thompson, *Modoc War*, 26–31, 146n3.

17. James. M. Sanderson, *Campfires and Camp Cooking: or Culinary Hints for the Soldier* (Washington: Government Printing Office, 1862), 6.

18. Orson A. Stearns, "Fort Klamath and 'The Bread Riot,' A Near Tragedy of Early Days," no date, Unpublished handwritten manuscript, Oregon Historical Society, Portland, Oregon, 21.

19. J.W. Berry to Lieutenant E. R. Reames, 6 January 1873, Applegate Collection.

20. Bancroft, *History of Oregon*, 2:399.

21. Meacham, *Wigwam and Warpath,* 394.
22. Wheaton to Canby, 28 December 1872, *House Document 122,* 49.
23. E. W. Stone to Canby, 28 December 1872 Fisher Papers, 3:425. This episode is sometimes called the "Battle of Land's Ranch." Wheaton a few days later tried to cast the outcome in a better light: "The Indians being in open ground fled in confusion to the Lava beds 4 of them were killed several wounded all their horses captured many Indians threw their rifles into Tule Lake as they fled to their main stronghold in the rocks." Wheaton to Assistant Adjutant General, 27 January 1873, Fisher Papers, 4:599. Bernard, who was there, reported that the men claimed they killed four Modocs, but in fact only "one dead Indian was left on the field." R. F. Bernard to Samuel Breck, 26 January 1873, Fisher Papers, 4:591.
24. *Yreka Union,* 4 January 1873, reported in Thompson, *Modoc War,* 147n21.
25. Wheaton to Canby, 26 December 1872, Fisher Papers, 3:458.
26. This is Meacham's list, in *Wigwam and Warpath,* 397.
27. Wheaton to Canby, 15 January 1873, *House Document 122,* 50.
28. F. W. Hamont, "The Modoc Indian War by One Who Was There," in Cozzens, *Wars for the Pacific Northwest,* 269.
29. Wheaton to Canby, 15 January 1873, *House Document 122,* 50.

Chapter 18: Modoc Victory at the Stronghold

1. Meacham, *Wigwam and Warpath,* 400.
2. Maurice Fitzgerald, "The Modoc War," in Cozzens, *Wars for the Pacific Northwest,* 117.
3. Boyle, *Personal Observations,* 15.
4. Meacham, *Wi-ne-ma,* 143.
5. Reported in Ray, *Primitive Pragmatists,* 67-68. The woman who reported this scene was the daughter of Schonchin John. When the soldiers later crossed the string, her father no longer believed in doctors. "We'll ask them no more," he said.
6. William Simpson, *Illustrated London News,* 7 June 1873.
7. Spier, *Klamath Ethnography,* 271. For variant feathered wands made by tribes in central California and the Southwest, see Kroeber, *Indians of California,* 867-68.
8. Murray, *Modocs and Their War,* 100-101.
9. "Fritz" appears to be Fritz Munz, a German cattle-man, who in September 1886 shot a Modoc from his horse and killed the man. Munz was arrested and placed under bond, but fled the country for Europe. "The Indians are much dissatisfied at his escape from justice," wrote the Indian agent. *Annual Report* (1887).
10. Murray, *Modocs and Their War,* 97-100, and Bancroft, *History of Oregon,* 2:578-80.
11. Boutelle, "Duel," in Brady, *Fights and Fighters,* 270.
12. James Jackson, "The Modoc War—Its Origin, Incidents, and Peculiarities," in Cozzens, *Wars for the Pacific Northwest,* 104.
13. Bancroft, *Inter Pocula,* 495.
14. Boyle, *Personal Observations,* 22.
15. General David Perry, "First and Second Battles in the Lava-Beds," in Brady, *Fights and Fighters,* 294.
16. Jackson, "The Modoc War," in Cozzens, *Wars in the Pacific Northwest,* 105.
17. Ibid.
18. Boyle, *Personal Observations,* 23
19. Albert Manucy, *Artillery Through the Ages* (Washington, D. C.: Division of Publications National Park Service, 1949) (Reprint 1985), 57.
20. [O. C. Applegate?], Untitled 13 page manuscript, Applegate Collections, 5-6. Though authorship is unidentified, the hand writing is that of O. C. Applegate, and describes events he witnessed. The manuscript states: "The howitzer practice amounted to nothing,

for the fog concealed the whereabouts of the main stronghold and there was great danger to Bernard's Command on the Eastside. I am told that shells from the howitzers actually passed over the heads of Bernard's men and struck in the lake beyond."

21. Jasper N. Terwilliger, from *Winners of the West* (30 April 1926), reprinted in Jerome A. Greene, ed., *Indian War Veterans: Memories of Army Life and Campaigns in the West 1864-1898* (New York: Savas Beatie, 2007), 355.

22. John Green to Acting Assistant Adjutant-General, District of the Lakes, 25 January 1873, *House Document 122*, 59.

23. Perry, "First and Second Battles," in Brady, *Fights and Fighters*, 296.

24. Anonymous in *Oregon Herald*, 16 February 1873 [dateline 22 January 1873], in Cozzens, *Wars for the Pacific Northwest*, 136.

25. [O. C. Applegate?], "Untitled Manuscript," Applegate Collection, 4.

26. Green's tactics as told in Thompson, *Reminiscences,* 101.

27. Bancroft, *Inter Pocula*, 496.

28. Thompson, *Modoc War,* 40.

29. Boyle, *Personal Observations,* 30.

30. Thompson, *Reminiscences,* 102.

31. Bancroft, *Inter Pocula,* 503.

32. O. C. Applegate to General John E. Ross, 2 February 1873, Fisher Papers, 4:665-67.

33. *San Francisco Bulletin,* 21 January 1873.

34. Bancroft, *Inter Pocula*, 500. Jerry Crook died the first week of February. *San Francisco Bulletin,* 8 February 1873.

35. Thompson, *Reminiscences,* 104.

36. *San Francisco Bulletin,* 21 January 1873.

37. Gatschett, *Klamath Indians*, 37–38.

38. Figures from Thompson, *Modoc War*, 43. Thompson did extensive examination of army communications and documents to arrive at his estimates.

39. Wheaton to Canby, 7 February 1873, *House Document 122*, 55.

40. Thompson, *Reminiscences*, 105

41. Wheaton to Canby, 19 January 1873, *House Document 122*, 51.

Chapter 19: The Army Licks Its Wounds

1. *San Francisco Chronicle,* 31 December 1872.

2. Thompson, *Reminiscences,* 107.

3. Bernard to Major Sam'l Breck, 23 January 1873, Fisher Papers, 4:589.

4. *New York Herald*, June 23, 1873, in Cozzens, *Wars for the Pacific Northwest*, 296. The report describes the court martial of deserters on June 9 at Boyles' Camp.

5. Jef. C. Davis to Headquarters, Department of the Columbia, 1 November 1873, *House Document 122*, 107, 109.

6. *Napa Valley Register,* 25 January 1873; 15 Feburary 1873.

7. *San Francisco Bulletin,* 23 January 1873.

8. Quotes from *San Francisco Bulletin,* 21 January 1873.

9. *New York Times,* 21 January 1873.

10. Canby to General W. T. Sherman, 30 January 1873, *House Document 122, 64.*

11. *Sacramento Daily Union,* 15 February 1873.

12. Ibid., 17 February 1873.

13. Wheaton to Canby, 5 May 1873, *House Document 122*, 58. Wheaton forwarded this letter to Canby with other correspondence on May 5, 1872. The letter as reproduced in *House Document 122* does not bear a date.

14. Wheaton to Canby, 19 January 1873, *House Document 121*, 50-51.

15. *San Francisco Bulletin,* 30 January 1873.
16. Bernard to Major Sam'l Breck, 23 January 1873, Fisher Papers, 4:588.
17. J. Q. Adams to Stephen P. Jocelyn, no date, quoted in Jocelyn, *Mostly Alkali,* 177.
18. *San Francisco Chronicle,* 26 January 1873.
19. *San Francisco Chronicle,* 30 January 1873.
20. *Daily Oregonian,* 9 January 1873.
21. Thompson, *Reminiscences,* 107.
22. Erwin Thompson describes the strategy of "gradual compression" in detail. Thompson, *Modoc War,* 46-47.
23. Brigadier General Canby, Special Orders No. 16, Fisher Papers, 4:565.
24. Gillem to Canby, 9 February 1873, in Fisher Papers, 5:741-47.
25. Francis B. Heitman, *Historical Register of the United States Army* (Washington: Government Printing Office, 1903), 1:457.
26. Gillem to Canby, 11 February 1873, Fisher Papers, 5:758.
27. *San Francisco Bulletin,* 17 February 1873.
28. Maurice Fitzgerald, "The Modoc War," in Cozzens, *Wars in the Pacific Northwest,* 121. "Squaw man" was a derogatory term for white men who had Indian wives.
29. Fitzgerald, "Modoc War," in Cozzens, *Wars in the Pacific Northwest,* 121.
30. Robt. Pollock to Post Trader, 21 February 1873, Fisher Papers, 5:779.
31. Paymaster V. G. Eggleston to Major David Taggart, 14 February 1873, Fisher Papers, 5:762.
32. Fitzgerald, "Modoc War," in Cozzens, *Wars in the Pacific Northwest,* 118-19.
33. *San Francisco Chronicle,* 9 February 1873.
34. *San Francisco Bulletin,* 19 February 1873.
35. Moore to My Dear____ [name omitted], 29 April 1873, in Moore, "Letters," typescript in Lava Beds National Monument, 1-2.
36. Fairchild's appears to have been a convenient meeting place for various groups. For example, three Modoc warriors rode into Fairchild's on February 26 to "have a big talk" with the Klamath chief. *New York Times,* 1 March 1873.
37. Moore, 29 April 1873, in "Letters." Even with dress precautions, "a much larger percentage of officer, non-commissioned officers and buglers" were killed and wounded than private soldiers. "Letter from the Lava Beds," *Bellows Falls* [VT] *Times,* 17 May 1873.
38. Moore, 29 April 1873, in "Letters."
39. William Murray, "Modoc War Diary: 1873," unpublished handwritten manuscript, Huntington Library Special Collections, San Marino, CA. Murray's sometimes breathless 120-day diary of his participation in the Modoc War captures both the eager anticipation of a good fight and the reality of suffering when real combat began.
40. Gilbert Davis, "Diary 1873," unpublished notebook, Oregon Historical Society, Portland.

Chapter 20: Trouble in the Stronghold

1. *Daily Alta California,* 2 February 1873.
2. Wheaton to Adjutant General, 5 February 1873, Fisher Papers, 5:697-700.
3. The account and quotations are from *New York Herald,* 12 February 1873, in Cozzens, *Wars for the Pacific Northwest,* 168 and Frank Wheaton to Adjutant General, 5 February 1873, in Fisher Papers, 5:697-700. Wheaton's report is the only place the name "Big Dick" occurs, although there are records of a "Big Duck" and "Big Ike" among the fighters.

Chapter 21: The Reporters

1. Boyd Cothran's excellent study *Remembering the Modoc War* was published in 2014, not long after author Jim Compton's death, preventing him for taking into account Cothran's exhaustive research and thoughtful conclusions. Cothran argues that the images and popular news coverage of the Modoc War "transformed complicated and nuanced explanations into simple arguments that established, sustained, and promoted American innocence."

2. *Sacramento Daily Union*, 12 July 1873.

3. Knight, *Following the Indian Wars*, 115.

4. Edward Fox, *New York Herald*, 21 February 1873, in Cozzens, *Wars for the Pacific Northwest,* 157.

5. Knight, *Following the Indian Wars*, 109.

6. *New York Herald*, 21 February 1873, in Cozzens, *Wars for the Pacific Northwest,* 157-58.

7. Ibid., 179-84.

8. Ibid., 224. Wilkins Micawber is a fictional character from Charles Dickens' novel *David Copperfield* known for his hopeful expectations in the face of mounting difficulties.

9. Ibid., 181.

10. Fox's account of his trip to Jack's cave was published 28 February 1873 in the *New York Herald.* The account that follows is distilled from his report. The account appears in Cozzens, *Wars for the Pacific Northwest,* 184-93.

Chapter 22: The Applegates Meet the Press

1. *Daily Alta California*, 19 February 1873.

2. *San Francisco Chronicle*, 9 February 1873.

3. *San Francisco Chronicle,* 17 February 1873.

4. *San Francisco Chronicle*, 3 February 1873. There may have been substance to the claims that the Applegates abused funds for cattle and blankets. An audit of reservation funds in October 28, 1872, reported that 2,000 pounds of beef and blankets for the Indians were never accounted for. Department of Interior, Office of Indians Affairs to L. Applegate, 28 October 1872, Applegate Collection.

5. *San Francisco Chronicle*, 17 February 1873. There may have been grounds for the charges of cowardice against Oliver Applegate. A few days after the ill-fated assault on the Stronghold, Applegate abruptly resigned from the Volunteers. O. C. Applegate to E. Ross, 22 January 1873, Fisher Papers, 4:561. Lieutenant Hyzer wrote to Applegate the same day, assuring him: "Your name and actions are criticized consisderably by those on the field who know more than we do but rest assured you have some true friends here who will not forsake you." J. Harry Hyzer to Capt. Applegate, 22 January 1873, Fisher Papers, 4:564.

6. *San Francisco Chronicle*, 26 February 1873.

7. *Daily Alta California*, 20 February 1873.

8. *Daily Alta California,* 22 February 1873.

9. *San Francisco Chronicle*, 3 February 1983.

10. *San Francisco Chronicle*, 19 February 1873.

11. *San Francisco Chronicle*, 23 February 1873.

12. *Oregon Sentinel,* 3 April 1873.

13. O. C. Applegate to L. B. Applegate, 20 February 1873, Fisher Papers, 5:789. Transcript of Interview, "The Kenneth McLeod Discussion of the Facts of the Modoc War," Lava Beds National Monument, 30 November 1961.

14. O. C. Applegate to L. B. Applegate, 20 February 1873, Fisher Papers, 5:789.

15. *San Francisco Bulletin,* 10 February 1873.

16. McCall to O. C. Applegate, 25 February 1873, Fisher Papers, 5:823-24.

17. O.C. Applegate to Dear Father, 26 February 1873, Applegate Collection.

18. *San Francisco Chronicle*, 27 February 1873. The same account by Oliver Applegate appeared a day earlier in the *San Francisco Evening Bulletin*, 26 February 1873.

19. L[indsay] Applegate to Oliver [Applegate], 26 January 1873, Applegate Collection. Phinney, "Meacham," 184 attributes this letter to Lucien Applegate, but it is signed "Your affectionate father," which clearly identifies the author as Oliver's father, Lindsay Applegate.

20. *Daily Oregon Statesman*, 27 February 1873.

21. Reprinted in several papers, including *San Francisco Chronicle*, 23 February 1873.

22. L[indsay] Applegate to Oliver, 26 January 1873, Applegate Collection.

Chapter 23: The Peace Commission

1. Robert Utley, *Frontier Regulars: The United States Army and the Indian, 1866-1891* (Lincoln: University of Nebraska Press, 1973), 188–214.

2. Delano to Belknap, 30 January 1873, in *House Document 122*, 65. Delano wrote that "in pursuance of the understanding between the President, yourself, and myself," he would send a commission to the scene of the difficulties.

3. E. D. Townsend, Adjutant General to The General of the Army, 30 January 1873, in *House Document 122*, 66.

4. Sherman to Canby, 31 January 1873, in *House Document 122*, 65.

5. Bancroft, History of *Oregon*, 2:595n59. In addition to Meacham and Applegate, the Oregonians included S. A. Clarke, newspaperman and politician from Salem who would later report on the war for the *New York Times*; D. P. Thompson; M. P. Berry; R. H. Kincaid; Daniel Chaplin; Jacob Stitzel; and "a few other Oregon gentlemen." Clarke, *Pioneer Days of Oregon History* (Portland: J. K. Gill, 1905), 119.

6. E. L. Applegate to Dear Brothers, 7 March 1873, Fisher Papers, 6:872.

7. By Yai-nax, the Oregonians were probably referring to the Yahooskins, a band of Snakes who had been sent to live on the Klamath reservation. The letter to Delano, 27 January 1873, is quoted in Meacham, *Wigwam and Warpath*, 417-20.

8. Meacham, *Wigwam and Warpath*, 415.

9. H.R. Clum to Meacham, 5 February 1873, and H. R. Clum to Meacham, 6 February 1873, in *House Document 122*, 245-46, 248.

10. Bancroft, *History of Oregon*, 2:596.

11. Oliver Applegate wrote a succinct statement of the family position to his brother Lucien: "The Oregon platform is as follows: (1) Unconditional Surrender of Jack and people, (2) Execution of the Murderers, (3) Transportation of the remainder to a distant Resvn [*sic*]," O. C. Applegate to L. B. Applegate, 20 February 1873, Fisher Papers, 5:789-90.

12. O. C. Applegate to L. B. Applegate, 21 February 1873, Applegate Collection.

13. O.C. Applegate to L. B. Applegate, 20 February 1873, Fisher Papers, 5:789-90.

14. [Major Quincy A.] Brooks to Dear Oliver, 23 February 1873 [from Jacksonville], Appplegate Collection.

15. O. C. Applegate to Dear Father, 26 February 1873 [from Yainax], Applegate Collection.

16. H.R. Clum to Jesse Applegate, 5 February 1873, in *House Document 122*, 246-7.

17. O.C. Applegate to Dear Father, 26 February 1873, Fisher Papers, 5:827.

18. Jesse Applegate to Honorable H. R. Clum, 26 February 1873, in *House Document 122*, 258.

19. H. R. Clum to Jesse Applegate, 19 March 1873, and C. Delano to Rev. E. Thomas, 19 March 1873, in *House Document 122*, 275.

20. *New York Herald*, 14 March 1873, in Cozzens, *Wars for the Pacific Northwest*, 224.

21. O.C. Applegate to John E. Ross, 5 March 1873, Fisher Papers, 5:853.

22. Jesse Applegate to H.R. Clum, 9 March 1873, in *House Document 122*, 265-6.

23. John H. James to The President of the United States, 15 January 1872, in *House Document 122*, 238.

24. Later, a lengthy Quaker appeal to President Grant by Alfred Love, Lucretia Mott et al., 12 Seventhmonth (July) 1873, asked leniency for the four Modocs condemned to death. *House Document 122*, 309–11.

25. Henry G. Waltman, "Circumstantial Reformer: President Grant and the Indian Problem," *Arizona and the West* 13, no. 4 (1971), 323. William S. McFeely, *Grant, a Biography* (New York: Norton, 1981), 305–18, has an excellent discussion of Grant's Indian policies and problems.

26. Sherman to Canby, 13 March 1873, in *House Document 122*, 70-71.

27. Canby to Sherman, 14 March 1873, in *House Document 122*, 71.

28. Canby to Sherman, 16 March 1873 [from Van Bremer's], in *House Document 122*, 72.

Chapter 24: Talking Peace

1. Meacham to Commissioner of Indian Affairs, 16 February 1873, *House Document 122*, 249.
2. The *Sacramento Daily Union* reported that on February 14, a Jacksonville grand jury indicted "Scar-faced Charley, Hocker Jim, Long Jim, One-Eyed Mose, Old Doctor Humphrey, Little Jim, Boston Charley and Dave." The paper mistakenly reported that they belonged "to Captain Jack's band." *Sacramento Daily Union*, 15 February 1873.
3. L. F. Grover, Govr. of Oregon to The Commissioners appointed to conclude Peace with the Modoc Indians, 10 February 1873, Fisher Papers, 5:750-53. The State of Oregon tried several times to wrest criminal jurisdiction away from the federal government. However, as early as 1854, Congress gave the federal government exclusive jurisdiction over the punishment of crimes committed in Indian country, except for crimes that were punished by tribal law, when it enacted the *Indian Country Crimes Act*, Rev. Stat. §2145-6 (1854); 18 U.S.C. §1152. Under the Act, an Indian who commits certain designated federal crimes (including murder) is subject to exclusive federal jurisdiction.
4. *New York Herald*, 20 February 1873, in Cozzens, *Wars for the Pacific Northwest*, 176. The meeting was in Linkville, and correspondent Edward Fox was present.
5. Captain Jack as quoted in *San Francisco Bulletin*, 7 March 1873.
6. *New York Herald*, 1 March 1873, in Cozzens, *Wars for the Pacific Northwest*, 174.
7. *New York Herald*, 22 February 1873, in Cozzens, *Wars for the Pacific Northwest*, 180.
8. Ibid., 179. The three Modoc women—Artinie Choakus, Queen Mary (Captain Jack's sister), and One-Eyed Dixie spoke English and were frequently used as translators and messengers by the Modocs, the army, and the peace commissioners.
9. Ibid.
10. Captain Jack as reported in the *New York Herald*, 8 March 1873 [date line February 22, 1873], in Cozzens, *Wars for the Pacific Northwest*, 181-83. The story is also reported in *Daily Alta California*, 26 February 1873. Perhaps in a crude attempt to manage the news, the official report Meacham gave to the reporters did not include Captain Jack's bitter remarks about the attack on his Lost River village and the murder of the woman and babies. Fox heard about this part of the talks from a private conversation with Bob Whittle, who had spoken with his wife Matilda. The reporter for the *Alta California* picked up the information on the murder of the Modoc woman and two babies from Artinie rather than from Meacham's official press release.
11. *New York Herald*, 8 March 1873 [dateline February 22, 1873], in Cozzens, *Wars for the Pacific Northwest*, 182.
12. Ibid., 183-14.
13. The account is based on Fox's reporting. The *Herald* printed two separate dispatches from Fox's trip: *New York Herald*, 28 February 1873 [dateline February 25-26], and *New York Herald*, 17 March 1873 [dateline March 1, 1873], both in Cozzens, *Wars for the Pacific Northwest*, 184-92, 196-212.
14. *New York Herald*, 17 March 1873, in Cozzens, *Wars for the Pacific Northwest*, 208. Captain Jack was too sick to participate in several of the peace talks during this period. One unconfirmed report said he suffered from pneumonia. *San Francisco Chronicle*, 27 February 1873.
15. Captain Jack quoted in Riddle, *Indian History*, 189.
16. The reporters are identified in Cozzens, *Wars for the Pacific Northwest*, 736n33.
17. *New York Herald*, 6 March 1873 in Cozzens, *Wars for the Pacific Northwest*, 215.
18. *New York Herald*, 3 March 1873, in Cozzens, *Wars for the Pacific Northwest*, 213
19. *San Francisco Chronicle*, 5 March 1873.
20. Meacham, *Wigwam and Warpath*, 428.
21. *New York Herald*, 3 March 1873, in Cozzens, *Wars for the Pacific Northwest*, 212-3.
22. Meacham, *Wigwam and Warpath*, 428.

23. Canby to Sherman, 2 March 1873, Fisher Papers, 5:832.

24. Quoted in Meacham, *Wigwam and Warpath*, 428. Emphasis in original.

25. *San Francisco Chronicle*, 11 March 1873.

26. Meacham, *Wigwam and Warpath*, 429.

27. The events and quotations from the first day are from *New York Herald*, 5 March 1873 in Cozzens, *Wars for the Pacific Northwest*, 216-23.

28. Unless otherwise noted, the following account is taken from *San Francisco Chronicle*, 11 March 1873. The *Chronicle* story, told in the first person, was written by Robert Atwell, the only reporter on the trip with Steele.

29. *New York Herald*, 6 March 1873, in Cozzens, *Wars for the Pacific Northwest*, 215.

30. Meacham, *Wigwam and Warpath*, 431.

31. Quoted in *New York Herald*, 5 March 1873, in Cozzens, *Wars for the Pacific Northwest*, 215.

32. Meacham to H. R. Clum, 8 March 1873, in *House Document 122*, 264-65.

33. Delano to Meacham, 5 March 1873, in *House Document 122*, 261.

34. Trial Transcript, *House Document 122*, 175.

35. Bancroft, *History of Oregon*, 2:604.

36. Clipping from *Daily Oregon Herald*, 6 March 1873, Fisher Papers, 5:859.

37. Quoted in Heyman, *Prudent Soldier*, 373–74.

Chapter 25: A Lethal Decision

1. Canby to Sherman, 17 March 1873, in *House Document 122*, 272-73.

2. The account of this meeting is taken from Fox, *New York Herald*, 24 March 1873, in Cozzens, *Wars for the Pacific Northwest*, 228-33.

3. Canby to Colonel W. D. Whipple, 24 March 1873, in *House Document 122*, 279-80.

4. Delano to Belknap, 24 March 1873, in *House Document 122*, 73-74.

5. Delano to Meacham, 4 March 1873, in *House Document 122*, 259.

6. Canby to Sherman, 17 March 1983, in *House Document 121*, 272-73.

7. Murray, *Modocs and Their War*, 168.

8. The account of the meeting and conversation with Captain Jack is from Meacham, *Wigwam and Warpath*, 440-52.

9. Ibid., 485-86.

10. Meacham, *Wigwam and Warpath*, 453. Meacham and reporter Fox both say it was William, Wild Girl's Man. Riddle calls him Weium. *Indian History*, 77-8.

11. Riddle, *Indian History*, 80.

12. Ibid., 84. Riddle says Winema later jumped up on a big rock and told Captain Jack she really did not dream the warning, but that she would never disclose who gave her the information.

13. The events inside what Jeff Riddle calls the "war council" are recounted in his *Indian History*, 69-73.

14. Gatschet, *Klamath Indians*, 40.

15. From Ray, *Primitive Pragmatists*, 136.

16. "Trial Transcript," 176.

17. Riddle, *Indian History*, 76.

18. Meacham, *Wigwam and Warpath*, 465-66.

Chapter 26: The Fateful Meeting

1. Meacham, *Wigwam and Warpath*, 472.

2. Mathew Deady, *Pharisee among Philistines*, ed. Malcolm Clark Jr. (Portland: Oregon Historical Society Press, 1975), 150. I am grateful to Philip Niles for bringing this work to my attention.

3. Meacham, *Wigwam and Warpath*, 475.

4. Canby as quoted in "Trial Transcript," 162.
5. Canby to My Dear Wife, 8 April 1873, quoted in Heyman, *Prudent Soldier*, 374.
6. "Trial Transcript," 139.
7. Meacham, *Wigwam and Warpath*, 470, emphasis in the original.
8. Meacham, *Wigwam and Warpath*, 470.
9. Riddle, *Indian History*, 86.
10. "Trial Transcript," 141.
11. Oliver C. Applegate, "The Modoc Peace Commission Massacre," in Cozzens, *Wars for the Pacific Northwest*, 271.
12. Direct quotes are from Meacham, *Wigwam and Warpath*, 471-74.
13. The account that follows relies heavily on the trial testimony of Frank Riddle, Dyar, and Meacham, as well as Meacham's dramatic version in *Wigwam and Warpath*. "Trial Transcript," 136-66; *Wigwam and Warpath*, 478-507. The Modocs' testimony in their defense is reported in "Trial Transcript," 169-78.
14. "Trial Transcript," 141-42.
15. Meacham wrote that although he fully understood the import of Hooker Jim's actions, he "assumed indifference." *Wigwam and Warpath*, 486.
16. Murray, *Modocs and Their War*, 188. Cheewa James interprets Captain Jack's odd behavior as a signal for action. James, *Modoc*, 112.
17. Meacham, *Wigwam and Warpath*, 491.
18. Ibid., 492.
19. There are different reports on the exact details of Canby's murder. Meacham says Captain Jack held Canby while Ellen's Man George cut his throat. *Wigwam and Warpath*, 492. Bogus Charley later claimed that he killed Canby, assisted by Steamboat Frank. *Sonoma Democrat*, 11 October 1873. Reporter Edward Fox, based on an interview with Dyar, says Canby ran off to the left after the second shot but "was speedily shot down and killed instantly." Fox, *New York Herald*, 13 April 1873, in Cozzens, *Wars for the Pacific Northwest*, 235.
20. Meacham, *Wigwam and Warpath*, 495-99.
21. *New York Herald*, 13 April 1873, in Cozzens, *Wars for the Pacific Northwest*, 235.
22. James, *Modoc*, 113. Meacham states that Winema called out "Bosteen-wa sojeers, Kot-pumbla!" ("White soldiers are coming!") in Chinook dialect. *Wigwam and Warpath*, 499. Riddle says she called out in Modoc, "Ut nah sholgars kep ko" ("Now the soldiers are coming.") *Indian History*, 97.
23. Fitzgerald, "Modoc War," in Cozzens, *Wars for the Pacific Northwest*, 123.
24. Reporter Fox saw the "half-written note" that Gillem penned to warn Canby. *New York Herald*, 13 April 1873, in Cozzens, *Wars for the Pacific Northwest*, 235.
25. Meacham, *Wigwam and Warpath*, 503.
26. *San Francisco Chronicle*, 14 April 1873.
27. Fox's account appears at *New York Herald*, 13 April 1873 in Cozzens, *Wars for the Pacific Northwest*, 234-43.
28. Meacham, *Wigwam and Warpath*, 504.
29. Atwell replaced Bogart as the correspondent for the *San Francisco Chronicle*. Atwell's lengthy report with a map of the "Scene of the Modoc Massacre" appeared on 13 April 1873, two days after the killings. A second full page piece appeared the following day. *San Francisco Chronicle*, 14 April 1873.
30. *San Francisco Chronicle*, 13 April 1873.
31. *New York Herald*, 13 April 1873, in Cozzens, *Wars for the Pacific Northwest*, 234.
32. *New York Herald*, 11 April 1873; *San Francisco Chronicle*, 13 April 1873; *San Francisco Chronicle*, 14 April 1873; *San Francisco Call*, 11 April 1873; *The New York Times*, 14 April 1873.
33. *San Francisco Chronicle*, 13 April 1873.

Chapter 27: Outrage!

1. Sherman to Gillem, 12 April 1873, reprinted in *New York Times,* 15 April 1873.
2. Sherman to W.W. Belnap, 3 June 1873, in *House Document 122,* 84-85.
3. Wheaton to O.C. Applegate, 2 May 1873, *Fisher Papers,* 7:45.
4. *Daily Evening Bulletin,* 14 April 1873.
5. William D Whipple to Heaquarters of the Army, 14 April 1873, in *House Document 122,* 77-78.
6. *Portland Oregonian,* 14 April 1873.
7. William D. Whipple to Headquarters of the Army, 14 April 1873, in *House Document 122,* 77-78.
8. *Portland Morning Oregonian,* 16 April 1873.
9. *Portland Morning Oregonian,* 15 and 16 April 1873.
10. *Daily Alta California,* 13 May 1873.
11. *San Francisco Chronicle,* 15 May 1873.
12. *Marysville Daily Appeal,* 18 May 1873. "General E. R. S. Canby Funeral March," (San Francisco: M. Gray, 1873) is in the sheet music collection at Univeristy of California in Los Angeles.
13. Events inside the Indian camp from Meacham, *Wigwam and Warpath,* 509-10.
14. *San Francisco Chronicle,* 5 May 1873.
15. *Daily Rocky Mountain Gazette,* 22 April 1873.
16. Ibid., 29 April 1873.
17. *San Francisco Bulletin,* 16 April 1873.
18. *Nevada State Journal,* 12 February 1873.
19. H. Clay Wood to Jeff C. Davis, 25 April 1873, Fisher Papers, 7:1106-7.
20. Bob Pollock to L. S. Dyar, 1 May 1873, Fisher Papers, 7:1133-34.
21. Ivon [sic] to "Dear Brother," 13 April 1873, and Ivon [sic] to "Dear Brother," 20 April 1873, Fisher Papers, 7:1059, 1097.
22. Medical report quoted in *San Francisco Evening Bulletin,* 16 April 1873.
23. Meacham to C. Delano, 16 April 1873, in *House Document 122,* 286-7.
24. *Daily Rocky Mountain Gazette,* 17 April 1873.
25. *New York Times,* 16 April 1873.
26. *New York Times,* 17 April 1873.
27. *Daily Rocky Mountain Gazette,* 30 April 1873.
28. *New York Times,* 16 April 1873. If the anonymous writer thought the Modocs had a rationale for rebellion, it did not lessen his racism: "An Indian has all the instincts of a dog, and as that quadruped never forgets a whipping from a stranger, so the red man remembers the wrongs that are done him, and never forgives an enemy."
29. O. K. Luttrell to C. Delano, no date, reprinted in Riddle, *Indian History,* 289-99.
30. Transcriptions of newspapers, dated 1873, Fisher Papers, 8:1310-13.
31. *New York Times,* 16 April 1873.
32. Lucretia Mott et al. to Ulysses S. Grant, 13 July 1873; John Beeson to U.S. Grant, 18 July 1873, in *House Document 122,* 309-11; 313-16.
33. Captain Rob Pollock, Twenty-first Infantry, to Assistant Adjutant General [Portland], 21 May 1873, Fisher Papers, 8:1135-36.

Chapter 28: Second Attack on the Stronghold

1. Gilbert Davis, *Diary,* 11 April 1873.
2. Boyle, *Personal Observations,* 41.
3. Fitzgerald, "Modoc War," in Cozzens, *Wars for the Pacific Northwest,* 124.

4. Meacham, *Wigwam and Warpath*, 457.

5. Thompson, *Modoc War,* 67–78. Erwin Thompson's book is the indispensible source on military movements, and I have used his well-researched accounts of the order of battle for the second attack on the Stronghold.

6. Invented in Holland in 1674 by Menno van Coehorn, a Dutch soldier and military engineer, a Coehorn could wreak destruction behind enemy lines by firing "mortar bombs" on a high looping trajectory. The small light versions used in the Civil War were still called Coehorns.

7. Gillem to Canby, 11 February 1873, Fisher Papers, 5:757. Emphasis in the original.

8. Gillem to Canby, 9 February 1873, Fisher Papers, 6:741.

9. As reported by Fox in *New York Herald,* 6 March 1873, in Cozzens, *Wars for the Pacific Northwest,* 214.

10. Riddle, *Indian History,* 56.

11. Thompson, *Modoc War,* 181. The Springfields' power and long range were good, but sometimes its single-shot firing capability left troops at a disadvantage.

12. The Warm Springs scouts under McKay played a role in several episodes of fighting during the Modoc War. Some later believed the Warm Springs had struck a deal with the Modocs to stand by when the Modoc warriors ambushed a patrol and killed seventeen officers and men. But in the beginning, Gillem thought it was good policy to have Indians fight Indians, and he hoped that the Warm Springs would frighten the Modocs. He found out later that Captain Jack and his warriors were unimpressed. Keith Clark and Donna Clark, eds., *Daring Donald McKay Or the last war-trail of the Modocs* (Chicago: Rounds Brothers, 1881; reprinted Portland: Oregon Historical Society, 1971), xi.

13. Fitzgerald, "Modoc War," in Cozzens, *Wars for the Pacific Northwest,* 125.

14. Ibid., 126.

15. Fox, *New York Herald,* 5 May 1873, in Cozzens, *Wars for the Pacific Northwest,* 245.

16. Fitzgerald, "Modoc War," in Cozzens, *Wars for the Pacific Northwest,* 127. Fitzgerald's unit was "Troop K," not "Company K."

17. Murray, "Modoc War Diary," 69-70.

18. Ibid.

19. Ibid., 48-49; Meacham, *Wigwam,* 524-26.

20. Murray, "Modoc War Diary," 58.

21. Fitzgerald, "Modoc War," in Cozzens, *Wars for the Pacific Northwest,* 128.

22. Fox, *New York Herald,* 7 May 1873 in Cozzens, *Wars for the Pacific Northwest,* 252.

23. Murray, "Modoc War Diary," 75.

24. Fitzgerald, "Modoc War," in Cozzens, *Wars for the Pacific Northwest,* 128

25. *San Francisco Chronicle,* 19 April 1873.

26. Corporal Pentz, "Journal," 25 April 1873, unpublished manuscript, Lava Beds National Monument.

27. Fitzgerald, "Modoc War," in Cozzens, *Wars for the Pacific Northwest,* 131.

28. Ibid.

29. Murray, "Modoc War Diary," 83.

30. One paper reported that Scarface Charley was scalped and dead. *Daily Rocky Mountain Gazette,* 23 April 1873. Another reported that the body of Scarface Charley was found in the cave, wounded and scalped. *Eureka Union,* 19 April 1873. Yet another report said that Scarface Charley was not killed, but that the body found was a Modoc by the name of Shacknasty Frank. *The New York Times,* 24 April 1873.

31. Murray, "Modoc War Diary," 87.

32. Fitzgerald, "Modoc War," in Cozzens, *Wars for the Pacific Northwest,* 130.

33. Murray, "Modoc War Diary," 88.

34. Fitzgerald, "Modoc War," in Cozzens, *Wars for the Pacific Northwest,* 129-30.

35. Ibid.

36. *Rochester* [NY] *Democrat and Chronicle,* 23 April 1873.

37. Boyle, *Personal Observations,* 44-45.

38. Simpson, *Illustrated London News,* 31 May 1873.

39. Riddle, *Indian History,* 111.

40. Fitzgerald, "Modoc War," in Cozzens, *Wars for the Pacific Northwest,* 129-30; Murray, "Modoc War Diary Campaign," 86.

41. Simpson, *Meeting the Sun,* 379.

42. Simpson, *Illustrated London News,* 7 June 1873.

43. Thompson, *Modoc War,* 78.

Chapter 29: The Thomas-Wright Battle

1. Boutelle, "Disaster," in Brady, *Fights and Fighters,* 305.

2. Thompson, *Modoc War,* 83-84.

3. Jocelyn, *Mostly Alkali,* 181.

4. Murray, *Modocs and Their War,* 114-15.

5. The expedition is described by P. W. Hamont, "The Modoc Indian War, by One who was There," in Cozzens, *Wars for the Pacific Northwest,* 264-67. Company E was criticized for disobeying orders. Lieutenant Kingsbury later published a defense of the conduct of the officers and Company E. George Kingsbury, "The Twelfth U.S. Infantry in the Lava Beds," in Cozzens, *Wars for the Pacific Northwest,* 274-75.

6. Murray, *Modocs and Their War,* 228.

7. Simpson, *Meeting the Sun,* 382.

8. Murray, *Modocs and Their War,* 229.

9. Thompson, *Modoc War,* 87.

10. Moore, "Letters," 7.

11. Francis "Van" Landrum, "The Ambush of Captain Thomas' Patrol," ca. 1975, unpublished typescript in author's collection, 50.

12. Murray, *Modocs and Their War,* 230. Buglers were in special danger during the war. "The Indians soon learn that the soldiers act from the bugle calls and the buglars [*sic*] are therefore mistaken for Tyees and consequently selected as objects upon which to wreak their vengeance." *Bellow Falls Times,* 17 May 1873. Three buglers (also listed as "trumpeters") died—two from the Fourth Artillery, and one from the First Cavalry—during the Modoc War.

13. Boyle, *Personal Observations,* 52.

14. Pentz, "Journal," 25 April 1873.

15. Boutelle, "Disaster," in Brady, *Fights and Fighters,* 307.

16. J. G. Trimble, "Carrying a Stretcher in the Lava–Beds," in Brady, *Fights and Fighters,* 314.

17. Boutelle, "Disaster," in Brady, *Fights and Fighters,* 307

18. Boyle, *Personal Observations,* 53.

19. To Dear Girl, 1 May 1873, Boutelle, "Letters."

20. Boyle, *Personal Observations,* 54.

21. Fitzgerald, "The Modoc War," in Cozzens, *Wars for the Pacific Northwest,* 132.

22. Boutelle, "Disaster," in Brady, *Fights and Fighters,* 310.

23. Trimble, "Carrying a Stretcher,"in Brady, *Fights and Fighters,* 315.

24. Ibid., 318-19.

25. Boyle, *Personal Observations,* 53.

26. Boutelle, "Disaster," in Brady, *Fights and Fighters,* 308.

27. Gillem to Sherman, 29 April 1873, in *House Document 122,* 82.

28. Thompson, *Reminiscences,* 119. Historian Van Landrum also argued that Gillem's resentment

against the sons of privilege led him to put the generals' sons in harm's way. Interview with the author, March 1990.

29. *Army and Navy Journal*, 3 May 1873, quoted in Thompson, *Modoc War*, 91.

30. Jefferson C. Davis to Headquarters, 4 May 1873, in *House Document 122*, 83-4.

31. Boutelle, "Disaster," in Brady, *Fights and Fighters*, 305.

32. Prucha, *The Great Father*, Kindle edition.

33. This episode in the Modoc War is called by many historians the "Thomas Wright Massacre" because of the involvement by Evan Thomas and Thomas Wright. But, as historian Van Landrum pointed out, it was so named because the Indians won. Cheewa James refers to the event as the Thomas-Wright Battle, and we have followed her nomenclature.

Chapter 30: The Battle of Sorass Lake

1. See Nathaniel Cheirs Hughes Jr. and Gordon D. Whitney, *Jefferson Davis in Blue: The Life of Sherman's Relentless Warrior* (Baton Rouge: University of Louisiana Press, 2002), 309. When Sherman and Grant requested that Davis be promoted to full brigadier general, Congress declined. His biographers wrote, "Congress was ashamed of this soldier, and would never confirm his further promotion." Ibid., 314.

2. Jeff. C. Davis to Assistant Adjutant–General, 14 May 1873, in *House Document 122*, 84.

3. Thompson, *Modoc War*, 95.

4. Davis to J. M. Schofield, 8 May 1873, in *House Document 122*, 84. Keith Murray notes although that official reports say little about this incident, sometimes called the Battle of Scorpion Point, "It was evident that no one was very proud of himself." Murray adds, "It is equally noticeable that the troops were in no condition, mentally or physically, to stand up and fight when they heard a Modoc yell followed by a few rifle shots." Murray, *Modocs and Their War*, 244.

5. *Daily Rocky Mountain Gazette*, 28 May 1873.

6. Ibid.

7. H. C. Hasbrouck, "The Last Fight of the Campaign," in Brady, *Fights and Fighters*, 321. The account of the battle of Sorass Lake is based on Hasbrouck's account.

8. Thompson, *Reminiscences*, 121.

9. Bancroft, *History of Oregon*, 2:624. This account and several others says that Captain Jack led the attack wearing General Canby's uniform.

10. Charles B. Hardin from *Proceedings, Order of Indian Wars*, January 24, 1931, in Rickey, *Forty Miles a Day*, 286.

11. Hasbrouck, "Last Fight," in Brady, *Fights and Fighters,* 322.

12. James, *Modoc*, 138. The description of the cremation of Ellen's Man George body is told with a literary flourish in Quinn, *Hell with the Fire Out* 160-61, and also in Murray, *Modocs and Their War*, 250-51. The source of the story is not known.

13. *New York Herald*, 14 May 1873. Francis Fuller Victor said the Modocs got ammunition for the attack from "illicit commerce with persons in or about Yreka." *History of Oregon*, 2:625n88.

Chapter 31: The Bloodhounds

1. Riddle, *Indian History,* 123.

2. Hasbrouck, "Last Fight," in Brady, *Fights and Fighters*, 324.

3. *Sonoma Democrat,* 31 May 1873.

4. Ibid.

5. Reported in *Daily Rocky Mountain Gazette*, 28 May 1873; *Bellows Falls* [VT] *Times*, 30 May 1873.

6. *Daily Rocky Mountain Daily Gazette*, 28 May 1873.

7. *Bellows Falls* [VT] *Times,* 30 May 1873.

8. Ibid.

9. Bancroft, *History of Oregon*, 2:627.
10. *San Francisco Evening Bulletin,* 26 May 1873.
11. Gatschet, *Klamath Indians,* 55-57n14.
12. Jefferson Davis, "Annual report of Military Operations to Headquarters, Department of the Columbia," 1 November 1873, in *House Document 122,* 111.
13. *Daily Alta California,* 2 June 1873.
14. Ibid.
15. Ibid.
16. Jeff C. Davis to H. Clay Wood, 22 May 1873, Fisher Papers, 8:1218.
17. *Sacramento Daily Union,* 3 June 1873.
18. *San Francisco Evening Bulletin,* 2 June 1873.
19. *Sacramento Daily Union,* 3 June 1873.
20. *New York Times,* 17 June 1873.
21. Ibid.
22. General Davis to Assistant Adjutant General, Division of Pacific, 1 June 1873, Fisher Papers, 8:1249.

Chapter 32: The Capture of Captain Jack

1. Ray, *Primitive Pragmatists,* 208. Ray includes a useful map of the Modoc villages showing the location of cremation places.
2. Ibid., 206–9.
3. Davis to Headquarters Department of the Columbia, 1 November 1873, in *House Document 122,* 110.
4. *New York Herald,* 16 June 1873, in Cozzens, *Wars for the Pacific Northwest,* 292.
5. Davis to Headquarters Department of the Columbia, 1 November 1873, in *House Document 122,* 110.
6. *Sacramento Daily Union,* 7 June 1873.
7. Perry, "First and Second Battles," in Brady, *Fights and Fighters,* 304.
8. Putnam, "Incidents," 12.
9. *New York Times,* 17 June 1873.
10. McCarthy, "Sketchbook," 7.
11. Ibid., 5.
12. Davis to Headquarters Department of the Columbia, 1 November 1873, in *House Document 122,* 105-13, at 111.
13. *New York Times,* 19 June 1873.
14. *New York Times,* 2 June 1873.
15. *New York Times,* 17 June 1873.
16. McCarthy, "Sketchbook," 7.
17. Putnam, "Incidents," 12.
18. *San Francisco Bulletin,* 7 June 1873.
19. *New York Times,* 17 June 1873.
20. *Daily Alta California,* 3 June 1873.
21. *New York Herald,* 23 June 1873.
22. *Marysville Daily Appeal,* 7 June 1873.
23. Putnam, "Incidents," 12.
24. McCarthy, "Sketchbook," 7.
25. *Daily Alta California,* 3 June 1873.
26. *New York Herald,* 1 October 1873.
27. Jeff C. Davis to Assist. Adjut. General, 1 June 1873, *Fisher Papers,* 8:1250..
28. *New York Times,* 17 June 1873.

Chapter 33: Captain Jack Will Be Tried

1. Kingsbury, *Bellows Falls* [VT] *Times*, 5 June 1873.

2. *San Francisco Bulletin*, 7 June 1873.

3. *Marysville Daily Appeal*, 14 June 1873.

4. Sixty-six years later another captive group— more than eighteen thousand Japanese-Americans who had been classified as troublemakers in other processing centers—were segregated at the same location in the notorious Tule Lake Internment Camp. Jeffrey F. Burton, "Confinement and Ethnicity: An Overview of World War II Japanese American Relocation Facilities," National Park Service (May 3, 2005). www.digitalhistory.uh.edu/active_learning/explorations/japanese_internment/confinement_ethnicity_nps_sm.pdf.

5. *San Francisco Bulletin*, 24 June 1873.

6. *Army and Navy Journal* (14 June 1873), 697, quoted in Thompson, *Modoc War,* 162n3.

7. *Willamette Farmer* [Salem], 21 June 1873.

8. Meacham, *Wigwam and Warpath,* 596-97.

9. Reported in *Daily Alta California*, 10 June 1873.

10. Thompson, *Reminiscences*, 130.

11. Davis to H. Clay Wood, 5 June 1873, Fisher Papers, 8:1260.

12. *New York Times*, 13 June 1873.

13. *Daily Rocky Mountain Gazette*, 10 June 1873.

14. Davis to Assist Adjut General, 5 June 1873, Fisher Papers, 8:1259.

15. *Daily Alta California*, 13 June 1873.

16. Sherman and J.W. Schofield to Davis, 3 June 1873, Fisher Papers, 8:1255.

17. Davis to Clay Wood, Assistant Adjutant General, 5 June 1873, Fisher Papers, 8:1260.

18. *The Lieber Code of 1863*, General Orders No. 100. 24 (April 1863). Although the army had been moving away from summary execution of Indians for a decade, trial by military commissions had just as certain a result—executions were almost always ordered, raising the question of why U.S. officials held trials at all. John Fabian Witt examines the application of the laws of war to the Modocs in *Lincoln's Code* (New York: Free Press, 2012), 328–35.

19. Geo. H. Williams to The President, 7 June 1873, in *House Document 122*, 88-90. The Attorney General's opinion can also be found at 14 Ops. Attys Gen. 249 (1873).

20. Williams to The President, 7 June 1873, in *House Document 122*, 90. Also quoted in Foster, "Imperfect Justice," 254. Foster points out that even though there was in fact no "white flag" when Canby and Thomas were killed, the government later explained that "white flag" was intended to mean there was a truce between the parties. Ibid., 284n13.

    The Williams decision on the Modocs would have echoes for more than a century. It was cited 130 years later in a memo to counsel for President George W. Bush permitting trial and punishment (even to death) of suspected terrorists captured after the September 11, 2001 attacks. Patrick F. Philbin, "Memorandum Opinion for the Counsel to the President: Legality of the Use of Military Commissions to Try Terrorists," 6 November 2001. nsarchive.gwu.edu/torturingdemocracy/documents/20011106.pdf. A secret memo prepared in March 2003 for the Bush administration (later declassified) again cited the Modoc opinion to justify torture of suspected terrorists at Guantanamo and elsewhere outside the United States. John C. Yoo, "Memorandum for William J. Haynes II, General Counsel of the Department of Defense *Re:* Military Interrogation of Alien Unlawful Combatants Held Outside the United States," 14 March 2003. See also, John C. Yoo to Alberto R. Gonzales, 1 August 2002.

21. *Willamette Farmer,* 21 June 1873.

22. Luttrell to Hon. C. Delano, 17 June 1873, Fisher Papers, 8:1332-34.The letter was published in the *Sacramento Daily Union*, 30 June 1873.

23. The account of the meeting and quotations are from *Sacramento Daily Union*, 14 June 1873.

24. The government also dispatched Eadweard J. Muybridge, the famous photographer, to the Lava Beds to take "photographic views of the different approaches to the lava bed and of Captain Jack's famous cave and fortifications." *San Francisco Chronicle*, 29 April 1873. Heller and Muybridge both photographed battle sites, sometimes staging scenes for dramatic effect. Peter Palmquist, "Image Makers of the Modoc War: Louis Heller and Eadweard Muybridge," *Journal of California Anthropology* 4, no. 2 (1977), 213.

25. Boyd Cothran contends that the popularity of these photographs, along with other Modoc War memorabilia, transformed "traces of brutal violence into commodity goods." *Remembering the Modoc War*, 14.

26. Photo session as reported in *Sacramento Daily Union*, 14 June 1873.

27. *New York Times*, 28 June 1873.

28. *New York Times*, 13 June 1873. Davis granted the interview to the reporter for the *San Francisco Bulletin* on June 11, and it was reprinted in several other papers.

29. Quoted in *New Oreleans Republican*, 15 June 1873.

30. Riddle, *Indian History*, 156-7.

Chapter 34: The Trial of Captain Jack

1. Sherman to J. M. Schofield, 3 June 1873, *House Document 122*, 86.

2. "Letter from Fort Klamath: Correspondence of the Bellows Falls Times," in *Bellows Falls* [VT] *Times,* 25 July 1873.

3. *Bellows Falls* [VT] *Times*, 25 July 1873.

4. The reconstructed guardhouse now houses the Fort Klamath Museum collection of artifacts and photographs from the Modoc War. The guardhouse burned down twice, and each time has been rebuilt as the last remaining historic building at Fort Klamath.

5. George Kingsbury of the *Bellows Falls* (VT) *Times*, 25 July 1873, listed the prisoners except Barncho and Slolux, who were later identified by the *San Francisco Chronicle*, 3 October 1873. Following quotes are from *San Francisco Daily Evening Bulletin*, 5 July 1873.

6. McCarthy, "Sketchbook," 9.

7. Ibid., 8.

8. Ibid.

9. The charges were read on the second day of the trial. "Trial Transcript," 134-36.

10. Curtis to J.C. Kelton, 8 July 1873, in *House Document 122*, 93-94.

11. Meacham, *Wigwam and Warpath*, 635.

12. Curtis to J.C. Kelton, 8 July 1873, in *House Document 122*, 93.

13. Meacham, *Wigwam and Warpath*, 448.

14. *Yreka Union*, 14 June 1873, cited in Doug Foster, "Imperfect Justice, The Modoc War Crimes Trial of 1873," *Oregon Historical Quarterly* (Fall 1999): 258.

15. Curtis to an officer in the Judge-Advocate-General's Office, "Extract from a private letter," no date, in *House Document 122,* 190; Curtis to Gen. J.M. Schofield, 2 September 1873, in *House Document 122*, 198-99.

16. "Trial Transcript," 134. Modern army rules for military courts provide that defendants have a right to counsel, either military or civilian. *Manual for Courts-Martial United States* (2012), Rule 506.

17. Henry Copée, *Field Manual of Courts-Martial* (Philadelphia: J.B. Lippincott, 1863), 71.

18. J.K. Luttrell to Hon. C. Delano, 17 June 1873, Fisher Papers, 8:1333-34.

19. *Marysville Daily Appeal*, 6 July 1873; Meacham, *Wigwam and Warpath*, 634.

20. Meacham, *Wigwam and Warpath,* 628. Meacham's account has a whiff of his penchant for self-aggrandizement. His health did not seem problematic; he was lecturing about Indian affairs in San Francisco three days earlier, and he had been able to travel to Washington, D.C., and back. His biographer Edward Phinney speculated that "[Meacham's] offer to serve as counsel for the Indians . . . may have been the product of later imagination." Phinney, "Meacham," 217.

21. Atwell to Honorable C. Delano, 30 July 1873, Fisher Papers, 9:1471.

22. "Trial Transcript," 141. Unless otherwise noted, the quotations and references to trial testimony are taken from "Trial Transcript," 151-173.

23. *New York Times,* 23 July 1873.

24. As reported in *San Francisco Bulletin,* 7 June 1873.

25. "Trial Transcript," 172-77.

26. Ibid., 182-3.

Chapter 35: The Execution

1. F[razier] to My dear Dolly, 15 July 1873, Boutelle, "Letters."

2. *San Francisco Chronicle,* 3 October 1873.

3. *San Francisco Daily Evening Bulletin,* 5 July 1873.

4. H. Clay Wood to J.C. Davis, 5 August 1873, *House Document 122,* 324-25.

5. *San Francisco Chronicle,* 3 October 1873.

6. *New York Times,* 5 October 1873.

7. *New York Star,* 23 July 1873, reprinted as attachment to letter from H.R. Clum to E.C. Kemble, Esq., 21 July 1873, in *House Document 122,* 316-17.

8. Transmitted by telegram, Clay Wood to Jeff C. Davis, 8 October 1873 Fisher Papers, 10:1660-1. Reported in *Marysville Daily Appeal,* 5 October 1873.

9. Grover to Jeff C. Davis, 4 October 1873, in *House Document 122,* 101.

10. Jeff C. Davis to Frank Wheaton, 9 October 1873, Fisher Papers, 10:1662.

11. Meacham, *Wigwam and Warpath,* 647.

12. *New York Times,* 5 October 1873.

13. Meacham, *Wigwam and Warpath,* 649.

14. *San Francisco Chronicle,* 3 October 1873.

15. Case, "Diary."

16. *Sonoma Democrat,* 11 October 1873.

17. Ibid.

18. *Daily Alta California,* 4 October 1873.

19. "General Court Martial Orders No. 34," U.S. Grant to Attorney General, 10 September 1873, in *House Document 122,* 98. Grant ordered that the order commuting the sentences of Barncho and Slolux should not be promulgated until "shortly before the time of executing the death-sentence upon Captain Jack." E. D. Townsend to J. M. Schofield, 12 September 1873, Ibid.

20. *Sonoma Democrat,* 11 October 1873.

21. Details of the execution are from *New York Times,* 2 October 1873, and *San Francisco Chronicle,* 4 October 1873.

Chapter 36: Exile

1. Sherman to Belknap, 3 June 1873, in *House Document 122,* 84-85.

2. John M. Spear to Grant, 30 July 1873, in *House Document 122,* 322.

3. Delano, *Report of the Secretary of the Interior* (Washington, D.C.: Government Printing Office, 1874), 31 October 1873.

4. Wm. W. Belknap to E. D. Townsend, to J. W. Schofield, 13 September 1873, in *House Document 122,* 99.

5. E.D. Townsend to J. W. Schofield, 13 September 1873, in *House Document 122*, 99.

6. Lieutenant Colonel J. C. Kelton to Comd'g Officer Fort Klamath, 22 September 1873, Fisher Papers, 10:1612-3.

7. Wheaton to Assistant Adjutant General, Portland, 30 September 1873, Fisher Papers, 10:1620.

8. Sherman to Headquarters of the Army, 6 October 1873, in *House Document 122*, 100.

9. *Daily Alta California*, 26 October 1873.

10. Ibid.

11. J. J. Reynolds, 29 October 1873, in *House Document 122*, 102

12. Wm. W. Belknap to Secretary of Interior, 1 November 1873, in *House Document 122*, 103.

13. M C. Wilkinson, "Report" 12 December 1873, in *Annual Report* (1873), 82.

14. Lucile Martin, "The Modocs in Indian Territory," in *The Northwest Tribes in Exile*, ed. Cliff Trazer (Sacramento, CA: Sierra Oaks Publishing Co., 1987), 15.

15. *Annual Report* (1873), 82.

16. Ibid.

17. *Annual Report* (1874), 229.

18. Martin, "Modocs in Indian Territory," 16-18.

19. *Annual Report* (1874), 20.

20. *Annual Report* (1880), 88.

21. *Annual Report* (1886), 140.

22. *Annual Report* (1874), 81.

23. *Annual Report* (1875), 348.

24. *Annual Report* (1874), 81.

25. Ibid.

26. Hurtado, "The Modocs and the Jones Family Indian Ring," 89. Bogus Charley's comments are from Inspector Arden Smith's report, 2 February 1878, as quoted in Hurtado, 100-1.

27. Ibid., 91-93.

28. Ibid., 94-95.

29. Ibid., 100-1.

30. E.A. Hayt, *Annual Report* (1878), xxxv.

31. Quoted in Hurtado, 102.

32. "Ex-Indian Commissioner Hayt," *New York Times* 11 February 1880.

33. *Annual Report* (1887), 91.

34. *Annual Report* (1884), 90.

35. W. K. Davis, Agency Physician, *Annual Report* (1887), 93.

36. John S. Lindley, Agency Physician, in *Annual Report* (1890), 89.

37. W. K. Davis, Agency Physician, in *Annual Report* (1887), 93.

38. Dr. John S. Lindsay, Agency Physician, in *Annual Report* (1890), 88.

39. Ibid.

40. Ibid., 89.

41. *Medford Mail*, 2 August 1901.

42. *Annual Report* (1904), 182.

43. Cora Hayman, interview by Nannie Lee Burns, Investigator (21 October 1937), Indian Archives, Oklahoma Historical Society.

Chapter 37: The Skull of Captain Jack

1. The account of Ken McLeod's role in uncovering the mystery of the skulls is from Landrum, *Guardhouse*, 79-80.

2. The Army Medical Museum was housed at Ford's Theater in Washington, D.C. where President Lincoln was assassinated. Later its specimen collection was transferred to the Smithsonian.

3. Landrum, *Guardhouse*, 80-81.

4. "Jack and Schonchin Decapitated," *San Francisco Chronicle*, 12 October 1873. Oliver Knight identifies the *San Francisco Chronicle* reporter who was covering the execution as City Editor Col. H. S. Shaw. Knight, *Following the Indian Wars*, 154. Shaw accompanied Ohio visitor Leonard Case.

5. "Form No. 5 Receipt," 17 October 1873; Henry McElderry to Surgeon General, U.S. Army, 25 October 1873, National Anthropological Archives, Smithsonian Institution Army Medical Museum, AMM 1018-1021. [Hereafter "AMM."]

6. Army Museum records show that several years earlier, McElderry had submitted specimens from Fort Griffin, Texas, including the skulls of Chippewa and Arapaho natives. 17 December 1869, AMM 773-74.

7. Handwritten note, 23 January 1874, AMM 1015-21.

8. Handwritten note, 27 April 1873, AMM 995.

9. A handwritten note with the record for the four Modoc skulls states: "Scalps of these crania in Anatomical Laboratory, Sept. 13, 1894." AMM 1018-21.

10. Ann Fabian, *The Skull Collectors: Race, Science, and America's Unburied Dead* (Chicago: University of Chicago Press, 2010): 183.

11. Including McElderry, there were at least ten army surgeons assigned to Fort Klamath during the Modoc war. Thompson, *Modoc War*, 173-79. Of these, six were collectors, donors, or correspondents to the Army Medical Museum: Edwin Bentley, Calvin DeWitt, H.K. Durant, Thomas McMillin, J.O. Skinner, and Henry McElderry. See, "Correspondents in the Records of the US Army Medical Museum," *Guide to the Collections of the National Anthropological Archives*, Smithsonian Museum of Natural History, anthropology.si.edu/naa/guide/jrg514c.htm.

12. *Sacramento Daily Union*, 7 May 1873.

13. William Murray, "Modoc War Diary," 85. Murray described the grotesque scene in his diary: "The heads were afterwards secured by Asst. Surgeon Bentley, U.S.A., who placed them carefully in a gunny sack for the purpose of having them sent to Camp."

14. United States Army Medical Museum, Anatomical Section, "Records relating to Specimens Transferred to the Smithsonian Institution," *Guide to the Collections of the National Anthropological Archives*, Smithsonian Museum of Natural History, anthropology.si.edu/naa/guide/_uv.htm.

15. Lee Juillerat, "4 Modoc Skulls at Smithsonian," *Klamath Falls Herald & News*, 18 November 1979.

16. Ibid.

17. Douglas H. Ubelaker to Debra L. Herrera Riddle, 16 August 1983. Letter in the author's collection.

18. Shipping Invoice, 26 January 1984, Smithsonian Institution, ACC 42109. The skulls are identified with the numbers assigned by McElderry. Riddle also received the skull of a Modoc woman who died near Lost River on November 28, 1873. Ibid.

19. "Warriors' descendant becomes keeper of the skulls," *The Sunday Oregonian*, 21 January 1996.

20. Debra Riddle, interview with the author, Klamath Falls, OR, 24 April 2012.

Epilogue: The Aftermath

1. *Letter from Secretary of War Transmitting Reports of the Quartermaster-General of Subsistence, giving in detail the costs to those Departments of the Modoc War*, 43rd Cong. 2nd sess., H. R. No. 131, 1 (1874).

2. Richard Dillon, "Costs of the Modoc War," *California Historical Quarterly* 28, no. 2 (June 1949): 161.

3. Thompson, *Modoc War*, 168-71.

4. *Annual Report* (1901), 218.
5. Quoted in James, *Modoc*, 216–17.
6. *Los Angeles Herald*, 21 March 1874.
7. Bancroft, *History of Oregon*, 2:659n42.
8. Quoted in Neiderheiser, *Jesse Applegate*, 254-7.
9. Jesse Applegate to My Very Dear Son, 22 July 1881. Landrum Collection, Shaw Historical Library, Klamath Falls, Oregon.
10. Account of Jesse Applegate's commitment and quotations from Neiderheiser, *Jesse Applegate*, 300.
11. Meacham, "Preface," *Wi-Ne-Ma*, no page.
12. Rebecca Bales, "Winema and the Modoc War," *Prologue Magazine* 37, no. 1 (2005), www.archives.gov/publications/prologue/2005/spring/winema.html.
13. James, *Modoc*, 103.
14. Alfred Meacham to O. C. Applegate, 9 August 1873, Fisher Papers, 9:1522.
15. *San Francisco Alta California*, 3 October 1873. Meacham's biographer wrote in 1963 that he had "a natural, but not fully developed, facility of expression." Phinney, "Meacham," 220.
16. *Annual Report* (1881), 325, 212.
17. *Salt Lake City Herald*, 7 October 1880; 10 May 1881.
18. T. A. Bland, *Life of Alfred B. Meacham* (Washington, D. C.: Bland Publishers, 1883), 13.
19. Phinney, "Meacham," 306.
20. Prucha, *The Great Father*, Kindle edition.
21. Chris Clements, "Federal Termination and Its Effects on the Land, Culture, and Identity of the Klamath Indian Tribe" (New Brunswick, New Jersey, 2009), 28. Clements' thesis offers an overview of the Tribe's efforts to restore its economic prosperity and cultural identity.
22. Ibid., 47-63.
23. Reed Benson, "Giving Suckers (and Salmon) an Even Break: Klamath Basin Water and the Endangered Species Act," *Tulane Environmental Law Journal* 15, no. 2 (Summer 2002): 236–38. The parties reached a separate agreement in 2016 to remove the dams on the Klamath River.
24. A recent agreement calls for removal of dams on the Klamath River. Emma Marris, "In the Dry West, Waiting for Congress," *New York Times*, November 6, 2015. Press Release, "Two New Klamath Basin Agreements Carve Out Path for Dam Removal and Provide Key Benefits to Irrigators," 6 April 2016, U.S. Department of the Interior.
25. Capt. Seth Hardinge, *Modoc Jack: or the Lion of the Lava Beds* (New York: Robert M. DeWitt, 1873), 73.
26. *Drum Beat* (Warner Brothers, 1954), directed by Delmer Davis. Dell Publishing Co, New York, published the comic in 1954.
27. The author is grateful to Lee Juillerat of the *Klamath Falls Herald and News*, for his guidance on literature of the war. See Lee Juillerat, "The Modoc War: Novel Ways of Playing with History," *Unforgiving Landscape*, (Klamath Falls: Shaw Historical Society, 2011), 97. *Also see* Boyd Cothran's discussion of the significance of some of the later literature in *Remembering the Modoc War*, 98-105, 130-35.
28. Arthur Sainer, *The Village Voice*, 9 April 1970. Reprinted at www.michaeltownsendsmith.com/captain-jack-s-revenge.
29. Interview with the author, April 1998.
30. Christine, who is a little deaf, likes to yodel, and it emerges that she plays the harmonica and tap-dances as well. She likes to tell mirthful stories about her grandfather Jeff Riddle.

Afterword

1. Jeffrey M. LaLande and Peter Skene Ogden, *First Over the Siskiyous: Peter Skene Ogden's 1826-1827 Journey Through the Oregon-California Borderlands* (Portland: Oregon Historical Society Press, 1987), 10.

2. Andrew C. Isenberg, *Mining California: An Ecological History* (New York: Hill and Wang, 2006) 131-61.

3. Cothran, *Remembering the Modoc War*, 113-40.

4. For a sample of the larger debate over whether or not the United States' treatment of Indigenous peoples in the nineteenth century qualifies as genocide, see Gary Clayton Anderson, "The Native Peoples of the American West: Genocide or Ethnic Cleansing," *Western Historical Quarterly* 47: 4 (Winter 2016): 407-34 and "A Roundtable of Responses to Gary Clayton Anderson," *Western Historical Quarterly* 47: 4 (Winter 2016): 435-61.

Bibliography

INTERVIEWS
Debra Riddle Herrera, Modoc descendant.
Cheewa James, historian and descendant.
Perry Chocktoot, tribal historian.
Francis "Van" Landrum, historian and collector.
Helen Crum Smith, last speaker of the Modoc language.
Steve Kandra, rancher.
Lee Juillerat, reporter, *Klamath Falls Herald and News*.
Ryan Bartholomew, local historian.
Bert Lawvor, Tribal Council.
Don Gentry, Vice Chairman, Tribal Council.
Jeff Mitchell, Tribal Council.
Charles Kimbol, Senior Tribal Council.
Taylor David, Tribal Communications Director.

SELECTED NEWSPAPERS

Alta California [San Francisco]
Bellows Falls [VT] *Times*
Boston Daily News
Daily Graphic [NY]
Eureka Union
Frank Leslie's Illustrated Newspaper
Harper's Weekly
Jacksonville [OR] *Sentinel*
Kansas City Gazette
Klamath Falls Evening Herald
Klamath Falls Herald and News
Los Angeles Herald
Marysville [CA] *Daily Appeal*
Medford [OR] *Mail*
Morning Oregonian [Portland]
Napa Valley [CA] *Register*
Nevada State Journal [Reno]
New Northwest [Portland, OR]
New Orleans Republican
New York Daily Graphic

New York Herald
The New York Times
New York Tribune
Oregon Sentinel
Oregon Statesman [Salem]
Portland Oregonian
Postville [IA] *Review*
Rochester [NY] *Democrat and Chronicle*
Rocky Mountain Gazette [Helena, MT]
Russian River Flag
Sacramento Bee
Sacramento Daily Union
Salt Lake City Herald
San Francisco Evening Bulletin
San Francisco Call
San Francisco Chronicle
Sonoma Democrat
Willamette Farmer
Yreka Journal
Yreka Union

Books, Articles, and Manuscript Materials

Applegate Collection. Lindsay Applegate Papers, 1863-1891 and Oliver Cromwell Applegate Papers, 1841-1938. Special Collections and University Archives, University of Oregon Libraries, Eugene, Oregon.

Applegate, Ivan D. "The Initial Shot of the Modoc War." In Peter Cozzens, ed. *Eyewitnesses to the Indian Wars 1865-1890.* Vol. 2, *The Wars for the Pacific Northwest,* 110-14. Mechanicsburg, PA: Stackpole Books, 2002.

Applegate, Jesse. "The Great Stock Farm of the Hon JESSE D. CARR." Survey map. Johnston Papers, Shaw Historical Library, Klamath Falls, Oregon.

Applegate, Lindsay. "The South Road Expedition: Notes and Reminiscences of Laying Out and Establishing The Old Emigrant Road Into Southern Oregon in the Year 1846." *Oregon Historical Quarterly* 22, no. 1 (March 1921): 12-45.

Applegate, Oliver Cromwell (?). "The Last Conflict of the Races." Unpublished typescript ca. 1938. Special Collections and University Archives, University of Oregon Libraries, Eugene, Oregon.

———. "The Battle on the East Side of Lost River." Unpublished manuscript (n. d.). Special Collections and University Archives, University of Oregon Libraries, Eugene, Oregon.

———. Notebook containing letter to Major General C. G. Martin, 5 September 1924, with detailed plan for tour of Modoc War sites. Unpublished handwritten manuscript. Oregon Historical Society Library, Portland.

Bales, Rebecca Anne. "You Will Be Bravest of All: The Modoc Nation to 1909." Ph.D. thesis, Arizona State University, 2001.

Bancroft, Hubert Howe. *California Inter Pocula.* San Francisco: The History Co., 1888.

———. *History of Oregon*, 2 vols. San Francisco: The History Company, 1888. Reprint, Baltimore: Bancroft Press, 1978.

———. Papers. Bancroft Library, University of California, Berkeley.

Barrett, S A. *The Material Culture of the Klamath Lake and Modoc Indians of Northeastern California and Southern Oregon.* Berkeley: University of California Press, 1910. Facsimile Reprint, Salinas, CA: Coyote Press, no date.

Bartholomew, Ryan. "Jesse Carr's Cattle Empire." In "Buckaroos and Barons: Cattle Ranching in the Land of Lakes." *Journal of the Shaw Historical Library* 25 (2011): 2-11.

Beckham, Stephen Dow. *Applegate Trail: Impression and Experiences of Emigrants and Other Travelers.* Oswego, OR: Applegate Trail Coalition, 1995.

Biddle, Ellen McGowan. *Reminiscences of a Soldier's Wife.* Philadelphia: J. B. Lippincott, 1907.

Bilby, Joseph G. *Civil War Firearms.* Conshohocken, PA: Combined Publishing, 1996.

Bland, T. A. *Life of Alfred B. Meacham, Together with his Lecture, The Tragedy of the Lava Beds.* Washington, D.C.: T. A. & M. G. Bland, 1883.

Boutelle, Frazier Augustus. "Letters." Special Collections, University of Oregon.

Boyle, William H. *Personal Observations on the Conduct of the Modoc Indian War,* ed. Richard H. Dillon. Los Angeles: Westernlore Press, no date, 19.

Brady, Cyrus Townsend, ed. *Northwestern Fights and Fighters.* Lincoln: University of Nebraska Press, Bison Book Edition, 1979.

Canby, Gen. E. R. S. Letter to Louisa. Shaw Historical Library, Klamath Falls, Oregon.

Case, Leonard. Diary, September 29-October 3, 1873. Klamath County Museum, Klamath Falls, Oregon.

Clark, Keith and Donna, eds. *Daring Donald McKay, or The Last War Trail of the Modocs.* Chicago: Rounds Brothers, 1881. Reprint, Portland: Oregon Historical Society, 1971.

Clarke, Samuel A. "From the Modoc Expedition," Klamath County Museum Research Papers No. 2, Klamath Falls, Oregon.

———. Unpublished typescript from handwritten manuscript, five chapters. Special Collections and University Archives, University of Oregon.

Clements, Chris. "Federal Termination and Its Effects on the Land, Culture, and Identity of the Klamath Indian Tribe." Thesis submitted to the History Department, Rutgers, New Jersey, 2009.

Cothran, Boyd. *Remembering the Modoc War: Redemptive Violence and the Making of American Innocence.* Chapel Hill: University of North Carolina Press, 2014.

Cozzens, Peter, ed. *The Wars for the Pacific Northwest.* Vol. 2, *Eyewitnesses to the Indian Wars, 1865-1890.* Mechanicsburg, PA: Stackpole Books, 2002.

Curtin, Jeremiah. *Myths of the Modocs.* London: Sampson, Low, Marston & Company, 1912. Facsimile reprint, Salinas, CA: Coyote Press, n.d.

David, Robert James. "The Landscape of Klamath Basin Rock Art." Ph.D. thesis, University of California, Berkeley, 2012.

Davis, Delmer, director. *Drum Beat.* Warner Brothers, 1954. Videocassette [VHS].

Davis, Gilbert F. "Diary, 1873." Handwritten manuscript in small notebook. Oregon Historical Society, Portland, Oregon.

Delano, Columbus. *Report of the Secretary of the Interior.* 31 October 1873. Washington, D.C.: Government Printing Office, 1874.

Dennis, Elsie Frances. "Indian Slavery in the Pacific Northwest." *Oregon Historical Quarterly* 31, nos. 1-3 (1930): 69-82, 181-195, 285-296.

Dillon, Richard H. "Costs of the Modoc War." *California Historical Society Quarterly* 28, no. 2 (1949): 161-64.

————. *Burnt-Out Fires.* Englewood Cliffs, NJ: Prentice Hall, 1973.

————, ed. *William Henry Boyle's Personal Observations on the Conduct of the Modoc War.* Los Angeles: Dawson's Book Shop, no date.

Ditman, Barbara. "Introduction." In "Unforgiving Landscape: Lava Beds National Monument and the Modoc War." *Journal of the Shaw Historical Library* 23-24 (2011).

Douthit, Nathan. "Between Indian and White Worlds on the Oregon-California Border, 1851-1857: Benjamin Wright and Enos." *Oregon Historical Quarterly* 100, no. 4 (Winter 1999): 402-33.

Fabian, Ann. *The Skull Collectors, Race, Science, and America's Unburied Dead.* Chicago: University of Chicago Press, 2010.

Fisher, Don. Papers. Typescript compilation, 11 volumes. Klamath County Museum, Klamath Falls, Oregon. Available online at klamathcountymuseum.squarespace.com/fisher.

Foster, Doug. "Imperfect Justice, the Modoc War Crimes Trial of 1873." *Oregon Historical Quarterly* 100, no. 3 (Fall 1999): 246-87.

————. "Refugees and Reclamation: Conflicts in the Klamath Basin, 1904-1964." *Oregon Historical Quarterly* 103, no. 2 (2002): 150-87.

Freer, Samuel. "Jesse Applegate: An Appraisal of an Uncommon Pioneer." Masters thesis, University of Oregon, 1961.

Furtwangler, Albert. *Bringing Indians to the Book.* Seattle: University of Washington Press, 2005.

Gates, Paul W. "California's Embattled Settlers." *California Historical Society Quarterly* 41, no. 2 (1962): 99-130.

————. "Carpetbaggers Join the Rush for California Land." *California Historical Quarterly* 56, no. 2 (1977): 98-127.

Gatschet, Albert S. *The Klamath Indians of Southwestern Oregon.* Vol. 2, *Contributions to North American Ethnology.* Washington D.C.: Government Printing Office, 1890.

Gifford, Edward Winslow. *California Anthropometry.* Berkeley: University of California Press, 1926.

Goeres-Gardner, Diane L. *Necktie Parties: Legal Executions in Oregon, 1861-1905.* Caldwell, ID: Caxton Press, 2005.

Good, Rachel Applegate. *The History of Klamath County, Oregon.* Klamath Falls: Klamath County Historical Society, 1941.

Grover, La Fayette. *Report of Governor Grover to General Schofield on the Modoc War.* Salem, Oregon: Mart. V. Brown, State Printer, 1874.

Guide to the Collections of the National Anthropological Archives. Smithsonian Museum of Natural History, anthropology.si.edu/naa/guide/jrg514c.htm.

Gwynne, S.C. *Empire of the Summer Moon.* New York: Scribner, 2010.

Hagen, Olaf T. "Modoc War Correspondence, and Documents, 1865-1878." Typescript compilation. Lava Beds National Monument, Tulelake, California.

Hardin, Maj. Charles B. "The Modoc War, 1872-3." Unpublished typscript, 1925. In Rickey, *Forty Miles a Day.*

Hayman, Cora. Interview by Nannie Lee Burns, Investigator. 21 October 1937. Typescript. Indian Archives, Oklahoma Historical Society.

Haynal, Patrick M. "The Influence of Sacred Rock Cairns and Prayer Seats on Modern Klamath and Modoc Religion and World View." *Journal of California and Great Basin Anthropology* 22, no. 2 (2000): 170-85.

Hazelett, Stafford J., ed. *Wagons to the Willamette: Captain Levi Scott and the Southern Route to Oregon, 1844-1847.* Pullman: Washington State University Press, 2015.

Helfrich, DeVere. "Railroads to Klamath." *Klamath Echoes* (n.d.): 17-18.

Heyman, Max L. Jr. *Prudent Soldier: A Biography of Major General E. R. S. Canby, 1817-1873.* Glendale, CA: Arthur H. Clark, 1959.

Hoge, Colonel George. Letter to his brother. 4 October 1873. Unpublished manuscript. Cornell University, Special Collections, Ithaca, NY.

Howe, Carrol B. *Ancient Tribes of the Klamath Country.* Portland: Binford & Mort, 1968.

———. *Ancient Modocs of California and Oregon.* Portland: Binford & Mort, 1979.

Hughes, Cheairs Jr., and Gordon D. Whitney. *Jefferson Davis in Blue: The Life of Sherman's Relentless Warrior.* Baton Rouge: Louisiana State University Press, 2002.

Hurtado, Albert L. "The Modocs and the Jones Family Indian Ring: Quaker Administration of the Quapaw Agency, 1873-1879." In *Oklahoma's Forgotten Indians,* 86-107. Edited by Robert E. Smith. Oklahoma City: Oklahoma Historical Society, 1981.

Indian Country Crimes Act, Rev. Stat. §2145-6 (1854); 18 U.S.C. §1152.

James, Cheewa. "Modoc: An American Indian Saga," in *Roundup!* Edited by Paul Andrew Hutton. Cheyenne, WY: La Frontera Publishing, 2010.

———. *Modoc: The Tribe That Wouldn't Die.* Happy Camp, CA: Naturegraph Publishers, 2008.

Jocelyn, Stephen Perry. *Mostly Alkali.* Caldwell, ID: Caxton Printers, 1953.

Johnston, Robert B. "The Two Jesses." *Journal of the Shaw Historical Library* 5, nos. 1-2 (1991): 1-43.

———. Papers. Shaw Historical Library, Klamath Falls, Oregon.

Juillerat, Lee. "4 Modoc Skulls at Smithsonian." *Klamath Falls Herald & News*, 18 November 1979.

———. "The Modoc War: Novel Ways of Playing with History." In "Unforgiving Landscape," *Journal of the Shaw Historical Library*, 23-24 (2011): 97-105.

Kaliher, Michael. "The Applegate Trail, 1846 to 1853." *Journal of the Shaw Historical Library* 1, no. 1 (1986): 6-23.

Kandra, Steve. "Growing Up Boomer," *Journal of the Shaw Historical Library* 28 (2016): 97-112.

Kerr, James T. "The Modoc War of 1872-73." In *The Papers of The Order of Indian Wars*. Fort Collins, CO: The Old Army Press, 1975.

Kittredge, William. *Hole in the Sky: A Memoir*. New York: Vintage Books, 1992.

Knight, Oliver. *Following the Indian Wars; The Story of the Newspaper Correspondents Among the Indian Campaigners*. Norman: University of Oklahoma Press, 1960.

Kroeber, A. L. "Elements of Culture in Native California." In R. F. Heizer and M. A. Whipple, ed. *The California Indians, A Source Book*. Berkeley: University of Californian Press (1965): 3-67.

———. *Handbook of the Indians of California*. Berkeley: California Book Company, 3rd Printing, 1970.

LaLande, Jeff. "Fort Klamath: Diverse Legacies of a Military Outpost on Oregon's Eastern Frontier." *Journal of the Shaw Historical Library* 28 (2016): 35-49.

Landrum Collection. Shaw Historical Library, Klamath Falls, Oregon.

Landrum, Francis F. *Guardhouse, Gallows, and Graves*. Klamath Falls, OR: Klamath County Museum, 1988.

Limerick, Patricia Nelson. *The Legacy of Conquest: The Unbroken Past of the American West*. New York: Norton, 1987.

Lydecker, G. J. "No. 80 Reconnaissance of Lava Beds: Sketch of Route from Redding to Tule Lake and of the Surrounding Country." 19 June 1873. San Francisco: Engineer Office, Military Division of the Pacific.

———. "Preliminary Report of Captain G. J. Lydecker, Corps of Engineers, on Reconnoisance of the Lava-Beds, (Modoc Campaign)," Oregon. 28 May 1873. Pamphlet. National Park Service, Crater Lake National Park, Medford Oregon.

Manual for Courts-Martial United States, 2012 Edition. www.loc.gov/rr/frd/Military_Law/pdf/MCM-2012.pdf.

Manucy, Albert. *Artillery Through the Ages*. Washington, D.C.: Division of Publications National Park Service, 1949. Reprint 1985.

Mardock, Robert Winston. *The Reformers and the American Indian*. Columbia: University of Missouri Press, 1971.

Margolin, Malcolm. *The Way We Lived: California Indian Reminiscences, Stories and Songs*. Berkeley: Heyday Books, 1981.

Martin, Lucile. "The Modocs in Indian Territory." In *The Northwest Tribes in Exile*, 15-26. Edited by Cliff Trafzer. Sacramento: Sierra Oaks Publishing, 1987.

Martin, Lucille J. "A History of the Modoc Indians: An Acculturation Study." *Chronicles of Oklahoma* 47, no. 4 (1970): 398-446.

Mattson, Lu. *Shaman's Dream: The Modoc War*. eBookIt.com: 2012.

McCarthy, Michael. "From the Sketchbook of First Sergeant Michael McCarthy Troop H, 1ˢᵗ U. S. Cavalry." Compiled by Francis S. Landrum. *The Journal of the Shaw Historical Library* 9, no. 1 (1995): 7-14.

McLeod, Kenneth. Taped Interview. November 1961. Typed transcription. Lava Beds National Monument, Tulelake, California

Meacham, Alfred B. Papers, 1869-1873. Yale University Library. Microfilm, Oregon Historical Society, Portland, Oregon.

———. *Wigwam and War-Path, or the Royal Chief in Chains*. Boston: John P. Dale, 1875.

———. *Wi-Ne-Ma, (The Woman Chief), and Her People*. Hartford: American Publishing, 1876.

Miller, Joaquin. *Life Amongst the Modocs: Unwritten History,* London: Richard Bentley and Son, 1873.

Miller, William Haven. "Incidents of the Modoc War." Typescript. Lava Beds National Monument, Tulelake, California.

"Modoc War correspondence and documents assembled from various sources, 1865-1878." Microfilm. BANC MSS C-A 233 Reel 1. Bancroft Library, University of California, Berkeley.

Moore, Harry DeWitt. "Letters." Lava Beds National Monument, Tulelake, California.

Mullaly, Larry. "The Ashland Golden Spike: Part I: The Railroad comes to Oregon." 18 December 2012. Unpublished typescript in author's collection.

Murray, Keith A. *The Modocs and Their War*. Norman: University of Oklahoma Press, 1959.

Murray, William. "Modoc War Diary: 1873." Unpublished manuscript. Huntington Library, San Marino, California.

Nash, Phileo. "The Place of Religious Revivalism in the Formation of the Intercultural Community on Klamath Reservation." In *Social Anthropology of North American Tribes*, ed. Fred Eggan, et al. Chicago: University of Chicago Press (1937): 337-444.

National Anthropological Archives. Smithsonian Institution Army Medical Museum. Exhibits AMM 773-774; 1018-1021.

Neiderheiser, Leta Lovelace. *Jesse Applegate: A Dialogue with Destiny.* Mustang, OK: Tate Publishing, 2010.

Nixon, Robert J. "A Brief and Authentic History of the Modoc War." Unpublished typescript, ca. 1900. Author's collection.

O'Donnell, Terence. *An Arrow in the Earth: General Joel Palmer and the Indians of Oregon.* Portland: Oregon Historical Society Press, 1991.

Odeneal, Thomas Benton. *The Modoc War: Statement of its Origin and Causes Containing An Account of the Treaty, Copies of Petitions, and Official Correspondence.* Portland: "Bulletin" Steam Book and Printing Office, 1873. Reprint, Nabu Press, 2010.

Oregon Donation Land Act of 1850, 9 U. S. Stat. 496 (1850).

Palmberg, Walter H. *Copper Paladin: The Modoc Tragedy.* Bryn Mawr, PA: Dorrance Publishing, 1982.

Palmer, Joel. "Statement of Inhabitants of Southern Oregon and in Northern California in Regard to the Character and Conduct of the Modoc Indians." Unpublished manuscript. Oregon Historical Society, Portland Oregon.

Parke, John S. "A Visit to the Lava Beds." 11 April 1873. Unpublished typescript. U. S. Army Military History Institute Archives, Carlisle, PA.

Payne, Doris Palmer. *Captain Jack, Modoc Renegade.* Portland: Binford and Mort, 1938.

Pentz, Corporal. Diary. Unpublished manuscript. Lava Beds National Monument.

Peters, Dewitt C. *Kit Carson's Life and Adventures from Facts Narrated by Himself.* Hartford: Dustin, Gilman, 1875.

Phinney, Edward S. "Alfred B. Meacham, Promoter of Indian Reform." Ph.D. thesis, University of Oregon, 1963.

Piper, Alexander. "Reports and Journal." *Oregon Historical Quarterly* 69, no. 3 (1968): 223-68.

Powers, Stephen. "The California Indians—the Modocs," *Overland Monthly* 10, no. 6 (1873): 535-45.

———. *Tribes of California.* Washington, D.C.: Government Printing Office, 1877. Reissued, Berkeley: University of California Press, 1976.

Prucha, Francis Paul. *The Great Father: The United States Government and the American Indians.* Lincoln: University of Nebraska Press, 1984. Abridged Kindle edition.

Putnam, Charles. "Incidents of the Modoc War." *Journal of the Shaw Historical Library* 1, no. 2 (1987): 5-15.

Quinn, Arthur. *Hell with the Fire Out: A History of the Modoc War.* Winchester, MA: Faber and Faber, 1997.

Ray, Verne F. *Primitive Pragmatist: The Modoc Indians of Northern California.* Seattle: University of Washington Press, 1963.

Reed, Gregory A. *An Historical Geography Analysis of the Modoc War.* Masters thesis, California State University, Chico, 1991.

Rhode, Michael G. "The Rise and Fall of the Army Medical Museum and Library." *Washington History* 18, no. 2 (2006): 79-87.

Rickey, Don, Jr. *Forty Miles a Day on Beans and Hay: The Enlisted Soldier Fighting the Indian Wars.* Norman: University of Oklahoma Press, 1963.

Riddle, Jeff C. *The Indian History of the Modoc War, and the Causes That Led to It.* San Francisco: Marnell & Co., 1914. Reprint with introduction by Peter Cozzens, Mechanicsburg, PA: Stackpole Books, 2004.

Rogers, Amos. Correspondence, 1862-63. National Archives, Records of Department of the Interior, Oregon Superintendent of Indian Affairs, Letters Received. Microfilm Roll 20, 1862-1894.

Rutledge, Lee A. *Campaign Clothing: Field Uniforms of the Indian War Army 1872-1886.* Tustin, CA: North Cape Publications, 1997.

Sainer, Arthur. *The Village Voice,* 9 April 1970. Reprinted at www.michaeltownsendsmith.com/captain-jack-s-revenge [accessed February 1, 2014].

Santee, J. F. "Edward R. S. Canby, Modoc War, 1873." *Oregon Historical Quarterly* 33, no. 1 (1932): 70-78.

Scott, Leslie M. "Indian Diseases as Aids to Pacific Northwest Settlement." *Oregon Historical Quarterly* 29, no. 2 (1928): 144-61.

Simpson, William. *Illustrated London News* 62 (7 June 1873): 536.

———. *Meeting the Sun: A Journey All Round the World.* London: Longmans, Green, Reader, and Dyer, 1874.

Slotkin, Richard. *Regeneration through Violence: The Mythology of the Western Frontier, 1600-1860.* Middletown, CT: Wesleyan University Press, 1973.

Spier, Leslie. "The Ghost Dance of 1870 Among the Klamath of Oregon." *University of Washington Publications in Anthropology,* vol. 2, no. 2. Seattle: University of Washington Press, 1927.

———. *Klamath Ethnography.* Berkeley: University of California Press, 1930. In A. L. Kroeber and Robert H. Lowie, ed. *University of California Publications in American Archaeology and Ethnology,* vol. 30, 1930. Reprint, New York: Kraus Reprint Co., 1976.

Stearns, Orson A. "Fort Klamath and the Bread Riot: A Near Tragedy of Early Days." Unpublished manuscript, no date. Oregon Historical Society, Portland, Oregon.

Stern, Theodore, "The Trickster in Klamath Mythology." *Western Folklore* 12, no. 3 (1953), 158-74.

———. *The Klamath Tribe: A People and Their Reservation.* Seattle: University of Washington Press, 1965.

———. "Klamath Myth Abstracts." *Journal of American Folklore* 76, no. 299 (1963): 31-41.

———. "The Klamath Indians and the Treaty of 1864." *Oregon Historical Quarterly* 57, no. 3 (1956): 229-73.

Stone, Buena Cobb. *Fort Klamath*. Dallas: Royal Publishing, 1964.

The History Company. Time books [Payroll records], 1845-1887. Bancroft Library, University of California, Berkeley.

The Lieber Code of 1863. General Orders No. 100. 24 April 1863. avalon.law. yale.edu/19th_century/lieber.asp.

Thompson, Colonel William. *Reminiscences of a Pioneer*. San Francisco: no publisher, 1912.

Thompson, Erwin. *The Modoc War, Its Military History and Topography*. Sacramento: Argus Books, 1971.

Trafzer, Cliff, ed. *The Northwest Tribes in Exile*. Sacramento: Sierra Oaks Publishing, 1987.

Traub, Peter E. "Letter describing experiences in Modoc War." Unpublished 7-page typescript. U. S. Army Military History Institute Archives, Carlisle, Pennsylvania.

Trimble, Will J. "A Soldier of the Oregon Frontier." *Oregon Historical Quarterly* 8, no. 1 (1907): 42-50.

U.S. Army Military History Institute Archives, Carlisle, Pennsylvania.

U.S. Department of the Interior, National Park Service. Lava Beds National Monument. "A Brief History of the Modoc War." www.nps.gov/labe/ planyourvisit/upload/modoc%20war.pdf.

———. *Annual Report of the Commissioner of Indian Affairs to the Secretary of the Interior*. Washington, D.C.: U.S. Government Printing Office, 1873, 1874, 1875, 1878, 1880, 1884, 1886, 1887, 1890, 1904.

U.S. House of Representatives. *Letter from Secretary of War Transmitting Reports of the Quartermaster-General of Subsistence, giving in detail the costs to those Departments of the Modoc War*, 43rd Cong. 2nd sess., H. R. No. 131, 1874.

———. *Official Copies of Correspondence Relative to the War with Modoc Indians in 1872-73*. 43rd Cong., 1st Sess., Ex. Doc. 122.

U.S. Senate. *Letter from the Acting Secretary of the Interior Accompanying Information Called for by the Senate Resolution of January 8, 1873, relative to the Modoc and other Indian tribes in Northern California*. 42nd Cong., 2nd Sess., Ex. Doc. 29.

Victor, Frances Fuller. *The Early Indians Wars of Oregon, Compiled from the Oregon Archives and Other Original Sources: With Muster Rolls*. Salem: Oregon State Printer, 1894.

Wells, Harry L. *History of Siskiyou County*. Oakland: D. J. Stewart, 1881.

Wells, Harry S. "The Ben Wright Massacre." *The West Shore* 10 (1884): 314-20.

Wheeler-Voegelin, Erminie. "The Northern Paiute of Central Oregon: A Chapter in Treaty-Making, Conclusions." *Ethnohistory* 3, no. 3 (1961): 1-10.

Woodhead, Daniel, III, ed. *Modoc Vengeance: The 1873 Modoc War in Northern California & Southern Oregon as reported in the newspapers of the day.* San Francisco: Linden Publishing, no date.

Wooster, Robert. *The Military and United States Indian Policy, 1865-1903.* Lincoln: University of Nebraska Press, 1995.

Yoo, John C. "Memorandum for William J. Haynes II, General Counsel of the Department of Defense *Re:* Military Interrogation of Alien Unlawful Combatants Held Outside the United States." 14 March 2003. nsarchive. gwu.edu/torturingdemocracy/documents/20030314.pdf.

Yoo, John C. to Alberto R. Gonzales, Letter. 1 August 2002. nsarchive.gwu. edu/torturingdemocracy/documents/20020801-3.pdf.

Young, F. G. "The Financial History of the State of Oregon, Part II." *Oregon Historical Quarterly* 10, no. 4: 378-83.

Zakoji, H. "Klamath Culture Change." Masters thesis, University of Oregon, 1932.

Bill Stafford. *Photo by Stephanie Stafford.*

About the Photographer

As a small child Bill Stafford received a camera as a gift, and photography became his lifelong hobby. When an Air Force jet crashed a few blocks from his home in Wantagh, New York, twelve-year-old Bill rode his bike to the crash site and took photos that appeared on the front page of the *New York Daily News*. While in high school, he worked for a professional photographer. He honed his skills in the Nassau County Camera Club and was awarded Photo of the Year. He was both newspaper and yearbook photographer in high school and college.

Jim Compton in the Lava Beds. *Photo by Carol Arnold.*

About the Author

Jim Compton was a well-known journalist retired in Seattle. He graduated with honors from the Columbia University School of Journalism and twice received Fulbright Scholarships in Eastern Europe, most
recently to teach investigative reporting in Romania. He was NBC
correspondent in London and Cairo, covering Europe, Africa, and
the Soviet Union. He later created and hosted *The Compton Report*—an
award winning weekly prime time television news program that ran for
ten years on the Seattle NBC affiliate. He won numerous journalism
awards, including the Columbia-DuPont Silver Baton for outstanding
documentary. He was a member of the Seattle City Council from 1999
to 2006. Mr. Compton died suddenly in March 2014, two months after
completing the manuscript for this book.

Visitor's Guide to Modoc Country

Note: These driving directions are approximate. For detailed information, visit Klamath County Museum, Klamath Falls, OR, and the Visitors Center, Lava Beds National Monument, Tulelake, CA.

Applegate Trail
>The Applegate Trail is now part of the California Historic Trail. Can be seen on Oregon Route 66 between Klamath Falls and Ashland, OR. See also Landrum Wayside, 24800 US 97, Klamath Falls OR.

Lost River Battleground
>Site of the attack on Captain Jack's village, the first battle of the Modoc War. Historic marker located on Malone Road where it crosses Lost River, 23698 Malone Road, Merrill, OR.

Modoc Point
>Modoc Point is the section of the Klamath reservation where the Lost River Modocs lived from late 1869 to 1872. Visible on the cliff east of Upper Klamath Lake, on Route 97 about 15 miles north of Klamath Falls, OR.

Canby's Cross and the Peace Tent
>Site of the peace tent where General Canby was killed. State Route 139 and County Road 120, Lava Beds National Monument, Tulelake, CA. Detailed driving directions and maps are at the Visitor's Center and at www.nps.gov/labe.

Captain Jack's Stronghold
> Experience the Modoc Stronghold along a 0.7 mile rugged hiking trail. Highway 120, Lava Beds National Monument, CA.

Battle of Sorass Lake (now called Dry Lake)
> Site of the last battle of the Modoc War. State Route 139 near Dry Lake Forest Service Station, Modoc County, CA.

Fort Klamath Museum
> See the graves of the executed Modoc warriors, the guardhouse, artifacts, maps, and photos of the Modoc War. 51400 Highway 62, Fort Klamath, OR.

Gillem's Camp and Graveyard
> Original gravesite where the army dead were buried. Near the intersection of Hill Road and Highway 120, Lava Beds National Monument, CA.

Jacksonville Cemetery
> Site of the Boddy Memorial with inscription to the men "murdered by the Modoc Indians." Graves Cemetery Rd, Jacksonville, OR.

Jacksonville Courthouse
Historic former courthouse in picturesque Jacksonville. 206 North 5th Street, Jacksonville, OR.

Klamath County Museum
This museum holds a collection of photos and artifacts of the Modoc War. 1451 Main St., Klamath Falls, OR.

Klamath Lake
Upper Klamath Lake was part of the system of lakes and rivers that sustained the Modocs for millennia. State Highway 422 off Highway 97 north of Klamath Falls, OR.

Lost River Gap
This Modoc fishing site was the location of important talks leading up to the Modoc War. Historical marker just off of South Poe Valley Road, east of Klamath Falls, OR.

Natural Bridge
Anderson-Rose Dam was later built over the natural stone bridge that provided an easy crossing of Lost River at this site. Located about 3 miles southeast of Merrill, OR.

Thomas-Wright Battlefield and Schonchin Flow
Site of one of the most dramatic battles of the Modoc War. Follow 1.1 mile unpaved road off Highway 10, Lava Beds National Monument, CA.

Index

References to illustrations are in italic type.

Adams, John Quincy, 119, 124–25, 162
Ainsworth, J. C., 43
Allen, Christine Riddle, 255–56
American Indian Aid Association, 234, 240
Applegate ranch, 30, 102, 205, 207, 209–10, 213–15
Applegate Trail, 21–22, 25, 28–29, 42–45, 67, 70, 106, 265n4, 310
Applegate, Cynthia, 251
Applegate, Daniel Webster, 68, 209
Applegate, Elisha, 132, 135
Applegate, Flora, 209
Applegate, Ivan: attack on Lost River village, 78–83, 88; correspondence with family and others, 51, 58, 65, 72, 130–32; Klamath Reservation, 29, 35, 39, 48, 50, 140; negotiations with Captain Jack, 61–64, 76–78, 231; spelling of name, 274n6
Applegate, Jesse: Francis Fuller Victor, 26, 30–31; interest in Modoc country, 19, 26–30, *27*, 41–42; irrigation plans and Jesse Carr, 30, 66–70, 253; later years, 250–51, 253; Lost River reservation, 60–61, 73, 75–76, 271n5; battle observer, 180; Peace Commission 136–37, 139–40, 142; press coverage, 93, 131–33, 137, 13940; railroad plans and Ben Holladay, 41–45, 258, 269nn13–14; relatives involved in Modoc affairs, 29–31, 33, 39, 68, 88–89, 135, 209–10
Applegate, Lindsay, 19, 26–30, 33–34, 37, 39, 50–51, 133, 136–37
Applegate, Lucien, 30, 132, 136
Applegate, Oliver Cromwell (O. C.): attack on Lost River Village, 82, 84, 85–87, 95; correspondence with family and others, 30, 51, 136–37, 165, 281n11; criticism in press, 130–32, 273n18; first assault on Stronghold, 97–98, 100–101, 113–14, 280n5; Francis Fuller Victor, 26, 30–31; Klamath Reservation, 29, 39, 41, 59, 62, 167; Meacham's traveling show, 252; Peace Commission, 139–40, 156, 227
Applegate, Peter Skene Ogden, 68

Applegate, Sallie, 68, 209
Army Medical Museum, 8, 245–47, 293n2
Attorney General decision (precedent on enemy combatants), 217–18, 290n20
Atwell, H. Wallace, 128, 144, 146–47, 163, 226, 239

Bancroft, Herbert Hugh, 26, 31, 47, 114, 266n1
Barncho, 4, 153, 158, 223, 225, 236, 239, 292n19
Battle of Sorass Lake, 193–200, 219, 224, 311
Baxter Springs, KS, 239–40
Belknap, William, 118, 134, 237
Ben Wright massacre, 22–23, 31, 129, 144, 168, 266n15
Bentley, Edwin, 182, 247, 294n13
Bernard, Reuben Frank, 62, 99, 102, 109–13, 116, 118, 276n15
Berwick, Nate, 106, 147
Bill Dadd the Scribe. *See* Atwell, H. Wallace
Black Jim: *61*; attack on Lost River Village, 79, 81, 85; capture and imprisonment, 214, 217–18, 225; execution, 4, 7, 236; killing at peace tent, 153, 161; meeting with Jesse Applegate, 60–61; Modoc factions, 125, 15253; skull, 245–47
Blair, Charley, 57, 59, 145–46
Bloodhounds: 5, 22728, 231, 235–36, 238; decision not to charge, 217, 223; photographs, *203*, 219-20; traitors to Captain Jack, 199–207, 209–10
Boddy, Louisa, 87, 216–17
Boddy, William, 87, 89, 276n6, 311
Bogart, Robert D.: *San Francisco Chronicle* correspondent, 69, 116, 126–27, 144–45; criticism of Applegates, 131–32
Bogus Charley: *203*; attack on Lost River Village, 78, 83; Bloodhound, 5, 201–5, 209, 217, 223, 235; killing of peace delegation, 153, 155, 157–58, *159*–60, 166, 228, 284n19; Oklahoma exile, 241–42; Modoc factions, 103, 125, 143, 145, 150